Europe and the Mediterranean Economy

With the creation of the Mediterranean partnership and the recent move towards the creation of the Union for the Mediterranean in 2008, a new emphasis is placed on the Mediterranean in the study of European Integration.

This book brings together a collection of experts to address this important new area of study and discuss issues such as development, aid, labour, markets, human capital investment, Europeanization and institutional reform.

This book is the first and possibly the most updated book on the economics and political economy of the Mediterranean. It is an ambitious manuscript that aims at first providing a wide overview of the institution-building and regionalization process that is taking place in the Mediterranean, containing a broad discussion of the successes and limitation in building a Mediterranean space in the midst of the construction of Europe. Second, the book contains an economic and policy analysis of the process of economic liberalization and its effects in macroeconomic performance. Specifically, the book contains chapters addressing questions on trade liberalization, the effects of the global financial crises in the Euro-Mediterranean area, as well as how liberalization has impacted economic growth. Third, the book contains a section that addresses problems with microeconomic reforms, and more specifically privatization and labour market stability, alongside productive efficiency in the area. Finally, three chapters of the book address the question of how reforms in the Mediterranean have affected welfare and, more specifically, poverty, migration and the environment

Joan Costa-Font is Reader in Political Economy at the London School of Economics, UK.

Routledge studies in the European economy

1 **Growth and Crisis in the Spanish Economy, 1940–1993**
Sima Lieberman

2 **Work and Employment in Europe**
A new convergence?
Edited by Peter Cressey and Bryn Jones

3 **Trans-European Telecommunication Networks**
The challenges for industrial policy
Colin Turner

4 **European Union – European Industrial Relations?**
Global challenges, national developments and transnational dynamics
Edited by Wolfgang E. Lecher and Hans-Wolfgang Platzer

5 **Governance, Industry and Labour Markets in Britain and France**
The modernizing state in the mid-twentieth century
Edited by Noel Whiteside and Robert Salais

6 **Labour Market Efficiency in the European Union**
Employment protection and fixed-term contracts
Klaus Schömann, Ralf Rogowski and Thomas Kruppe

7 **The Enlargement of the European Union**
Issues and strategies
Edited by Victoria Curzon-Price, Alice Landau and Richard Whitman

8 **European Trade Unions**
Change and response
Edited by Mike Rigby, Roger Smith and Teresa Lawlor

9 **Fiscal Federalism in the European Union**
Edited by Amedeo Fossati and Giorgio Panella

10 European Telecommunications Liberalisation
Edited by Kjell A. Eliassen and Marit Sjøvaag

11 Integration and Transition in Europe
The economic geography of interaction
Edited by George Petrakos, Gunther Maier and Grzegorz Gorzelak

12 SMEs and European Integration
Internationalisation strategies
Birgit Hegge

13 Fiscal Federalism and European Economic Integration
Edited by Mark Baimbridge and Philip Whyman

14 Financial Markets in Central and Eastern Europe
Stability and efficiency
Edited by Morten Balling, Frank Lierman and Andy Mullineux

15 Russian Path Dependence
Stefan Hedlund

16 The Impact of European Integration on Regional Structural Change and Cohesion
Edited by Christiane Krieger-Boden, Edgar Morgenroth and George Petrakos

17 Macroeconomic Policy in the European Monetary Union
From the old to the new stability and growth pact
Edited by Francesco Farina and Roberto Tamborini

18 Economic Policy Proposals for Germany and Europe
Edited by Ronald Schettkat and Jochem Langkau

19 Competitiveness of New Europe
Papers from the second Lancut economic forum
Edited by Jan Winiecki

20 Deregulation and the Airline Business in Europe
Sean Barrett

21 Beyond Market Access for Economic Development
EU–Africa relations in transition
Edited by Gerrit Faber and Jan Orbie

22 **International Trade, Consumer Interests and Reform of the Common Agricultural Policy**
Edited by Susan Mary Senior Nello and Pierpaolo Pierani

23 **Economic Governance in the EU**
Willem Molle

24 **Financial Integration in the European Union**
Edited by Roman Matoušek and Daniel Stavárek

25 **Europe and the Mediterranean Economy**
Edited by Joan Costa-Font

Europe and the Mediterranean Economy

Edited by Joan Costa-Font

Routledge
Taylor & Francis Group
LONDON AND NEW YORK

FEMISE

EUROMED

First published 2012
by Routledge
2 Park Square, Milton Park, Abingdon, Oxon OX14 4RN

Simultaneously published in the USA and Canada
by Routledge
711 Third Avenue, New York, NY 10017

Routledge is an imprint of the Taylor & Francis Group, an informa business

British Library Cataloguing in Publication Data
A catalogue record for this book is available from the British Library

Library of Congress Cataloging in Publication Data
A catalog record has been requested for this book

ISBN: 978-0-415-66765-4 (hbk)
ISBN: 978-0-203-11989-1 (ebk)

Typeset in Times New Roman
by Wearset Ltd, Boldon, Tyne and Wear

MIX
Paper from responsible sources
FSC® C004839
FSC www.fsc.org

Printed and bound in Great Britain by
TJ International Ltd, Padstow, Cornwall

Contents

Figures

Tables

Contributors

Hüseyin Ağır is an assistant professor at Kahramanmaraş Sütçü İmam University (KSU) in Kahramanmaraş, Turkey. He obtained his Masters degree at this university (2004) and his PhD at Adnan Menderes University, Aydın, Turkey (2009). His research interests are concerned with financial liberalization, financial development and economic growth.

Hedi Bchir joined UNESCWA as an economic affairs officer in October 2011. Previously he worked as Principal Country Economist at the African Development Bank between 2008 and 2011, and as Economic Affairs Officer at the UNECA between 2005 and 2008. He received his PhD in Economics from the University of Paris 1 Pantheon Sorbonne in 2004, and an engineering diploma from the polytechnic school of Tunisia in 1998. During his career, Mohamed Bchir has published a number of academic articles in fields related to trade, macroeconomics and labour.

Mhamed Biygautane is a research associate at the Dubai School of Government. Since joining the DSG in early 2010, he has actively contributed to the research department and produced studies on the political economy of development, knowledge management in the public sector, modernization and reform of the public sector, and governance challenges in the Arab World, and has also contributed to case studies that the DSG has co-published with the World Bank. He has presented at various conferences in the US, China, Australia, UK, Belgium, France and Poland, and in countries in the Arab World including Syria, Lebanon, the United Arab Emirates, Jordan and Morocco. Mr Biygautane graduated from Monash University, Melbourne Australia, with a Masters in Public Policy and Management (with distinction). He is the author of *The Arab State, Public Administration and Governance Models: In Search of Indigenous Identity* (forthcoming, 2012).

Mireia Borrell-Porta is an economist currently doing a PhD at the European Institute, London School of Economics. Her research focuses on the political economy of Europe and its neighbouring countries, more specifically on the relationship between culture, policy and economic development in the

Mediterranean area. She has also been involved in projects related to trade and foreign direct investment in this particular region.

Mohamed A. Chemingui holds a PhD in economics from Montpellier University, France. He is currently First Economic Affairs Officer at the United Nations Economic Commission for Africa, Addis Ababa, Ethiopia. He has been a research fellow of the Economic Research Forum and research scientist at the Kuwaiti Institute of Scientific Research. He served as consultant for many regional and international organizations, including the OECD, the World Bank, the European Commission, UNIDO, IFPRI, UNDP, GDN, ERF, etc. His research and publications have dealt with issues involving international trade, foreign direct investment, regional integration, economic growth and income distribution, public finances, the labour market and environmental economics.

Joan Costa-Font is an economist and social scientist specializing in economics of social policy, and with a particular interest in the Mediterranean. He holds three undergraduate degrees in Economics (Barcelona, 1996), Law, and Political Science; a Masters degree (MSc LSE, with distinction), a PhD in Economics (2000), and he was awarded a Marie Curie postdoctoral Fellowship based at LSE (2001). Currently he works as a Reader in Political Economy at the LSE, a joint appointment with the Department of Social Policy and European Institute, and he is affiliated to LSE Health , the Center of Economic Performance (CEP) and the Political Science and Political Economy group . Joan externally collaborates as a network research fellow with CESifo (Munich) and FEDEA , and has held teaching, visiting or research posts at the University of Barcelona, Pompeu Fabra University, the University of Oxford, the University of Munich, and the Iberoamerican University in Mexico City. His main academic responsibilities include being stream convener of the MPA public and social policy, co-editing the journal *Applied Economics, Perspectives and Policy*, the LEQS Discussion Paper Series, and has assisted the editing of a range of academic journals in his areas of specialism, including being a special issue editor of the *Oxford Review of Economic Policy* and *CESIfo Economic Studies*, among other journals. His research interests are in health economics, political economy, and social economics and policy. His work has been published in *Economic Policy*, *Journal of the European Economic Association*, *Public Choice* and *Journal of the Royal Statistical Society*, among others.

Reinout De Bock joined the International Monetary Fund in 2009. He worked as a desk economist in the Middle East and Central Asia Department before moving to the Monetary and Capital Markets Department in 2010. Prior to joining the IMF, Reinout worked as a G-10 FX strategist for Lehman Brothers and Barclays Capital. He received his PhD in Economics from Northwestern University in 2008, and was a dissertation fellow at the National Bank of Belgium, the European Central Bank and the Board of Governors of the Federal Reserve. He also holds an MSc in Economics from the London School of Economics.

Daniel Florea began his career in Romania, as a diplomat for the Ministry of Foreign affairs. After moving to Canada, he worked for Quebec's Department of Finance, where he was Director for Economic and Fiscal Studies and Economic Development. In 2010, he was appointed Director General for Macroeconomic Analysis and Forecast in the Department of Finance, a position he currently holds. He also worked as a senior analyst in the Financial Markets Department of the Bank of Canada in 2008–209 and as a senior economist for the International Monetary Fund in 2009–20. Daniel Florea holds Bachelor's degrees in economics and mathematics, and an MBA. He has published several research papers in the areas of macroeconomics, fiscal policy and economic modelling.

Clive George has recently retired as a senior research fellow at the Institute for Development Policy and Management, University of Manchester. He remains a visiting senior fellow at Manchester, and is a visiting professor at the College of Europe, Bruges, where he teaches impact assessment and policy analysis.

Bülent Güloğlu is an associate professor at Pamukkale University in Denizli, Turkey. He received his PhD and Masters from the University of Paris in 2000 and 1995, respectively. He taught at the Adnan Menderes University in Aydın from 2001 to 2005. He has been teaching at the Department of Economics at Pamukkale University since 2005. His research focuses on time-series and panel data econometrics, and monetary policy.

Muhsin Kar is a professor of macroeconomics. He obtained his undergraduate degree in Economics from the Faculty of Political Sciences in Ankara University (1992). He did his MA in Economic Development in Leicester University (1995) and his PhD in Economics in Loughborough University (2000), both in the UK. After completing his doctorate, he returned to Turkey and worked at Kahramanmaras Sütçü İmam University until April 2009, when he joined the staff at the University of Çukurova in Adana to continue his academic work. He was appointed as a Dean in the Faculty of Tourism in Konya University in Konya, Turkey, in August 2011. His fields of specialization are in the areas of financial liberalization, financial development, capital flows, savings and investment, and economic growth.

Mohamed Lahouel is Chief Economist in the Department of Economic Development, Government of Dubai. Previously, he held the positions of Professor of Economics and Associate Dean for Academic Affairs at the Dubai School of Government; Professor of Economics at the University of Tunis, Al Manar; and Visiting Professor at the Sorbonne University and the Nice Sophia-Antipolis University in France. He has also been a consultant to international institutions such as the World Bank, UNDP and OECD. His research and publications have focused on macroeconomic and international trade issues in developing countries. Mr Lahouel holds a Masters and PhD in economics from Harvard University.

Joaquín A. Millán is Associate Professor of Agricultural Economics, Technical University of Madrid (UPM). His research interests include energy, trade and regional modelling, especially from production economics perspectives.

Şaban Nazlioğlu is an assistant professor at Pamukkale University in Denizli, Turkey. He received his Masters degree and doctorate from Erciyes University in 2006 and 2010, respectively. He has been teaching at the Department of Econometrics at Pamukkale University since 2010. His research focuses on panel data econometrics, the macroeconomics of agriculture, and commodity prices.

Simon Neaime is Professor and Chair of the Department of Economics, American University of Beirut, Lebanon. He has had numerous academic journal articles published in high-ranking economics and finance journals on the economies of the MENA region, and has also published several graduate textbooks in financial, monetary, macroeconomics, and international economics fields. His most recent journal articles have appeared in the *Emerging Markets Review*, *Open Economies Review*, *Review of Middle East Economics and Finance*, *Journal of Economic Integration*, *North American Journal of Economics and Finance*, and *International Economic Journal*.

Nicolas Péridy is Professor of International Economics at the Université du Sud Toulon-Var, France. His research topics mainly include international trade, regional integration, FDI and migration. He has published more than 30 articles in international reviews, such as *World Economy*, *Review of World Economics*, *Journal of Economic Integration*, *Economics Letters*, *International Economic Journal*, *Economics Systems*, *Journal of World Trade*, etc. He is consultant for several international organizations, including the World Bank, the European Commission and the FEMISE network.

Mona Said is Assistant Professor of Economics in the School of Business, American University in Cairo; and Faculty Affiliate of the London Middle East Institute, School of Oriental and African Studies, University of London, UK. Her research interests include labour and human resource economics, gender-based inequality in earnings, and job quality and equity implications of trade policy. Her publications have appeared in the *Journal of Developing Areas*, *Comparative Economic Studies*, *Economic Development and Cultural Change*, *Review of Middle East Economics and Finance* and the *Review of Radical Political Economics*.

Alfred Tovias is the Walter Rathenau Professor in European Economics at the Department of International Relations of the Hebrew University. He has been Chairman of the Department since 1 October 2010; before this he served for five years as Director of the Leonard Davis Institute for International Relations at the same university (2005–2010). He has also held the EU-sponsored Jean Monnet Chair on External Economic Relations of the EU since 2001. After completing his PhD in Economics at the University of Geneva, he taught there for several years, moving in 1979 to the Hebrew University. He was Visiting Lecturer and Research Fellow at the London School of Economics and Political Science (LSE) in 1999–2000. In the past, he served for several years as Chairman of the Israeli Association for the Study of European Integration, as well as Deputy Director of the Institute for European Studies at The Hebrew University in Jerusalem. He has also been a consultant to the OECD, UNCTAD and the World Bank, and a research fellow of CEPS (Center for European Policy Studies) in Brussels. He is a member of the Steering Committee of the FEMISE (Forum Mediterraneen d'Instituts d'Etudes Economiques) and a member of the editorial boards of *European Union Politics*, *Mediterranean Politics* and *Revista de Economia Mundial*. He has published several books and articles in, among others, *Journal of Common Market Studies*, *Oxford Economic Papers*, *The World Economy* and *West European Politics*.

Joël Toujas-Bernaté started his professional career at the economic research department of the French National Institute of Statistics and Economic Research (INSEE, Paris). He joined the International Monetary Fund in 1993, where he successively worked as desk economist in the African Department and the Strategy and Review Department, before becoming mission chief and division chief in the Middle East and Central Asia Department. He was the IMF Senior Resident Representative for the Palestinian Territories from 2005 to 2008. He has been heading the division covering the French-speaking Maghreb countries since the end of 2008, leading in particular the teams covering Algeria and Tunisia. Joël Toujas-Bernaté graduated from École Polytechnique (Paris) and École Nationale de Statistiques et Administration Économique (ENSAE, Paris).

Preface

If Europe is something more than a cultural construction to respond to the challenges of globalization, and hence historical roots need to be found to justify Europe existence, then the Mediterranean is an essential part of the idea of Europe. This explains why the current Union for the Mediterranean (UfM) involves 43 members, 27 of which are EU Member States (the remaining 16 being Albania, Algeria, Bosnia and Herzegovina, Croatia, Egypt, Israel, Jordan, Lebanon, Mauritania, Monaco, Montenegro, Morocco, the Palestinian Authority, Syria, Tunisia, and Turkey). The Euro-Mediterranean process has become the natural extension of European influence in the area as a whole rather than through its member states. Institutionally, it provides a long list of opportunities as well as challenges. More specifically, it is a process that should not slow down existing European integration but instead it should encourage the diffusion of European political and social reforms that typically come along with new forms of economic organization and trade. With this in mind, this book is, to the best of my knowledge, the first attempt to bridge the existing fragmentation in the study of the Mediterranean and bring together an integrated picture of the economic issues that affect the labour markets, trade, financial and social protection of the Mediterranean economies.

The book contains an analysis of the effects of the set-up of the Euro-Mediterranean process. With the creation of the Union for the Mediterranean in 2008 and the new priority given to the Mediterranean within the context of European integration, the study of Mediterranean economies has become essential material for students of European economics, political economy and public policy. This book contains chapters from top scholars in the area – generally experts that do an excellent job demonstrating how the economy of the Mediterranean is an important area of study. Indeed, the story of the Mediterranean stands as one where issues related to development and aid share equal importance with the challenges of reforming labour markets and promoting human capital investment in the regions. Similarly, traditional questions on enhancing economic and capital exchange are examined alongside challenging ones such as the Europeanization and institutional reform in the region, including democracy and the absolute imperative of the rule of law.

The book has been organized into four main blocks covering the institutionalization of the Mediterranean as an area of economic activity, the process of economic liberalization and macroeconomic performance, the process of privatization and labour market reform and its impact on productivity, and, finally, the effects on social welfare and public policies concerning the environment. The four blocks attempt to provide an overview of the economic performance of the Mediterranean and its institutional reforms at both macro- and micro-level and, ultimately, how those reforms translate in terms of economic and social progress.

This book is the first and possibly the most updated piece on the economics and political economy of the Mediterranean. It is an ambitious manuscript that aims at first providing a wide overview of the institution-building and regionalization process that it is taking place in the Mediterranean. It contains a broad discussion of the successes and limitation in building a Mediterranean space in the midst of the construction of Europe. Second, the book includes an economic and policy analysis of the process of economic liberalization and its effects in macroeconomic performance. Specifically, the book includes chapters addressing questions on trade liberalization, the effects of the global financial crises in the Euro-Mediterranean area, as well as how liberalization has impacted economic growth. Third, the book devotes a section that addresses problems concerning microeconomic reforms, and more specifically privatization and labour market stability, alongside productive efficiency in the area. Finally, three chapters of the book address the question of how reforms in the Mediterranean have affected welfare and, more specifically, poverty, migration and the environment.

I can only hope that this book will answer some of the questions that the Euro-Mediterranean process brings to the fore, and that the reading of these chapters appeals to you as much as it has appealed to me.

Joan Costa-Font, London, September 2011

Acknowledgements

This book could not have been written without the enthusiasm of Mireia Borrell-Porta, who has assisted with editing of the book from its very beginning; the hard work of the authors in providing us with high-quality manuscripts; and the organizers of the two workshops that the European Institute of the London School of Economics arranged together with the CREMed centre of the Universitat Pompeu Fabra and that aimed at the study of the Mediterranean and the Euro-Mediterranean process in 2010 and 2011. Special thanks go to Eva Ventura for helping to organize this event. Finally, the editor's involvement in the process has been possible thanks to financial support from the Jean Monnet Chair that was granted to the European Institute to co-organize the above-mentioned workshops, as well as from FEMISE to edit this book.

Disclaimer

This edited volume has been produced with the financial assistance of the European Union through the FEMISE Association. The contents of this volume are the sole responsibility of the editors and authors and can under no circumstances be regarded as reflecting the position of the European Union.

Part I

Institutionalism and the Mediterranean area

1 The importance of institution-building in free trade agreements

Mireia Borrell-Porta

1 Introduction

Association agreements are developed under the assumption that institution-building can impact on economic exchange, and ultimately trigger economic integration.

This belief has underpinned numerous trade agreements between the EU and neighbouring countries. One of the most recent trade agreements is the one that constitutes the *Euro-Mediterranean Partnership* (EMP). The EMP qualifies as a partnership with non-European Mediterranean Countries to initially liberalize trade and eventually set up a free trade area in the region.

From then on, trade has increased between these two regions and large social and political changes have taken place. Yet the expectations held by some actors have not been fulfilled, and the EMP, far from confirming the positive effects of trade-enhancing institutions on economic exchange, has challenged this 'naïve view' of economic integration on several grounds. First, institution-building may be motivated by reasons other than trade, namely security. Second, positive effects of trade association agreements and removal of tariff barriers might be hampered if non-tariff barriers persist. And third, the success of the association agreements depends greatly on the political situation and the type of social norms of the affected economies.

Against the backdrop of agreements successfully promoting trade, this chapter analyses trade volume and its composition and, using the Europe Agreements signed between the Central and Eastern European Countries (CEECs) and the EU in the 1990s as a benchmark, questions the impact of the association agreements on the evolution of trade between the European Union and the Mediterranean Non-Member Countries (MNMCs). In an attempt to know the causes of the relatively poor trade outcomes, the chapter highlights on the one hand the economic-only rationale applied by the EU in their relationship to the MNMCs, which ignored the political situation of the MNMCs, and on the other hand the political unwillingness to put the relationship with MNMCs at the top of the EU agenda. The analysis therefore conveys that institutional building, in the case of the MNMCs, was incomplete and that it served another objective different from the one expressed by the EU.

2 The liberalization process of the MNMCs and CEECs

Officially, the Euro-Mediterranean Partnership (EMP) began in 1995 under the name of the Barcelona Process, with the aim of creating 'an area of shared prosperity' (European Union 2005). It is sometimes argued that its creation was more a realization of security concerns rather than economic interests. While a sense of hope in the European Union was embedded in the Oslo Agreements of 1993 and 1995, the instability present in the MENA (Mediterranean and North African) region instilled a hint of fear in the Member States. Concurrently, EU negotiations for accession were taking place with Eastern and Central European countries for the eventual enlargement in 2004, a fact that upset some Southern European countries, which were keener on developing a common European policy among the non-European Mediterranean countries (Brach 2006: 8).

In order to solve these security and political concerns, and following its own experience with previous integration processes, the EU opened up the door for a partnership based on an economic rationale which was meant to achieve sustainable socioeconomic development (Euromed 1995, cited in Brach 2006: 6) and, ultimately, to solve the security and political concerns. For this purpose, a Free Trade Area was established. This Free Trade Area was based on bilateral trade agreements, which would set the pace for liberalization of trade for every Mediterranean country involved in the agreements.

The current Union involves 43 members, 27 of which are EU Member States.[1] This chapter analyses the trade relationship between the 27 EU members and eight non-EU members (MNMC8), namely Algeria, Egypt, Israel, Jordan, Lebanon, Morocco, Syria and Tunisia.[2] These eight countries plus the Palestinian Authority are the ones which are included in the Euro-Mediterranean Association Agreements and enjoy a preferential trade relation with the EU. Before the Association Agreements, economic relations with the MNMCs were limited to bilateral and non-reciprocal cooperation agreements set in the mid- and late 1970s (Licari 1998: 3–4, Bensassi *et al.* 2010: 5).

This chapter focuses on one of the four pillars on which the Euro-Mediterranean Partnership is structured: the Economic and Financial Partnership (EFP), which is the pillar that covers the trade liberalization process.

At the same time, the EU signed trade agreements with ten Central and Eastern Countries,[3] to be known as *Europe Agreements* (EAs). These covered bilateral trade relations until 2004 between the EU and CEECs in both goods and services, with the exception of agricultural products, and envisage trade liberalization after a period of ten years. Unlike the association agreements with the MNMCs, which were designed to be an objective in themselves, the EAs were clearly set as a means to achieve an ultimate goal; namely, the entrance of the CEECs to the EU single market.

3 Trade analysis

The analysis of manufactured trade[4] (from now on, trade) is structured into two parts, namely trade evolution and trade composition.

The first part, trade evolution, aims at showing whether the EU trade agreements with both the CEECs and the MNMCs have caused an increase in trade. For this purpose, the analysis is carried out in three parts. First of all, a comparison between the evolution of trade of each region with the world and the average evolution of world trade is drawn. World trade is used as a benchmark, and it allows us to see whether the evolution of trade of each region follows the average world trade trend. The second comparison is drawn between the evolution of trade between the region and the world on one hand, and between the two regions bound by the Agreement on the other hand (EU15–CEECs, EU27–MNMCs[5]). The reason behind this comparison is to find whether trade between the two regions has evolved at the same pace as trade between one region and the world. In order to prove an institutional shock provoked by the Agreements, differences in evolution of trade should be appreciated by a greater extent in the latter comparison than in the former one. If a case is given where trade of the MNMC8/CEEC5 with the EU and with the World, respectively, increases at a similar percentage, it does not particularly imply that this increase has been due to the institutional shock, since it could well be a global shock affecting worldwide trade. These two sets of comparisons present data as a percentage change with respect to year *n*–1. Finally, the third part of the analysis consists of picturing the importance of one region's trade for another region, and seeing the evolution of its importance before and after the Agreements. This third part allows us to quantify the magnitude of the shock (if any) that may have been observed in the first two parts of the analysis. For this purpose, the share of trade of one region with the other region compared to total trade of the region with the world is drawn.[6]

The second part, trade composition, is aimed at corroborating or amplifying the results of the first part as well as at examining the trade patterns and composition of trade. For this purpose, the chapter uses different integration and trade theories. One early contribution to integration and trade theory was made in 1950 by Jacob Viner. He analysed the static effects of a customs union on trade and welfare, claiming that two opposite trade effects could arise as a result of the formation of a customs union: trade creation and trade diversion. Trade creation, he argued, takes place when

> one of the members of the customs union will from now on newly import from the other one but which it formerly did not import at all because the price of the protected domestic product was lower than the price at any foreign source plus the duty.
>
> (Viner 1950, cited in Kenen 2000: 250)

Therefore, the combined effect in the two countries must be net benefit, and thus the world as a whole benefits (Viner 1950, cited in Kenen 2000: 250). Instead, trade diversion occurs when

> one of the members of the customs union will from now on newly import from the other whereas before the customs union it imported them from a third country, because that was the cheapest possible source of supply even after payment of duty.
>
> (Viner 1950, cited in Kenen 2000: 250)

Therefore, the combined effect of the two countries would be a net loss (Viner 1950, cited in Kenen 2000: 250).

In another direction, trade has also been examined in terms of its margins. According to new–new trade theories, trade can increase in two ways (Bensassi *et al.* 2010): with its extensive margin, that is the number of new firms or products exported/imported; or with its intensive margin, meaning the average value (quantity or price) of traded goods that were already being exported/imported.[7]

Many authors have used these theories for empirical analysis by employing a common model: the gravity model. According to several authors (Bergstrand 1985, Eichengreen and Irwin 1998, Feenstra, Markusen and Rose 2001, Kandogan 2009), the gravity model has succeeded in explaining international trade flows since its development by Tinbergen in 1952 (Nello 2005: 125). In its simplest form, it claims that bilateral trade is explained by the income of the exporter and the importer, which affects bilateral trade positively; and by the transaction costs, proxied by the geographical distance between the two countries and which affects trade negatively:

$$T_{ij} = \alpha + \beta_1 d_{ij} + \beta_{2i} Y_i + \beta_{2j} Y_j + \phi_{ij}$$

where T_{ij} is the average volume of total trade between countries i and j, d_{ij} is the distance between the two countries (i,j), and Y is the GDP of countries i and j (Kandogan 2009: 596)

According to the definitions above of extensive and intensive margin and trade creation and diversion, it can be claimed that an increase in the extensive margin of trade may happen because of trade creation or trade diversion; therefore, both trade effects can be regarded as a decomposition of the structure of the extensive margin. Following this reasoning, the analysis of trade composition will examine the evolution of the intensive and extensive margin of trade of both the MNMCs' and CEECs' bilateral trade flows with the EU, and, inside the analysis of the extensive margin, trade creation and diversion effects will be examined as well.[8]

3.1 Mediterranean countries' trade analysis

The graphics for the MNMC8 (Figures 1.1 and 1.2) illustrate that trade between the EU27 and MNMC8 increases, but so does trade between the World and the MNMC8. Therefore, it is not clear that such an increase is the result of the EMAAs, as it could well have been caused by a global shock (e.g. a general reduction in tariffs or an economic boom) that would affect the World and the EU27 trade likewise.

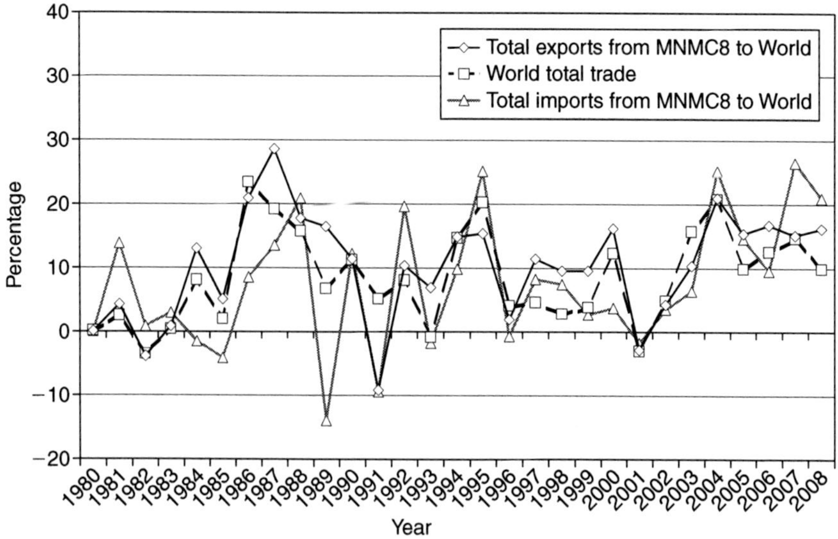

Figure 1.1 Comparison: World total trade vs trade from MNMC8 to World in yearly percentage change – period 1980–2008 (source: yearly percentage change based on WTO 2010).

The share of EU trade with the MNMC8 (Figure 1.3) is no more encouraging, and shows a decrease of the importance of the EU for MNMC8 trade, which might account for a null impact of the Agreements.

However, this would be a precipitate conclusion. The figures tells us that MNMC8 trade with both the World and the EU has increased, so actually we could be facing two different shocks, one of them being the Euro-Mediterranean Agreements. Moreover, the fact that the importance of the EU27 in MNMC8 trade is decreasing does not mean that the Agreements have not had any impact. It could well be that trade between both regions still increases, but trade between the MNMC8 region and the world has increased at a higher percentage. Thus, although MNMC8 trade with the EU and the World has increased, we do not have enough information to conclude whether it is precisely because of the Agreements. The evolution of trade composition is needed to shed more light on which interpretation reflects the reality.

The analysis of the MNMCs' composition of trade is based on the result of two papers. One of them, authored by Bensassi *et al.* (2010), provides us with a thorough analysis of the margins of trade of the Euro-Mediterranean Agreements. The other one, Kandogan (2009), analyses trade creation and diversion effects by using a gravity model.[9]

Bensassi *et al.* (2010) show in their paper that the Euro-Mediterranean Agreements had a very slight negative effect on the extensive margin and a positive and significant effect on the intensive margin on EU imports (p. 20).

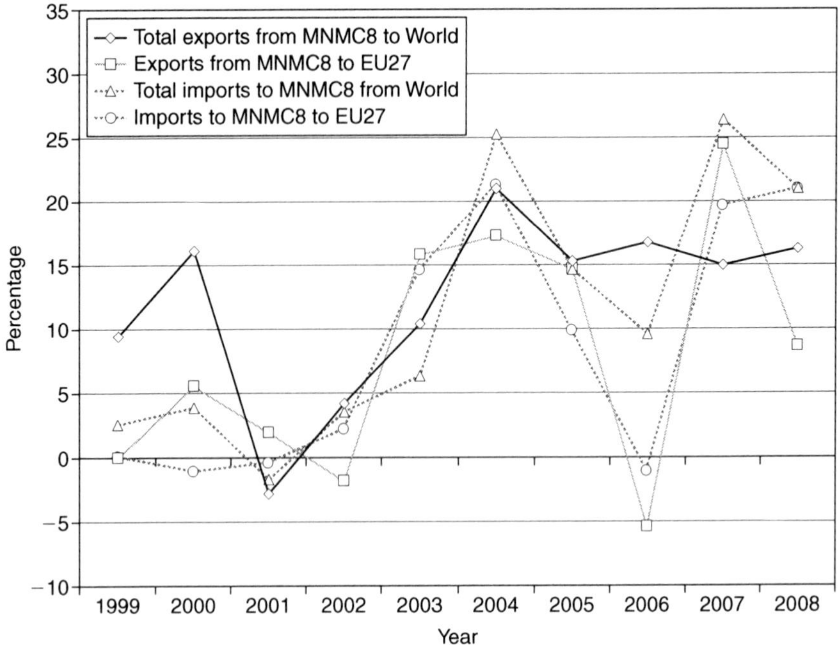

Figure 1.2 Comparison in MNMC8 trade flows of manufactured goods with the World and with the EU27 (percentage change) (source: yearly percentage change based on WTO 2010 and Eurostat 2010).

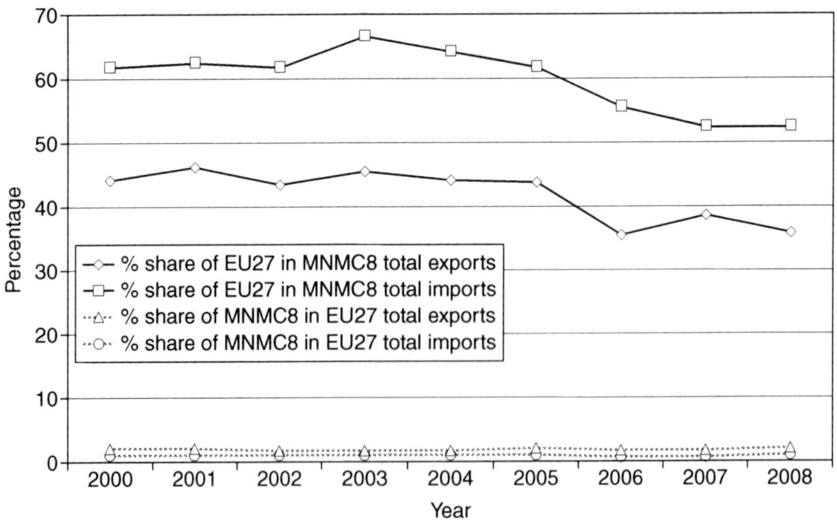

Figure 1.3 Percentage share of EU27 in MNMC8 trade and percentage share of MNMC8 in EU27 trade 1999–2008 (source: percentage share based on WTO 2010 and Eurostat 2010).

The almost null effect on the extensive margin is corroborated by the findings of Kandogan (2009), who claims in his paper that the Euro-Mediterranean Agreements have caused no trade creation or diversion. Specifically, he states that the Euro-Mediterranean Agreements have created no trade in both EU and MNMCs' imports (pp. 612, 613), and that trade diversion has been small in MNMCs' imports (p. 612). With regard to the positive and significant impact on the intensive margin on EU imports, the findings of Bensassi *et al.* (2010) shed some light on the impact of the Euro-Mediterranean Agreements on EU27–MNMC8 trade. They find that EU imports have increased due to the Euro-Mediterranean Agreements; that is, they claim that '[the] variable of interest, the implementation of Free Trade Agreements between the MENA countries and the EU, has a positive and significant effect on the intensive margin (...)' (p. 20).

Thus, after examining the trade evolution and composition of the Euro-Mediterranean Agreements, we can determine that the Euro-Mediterranean Agreements have had a null impact on the extensive margin of trade, being unable to create or divert trade, and a positive impact on the intensive margin of EU imports, although this impact has not been strong enough to stop the decrease in the importance of the EU27 in MNMC8 trade.

3.2 Central and Eastern European Countries

The findings regarding the CEECs differ greatly from the results regarding MNMC8 and EU27 trade evolution. Both comparisons (the first one being between the average World and the CEEC5–World trade evolution, and the second one being between the CEEC5–World and CEEC5–EU) show a strong relative increase in the CEEC5–EU15 trade since 1992 (Figures 1.4 and 1.5)

Moreover, it can be claimed that the magnitude of the institutional shock (i.e. the Europe Agreements) was very large, as the share of EU15 in CEEC5 trade flows of manufactured goods increases substantially and so does the share of CEEC5 in EU15 (Figure 1.6)

Trade composition analysis of CEEC5 corroborates and amplifies the results stated above. The analysis is based on the results of a paper by Tkachuk and Popko (2009) that analyses the evolution of the extensive and intensive margins, and on the results of Kandogan's paper (2009) analysing trade creation and diversion effects.

Tkachuk and Popko (2009) demonstrate in their paper that the Europe Agreements caused an increase in EU imports due mainly to the rise of the intensive margin, and that the role of the extensive margin was lower (p. 22). Kandogan (2009), on the other hand, focuses on the role of the extensive margin (trade creation and diversion), claiming that its increase was provoked more by trade diversion effects rather than by trade creation effects. Therefore, after analysing the trade evolution and its composition, it can be claimed that the Europe Agreements have managed to have a positive impact on the extensive margin, creating and diverting trade, as well as a strong and positive impact on the intensive

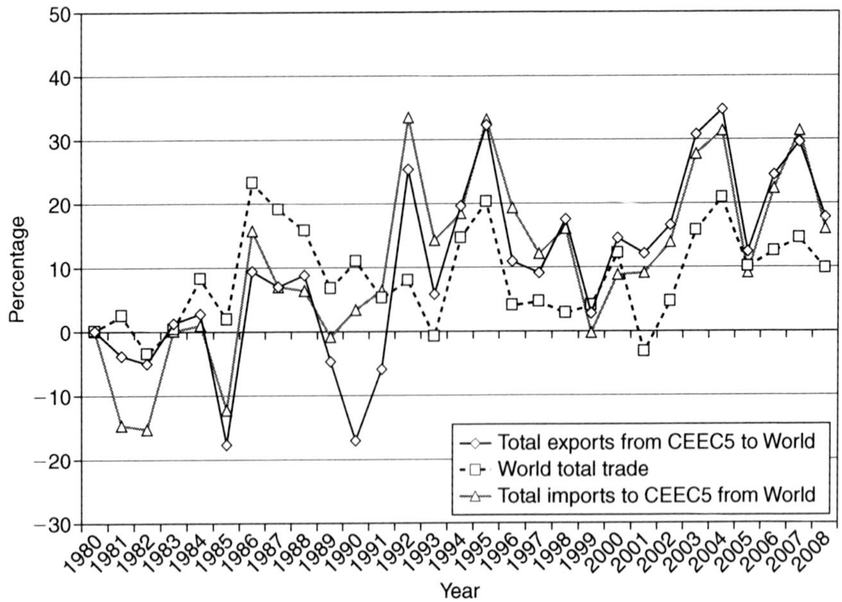

Figure 1.4 Comparison: World total trade vs trade from CEEC5 to World in yearly percentage change – period 1980–2008 (source: yearly percentage change based on WTO 2010).

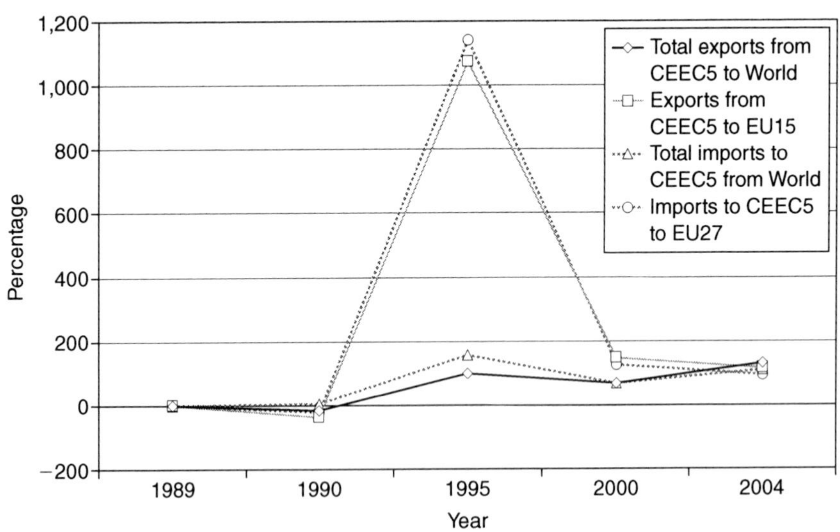

Figure 1.5 Comparison in CEEC5 trade flows of manufactured goods with the World and with the EU15 (percentage change) – period 1989–2004 (source: yearly percentage change based on WTO 2010 and UN Comtrade 2010).

margin of trade. Thus, the Europe Agreements have, on the whole, had a strong and positive impact on the bilateral trade flows of manufactured goods.

Comparing the two conclusions for MNMCs and CEECs, it is easy to note that the Europe Agreements had a stronger impact than the Euro-Mediterranean Agreements, and that the latter have proved, in themselves, to be weak. One possible explanation for this is the fact that the MNMCs had already been enjoying a preferential trade treatment with the EU since the late 1970s, when Cooperation Agreements were signed with Algeria, Tunisia, Morocco, Egypt, Jordan, Syria and Lebanon. However, previous papers, such as that of Joffé (in Fernandez and Youngs 2005), give us a broad idea of the weak impact of the 1970s Agreements, forcing us to search for other plausible reasons that explain the weak impact of the Euro-Mediterranean Agreements.

4 Plausible explanations for weak impact of the EMAAs

One feature common to all the MNMCs between the 1990s and 2009 was their political situation. Although different types of political regimes cohabited in the region, most of them shared several features that are worth noting. Despite labelling themselves as democracies, most of their heads of state had in common a strong desire for power, which moves them away from the democratic Western standards. Moreover, and despite the embracing of democracy and human rights

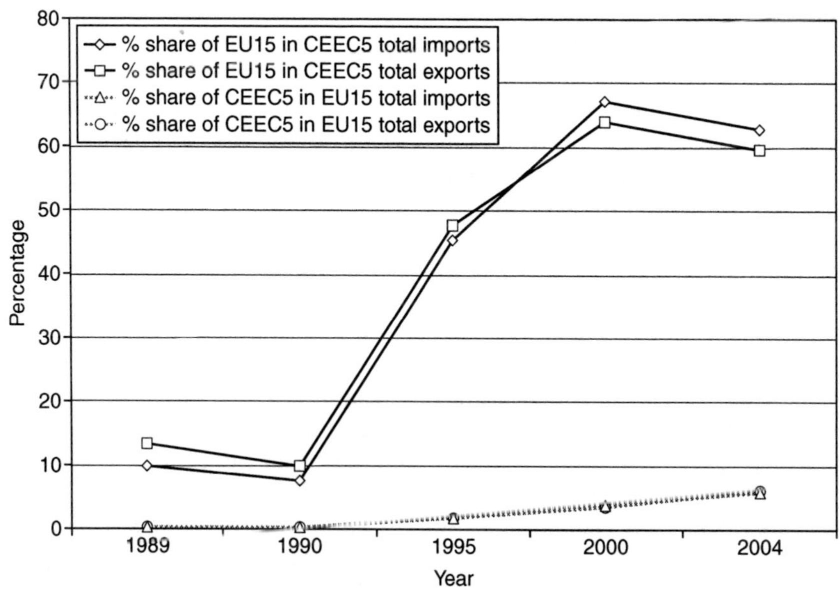

Figure 1.6 Percentage share of EU15 in CEEC5 trade and percentage share of CEEC5 in EU15 trade 1989–2004 (source: yearly percentage change based on WTO 2010 and UN Comtrade 2010).

in legal texts, 'Western' features of democracy such as freedom of expression or association were, in many cases, limited (ADE-EPU-NTUA-IBM Report 2003: 5). The economic situation was generally tough, and rent-seeking behaviour on the part of both the government and the society highly persistent. All these features combined to contribute to deterring investors and businessman, and as a whole 'the entire market mechanism is largely ruled out' (Schlumberger 2000: 250).

Concerning the political situation of the Mediterranean region as a whole, relations *amongst* the MNMCs were, up to 2003, almost non-existent (Brach 2006: 19), which made it difficult to create a whole area of shared prosperity. As Ghesquiere (1998, cited in Brach 2006) puts it, 'South–South integration represents a key element for the success of the region as a whole' (p. 22). With the creation of the Agadir Process in 2003, South–South relations have improved, but there is still a long way to go.

As the figures in the Appendix to this chapter show, the CEECs seem to be some steps ahead of the MNMCs in regard to their political situation. The figures capture the regime authority spectrum, with a range that goes from −10 (hereditary monarchy) to +10 (consolidated democracy).[10] From −10 to −6 the regime is labelled as an 'autocracy', from −5 to +5 as an 'anocracy', and from +6 to +10 as a 'democracy'. Whereas most Mediterranean countries have been considered 'anocracies'[11] from the time of the entry in force of the agreements onwards, all the CEEC5 have been labelled as democracies from the 1990s onwards (when the Europe Agreements took place). Therefore, and despite the improvements made with the Agadir process in terms of South–South integration, one can claim that lack of political stability has affected trade in the MNMCs.

If the first reason – the internal political situation – pointed at the MNMCs for the partial failure of the Agreements, the second reason points directly at the EU and its unwillingness to put the Euro-Mediterranean issue at the top of the EU agenda. In this direction, Montanari (2007) provides a valuable analysis of the Agreements, arguing that the design of trade agreements depends largely on the final objective of the bilateral relationship. In his paper, he suggests that whereas the final goal of the EU when negotiating with the CEECs was EU membership, this was not the case for the MNMCs, whose Agreements with the EU had the final objective of creating an FTA (p. 1022). Therefore, if the CEECs were to enter the single market eventually, the Agreements had to make sure that after ten years the CEECs would be ready to absorb the *acquis communautaire* and developed enough to fulfil the economic, political and social obligations that EU membership entails.

This is not to say that the failure arises from the decision not to include the MNMCs in the single market program. What it means is that, knowing that the final objective of the Agreements with the MNMCs was not that of entering the single market, many EU countries that are geographically further away from the Mediterranean did not want to devote time and money to an area where they had little vested political and economic interest. And this is what Montanari

(2007) refers to as the 'bargaining game of the EU'. In the first level of bargaining, domestic groups compete in the level of market openness: whereas industrial producers aspire to free access to MNMCs' markets, agricultural producers will fight for protection. At the second level (among countries), financial aid is negotiated: larger contributors to the EU budget will resist large financial aid, whereas larger beneficiaries will prefer the opposite. The outcome at both levels will therefore depend on the bargaining power of each group. In the case of the EU, agricultural producers have always had very strong bargaining power, probably explained by the 'logic of collective action' (Olson 1965). As for financial aid, net contributors have managed to keep the budget under control (Montanari 2007: 1019–1020). Therefore, the outcome that one should expect at the first two levels is a high level of protectionism and low level of aid. Furthermore, this lack of vested interest on the part of some EU countries in the Mediterranean prevents two important issues from being included in the Agreements, namely trade liberalization in services and regulatory harmonization (Montanari 2007: 1021; Brenton and Manchin 2003;4, 9; Reiffers and Tourret 2000: 16, 18, 21), which were given much more relevance in the CEECs' Agreements.

4.1 How have these outcomes influenced trade?

Aid to the Mediterranean countries has been clearly small and lower than that to the CEE countries (Montanari 2007: 1022; Brach 2006: 26; García-Álvarez-Coque 2002: 414; Licari 1998: 17). This fact seems to be indirectly (and negatively) related to trade. As Brach (2006) puts it, a large amount of aid gives an economic incentive to countries to pursue economic transition. The lack of economic incentives to reform the economy implies that state intervention remains very high and private business activity very low, thus affecting grade and levels of FDI negatively. Therefore, one can claim that the small amount of aid received by the MNMCs has had a negative impact on trade through the lack of incentives to reform their economic structure, which has moved business and FDI away.

Regarding agriculture liberalization, it is widely known that all sectors in an economy are highly related, and, from this, the importance of agriculture liberalization for trade in manufactured goods. Despite agriculture being one of the key sectors in many MNMCs, agriculture liberalization was not included in the EMAAs, and the MNMCs had to wait until the Marrakech Conference in 2006 to extract a commitment to a progressive liberalization. Therefore, not having liberalized agriculture trade earlier can be understood as a barrier for the MNMCs to exploit their comparative advantage.

Nonetheless, there are some reasons to think that the impact of agriculture liberalization is overestimated. Reiffers and Tourret (2000) show that already in 1997 many MNMCs had, aside from a comparative advantage in agriculture products, a potential comparative advantage in manufactured products such as chemicals and paper, among others (p. 11). Other authors emphasize the fact that by simply removing tariffs agriculture trade will not increase: agricultural products in the MNMCs, despite having a lower 'farm-gate' price, face higher logistic and transport costs (García-Alvarez-Coque 2000: 408); moreover, they have to adapt to EU requirements regarding safety and pest detection, among others (Brenton and Manchín 2003: 3). Finally, it is important to mention that the Europe Agreements did not involve any agriculture liberalization, and yet the CEECs' manufactured trade was boosted with the EAs (as stated in Section 3). Therefore, and taking all these statements into account, one can assert that even though agriculture liberalization might have a potential impact on local levels, this is not in itself a key factor needed for boosting manufactured trade and definitely is not a factor that has caused the difference in the impact between the EAs and the EMAAs.

Liberalization of trade in services has been effectively excluded from the Agreements. Only in 2003 was it agreed in the Palermo Conference of Trade that a Framework Protocol would be established (European Union 2003), and in 2006 the negotiations in conformity with WTO rules were launched (European Union 2006). Nonetheless, in the last conference in Brussels in 2009 (European Union 2009), negotiations were not concluded with any country. This situation differs greatly from that of the EAs with the CEECs in the early 1990s, which covered the movement of workers and the establishment and supply of services.

Moreover, liberalization of trade in services is considered by many authors to be an important issue affecting the level of trade, economic growth and FDI. Montanari (2007: 1021) and Brenton and Manchin (2003: 3) agree in considering liberalization of trade in services a source of economic growth, asserting that liberalization can lead to efficiency gains in both the service sector and the other sectors of the economy, and highlighting the technology spillovers that can be produced by liberalization.

Therefore, the clear difference witnessed between the level of liberalization of trade in services in the CEECs and the MNMCs on one hand, and the proven importance of the said liberalization in economic growth, trade and FDI on the other hand, proves the lack of liberalization of trade in services as an important factor affecting trade in manufactured goods negatively.

Regulatory harmonization concerning safety, environmental or health issues, among others, was not given much importance in the EMAAs. Instead, in the EAs in the 1990s this issue played an important role, and the EU even provided technical assistance to the CEECs. Brenton and Manchin (2003) provide a thorough analysis of the importance of regulatory standards and harmonization, claiming that the lack of standards acts as a non-tariff barrier that segments the market and therefore reduces trade (p. 7). The FEMISE Report in 2000 written by Reiffers and Tourret goes beyond by stating that the lack of harmonization is clearly an obstacle to FDI (p. 16), which in turn affects trade. Therefore, given the impact that regulatory harmonization has in the market, FDI and trade, we consider it a factor which negatively affects trade.

To summarize, one can claim that the weak impact of the EMAAs on trade has its roots in the following factors: the internal political situation of most of the MNMCs; the small amount of aid provided by the EU; and the lack of liberalization of trade in services and of regulatory harmonization, which are the result of political unwillingness to put the issue at the top of the EU agenda.

5 Conclusions

Institutional building in the shape of trade agreements has proved insufficient to achieve the main goal put forward in the Barcelona Declaration in 1995 – namely, to achieve an area of shared prosperity (European Union 2005). Even the rather *unofficial* goal of achieving security through an economic-driven partnership has not been accomplished. This has been shown by the evolution and composition of trade, described in the first half of this chapter.

In this part we have demonstrated, with trade theories and models, that the extensive margin of trade has not been affected by the EMAAs – that is, no trade has been created or diverted with the EMAAs – and the increase in the intensive margin has not been strong enough to stop the decline of the EU27 in MNMC8 trade. Taking into account the results and the comparison with the EAs, the conclusion is that the EMAAs have generated a positive impact on the aggregate flows of manufactured goods via the intensive margin, although this impact has not been strong compared to the impact that the EAs had on bilateral aggregate trade flows of manufactured goods.

What has failed? Why has the partnership not produced the expected outcomes? During the second half of the chapter we have aimed at disentangling the reasons for such an outcome, taking a political economic approach and comparing each of the plausible reasons with the situation of the CEECs.

The chapter has argued that persistent political instability and the hardly existent political and economic relationship among the MNMCs has affected trade negatively. Also, it shows that the political situation in the 1990s was better compared to that of the MNMCs, so we can infer that political instability can also account for the difference between the CEECs and the MNMCs regarding the outcome in trade.

The EU's political unwillingness to put the EMAAs at the top of the EU agenda has also affected several aspects of the Agreements. The comparison between CEECs and MNMCs shows that the MNMCs have received much less aid than the former countries. This smaller amount of aid has proven detrimental for economic transition, and has delayed the participation of private enterprises in the economy. Trade in agriculture has proven a less important reason hampering trade. Bilateral trade flows have been definitely affected through the refusal of liberalization of trade in services and a lack of regulatory harmonization. Both liberalization of trade in services and regulatory harmonization played an important role in the EAs, and therefore the chapter confirms that they account for the difference between the success of the EAs in enhancing trade and the relative failure of the EMAAs.

Although all the reasons for the weak outcome are already being dealt with and some improvements have been achieved – financial aid is better managed, liberalization in agriculture and trade are being negotiated, South–South integration is being encouraged and regulatory harmonization is being addressed – the pace of negotiations is still exceedingly slow, and it seems that the EU is still neglecting to give the issue high priority. On the other hand, a more social focus should be given to the partnership in order to tackle the political instability and rent-seeking behaviour of both government and society actors. The EU has to realize that the Mediterranean basin is an area with vast potential but also with great threats, and therefore some issues of utmost importance must be coped with before disappointment and frustration spread throughout the Mediterranean region.

Appendix: democratization levels in CEEC5 and MNMC8

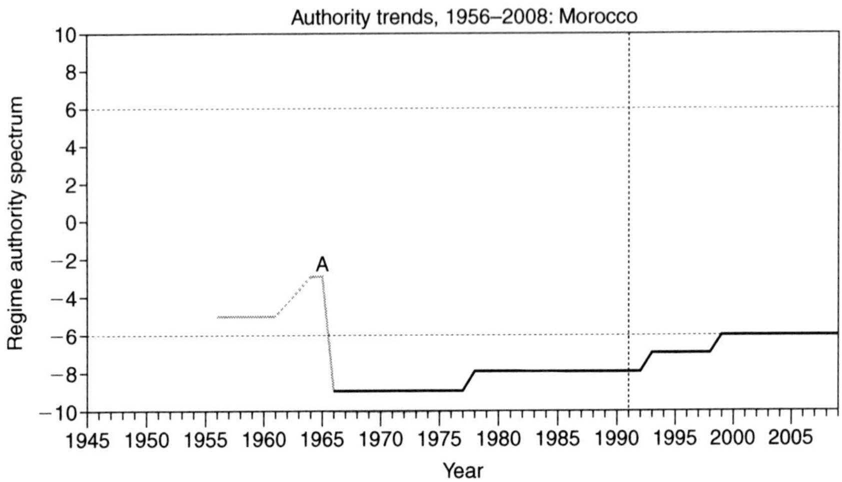

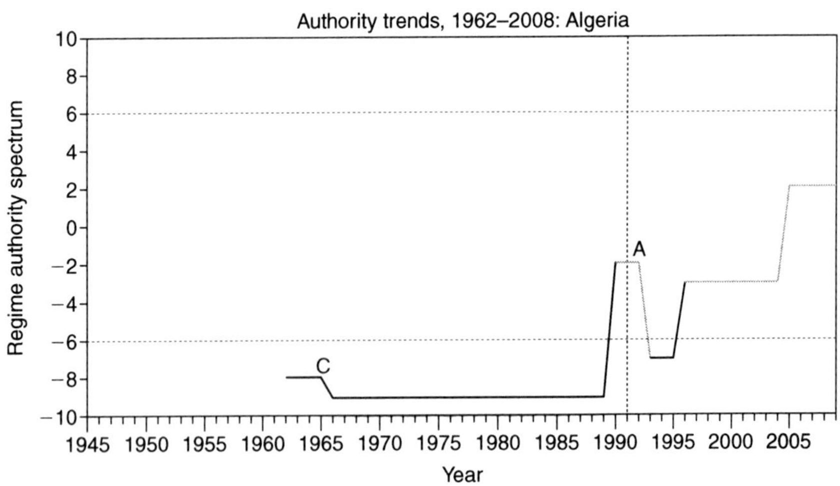

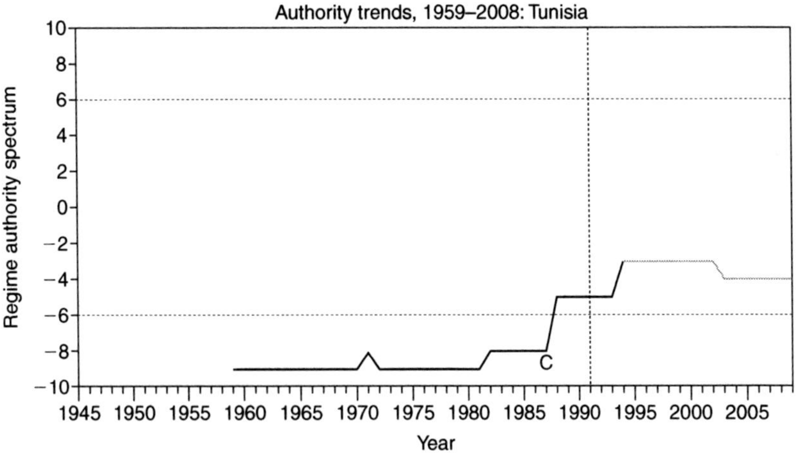

Authority trends, 1959–2008: Tunisia
Regime authority spectrum
10
8
6
4
2
0
−2
−4
−6
−8
−10
C
1945 1950 1955 1960 1965 1970 1975 1980 1985 1990 1995 2000 2005
Year

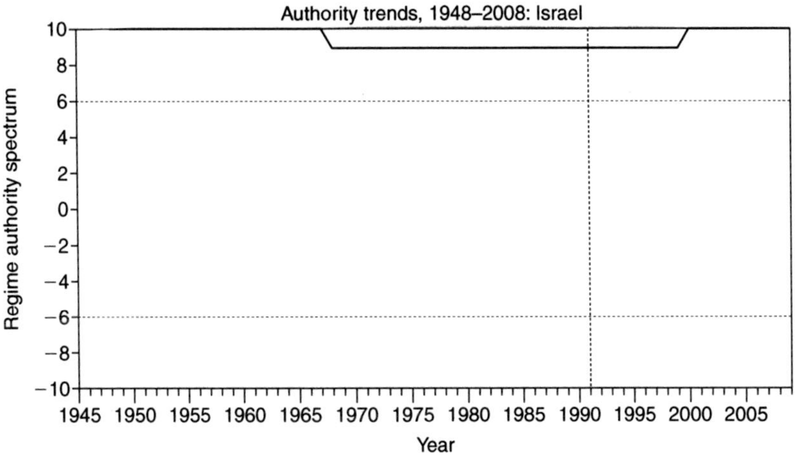

Authority trends, 1948–2008: Israel
Regime authority spectrum
10
8
6
4
2
0
−2
−4
−6
−8
−10
1945 1950 1955 1960 1965 1970 1975 1980 1985 1990 1995 2000 2005
Year

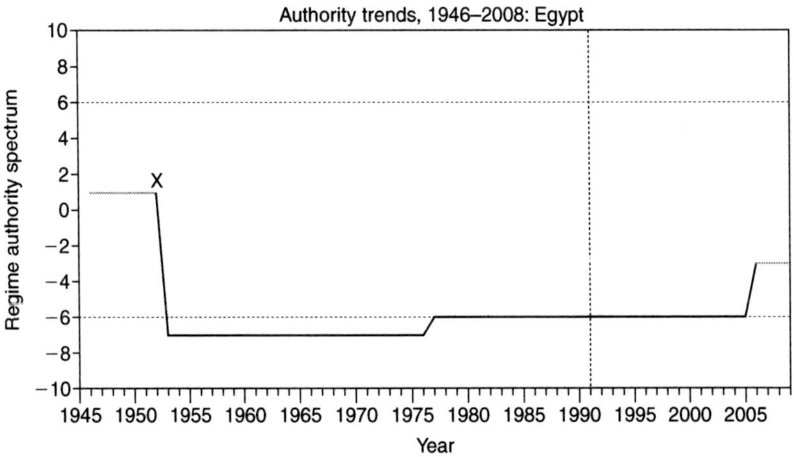

Authority trends, 1946–2008: Egypt
Regime authority spectrum
10
8
6
4
2
0
−2
−4
−6
−8
−10
X
1945 1950 1955 1960 1965 1970 1975 1980 1985 1990 1995 2000 2005
Year

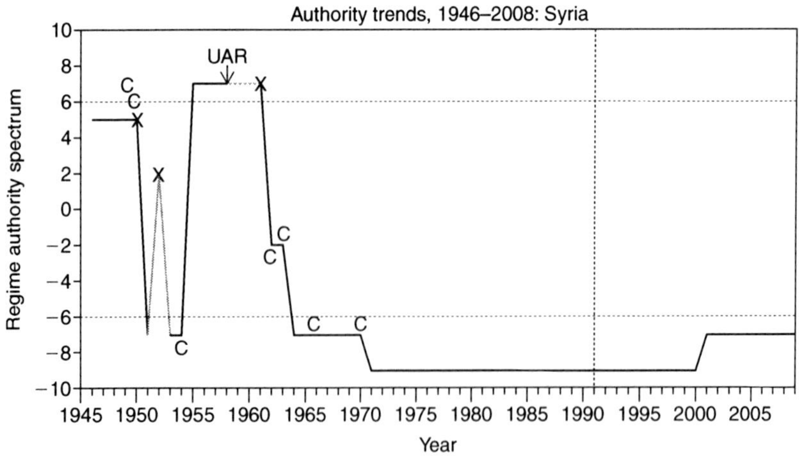
Authority trends, 1946–2008: Syria
Regime authority spectrum
Year
UAR
C
X
10
8
6
4
2
0
−2
−4
−6
−8
−10
1945
1950
1955
1960
1965
1970
1975
1980
1985
1990
1995
2000
2005

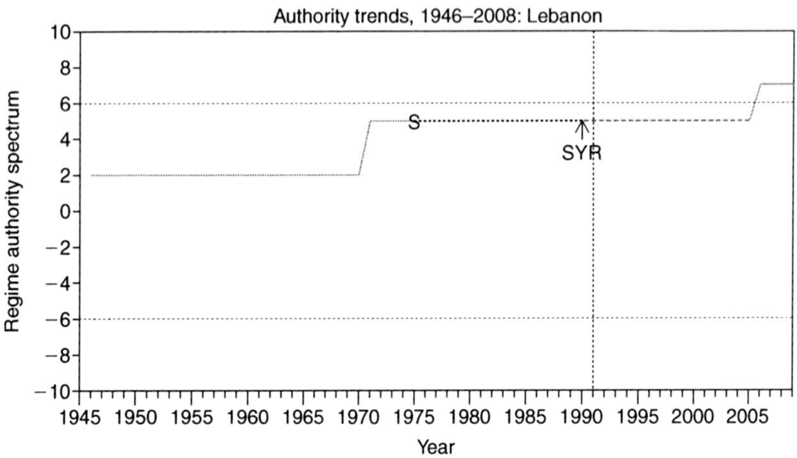
Authority trends, 1946–2008: Lebanon
Regime authority spectrum
Year
S
SYR
10
8
6
4
2
0
−2
−4
−6
−8
−10
1945
1950
1955
1960
1965
1970
1975
1980
1985
1990
1995
2000
2005

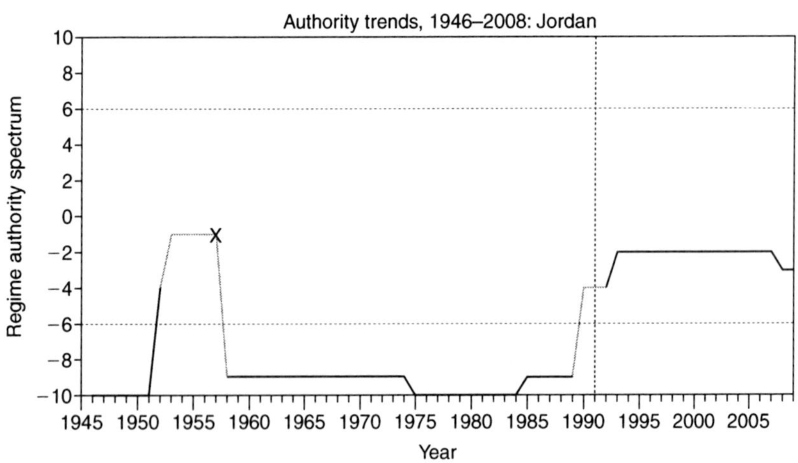
Authority trends, 1946–2008: Jordan
Regime authority spectrum
Year
X
10
8
6
4
2
0
−2
−4
−6
−8
−10
1945
1950
1955
1960
1965
1970
1975
1980
1985
1990
1995
2000
2005

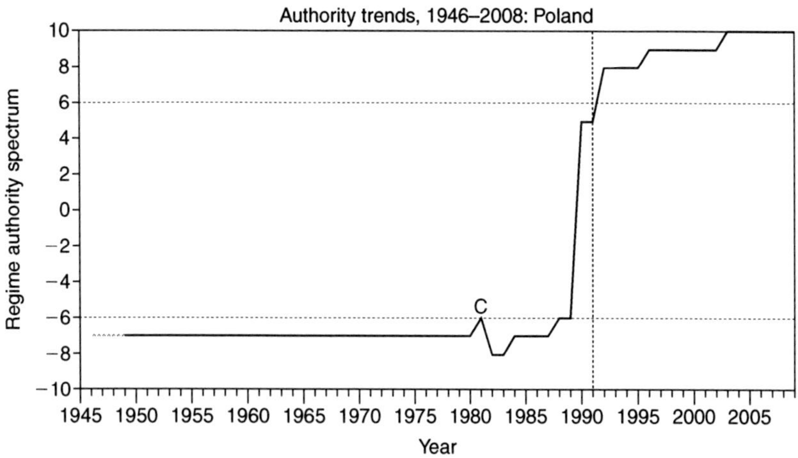
Authority trends, 1946–2008: Poland
Regime authority spectrum
10
8
6
4
2
0
−2
−4
−6
−8
−10
C
1945 1950 1955 1960 1965 1970 1975 1980 1985 1990 1995 2000 2005
Year

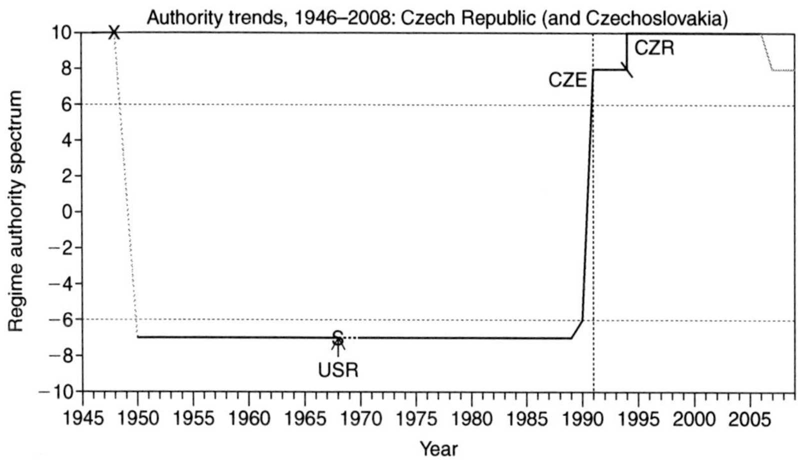
Authority trends, 1946–2008: Czech Republic (and Czechoslovakia)
Regime authority spectrum
10
8
6
4
2
0
−2
−4
−6
−8
−10
X
CZR
CZE
S
USR
1945 1950 1955 1960 1965 1970 1975 1980 1985 1990 1995 2000 2005
Year

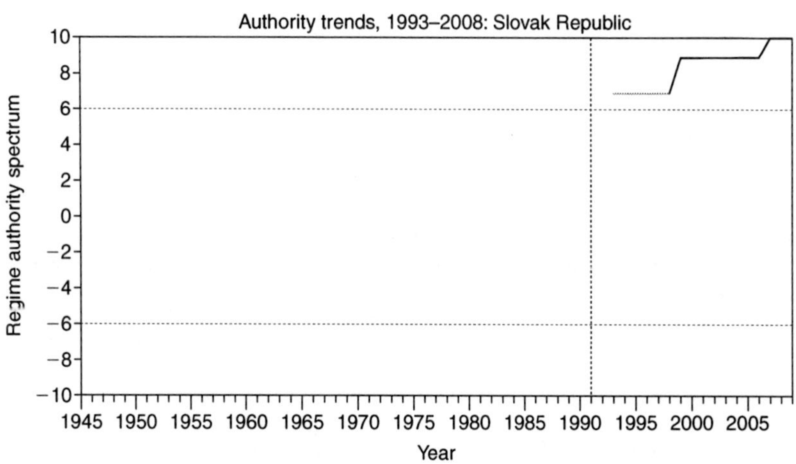
Authority trends, 1993–2008: Slovak Republic
Regime authority spectrum
10
8
6
4
2
0
−2
−4
−6
−8
−10
1945 1950 1955 1960 1965 1970 1975 1980 1985 1990 1995 2000 2005
Year

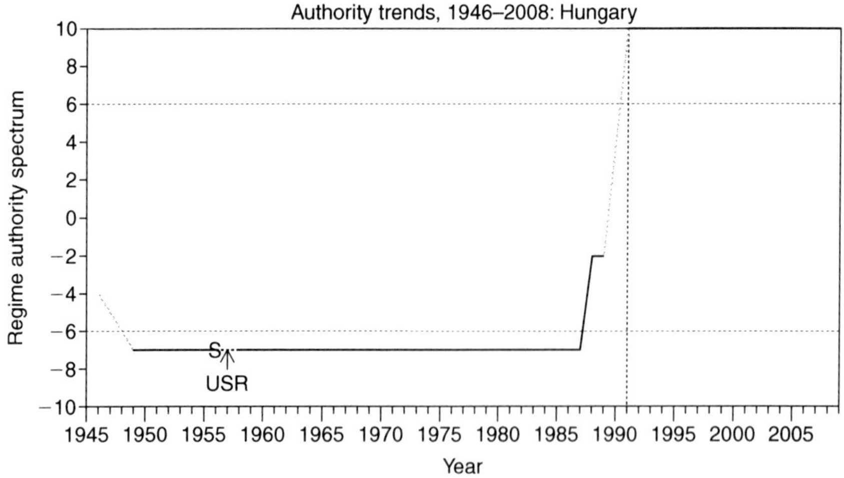

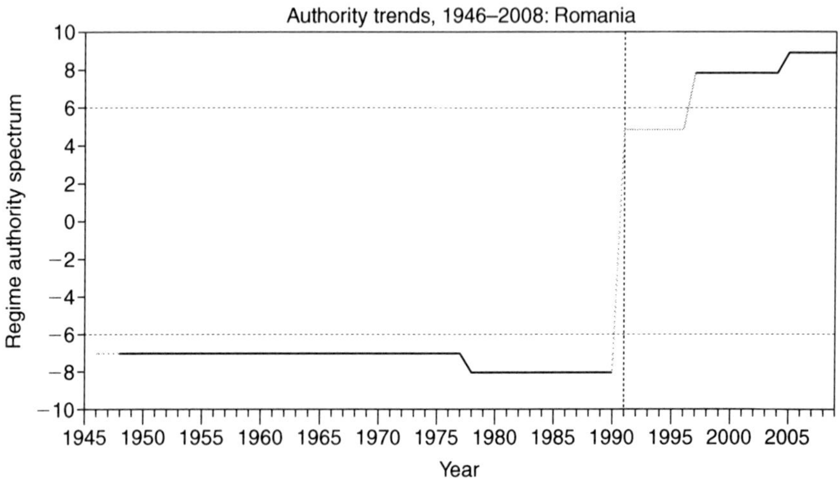

Notes

1 The remaining 16 are Albania, Algeria, Bosnia and Herzegovina, Croatia, Egypt, Israel, Jordan, Lebanon, Mauritania, Monaco, Montenegro, Morocco, the Palestinian Authority, Syria, Tunisia and Turkey (Europa.eu).
2 The Palestinian Authority is left aside because of lack of data.
3 Data for the CEECs in this chapter will only refer to Poland, the Czech Republic, Hungary, Romania and Slovakia because data regarding the other countries were not available.
4 Since both the EAs and the Euro-Mediterranean Agreements (EMAAs) are focused mainly on manufactures, the focus of the analysis is manufactured goods (SITC 5, 6, 7, 8).
5 CEECs are compared with EU15 (and not EU27), as the EAs entered in force in the 1990s, much before the entrance of the CEECs into the EU. MNMCs are compared with EU27, as the effects of the Agreements are analysed until 2008.

6 Data for all figures are taken from different databases according to availability. The three sources are the WTO 2010 (with data available from 1980 to 2008), UNComtrade 2010 (with data available from 1976 to 2009) and Eurostat 2010 (with data available from 1999 to 2008). Data are presented in USD. For more information on data description, contact the author.
7 See Melitz (2003) for further explanations.
8 A limitation to the present chapter must be addressed. Unfortunately, both papers dealing with extensive and intensive margins for CEECs and MNMCs (Tkackuk and Popko 2009 and Bensassi *et al.* 2010) focus on EU imports, leaving EU exports aside, and no other paper has been found analysing extensive and intensive margins concerning EU exports. The paper by Kandogan (2009) provides us with information about the extensive margin (by analysing trade creation and diversion) of both EU imports and exports for CEECs and MNMCs; therefore, an important limitation of this analysis and this chapter will be on the intensive margin of EU exports.
9 The two papers cover different countries: whereas Bensassi *et al.* (2010) covers all MENA countries, Kandogan (2009) only covers Tunisia, Israel, Morocco, Algeria and Jordan. However, for the purpose of our analysis, this difference is not considered relevant.
10 Data taken from Polity IV dataset project (Marshall 2010).
11 The exceptions being Israel, considered a democracy since 1946 (first available data); Lebanon, considered a democracy since 2005; and Syria, considered an autocracy since the early 1960s.

References

ADE-EPU-NTUA-IBM (2003) 'Evaluation of economic cooperation between the EC and MED Countries', Final Report, Vol. 1. Available at: http: //ec.europa.eu/europeaid/how/evaluation/evaluation_reports/reports/med/951645_vol. 1_en.pdf [accessed 7 July 2010].

Bensassi, S., Márquez-Ramos, L. and Martínez-Zarzoso, I. (2010) *Economic Integration and the Two Margins of Trade: An Application to the Euro-Mediterranean Agreements*, The Selected Works of Inma Martinez-Zarzoso [unpublished]. Available at: http: //works.bepress.com/inma_martinez_zarzoso/21.

Bergstrand, J.H. (1985) 'The gravity equation in international trade: some microeconomic foundations and empirical evidence', *Review of Economics and Statistics*, 67(3): 474–481. Available through the JSTOR database at: www.jstor.org/stable/1925976 [accessed 14 July 2010].

Brach, J. (2006) 'Ten years after: achievements and challenges of the Euro-Mediterranean economic and financial partnership', German Institute of Global and Area Studies (GIGA) Working Paper No. 36. Available at: www.giga-hamburg.de/content/publikationen/pdf/wp36_brach.pdf [accessed 7 July 2010].

Brenton, P. and Manchin, M. (2003) 'Trade policy issues for the Euro-Med partnership', Center for European Policy Studies (CEPS), Working Paper No. 7. Available at: www.ceps.eu/book/trade-policy-issues-euro-med-partnership. [accessed 7 July 2010].

Eichengreen, B. and Irwin, D. (1998) 'The role of history in bilateral trade flows', in J. Frankel (ed.), *The Regionalization of the World Economy*, Chicago, IL: University of Chicago Press.

European Union (2003) *Conclusions of the Euro-Mediterranean Trade Ministerial Conference*, Palermo, 7 July 2003.

European Union (2005) *Barcelona Declaration and Euro-Mediterranean Partnership 1995*. Available at: http: //europa.eu/legislation_summaries/external_relations/relations_with_third_countries/mediterranean_partner_countries/r15001_en.htm [accessed 2 July 2010].
European Union (2006) *5th EUROMED Trade Ministerial Conference*, Marrackech, 24 March 2006.
European Union (2009) *8th Union for the Mediterranean Trade Ministerial Conference*, Brussels, 9 December 2009.
Eurostat database (2010) http: //epp.eurostat.ec.europa.eu/portal/page/portal/eurostat/home/.
Feenstra, R.C., Markusen, J.R. and Rose, A.K. (2001) 'Using the gravity equation to differentiate among alternative theories of trade', *Canadian Journal of Economics/Revue canadienne d'Economique*, 34(2): 430–447. Available through the JSTOR database at: www.jstor.org/stable/3131862 [accessed 14 July 2010].
Fernandez, H.A. and Youngs, R. (2005) *The Euro-Mediterranean Partnership and Foreign Investment*, Quinteral Servicios Gráficos, S.L. Available at: www.realinstitutoelcano.org/publicaciones/libros/Barcelona10_eng.pdf [accessed 6 July 2010].
García-Alvarez-Coque, J.M. (2002) 'Agricultural trade and the Barcelona Process: is full liberalization possible?', *European Review of Agricultural Economics*, 29(3): 399–422. Available through the Oxford Journal database at: http: //erae.oxfordjournals.org/cgi/reprint/29/3/399 [accessed 15 March 2010].
Kandogan, Y. (2009) 'Trade creation and diversion effects of Europe's Regional Liberalization Agreements', *International Economic Journal*, 23(4): 591–615. Available through the Informaworld database at: http: //dx.doi.org/10.1080/10168730903372257 [accessed 14 July 2010].
Licari, J. (1998) 'The Euro-Mediterranean Partnership: economic and financial aspects', *Mediterranean Politics*, 3(3): 1–20. Available through the Informaworld database at: http: //pdfserve.informaworld.com/761835_731224298_784385148.pdf [accessed 7 July 2010].
Marshall, M.G. (2010) *Polity IV Database Project: Political Regime Characteristics and Transitions, 1800–2009*. Available at: www.systemicpeace.org/polity/polity4.htm [accessed 15 August 2010].
Melitz, M.J. (2003) 'The impact of trade on intra-industry reallocations and aggregate industry productivity' *Econometrica*, 6: 1695–1725.
Montanari, M. (2007) 'The Barcelona Process and the political economy of Euro-Mediterranean trade integration', *Journal of Common Market Studies*, 45(5): 1011–1040. Available at: http: //onlinelibrary.wiley.com/doi/10.1111/j.1468–5965.2007.00758.x/pdf [accessed 15 March 2010].
Nello, S. (2005) *The European Union, Economics, Policies and History*, 2nd edn. Maidenhead: McGraw-Hill Education.
Olson, M. (1965) *The Logic of Collective Action: Public Goods and the Theory of Groups*. Cambridge, MA: Harvard University Press.
Putnam, R. (1988) 'Diplomacy and domestic politics: the logic of two-level games', *International Organization*, 42(3): 427–460. Available at: http: //b37.moelabs.org/Teoria_das_ri_I-Rafael_Pons/I_Semestre/Diplomacy_and%20_Domestic_Politics_The_Logic_of%20_JDN.pdf [accessed 16 July 2010].
Reiffers, J.L and Tourret, J.C (2000) 'Investing in a Euro-Mediterranean Free Trade Area', FEMISE Report, Institut de la Méditerranée. Available through FEMISE at: www.femise.org/PDF/Investment_en_InsMed.pdf [accessed 21 July 2010].
Schlumberger, O. (2000) 'Arab political economy and the European Union's Mediterranean policy: what prospects for development?', *New Political Economy*, 5(2): 247–268.

Available through the Informaworld database at: www.informaworld.com/smpp/content~db=all~content=a713687768~frm=abslink [accessed 3 July 2010].

Tkachuk, O. and Popko, D. (2007) *On the Patterns of Trade Convergence in European Transition Countries*, MPRA Paper No. 14109. Available at: http: //mpra.ub.uni-muenchen.de/14109.

UN COMTRADE database (2010) http: //comtrade.un.org/.

Viner, J. (1950) *The Customs Union Issue*, cited in Kenen, P.B (2000) *The International Economy*, Cambridge: Cambridge University Press. Available at: http: //books.google.es/books?id=Cy02FPQER_sC&printsec=frontcover#v=onepage&q&f=false [accessed 27 July 2010].

WTO database (2010) www.wto.org.

2 Cross-regionalism and MENA countries

Alfred Tovias

1 A brave new world

In his book *Nineteen Eighty-Four*, published in 1949, George Orwell pictured a world divided between three rival totalitarian powers – EastAsia, Oceania and Eurasia – which would be in perpetual war, always two of them allied against the third in sequence. Similarly, quite a few experts in international economic relations, whether economists or political scientists, were predicting less than a decade ago that the twenty-first century would be characterized by the emergence of trading or trade 'blocs' in the context of what was then baptized as the 'New Regionalism'.[2] Quite a number of books, reports and articles written in the second half of the 1990s contain in their title the word 'blocs', including from the most serious international institutions (see, for example, World Bank, 2000).

Even the former GATT's General Secretary, Renato Ruggiero, said in a speech in 1997 that the new RTAs (Regional Trade Agreements) were about 'securing regional spheres of influence in a world, marked by growing competition for markets, for investment and for technology' (quoted in Mathis, 2002: 127). Clearly, Ruggiero's scenarios remained in the setting of the 1930s. He feared the development of concentric circles around two focal points or hegemonic trade superpowers, namely the US and the EU. For him, it reflected an inability of the transatlantic community to coordinate its trade interests and vision, all being an outcome of the end of the Cold War. Some time previously, Huntington (1993), in his remarkable article on the clash of civilizations, had evoked the possibility of international friction, if not war, between different 'tectonic plates' – an idea bearing some commonality with the concept of 'blocs'. The world was suffering from a bout of so-called regionalism, namely a doctrine or ideology that argues that countries should promote trade preferably with countries of the same region[3] rather than with any other country in the world. This is the case for different reasons, be they political, cultural, defensive or, last but not least, economic. It may have potentially lethal consequences not only for the open multilateral world trade system as embodied by the laws of the WTO but also for world peace (Tovias, 2000a).

In the middle of this decade, and to the astonishment of many, the international business press started to report on the conclusion of trade agreements that not long ago would have been considered as belonging to the realm of political fiction. A good illustration, for instance, of what is mentioned here was the announcement posted in mid-2005 on the website of the General Directorate for Economic Affairs of Chile explaining that Brunei, Chile, New Zealand and Singapore were to conclude negotiations on a Trans-Pacific Strategic Economic Partnership Agreement, and which was presented as a 'bridge between Latin America, the Pacific and Asia'. In other news, the press revealed in November 2004 that Chile and China were to start negotiations towards the conclusion of a Free Trade Agreement.[4] Experts of the World Bank used the term 'additive regionalism' when relating to the new wave of agreements with multiple partners concluded by countries such as Singapore, Mexico, Chile and Israel, as it would be a new fashion or trend. The US concluded an FTA agreement with Bahrain in 2004 (see Table 2.1), whereas the latter country is a member of the Gulf Cooperation Council, aspiring to become a Customs Union. Obviously, sometimes new programmes or policies are launched and never come to fruition, but what seems important here is that they were openly publicized. For instance, the EU, an hegemonic trade superpower, has given a lot of publicity to negotiations with Mercosur since the early years of this decade, but has not been able to achieve the conclusion of an FTA with this entity, a Latin American scheme initially aiming at the creation of a Customs Union (hence allowing the EU to negotiate with it as a unit).

This chapter deals with this new wave in preferential trading which affects MENA countries as well, a fashion dating back only to the year 2000 (see Table 2.1 for a list of the agreements in force), which has alternatively been called different names by various experts: Cross-regionalism (Crawford and Florentino, 2005), Transoceanic Agreements (Péridy, 2004), Preferential Trade Agreements (Bhagwati and Panagariya, 1999), Polilateralism (De Sebastian, 1995), Competitive Regionalism (Abugattas Majluf, 2004) and, last, but not least, Additive Regionalism (Harrison *et al.*, 2002). A distinctive feature of this new trend is the simultaneous participation of countries in various FTAs, even if, in many cases, these agreements have very different trade rules (usually also being implemented over different periods) and include countries not belonging to the same geographic region. The launching of agreements of the new sort challenges geographical proximity as a necessary element for promoting and making integration viable. Economic distance is no longer perceived as a criterion for choosing preferred trading partners. These agreements challenge the classical notion of a region. This chapter has adopted the concept of 'cross-regionalism' used by Crawford and Florentino (2005) to describe the new trend.

About one-third of the FTAs currently under negotiation are among countries that belong to different world regions, with a growing share of North–South agreements. According to Crawford and Florentino (2005), cross-regional agreements have accounted for a large proportion of the total increase in PTAs (preferential trade agreements) in recent years.[5] Both the EU and the US try to encroach on the sphere of influence of the other. Some middle-income countries (such as Chile, Singapore and Mexico, but also Israel and Morocco) try to escape their initial uncomfortable status of a so-called 'spoke' by signing agreements with more than one 'hub'. The most daring of them go forward and also conclude agreements with other high-income 'spokes' (e.g. Israel with EFTA).

2 Historical background: first, second, third wave of regionalism – what is new?

In the 1950s, 1960s and 1970s, PTAs were among countries of similar development levels, usually in close geographical proximity, and focused on eliminating tariffs on industrial goods. They took the form of Customs Unions (e.g. the EC, UDEAC, Arab Common Market) or Free Trade Areas (e.g. EFTA, LAIA, the Andean Pact). One exception to this type of regionalism was the EC, which had already started signing some reciprocal trade agreements with countries or FTAs in its proximity (e.g. the 1972 EC agreements with individual EFTA countries). The rest of the EC cooperation agreements with developing countries (such as Mediterranean countries) were non-reciprocal.[6]

The turn to the second type of regionalism at the end of the 1980s was, according to different experts, the result of declining US hegemony and the world economic recession, combined with the demise of the Soviet empire. What was new then was that the US wanted to establish itself as a regional benevolent hegemon in the western hemisphere. Admittedly Latin America had been the backyard (and, for some, the private garden) of the US since at least the 1940s, but with the end of Cold War the US could take a more relaxed view of Latin America. It could, for instance, try to promote democracy and reform in Latin America without taking big security risks for itself. This could be done in a business-like manner by drawing up very enticing FTA agreements for Latin American candidates, namely tariff-free unimpeded and secured access to the largest national market of the world – the US (including agricultural markets). In exchange, Latin American countries would have to respect some US-imposed rules (labour standards, environmental norms, Intellectual Property Rights). Hence the rapidly concluded deal of NAFTA and the proposal for an FTAA (Free Trade Area of the Americas) made by the US government to Latin America. At the same time, the US administrations of the period felt the US could not any longer act as a global hegemon (as had been the case since 1945). As Woolcock showed, in Geiger and Kennedy (1996), in the first half of the 1990s the preoccupation of multilateralists in GATT, and as from 1994 in the WTO, was with the emergence of trading blocs, i.e. contiguous countries forming a region (exemplified by the EU, NAFTA and Mercosur and the project of ANZCERTA[7]) and the possible reaction to all this by ASEAN countries. Among others, this was due to the uncertainty about the fate of the Uruguay Round of multilateral trade negotiations which had started in 1986 and had become stuck at different instances. Another frequently mentioned factor in the relevant literature was the fear of seeing the emergence of Fortress Europe as an outcome of the Completion of the Single Market (the so-called EC1992 programme) together with the perspective of further EU Enlargements. Observe, as well, that the main tensions during the Uruguay Round were between the US and the EU, with middle-income and developing countries wondering if it was no time to get a separate deal with the local hegemon. This was the time of the so-called domino regionalism and the hub-and-spoke systems, popularized in Baldwin *et al.* (1995) and Baldwin and Venables (1995).

Since the formal initiation of the Doha Round in 2001, the fight has been between North and South (around the group of the G-20, captained by Brazil). The fear, then, is no longer that closed trading blocs will emerge as a result of the possible failure of the Doha Round. By now, every developing country has learned (and that includes Morocco, Jordan and Egypt), as some middle-income countries did a while before (e.g. Israel), that whereas a country can belong to only one Customs Union, it can be a member of an infinite number of Free Trade Areas. Nobody can prevent it from doing this – not the US or the EU.[8] Countries need to be a 'spoke' of only one 'hub', and they can become a 'hub' as well. This dynamic explains the 'free-for-all' atmosphere characterizing this new wave of preferentialism, including prominent MENA countries, which is the object of this chapter. It is a development going well beyond the so-called 'hub-and-spoke' pattern. What seems to be emerging now is a multipolar trade system, rather than the multilateral one envisaged by the architects of the WTO a decade ago (Mathis, 2002). Individual PTAs increasingly overlap one with another. This was exceptional in the past but is rapidly becoming the rule now. The hub-and-spoke model tends to disappear or at least to be diluted, not only because there are agreements between the spokes, but also because some of the spokes rebel against their hub by signing with other hubs. Some of them actually become hubs themselves (e.g. Turkey).

An answer to the 'spokes' rebellion developed quickly in 2001–2002, when the first US George W. Bush Administration launched what was denominated by its USTR Representative of the time, Robert Zoellick, 'competitive regionalism' – namely, that the US was open from now on to signing special preferential trade agreements (of course officially conforming with WTO rules and taking the form of FTAs) with any country in the world regardless of its location. *The Economist* (24 February 2004) reported that since the Cancun Summit ending in total discomfiture at the end of 2003, the US had turned bilateral.

The EU did not wait for the 'rebellion of the spokes' to unfold when it decided, as from 1999, to try to get a deal with Mercosur. This was violating the unspoken rule of division of the trade world into specific spheres of influence (see the first and second regionalism). At the time it seemed innocuous, as the US had not budged when the EU succeeded in signing a separate FTA deal with Mexico which entered into force in 2000. But maybe the reason for the US passivity then was that the EU presented the agreement as an answer to NAFTA's trade-diverting potential against the EU.

In any case, it is the impatience with the lack of progress at the WTO multilateral level that explains the present race. Pessimism about the fate of the Round reached a high point for the first time after the *sine die* formal suspension of the negotiations by the WTO's Director General, Pascal Lamy, on 24 July 2006.[9] A subsequent meeting of the G-4 (i.e. Brazil, the EU, the US and India), held in Potsdam on 19 June 2007 and failing to produce concrete results, has only confirmed the prevailing pessimistic prognosis for the present Round (see Kohr, 2007). Therefore it does not come as a surprise that some countries have actually felt for quite some time now that they could beat not only some other competing countries in this race but, more to the point, all of them, by betting on the fact that the Doha Round results would and will not succeed, or in any case will take a lot of time to be implemented if at all.

Confronted with this development, the WTO Secretariat has sharply reacted by stating that the multiplicity of preferential tariff rates depending on the countries, the groupings or the rules of origin would bring the system to a confusing state of affairs that private sectors would not enjoy (*The Economist*, 24 October 2003). The multiplicity of rules of origin might lead an exporter to tailor its products in accordance with a daunting array of product-specific criteria in order to reap benefits. In many cases, the exporter might give up. And, as is well known, enforcing origin rules has administrative costs, which in the case of EFTA have been estimated to be around 3% of the value of intra-EFTA and EFTA–EU trade (Baldwin and Venables, 1995: 1635). Moreover, small countries with limited human resources to examine and negotiate trade deals will be disadvantaged (see below).

3 Present, past and prospective cross-regional trade agreements

Table 2.1 provides a list of the most significant agreements considered in this chapter, in chronological order of the date of entry into force. The reason for indicating the latter is that it is neither the date of negotiations which is economically significant, nor the dates of signature or ratification, but the date of actual entry into force, as this is normally the date when an important share of mutual trade starts to be freed between the parties on a discriminatory basis. Agreements concerning MENA countries are in italics. From the table it appears that the number of actual cross-regional FTAs in force is still quite small but that among them a significant number involves one or another MENA country as a partner.

4 Economic analysis of cross-regionalism

Most theoretical models of the 1960s/1970s assumed implicitly that the reciprocal trade agreement was being signed between a small (A) and a large country (B), non-neighbours, while the Rest of the World (C) was huge and would not notice anything (Vanek, 1965; Kemp, 1969; Lipsey, 1970). Observe that transport costs were ignored. For instance, in all general equilibrium models presented in Kemp (1969), the small country was exclusively trading with its future partner, the large country, which was also trading with the Rest of the World, represented by given international terms of trade (world prices). In that context, A gains, B loses, and non members are indifferent. This simple model could be

Table 2.1 Cross-regional trade agreements and date of entry into force (in chronological order)

Israel–US	*8/1985*	
Bolivia–Mexico	1/1995	
Canada–Chile	7/1997	incl. services agreement
Israel–Canada	*9/1997*	
Chile–Mexico	8/1999	incl. services agreement
Israel–Mexico	*70/2000*	
EC–Mexico	7/2000	services agreement 3/2001
New Zealand–Singapore	1/2001	incl. services agreement
EFTA–Mexico	7/2001	incl. services agreement
US–Jordan	*12/2001*	*incl. services agreement*
Chile–Costa Rica	2/2002	incl. services agreement
Chile–El Salvador	6/2002	incl. services agreement
Canada–Costa Rica	11/2002	
EFTA–Singapore	1/2003	incl. services agreement
EC–Chile	2/2003	services agreement 3/2005
Singapore–Australia	7/2003	incl. services agreement
US–Singapore	1/2004	incl. services agreement
Chile–US	1/2004	incl. services agreement
Panama–Taiwan	1/2004#	
Republic of Korea–Chile	4/2004	incl. services agreement
Mexico–Uruguay	7/2004#	
EFTA–Chile	12/2004	incl. services agreement
Thailand–Australia	1/2005	incl. services agreement
US–Australia	1/2005	incl. services agreement
Mexico–Japan	4/2005	incl. services agreement
Thailand–New Zealand	7/2005	incl. services agreement
Jordan–Singapore	*8/2005*	*incl. services agreement*
US–Morocco	*1/2006*	*incl. services agreement*
Korea–Singapore	3/2006	incl. services agreement
Guatemala–Taiwan#	7/2006	
Japan–Malaysia	7/2006	incl. services agreement
US–Bahrain	8/2006	incl. services agreement
EFTA–Korea	9/2006	Incl. services agreement
Chile–China	10/2006	
Chile–New Zealand–Singapore–Brunei	not implemented yet	
Panama–Singapore	not implemented yet	
US–Malaysia	not implemented yet	
US–Oman	*not implemented yet*	
US–UAE	*not implemented yet*	
US–Republic of Korea	not implemented yet	
US–Thailand	not implemented yet	
US–SACU[1]	not implemented yet	
Peru–Thailand	not implemented yet	

Source: WTO and various other sources.

Notes
1 Southern African Customs Union.
= not notified to the WTO.

applied, then, to partial preferential agreements signed between the EC and small Mediterranean countries (such as Morocco, Tunisia or Israel), or the membership agreements between Portugal and the EC or Greece and the EC. Theoreticians thus questioned the economic wisdom of the EC signing these agreements; quite validly, they stressed that only political reasons could justify the EC's policy – the EC's wish to create its own sphere of political influence in the Mediterranean or its wish to consolidate democracy in Southern Europe.

With the emergence, though, of the new trade theories in the 1980s a new economic rationale was found in the EC to justify what it was doing: the EC, by signing FTAs with countries in its proximity and vicinity, could expect to gain from the establishment of intra-industry trade in some specific sectors (such as textiles): this is the outsourcing argument for FTA creation. Observe that the agreements between the EC and its neighbours were 'natural' for the latter but 'unnatural' for the EU, as its small partners each accounted for a very small share of the EU's total trade. Therefore these agreements were only 'semi-natural' (e.g. the EU might be the natural trading partner of Mediterranean countries, but the latter are not the natural trading partners of the EU). This stands in contrast to EU agreements with EFTA countries; they were probably natural trade partners for the EU. Therefore, we find that differential country size in semi-natural FTAs *with neighbouring countries* leads to economic gains for the small and political gains for the large trading partners.

The conclusion of cross-regional agreements between 'non-natural' trading partners in recent years is not that straightforward, and poses the theoretical question of why they are concluded.

First of all, independently of which of the two partners gains or loses, the overall diagnosis should follow Krugman (1990), Frankel (1998) and Baier and Bergstrand (2004) in that they do not increase welfare but rather decrease it. Politically, the proximity argument of the large country creating spheres of influence or consolidating democracy cannot be invoked, since the shares of trade of the large country in the small are far from being dominant. Economically, the only justifications seem to be:

1 to overcome Frankel's 'supernaturalism', i.e. to neutralize the deleterious effects derived from having previously signed with a neighbouring country leading to too much costly trade diversion; this argument applies in particular to the large country, which has an interest in having the preferences of neighbouring small countries being eroded.
2 for the small country to overcome the transport cost differential favouring non-preferred neighbours with preferential market access to the large country.

Since the economic rationale for the small country to sign with a far-away large country is less compelling if compared to the one of signing with a local hegemon, there must be non-economic (i.e. political) reasons invoked by the small, such as a reduction of dependence vis-à-vis the local hegemon. In other words, whereas, as stated above, differential country size in semi-natural FTAs with neighbouring countries leads to economic gains for the small and political gains for the large trading partners, in the case of cross-regional agreements (i.e non-natural FTAs) the two sides have both economic and political gains in sight.

A subset of small economies particularly attracted, in the last five to ten years, by these features are countries in the MENA region (e.g. Jordan, Morocco and Bahrain). A strategy consisting in multiplying the number of Free Trade Areas is perfectly suited to the latter. According to the old North–South pattern, the EU or the US concluded preferential deals mainly to reap the political benefit of extending their sphere of influence in their geographic neighbourhood. MENA countries sought the economic benefit of market access to the large EU market. Now a new pattern is emerging whereby the two partners to the bilateral preferential agreement (e.g. the US and Morocco) are motivated by both economic and political reasons. One clear result is that the EU's sphere of influence in the Mediterranean is on the wane, the creation of the Union for the Mediterranean (UfM) notwithstanding.

5 A policy-maker's perspective of why MENA countries would want to have a PTA with a non-neighbouring partner rather than with the EU

There are economic and political reasons for geographically discriminating in trade, i.e. for preferentialism, whether regional or non-regional. But why distinguish between distant and neighbouring or near-abroad/near-outside countries[10]? Are the aims of the small, emerging economies and developing countries identical as when striving to conclude an agreement with the trading hegemon in the neighbourhood? In what follows, reasons for and against have been carefully enumerated on the basis of examination of official documents, declarations and newspaper articles, paraphrasing the arguments typically put forward by policy-makers in the Arab World, Turkey and Israel and their 'natural' economic partner, namely the EU:

5.1 Political and other non-economic reasons

Mentioned by MENA and EU policy-makers alike

1 'several distant countries are more important military and/or political allies, than closer countries'; this is the sort of argumentation heard in the US regarding Jordan and vice versa.
2 'in a country as ours open to global trade, bilateral preferential agreements with neighbours are not as likely to prevent war with them as in the past. They are politically less necessary.' As argued by Martin *et al.* (2008), multilateral trade openness reduces the opportunity cost of going to war with any given country. Clearly, insofar as a country is increasingly trade-dependent on countries other than the neighbour(s), it will be less deterred in engaging in war against the latter. This argument is put forward in Israel

by those who do not see any relevance of the Jean Monnet argument in favour of PTAs with former enemies (e.g. France and Germany after 1945).
3 'our neighbours do not want to have PTAs with us; it is a matter of ideology' (e.g. heard after 1979 in Israel, regarding Egypt).

Mentioned by MENA policy-makers only

4 'neighbours are our enemies'; in some cases (as in the case of Israel) 'neighbours are boycotting us. Even if there is no Cold nor Hot War, there is only Cold Peace (e.g. the case of many Arab WTO member countries at present).'
5 'we will gain negotiating experience.' Among the typical motivations for having a PTA with any country is that it can be a laboratory for change; it provides the relevant country with valuable negotiating skills (argument heard typically in small countries, like Jordan or Israel).

5.2 Economic reasons

Mentioned by MENA and EU policy-makers alike

1 'our neighbours have small markets anyway' (a typical argument heard in Israel).
2 'we have already agreements with the region/the neighbours; we must improve market access elsewhere' (an argument stressed by Morocco, which has had access to industrial EU markets since 1977).
3 'our exports are distance-insensitive', such as financial/insurance/software/accountancy services, high-tech, diamonds, crude oil (an argument heard in Israel).

Mentioned by MENA policy-makers, rather than in the EU

4 'we need to secure demand for our goods and services in distant OECD markets.' There have been, for example, voices in Morocco in favour of increasing exports to the US to somehow diminish exclusive trade dependence on EU markets.
5 'we need to draw specific technologies via FDI from a particular OECD country which is distant from us.' Probably, the wish of Morocco to be less technologically dependent on the EU or France has played a certain role in its deciding to go for an FTA with the US.
6 'we need to compensate what Frankel (1998) calls *supernaturalism*: previous preferential agreements with our *natural* trading partners have made us artificially dependent on them; on top of it we bear a huge cost of trade diversion in their favour'; this is the sort of argument which led Israel to get an FTA with the US after the conclusion of the 1975 FTA with the EU; also argued is that 'with such an agreement we diminish our historical dependence on our local hegemon.'
7 'we must overcome the "spoke" syndrome and unravel the prevailing hub-and-spoke system.' This is an argument used in Israel by those that already

suggested in the 1990s engagement in FTA relations with Turkey and with Eastern European countries not yet in the EU.

8 'we must prevent the politicization of trade relations' (advanced as an argument in Israel).

9 'we must beat the Doha Round by several years.' This argument has been advanced by a large number of emerging and developing economies (such as Morocco) distressed by the fact that it is taking a lot of time to be concluded, if at all, successfully.

10 'we might be graduated out of the GSP'; this is a common fear in most South Eastern Asian countries at present. Some have actually already been graduated (e.g. Singapore). However, it could also become an argument in advanced MENA countries (Turkey, Tunisia, Israel, Lebanon)

6 A policy-maker's perspective of why MENA countries would refrain from having a PTA with a non-neighbouring partner

6.1 Political and other non-economic reasons:

Mentioned by MENA countries

1 'neighbours are more important than non-neighbours; potentially they constitute a more direct menace, therefore there is an additional reason to cooperate with them; we need to make them win from exchanging with us (and not only that we win from exchanging with them); our neighbours are also more important than non-neighbours because they are a bulwark in relation to outer-lying countries; being on good terms with them helps indirectly our security' (e.g. an argument in favour of Israel–Jordan or Israel–Egypt PTA relations, or between Maghreb countries).

2 'signing PTAs with non-neighbours will be looked upon by our neighbours as a treason and display of hostility to the region'; this is a fear that has been evoked by some Arab countries' policy circles in the past (applied both in relation to the Arab World and to the Euromed).

Mentioned by MENA and the EU alike

3 'the PTA with the far-away partner (e.g. the US) will not reduce the risk of political conflict with it, since mutual trade dependence is small' (e.g. between Tunisia and the US).

4 'such a PTA cannot constitute a political project towards creating a federation or political union' (contrasting, for example, with an FTA with other Maghreb countries or with other countries in the Arab League).

5 'there are no common environmental problems to be solved between us and distant countries, no common regional identity, we share nothing in common with them (language, religion, culture, values, ethnic origin, history, customs, folklore)'.

6 'we do not share a similar political and legal framework.'

6.2 Economic reasons

Mentioned by MENA countries

1 'there are too many potential external partners (EU, US, but also EFTA, Gulf countries, Canada, Mexico) and we have limited human resources to negotiate and/or monitor the agreements.'
2 'adding non-critical trade agreements will translate in a real mess for prospective exporters which will be confused and perplex, since they will face an array of different trade regimes; on top of it the bureaucratic power of our public officials will be enhanced since a lot of discretion in the hands of customs officers will become the rule; this might also increase corrupt practices.'
3 'concluding such agreements cannot replace unfortunately the usefulness of multilateral trade negotiations in important domains for us' (agricultural subsidies distorting trade between MENA and several OECD countries).

Mentioned by MENA countries and the EU alike

4 'there are no lock-in effects involved.' This refers to the external anchoring role that many PTAs and FTAs have for one of the two partners involved (e.g. for Mediterranean Arab countries having signed an association agreement with the EU under the Euro-Mediterranean Partnership).
5 'there is no potential for environmental cooperation, since there are no reasons for it'; while, in general, with neighbours there is a 'public good' dimension (e.g. Mediterranean weather, the same season, the same time, the same water, the same air) and a 'public bad' dimension (pollution, earthquakes) dimension, this does not exist in the case of distant countries; between neighbours there is more osmosis than with non-neighbours (a reason to favour, for example, the Union for the Mediterranean).
6 'there is no much scope for engaging in trade facilitation activities, since the latter are disproportionately related to contiguity and sharing common borders, thus pointing to a need in sharing common infrastructures' (an argument in favour of cross-border cooperation schemes in the context of the ENP or the Union for the Mediterranean).
7 'there is no much scope for intra-industry trade nor FDI flows linked to the latter and the possibilities of fragmenting production on a regional basis and reaping economies of scale are limited; the long distance to inputs supply for our producers is a handicap.'
8 'such a PTA would not enhance our bargaining power in the GATT/WTO or when a trade conflict arises, compared to Customs Unions which are almost always regionally-based' (an argument in favour of the Customs Union of Turkey with the EU).
9 'less gains from trade derive from these type of agreements compared with those with closer countries; in a region there is more trade potential, more gains from trade to exploit; this is due to similarity of demand structures *à la* Linder (common culture, language, religion, ways of life, political

systems)' (e.g. in the event of an FTA between Tunisia and the EU, marketing efforts to be made by Tunisia in the US are disproportionately larger compared to those to be made in the EU).

10 'servicing and maintenance of equipment bought by us from the preferred partner is problematic over long distances' (e.g. Boeing fleets compared to Airbus fleets).

7 Arguments in favour of MENA countries or the EU engaging in preferentialism, which is insensitive to distance (including preferences in services)

Mentioned by MENA countries

1 'a PTA frequently improves the terms of trade in trade with the partner (whether the EU or the US).'

2 'it allows for exploitation of scale economies (the local market is too small), whether with the EU or the US.'

3 'trade liberalization, even if done on a discriminatory basis, improves the competitive environment.'

4 'FDI will be attracted if agreement signed with OECD partners.'

5 'PTAs are insurance policies against retaliation by the large preferred partners in the case of a generalized trade war (important in relation to the EU and the US).'

Mentioned by MENA countries and the EU alike

6 'more market access is better than less market access.'

7 'prices for final and intermediary consumers will be cheaper (trade creation).'

8 'a PTA may help gain privileged access to strategic raw materials (e.g. for having FTAs with Canada or Mercosur and overheard over in Israel).'

9 'harmonization or mutual recognition of standards is a step in the right direction and is better than maintaining standards at the national level.'

Observe that all the arguments above are economic, with (almost) no political content.

8 MENA countries' arguments against preferentialism, which is insensitive to distance (including preferences in services)

1 'the cost of trade diversion (e.g. of 1975 EU–Israel agreement in favour of expensive cars originating in the EU compared to Japanese ones)'.

2 'it leads to a deterioration of relations with non members (e.g. negative impact of the 1975 Israel-EU agreement on Israel–US relations).'

3 'it undermines the non-discrimination principle ('most-favoured-nation') on which WTO is based (and which led to, for example, Israel reducing its tariffs unilaterally on an m.f.n. basis in 1991).'

4 'it increases administrative costs of monitoring imports at the national borders.'
5 'some issues cannot be solved at the bilateral level such as the subsidization of agricultural products (an argument which is important for Arab countries, such as Jordan, which dislikes the idea of free trade in agricultural products in bilateral FTAs for this reason).'
6 'it allows hegemons to impose rules which are theirs and not universal (labour/environmental standards); not only they are not universal; they might be unsuitable for developing countries. This is a sort of argument heard over in Egypt).'
7 'multilateral trade liberalization on a most-favoured-nation basis and, more generally, world trade globalization deters multilateral conflicts and global trade wars, which are the most costly in terms of human welfare (Martin *et al.*, 2005: 30). For instance Maghreb countries would suffer a very large onslaught on their exports if, in the absence of the WTO, widespread protectionism would ensue as a result of the financial crisis.'

Observe, again, that all the arguments above but the last one are economic, with (almost) no political content.

9 Concluding remarks

Until a decade ago, many observers in the trade policy sphere were predicting that a world of trading blocs or empires was bound to emerge sooner or later. One bloc would be built around the European Union, including most probably Mediterranean Non-Member countries as well as sub-Saharan Africa. A second trade bloc would have the United States at its centre and it would include all the other economies of the western hemisphere. At the time there were debates around the question of whether Japan would be led to counteract the moves of the other two economic powers by promoting the creation of a third bloc around it.

Clearly, nothing of the sort has taken place. In part this is due to technological innovations, particularly in the domain of air transport but also in telecommunications and of course the emergence of the Internet. It has made the world, more than ever before, a 'global village'. But, as this chapter contends, it is also due to trade policy innovations. On the one hand, many erstwhile small emerging economies in the past decade become sizable markets in their own right. These include several MENA countries (Turkey, Israel, Egypt and Morocco). They cannot be ignored any longer even by the large economic powers, such as the EU and the US. The latter will thus not refrain from opening negotiations with emerging economies which are not in their traditional sphere of influence (notably the US in the case of MENA countries). This is even done, if necessary, with countries belonging to the sphere of influence of rival economic powers, with the attendant political implications, if not costs. Typical examples are Morocco, Israel and Jordan, for the United States. In turn, these three countries have long realized that their exclusive dependence on one single (albeit large) export market to which they have gotten privileged access (namely the EU) is potentially dangerous. This perception has been visible for a while now among Israeli policy-makers. They sense there is a need for diversification of export markets, but the latter is only feasible if they engage in negotiations to gain preferential access in additional large markets.

This remarkable change in the trade policies of several key Mediterranean countries could lead, in the medium term, to a sort of meltdown of the still-existing, although loose, sphere of influence that the EU has in the Southern Mediterranean. Note that in a world of cross-regionalism, the least-developed countries tend to be the losers. In the case of MENA, that affects Yemen and the Sudan. This is due to the fact that neither the US or the EU, nor relevant Arab economies (e.g. the GCC or Egypt), consider the markets of Yemen or the Sudan wide enough to be covered by Free Trade Area agreements (which, by definition, are based on reciprocity).

Instead of presupposing that the meltdown of the EU sphere of influence in the MNMCs is already a fact, we could end by challenging the Euromed process. We could put it like this:

> With this new cross-regionalism trend, where does the Euromed process stands? Two possible answers:
>
> - Failure: and here put the entire above paragraph.
> - Success: The Euromed process will only survive if it strengthens political ties and drives democratic change, as cross-regionalism is NOT interested in this (correct?).
>
> The outcome, then, depends on the insights of the Euromed process, the failure/success until now, and what we have learnt from it.

Notes

1 Presented at the Workshop on Economics of the Mediterranean and the Euromediterranean Process, organized by CREMed (IEMed and Barcelona GSE) and the European Institute (LSE), Barcelona, 16–17 July 2010. This paper draws extensively from CEPII Working Paper number 3-2008, based on a report prepared for CEPII (France). I especially wish to thank Lionel Fontagne, Agnes Benassy and Matthieu Crozet of CEPII, and Daniela Persin of Hebrew University, for their comments on earlier drafts of the original report.

2 This would happen through a domino process of bloc creation. For instance, Frankel and Wei (1998) explain how the creation of a continental trade bloc (made up of natural trade partners) may lead to the creation of a competing second one, and so on.

3 A region is characterized by a geographical dimension in conjunction with its extra-regional perception and regional identity.

4 A Free Trade Agreement (FTA) refers in this document to a special type of Preferential Trade Agreement (PTA), in that tariff preferences applied on substantially all import trade originating in the partner country reach 100%.

5 As of January 2005, 312 PTAs had been notified either to the GATT (before 1994) or to the WTO since then. Of these, 170 were in force and 65 were operational but not

yet notified by that time. Also according to the WTO, between January 2004 and February 2005, 43 PTAs were notified to this organization; 70 other agreements were under negotiation. The number of PTAs quadrupled between 1990 and the end of 2004. Actual trade between PTA partners makes up nearly 40% of total trade, and this percentage increases to more than 50% if one includes prospective PTAs. For some WTO members, preferential trade covers now 90% of their total trade flows. In fact, but for the (in)famous exception of Mongolia, every country of the world is involved in one or more PTAs. On average, each WTO member is now in six agreements. Northern countries have 13 PTAs on average; the average developing country nowadays has five PTAs. There are, however, some exceptions – for example East Asian countries, which for the moment have very few agreements (World Bank, 2005).

6 Different GSP schemes (including the one of the EC) are not counted here, since they were based not on bilateral agreements but on unilateral temporary trade concessions made by developed countries to all developing countries without discrimination.

7 ANZCERTA is the Australia–New Zealand Closer Economic Relations Trade Agreement, which came into effect on 1 January 1983.

8 As strange as it might sound, Japan, Australia and many Eastern Asian countries seemed to have ignored this possibility until recently, although they must have had second thoughts. For instance, the *International Herald Tribune* of 17 December 1999 contained an article entitled 'WTO Flop Spurs Pacts at US expense' which argued that, as a result of the Seattle debacle, countries like Japan had begun to look for special deals, including one with Mexico, not in its region. The article underlined the dangers of Balkanization of the global economy but, quite interestingly, its author did not yet preach to the US government to make special deals with countries across the oceans.

9 At that date, the countries of the G-6 (Brazil, Argentina, India, the EU, Japan and the US) had not yet be able to narrow their positions regarding the main obstacle in this Round, namely agriculture concessions (see Decreux and Fontagné, 2006).

10 A term borrowed from Russian geo-politics and nowadays adopted sometimes by experts dealing with the new EU's Neighbourhood Policy, known as ENP; see, for example, Tovias and Magen (2005).

Bibliography

Abugattas Majluf, L. (2004) 'Swimming in the Spaghetti Bowl: Challenges for Developing Countries under the 'New Regionalism', UNCTAD, Policy Issues in International Trade and Commodities Study Series No. 27.

Baier, S. and Bergstrand, J. (2004) 'Economic Determinants of Free Trade Agreements', *Journal of International Economics*, 64(1): 29–63.

Baldwin, R. and Venables, A. (1995) 'Regional Economic Integration', in G. Grossman and K. Rogoff (eds), *Handbook of International Economics*, Vol. III, Amsterdam: Elsevier, 1597–1644.

Baldwin, R., Haaparanta, P. and Kiander J. (eds) (1995) *Expanding Membership of the European Union*, Cambridge: Cambridge University Press.

Bhagwati, J. (1991) *The World Trading System at Risk*, Princeton, NJ: Princeton University Press.

Bhagwati, J. (1995) 'US Trade Policy: The Infatuation with Free Trade Agreements', in J. Bhagwati and A. Krueger, *The Dangerous Drift to Preferential Trade Agreements*, Washington, DC: AEI Press.

Bhagwati, J. and Panagariya, A. (1999) 'Preferential Trading Areas and Multilateralism-Strangers, Friends, or Foes?', in J. Bhagwati, P. Krishna and A. Panagariya, *Alternative*

Approaches to Analyzing Preferential Trade Agreements, Cambridge, MA: MIT Press, pp. 33–100.

Clavin, P. (1996) 'Triumph of Regionalism over Globalism: Patterns of Trade in the Interwar Period', in T. Geiger and D. Kennedy (eds), *Regional Trade Blocs, Multilateralism and the GATT*, London: Pinter.

Crawford, J.A. and Florentino, R.V. (2005) 'The Changing Landscape of Regional Trade Agreements', WTO Discussion Paper No. 8.

Decreux, Y. and Fontagné, L. (2006) 'A Quantitative Assessment of the Outcome of the Doha Development Agenda', Document de travail CEPII, #2006–10

De Sebastian, L. (1995) 'Trading Blocs and The Stranded Countries', in E. Ahiram and A. Tovias (eds), *Whither Israel and the European Union?* Frankfurt: Peter Lang, 147–164.

Frankel, J. (ed.) (1998) *The Regionalization of the World Economy*, Chicago, IL: University of Chicago Press.

Frankel, J. and Wei, S. (1998) 'Open Regionalism in a World of Continental Blocs', IMF Working Paper WP/98/IO.

Geiger, T. and Kennedy D. (eds) (1996) *Regional Trade Blocs, Multilateralism and the GATT*, London: Pinter.

Grugel, J. (2004) 'New Regionalism and Modes of Governance–Comparing US and EU Strategies in Latin America', *European Journal of International Relations*, 10(4): 603–626.

Harrison, G., Rutherford, T. and Tarr, D. (2002) 'Trade Policy Options for Chile: The Importance of Market Access', *The World Bank Economic Review*, 16(1): 49–79.

Hirschman, A. (1945) *National Power and the Structure of Foreign Trade*, Berkeley, CA: University of California Press.

Huntington, S. (1993) 'The Clash of Civilizations?', *Foreign Affairs*, 72(3): 22–49.

Kemp, M. (1969), *A Contribution to the General Equilibrium Theory of Preferential Trading*, Amsterdam: North Holland Publishing.

Kohr, M. (2007) 'WTO: Why Potsdam Failed', *Economic and Political Weekly*, 30 June. Available at: www.epw.org.in/epw/uploads/articles/10768.pdf.

Krugman, P. (1990) 'Is Bilateralism Bad?,' in E. Helpman and A. Razin (eds), *International Trade and Policy*, Cambridge, MA: MIT Press.

Lipsey, R. (1970) *The Theory of Customs Unions: A General Equilibrium Analysis*, London: Weidenfeld & Nicolson.

Martin, P., Mayer, T. and Thoenig, M. (2008) 'Make Trade Not War?', *The Review of Economic Studies*, 75(3): 865–900.

Mathis, J. (2002) *Regional Trade Agreements in the GATT/WTO*, The Hague: T.M.C. Asser Press.

Michaely, M. (2004) *Trade Liberalization and Trade Preferences*, Aldershot: Ashgate.

Orwell, G. (1949) *Nineteen Eighty-Four*, London: Secker and Warburg.

Payne, A. (1996) 'The United States and its Enterprise for the Americas', in A. Gamble and A. Payne (eds), *Regionalism and World Order*, New York, NY: St Martin's Press, pp. 93–129.

Péridy, N. (2004) 'The New Trans-Ocean Free Trade Initiatives: Estimating Export and FDI Potentials From Dynamic Panel Data Models', *Economics Bulletin*, 6(9): 1–12.

Rollo, J. (1994) 'The EC, European Integration and the World Trading System', in V. Cable and D. Henderson (eds), *Trade Blocs? The Future of Regional Integration*, London: RIIA, pp. 35–58.

Sapir, A. (1997) 'The Political Economy of EC Regionalism', 12th Annual Congress of the European Economic Association, Toulouse.

Shibata, H. (1971) 'A Theory of Free Trade Areas', in P. Robson (ed.), *International Economic Integration*, Harmondsworth: Penguin, pp. 68–87.

Szymanski, M. and Smith, M. (2005) 'Coherence and Conditionality in European Foreign Policy: Negotiating the EU–Mexico Global Agreement', *Journal of Common Market Studies*, 43(1): 171–192.

Tovias, A. (1990) *Foreign Economic Relations of the European Community: The Impact of Spain and Portugal*, Boulder, CO: Lynne Rienner.

Tovias, A. (2000a) 'Regional Blocks and International Relations: Economic Groupings or Political Hegemons?', in T. Lawton, J. Rosenau and A.Verdun (eds), *Strange Power. Shaping the Parameters of International Relations and International Political Economy*, Aldershot: Ashgate, pp. 321–341.

Tovias, A. (2000b) 'The Optimum Strategy for a Spoke: Linking with Other Spokes or Other Hubs?', in M. Maresceau and E. Lannon (eds), *The EU's Enlargement and Mediterranean Strategies*, London: Macmillan, pp. 153–168.

Tovias, A. and Magen, A. (2005) 'Reflections from the New Near Outside: An Israeli Perspective on the Economic and Legal Impact of EU Enlargement', *European Foreign Affairs Review*, 10(5): 399–425.

Vaillant, M. and Ons, A. (2002) 'Preferential Trading Arrangements Between the European Union and South America: The Political Economy of Free Trade Zones in Practice', *The World Economy*, 25(10): 1433–1468.

Vanek, J. (1965) *General Equilibrium of International Discrimination*, Cambridge, MA: Harvard University Press.

Vasconcelos, A. (2001) 'European Union and MERCOSUR' in M. Telo (ed.), *European Union and New Regionalism: Regional Actors and Global Governance in a Post-hegemonic Era*, Burlington, VT: Ashgate, pp. 135–152.

Viner, J. (1965), *Studies in the Theory of International Trade*, Cambridge, MA: Harvard University Press.

World Bank (2000) *Trade Blocs*, Oxford: Oxford University Press.

World Bank (2005) *Global Economic Prospects: Trade, Regionalism and Development*, Washington, DC: World Bank.

3 Shallow versus deep integration scenarios in the Euro-Mediterranean area

A quantitative assessment[1]

Nicolas Péridy

1 Introduction

Since the conclusion of the Barcelona Agreement, an extensive literature has been dedicated to the assessment of the effects of the Euro-Mediterranean partnership. This literature generally concludes that the gains due to the conclusion of a free trade area (FTA) between the EU and its Mediterranean partners are positive but small (for a complete survey, refer to Lucke and Nathanson, 2007 as well as Péridy, 2010). This conclusion leads one to wonder to what extent additional steps toward regional integration, especially deep integration, would provide more significant gains.

Given the lack of quantitative analysis in this field, this chapter aims at paving the way for assessing the specific impact of shallow versus deep integration between Mediterranean (MED) countries[2] and their partners in the Euromed area. It relies on a new dataset concerning especially tariffs (as a proxy for shallow integration) and Non Tariff Measures (NTMs)[3] (as a proxy for deep integration) (Lopez Gonzalez and Mendez Parra, 2010). Additional data are also included in order to take into account other trade costs, especially transport costs and logistics costs in the framework of deep integration. In this regard, an original dataset of maritime freight cost (Maersk, 2007) will be introduced, as well as new data on logistics performance (World Bank, 2011).

The second section of this chapter is dedicated to calculating the magnitude of NTMs in terms of ad valorem tariff equivalent (AVEs). It relies on new research developments based on Kee *et al.* (2009). This makes it possible to get a first idea about the role of NTMs in Mediterranean trade and thus the cost of non-deep integration.

The third section estimates a gravity model from new theoretical and empirical developments. This model strongly relies on trade costs, following the literature initiated by Anderson and van Wincoop (2004). Consequently, the gravity model implemented makes it possible to calculate the specific impact of tariffs, NTMs as well as transport and logistics costs on trade of Mediterranean countries with their partners in the Euromed area. This provides a better understanding about the expected gains due to these cost reductions in the framework of shallow and deep integration.

These results pave the way for simulations of trade creation due to shallow and deep integration. The results are presented in Section 4. Section 5 then focuses on the simulations applied to South–South integration, i.e. within MED countries.

2 An estimation of tariff and NTMs protection between MED countries and the EU

This section attempts to provide an estimation of trade costs, especially tariffs and NTMs applied between MED and the EU. This will make it possible to (1) have a more precise and reliable idea about the level and magnitude of tariffs and NTMs in the countries considered; and (2) use these estimations as inputs in the gravity model in order to assess the effects of tariffs and NTMs in the MED/EU trade.

Starting with **tariffs**, Figure 3.1 summarizes MFN tariffs applied by MED countries at digit-2 level.

It shows that except for Israel, Lebanon and Turkey, other countries still show significant tariff protection, especially Tunisia, Egypt, Morocco and Algeria.

Table 3.1 complements these results by showing the average tariffs which are effectively applied overall and at bilateral level. It provides a slightly different

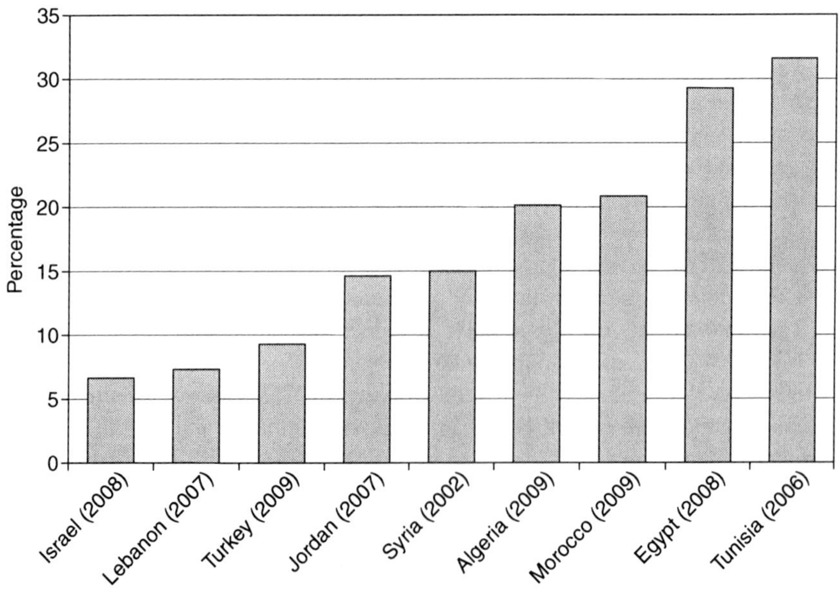

Figure 3.1 Average MFN tariffs applied by MED countries (unweighted average, %) (source: Lopez Gonzalez and Mendez Parra 2010, from TRAINS).

Note
Last year available in brackets.

Table 3.1 Average tariffs applied by MENA countries on their imports (%, unweighted average)

	Tariffs with all countries	*Tariffs with EU*	*Share of duty free EU lines*
Algeria (2009)	14.1	12.9	n.a.
Morocco (2009)	8.2	3.9	51.0
Tunisia (2006)	22.2	18.0	39.2
Egypt (2008)	9.4	10.1	6.2
Lebanon (2007)	5.1	5.4	n.a.
Israel (2008)	2.1	0.1	95.0
Jordan (2007)	10.1	11.0	38.3
Syria (2002)	12.8	14.1	n.a.
Turkey (2009)	1.2	0.1	n.a.

Source: TRAINS; De Wulf and Maliszewska (2009); n.a., not available.

picture by showing that Israel and Turkey have removed almost all tariff protection with regard to EU imports. Morocco and Lebanon have also made significant progress, with small average tariffs applied to EU imports. On the other hand, Tunisia, Syria and Algeria show the highest tariffs (up to 18% for Tunisia), whereas Jordan and Egypt are in intermediate positions. Basically, Table 3.1 shows that the shallow integration process is not fully completed between MED countries and the EU, with the exception of Israel and Turkey. In particular, Algeria, and Tunisia to a lesser extent, exhibit relatively high tariffs. This remark will have significant implications when assessing the impact of shallow versus deep integration with the gravity model.

With regards to the tariffs applied to MENA countries' exports by the partners considered in this study (i.e. all countries in the Euro-Mediterranean area), it must be remembered that they have been progressively removed both in the framework of the Barcelona Process and in the framework of the South–South integration process (GAFTA Agreement). As a result, the shallow integration is now completed with regard to MED countries' exports. Algeria is one exception, since this country is a GAFTA member but had not started the tariff liberalization process in 2005 (Ghoneim and Péridy, 2009). Israel and Turkey are two other exceptions, since these two countries are outside the GAFTA area.

The estimation of **NTMs** is a more difficult task. The corresponding data come from the TRAINS database, with eight groups of measures, including specific charges and taxes, administered process, financial measures, automatic licenses, non-automatic licenses and other quantitative restrictions, monopolistic measures as well as technical or quality regulations (for a complete description, refer to Lopez Gonzalez and Mendez Parra, 2010). One drawback with this dataset is that data are incomplete and available for one year only (generally 1999 or 2001). Nevertheless, it provides a first insight into NTMs in MED countries. Another drawback is that the available data indicate the number of NTMs applied at bilateral level. Consequently, they do not provide any direct indication about the effectiveness of NTMs as a protection tool. In particular, it is not possible to compare the magnitude of the protection due to NTMs to that due to tariffs, since these two variables are not measured in the same way. However, this major problem can be solved by calculating tariff ad valorem equivalents (AVEs) of NTMs. This can be achieved by using the recent methodology developed by Kee *et al.* (2009), which is sometimes referred to as KNO (2009). This methodology is applied here. It is fully described in the technical annex (Appendix A)

The calculations of the corresponding AVEs applied to MED countries are reported in Figure 3.2. They provide a first picture about the magnitude of NTMs. In this regard, it can be observed that protection due to NTMs is very significant for Algeria but also Jordan (due to low import demand elasticity in absolute value).[4] In these two countries, NTMs amount to more than 33% in tariff equivalent. It is striking to observe that these countries also show the highest number of NTMs in the database (up to 309,800 for Jordan). Conversely, Morocco, Tunisia but also Egypt (due to high import demand elasticity in absolute value) exhibit the lowest AVEs (less than 25%). Interestingly, these countries show the lowest number of NTMs in the database (about 20,000 each).

Summing tariffs and NTMs, the overall protection is presented in Figure 3.3. It is worth mentioning that all Mediterranean countries exhibit NTMs which are greater than tariff. Overall, Algeria, Jordan but also Tunisia (due to significant tariffs) show protection levels which range between 43% (Jordan) and 50% (Algeria). In the other countries, protection is also significant, but to a lesser extent (about 30% in Morocco, Egypt and Lebanon).

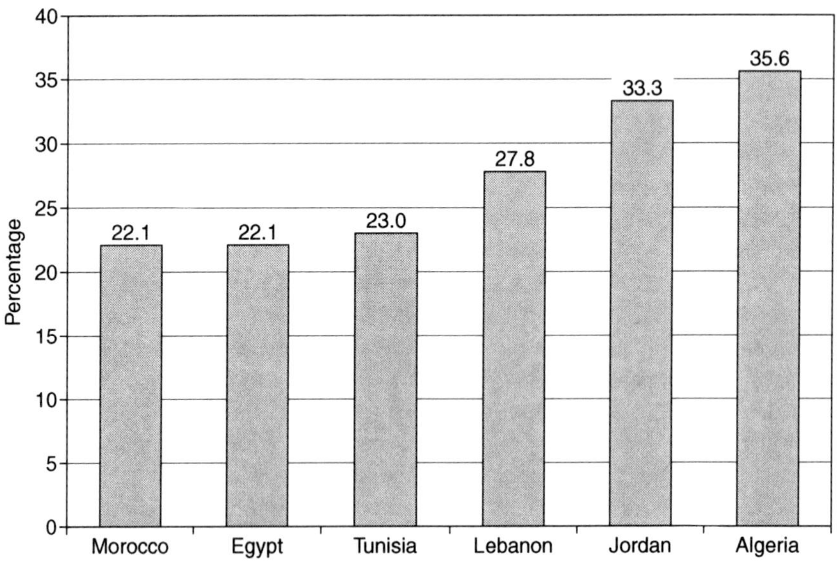

Figure 3.2 An estimation of AVEs in Mediterranean countries (%).

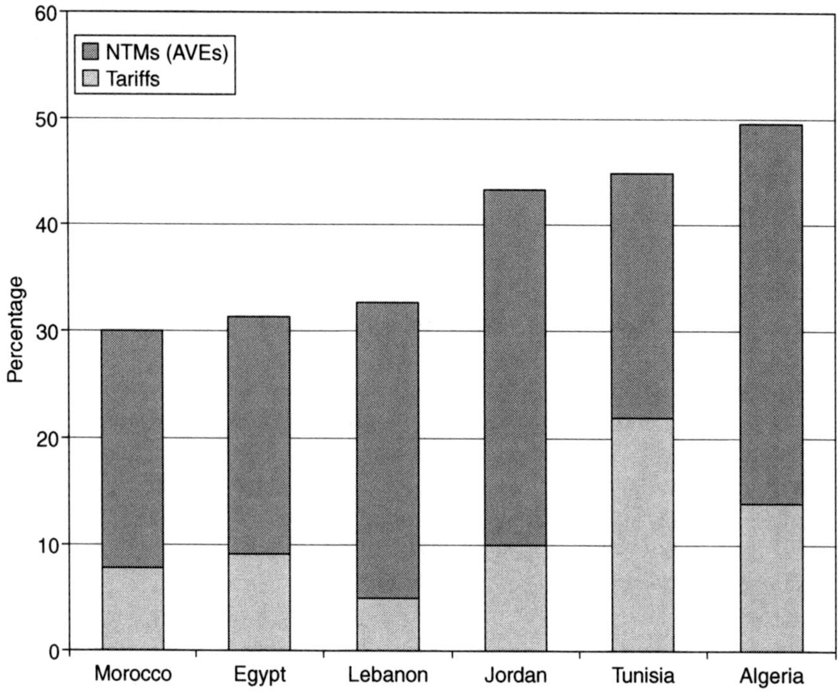

Figure 3.3 Overall protection in Mediterranean countries: tariffs and NTMs (%).

Given these high protection levels, it is expected that the trade impact of both tariffs and NTMs is significant on Mediterranean imports from their partners. The story is somehow different when looking at Mediterranean exports to their partners. In this regard, it must be observed that the EU has fully removed its tariff protection applying to these countries since the early 1990s. In addition, the NTMs applied by the EU also seem to be of lower importance. For example, Kee *et al.* (2009) show that the AVE applied by the EU to its imports is equal to 13.4%. This is much lower that AVEs applied by Mediterranean countries to their own imports. Consequently, NTM removal between the EU and Mediterranean countries is expected to produce smaller effects with regard to Mediterranean exports than Mediterranean imports. This question will be investigated in the following sections.

3 The econometric model, the scenarios and the simulation

This section is dedicated to the presentation of the econometric model which will be used for simulating the impact of shallow versus deep integration between MED countries and their partners. The theoretical background can be found in Appendix B, whereas the model specification, the scenarios and the simulation methodology will be explained in this section.

3.1 Model specification, data and sources

The new framework of gravity models makes it possible to derive the following empirical equation which will be tested for the Mediterranean countries' trade relationships (refer to Appendix B for technical details):

$$\ln X_{jk} = \alpha_0 + \alpha_1 \ln SUMGDP_j + \alpha_2 \ln TAR_{jk} + \alpha_3 NTMs_{ijk} + \alpha_4 \ln TRANSCOST_j + \alpha_5 \ln LANG_j + \alpha_6 \ln COL_j + \varphi_j + \phi_k + \varepsilon_{ijt} \quad (1)$$

where X_{jt} corresponds to MED countries' exports to country j at year t. Given that data for NTMs are only available for one year, the gravity equation will only be estimated for this year. This is why the temporal pattern of the equation is disregarded. In addition, the equation is estimated for each Mediterranean country *i*. As a result, the equation does not include the GDP of the origin and destination country separately, but the sum of the GDP (*SUMGDP*) of each Mediterranean country with its partner *j*.[5] This particular specification is frequently used both in the theoretical and in the empirical literature based on the new trade theory (NTT) (Helpman and Krugman, 1985). Finally, subscript *k* denotes the product decomposition level (digit 2).

Interestingly, bilateral trade costs are considered with three variables. The first corresponds to bilateral tariffs (TAR_j). This variable will be used as a proxy for shallow integration whose process has been initiated in the Barcelona Agreement and its related association agreements. As in Section 2, the MFN tariffs have been used for the estimation of the model, given the possible biases related to the use of the AHS tariffs. Data are derived from the UNCTAD TRAINS database.

NTMs will be considered as a proxy for deep integration. We will use the same proxy as in Section 2, i.e. a binary variable which takes the value of unity in case of NTMs and 0 otherwise.

TRANSCOST is an original measure of transportation costs. It is based on statistics developed by Maersk, which is one of the leading liner shipping companies in the world. It must also be remembered that maritime transport accounts for about 80% of world trade. The variable used in the model corresponds to the freight costs in US dollars for a standard container (20 feet long) from a port of origin to a port of destination (year 2007).

As a sensitivity analysis, alternative variables are also used for transport costs. The most interesting one is related to the logistics performance index (LPI) (World Bank, 2011). This indicator is built from information gathered in a worldwide survey of the companies involved in logistics services. Seven areas are covered by this index, namely: efficiency of the clearance process by customs and other border agencies, quality of transport and information technology infrastructure for logistics, ease of arranging international shipments, competence of the local logistics industry, ability to trace and check international shipments, domestic logistics costs, and timeliness of shipments in reaching destination. The LPI is a weighted average of these variables. It ranges from 1 (worst) to 5 (best).

Overall, the LPI is particularly relevant for our study since it measures not only transport costs, but more generally the efficiency of logistics in a given country. It is expected that countries with the best LPI score trade more than other countries (everything being equal).

Figure 3.4 shows the country ranking of the countries included in the present study. The most striking feature is the gap between the EU and MED countries. As a matter of fact, 11 EU countries are ranked in the world top-20 countries. In particular, Germany, Sweden and The Netherlands are respectively ranked at the first, third and fourth places in the world for their logistics performance (Singapore is in the second place). These three EU countries are major global transport and logistics hubs which are very efficient. These countries are followed by most Northern EU countries. On the other hand, MED countries are ranked well behind, except for Israel, Lebanon and Turkey (ranked 31, 33 and 39 respectively), which are close to Southern and Eastern EU countries.

In particular, Algeria and Libya are placed at the bottom of the country ranking (at 130 and 132, respectively). This reveals major inefficiency problems for transport and logistics in these two countries. Syria, Egypt, Jordan and Morocco also show poor results in terms of LPI. However, Tunisia, ranked 61, shows significant progress. In this regard, the World Bank (2007) notes that the difference in country ranking between Tunisia and Morocco may be explained by the fact that Tunisia implemented the core reforms earlier than Morocco, and has just reaped the benefits of these reforms. Nevertheless, Morocco has recently

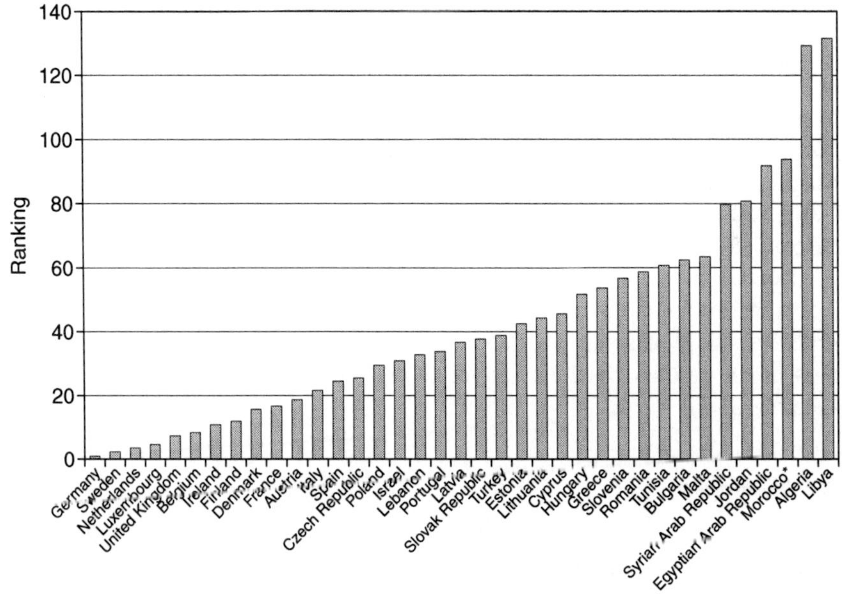

Figure 3.4 Country ranking for LPI (rank 2010* over 155 countries) (source: World Bank (2011); *year 2007 concerning Morocco).

implemented exemplary customs and port reforms which should significantly improve its ranking in the coming years. It must also be noticed that data for 2010 are unavailable for Morocco.

As a last alternative proxy for transport costs, the distance between MED countries and their EU partners is also used. It is measured by a weighted index which takes into account the spatial distribution of the population within each country (source: CEPII, 2007a).

$LANG_{ij}$ is a dummy variable which takes the value of 1 if a common language is spoken by at least 10% of the population in each country pair (exporter and importer), and 0 otherwise (source: CEPII, 2007b).

COL_{ij} reflects colonial relationships over a long period of time, with substantial participation in the colonized country's governance (source: CEPII, 2007b). This variable is equal to 1 in case of colonial links and 0 otherwise. This variable accounts for cultural and historical relationships which are expected to increase trade flows between some EU countries and Mediterranean countries.

Finally, specific country and product effects are introduced in the model (φ_j and φ_k). These effects make it possible to capture the heterogeneity of the data. They also capture the effects of potential omitted variables (Egger, 2004). In particular, the price effects included in the theoretical equation are captured by the country-specific effect (φ_j).[6] In addition, the product effect φ_k takes into account potential omitted variables at product level. All these specific effects can be considered as fixed or random, depending on the specification of the model.

Finally, as an additional sensitivity analysis, the estimators are also controlled for cross-sectional heteroskedasticity as well as serial correlation of the error term by using appropriate Feasible GLS.

Equation (1) is estimated for the imports of the nine MED countries described above. However, data for Syria proved to be of poor quality, so this country was eventually removed. The partner countries include the whole Euromed area, i.e. the EU-15, Central and Eastern European countries (CEECs) as well as the eight Mediterranean countries described above (after Syria has been excluded, besides Libya and Palestine, due to lack of data in the trade, transport and other databases). Thus, 33 partner countries are included. The dataset also includes a product decomposition level at digit-2.

Estimations are implemented with the Heckman two-stage procedure. Appropriate sensitivity analysis has also been carried out in order to check the robustness of the results (fixed-effects vector decomposition, Hausman and Taylor, Feasible GLS).

3.2 Simulations

According to the trade modeling developed previously and given the data available, Table 3.2 shows the various simulations and scenarios which will be implemented. In each case, we will distinguish on the one hand a partial move towards shallow and deep integration (pessimistic scenario), and full integration on the other (optimistic scenario).

Table 3.2 Simulations used for shallow and deep integration

Shallow integration		*Deep integration*			
Partial (pessimistic scenario)	*Full (optimistic scenario)*	*Partial (pessimistic)*		*Full (optimistic)*	
Tariffs	Tariffs	NTMs	LPI	NTM	LPI
Marginal cut	Complete removal	Marginal cut	Marginal cut	Complete removal	Increase to 3.05

Basically, the simulations for shallow integration will consider the marginal effect of tariff reductions as the pessimistic scenario (partial liberalization), as well as their complete removal as the optimistic scenario (full liberalization).

Deep integration includes two tools. The first is NTMs, for which we also consider marginal effects in the reduction of NTMs and a complete removal (pessimistic and optimistic scenarios). The second tool includes transport costs or more generally logistics inefficiencies, which can also be considered as trade barriers, although they are not product-specific. Given that LPI is a wider concept than transport costs, it will be used as the reference variable for the scenarios. In the simulations, the pessimistic scenario will be built upon the assumption of a marginal increase in LPI, whereas in the optimistic scenario it will be assumed that LPI improves to the level reached in middle-income countries, such as Mexico, Argentina and Central and Eastern European countries (i.e. 3.05). This level also corresponds to the case where countries reach the 66% of highest performers (World Bank, 2011).

Partial integration can be captured by the marginal effects shown directly by the parameter estimates corresponding to tariffs, NTMs and LPI, estimated from equation (1). In this case, the parameter estimates directly show the effects of a 1% decrease in trade costs on trade in Mediterranean countries.[7] These marginal effects will be reported in the results as the trade creation due to partial shallow or deep integration (pessimistic scenario).

One the other hand, full integration cannot be grasped by the marginal effects, since it corresponds to a 100% reduction in trade costs (except logistics) or at least to a very significant reduction, i.e. towards levels reached in middle-income countries. Consequently, a specific methodology must be implemented in order to capture the full effects of tariff and NTMs removal. The methodology proposed here has been commonly used in the literature for the calculation of trade creation due to regional integration from a standard dummy variable (refer, for instance, to Péridy, 2005). This methodology is refined here by considering specific variables corresponding to tariffs and NTMs. Basically, it starts from equation (1) and uses the parameter estimates corresponding to tariffs, NTMs and LPI in order to calculate the gross trade creation due to shallow and deep integration (refer to Appendix C for all technical details).

4 Estimation results: the calculation of trade creation from shallow and deep integration

Tables 3.3 and 3.4 exhibit the estimation results and the sensitivity analysis of the gravity model specially estimated for the simulations.[8]

Using the parameters corresponding to tariffs, NTMs and LPI in Table 3.3, this section will first present the trade creation due the full integration corresponding to shallow and deep integration (optimistic scenario). Thereafter, it will also present the marginal effects expected from partial integration (pessimistic scenario), using parameters from Table 3.4.

4.1 Trade creation due to shallow and deep integration (full removal of tariffs and NTMs): the optimistic scenario

Table 3.5a and Figure 3.5a show the results of trade creation as a percentage of Mediterranean imports corresponding to equations (1.13a), (1.13b) and (1.14) in Appendix C. For each country, three columns are presented first. They correspond to the trade creation due to the removal of tariffs, NTMs and both, respectively. As already explained previously, the trade creation due to tariffs and NTMs cannot be strictly added. This is why the trade creation presented in the last column is not equal to the sum of that calculated in the first two columns. When the parameter estimates corresponding to tariffs are statistically insignificant, we assume that trade creation due to shallow integration (tariff removal) is also insignificant. In this case, the overall effect is the same as that corresponding to the removal of NTMs (deep integration). Besides, a fourth column is introduced to take into account additional trade creation due to improvement of logistics. In the optimistic scenario, it is assumed that MED countries improve their LPI toward the 66% of highest performers, i.e. an LPI index equal to 3.05. This level is recorded in several middle-income countries, such as Mexico, Argentina and Chile, as well as some Central and Eastern EU countries.

In addition, three lines are presented for each country. They reflect the minimum, maximum and average trade creation. These are calculated from Table 3.3 by taking, respectively, the lowest, highest and average parameter estimates amongst the four available estimators (Heckman two-step, FEVD, Hausman and Taylor as well as FGLS). This makes it possible to define margins of errors in the calculation of trade creation. In this regard, it can be observed that this margin is generally very thin. This is an indication regarding the fair robustness of the econometric results. Concerning the column related to LPI, the minimum and maximum are calculated by taking −10% or +10% from the average scenario.

A first crucial result is that **trade creation due to deep integration** (removal of NTMs) is very significant in all countries. In particular, the trade creation for Algeria amounts to 60.4% of its current imports (remember that the maximum is 100%). Egypt, Jordan and Lebanon also exhibit high potentials of import increases if they remove their NTMs (from 32% in Lebanon to 39% in Egypt). Tunisia and Morocco show the lowest trade creation (about 25%), although this percentage is still very significant.

Table 3.3 Parameter estimates used for full liberalization (dependent variables: MENA countries' imports)

Heckman Twostep	*Algeria*	*Egypt*	*Jordan*	*Lebanon*	*Morocco*	*Tunisia*	*Israel*	*Turkey*
Independent:								
no NTM	0.906***	0.510***	0.496***	0.382***	0.277***	0.355***	–	–
no tariffs	0.848**	0.490	0.071	0.072	0.281	0.564*	0.001	0.029
transport	−3.100***	0.030	−1.382***	−4.722***	−2.483***	−1.758***	−3.671***	
sum GDP	0.650***	0.676***	0.252***	0.304***	0.912***	1.047***	1.157***	1.929***
colony	1.447***	0.340*	0.079	0.296***	0.830***	0.900***	0.077	–
common language	0.082	−0.137	0.445***	0.26***	0.811***	0.593***	0.310	–
constant	19.041**	−3.939	−0.449	8.260***	1.555***	8.933**	1.060	6.984*
Selection								
partner type	−0.264**	−0.415**	−0.345***	−0.398***	−0.372**	−0.291**	−0.440***	−0.353***
number of obs.	1560	1657	1606	1984	1820	1959	2232	2930
censored obs	68	451	172	203	328	275	395	722
Sensitivity analysis								
partner's LPI	0.413	0.947	1.096	1.625	1.173	1.141	2.177**	3.885***
MENA countries' LPI	1.95**	1.95**	1.95**	1.95**	1.95**	1.95**	1.95**	1.95**
Fixed-effects vector decomposition (FEVD, product-invariant and endogeneity)								
no NTM	0.919***	0.498***	0.514***	0.383***	0.262**	0.341**	–	–
no tariffs	0.867***	0.424	0.101	0.081	0.410	0.512	0.001	0.023
transport	−3.099***	−0.234	−0.130	−1.362***	−3.903***	−2.491***	−1.685***	−3.481***
Hausman-Taylor (endogeneity)								
no NTM	0.947***	0.498***	0.514***	0.384***	0.262***	0.341***	–	–
no tariffs	0.919*	0.424	0.101	0.082	0.411	0.512	0.001	0.023
transport	−3.221***	−1.041	−2.597	−1.264***	−5.085***	−2.214***	−1.374***	−4.580***
FGLS (panel heteroskedasticity and autocorrelation)								
no NTM	0.915***	0.485***	0.489***	−0.401***	0.281***	0.279**	–	–
no tariffs	0.810*	0.418	0.07	0.08	0.187	0.556	0.001	0.045
transport	−2.917***	−0.160	−0.143	−1.317***	−3.475***	−2.567***	−1.637***	−3.359***

Table 3.4 Parameter estimates used for partial liberalization (marginal effects) (dependent variable: MENA countries' imports)

Heckman Twostep	*Algeria*	*Egypt*	*Jordan*	*Lebanon*	*Morocco*	*Tunisia*	*Israel*	*Turkey*
Independent:								
NTMs	−0.115***	−0.012*	0.01	−0.046***	−0.0033*	−0.014***	–	–
tariffs	−1.076***	−0.679***	−0.240***	−0.060**	−0.300***	−0.907***	−0.052***	−0.034***
transport	−3.124***	−0.266	−0.224	−1.397***	−4.688***	−2.404***	−1.568***	−4.126***
sum GDP	0.675***	0.704***	0.261***	0.304***	0.908***	1.099***	1.177***	1.977***
colony	1.403***	0.394*	0.118	0.295***	0.833***	0.802**	0.045	–
common language	0.190	−0.188	0.485***	0.210***	0.807***	0.684***	0.209	–
constant	17.162**	−2.612	−0.111	8.228***	1.081***	6.992**	1.057	8.789**
Selection:								
partner type	−0.264**	−0.414**	−0.361***	−0.398***	−0.372**	−0.296**	−0.455***	−0.366***
number of obs.	1544	1655	1533	1984	1820	1944	1937	2740
censored obs.	68	451	172	203	328	275	395	722
Sensitivity analysis								
partner's LPI	1.663	1.870	1.203	1.612	1.293	1.704	2.818***	3.932***
MENA countries' LPI	1.95**	1.95**	1.95**	1.95**	1.95**	1.95**	1.95**	1.95**

Fixed-effects vector decomposition (FEVD, product-invariant and endogeneity)								
NTMs	−0.115***	−0.023***	0.01	−0.046***	−0.0033*	−0.014***	–	–
tariffs	−1.056***	−0.681***	−0.241***	−0.055**	−0.292***	−0.824***	−0.047***	−0.034***
transport	−3.124***	−0.266	−0.224	−1.376***	−3.921***	−2.406***	−1.607***	−3.954***
Hausman-Taylor (endogeneity)								
NTMs	−0.115***	−0.012*	0.01	−0.047***	−0.0095**	−0.014***	–	–
tariffs	−1.066***	−0.681***	−0.241***	−0.055**	−0.292***	−0.824***	−0.047***	−0.035***
transport	−3.821***	−0.648	−0.984	−1.264***	−5.010***	−2.256***	−1.439***	−4.555***
FGLS (panel heteroskedasticity and autocorrelation)								
NTMs	−0.115***	−0.012*	0.01	−0.048***	−0.0033*	−0.014***	–	–
tariffs	−1.069***	−0.667***	−0.256***	−0.059**	−0.295***	−0.872***	−0.050***	−0.037***
transport	−2.921***	−0.168	−0.251	−1.331***	−3.515***	−2.519***	−1.611***	−3.702***

Overall, these results can, interestingly, be related to the calculation of AVEs and the results of the gravity model presented in Section 2 (Figure 3.2). Indeed, it has been shown that the most trade-reducing impact of NTMs concerned Algeria and the smaller impact involved Morocco and Tunisia. Hence, the results for trade creation strongly correlate with our previous conclusions. However, these results go further since they make it possible to quantify and scale from 0% to 100% the specific impact of deep integration (NTM reduction). In particular, it shows that this impact is huge for Algeria. These results are also consistent with those found in De Wulf and Maliszewska (2009) which state that deep integration could lead to significant trade gains.

The gains due to deep integration can also be increased by logistics improvement. As a matter of fact, Table 3.5a and Figure 3.5a show that these gains are very significant for Algeria (+57%). This is due to the fact that this country faces a very poor logistics performance (the LPI is currently equal to 2.36). Consequently, an improvement toward middle-income countries' LPI (3.05) would lead to very significant import increases. Significant trade gains are also expected for Morocco (44%). However, it must be remembered that this gain is based on

Table 3.5a Percentage change in Mediterranean countries' imports (optimistic scenario) (from significant parameter estimates only)

		Tariffs (%)	*NTMs (%)*	*Both (%)*	*TPI (%)*
Algeria	min	57.2	59.6	82.7	51.2
	max	60.1	61.2	84.5	62.6
	average	58.6	60.4	83.6	56.9
Egypt	min	ns	38.4	38.4	29.5
	max	ns	40.0	40.0	36.1
	average	ns	39.2	39.2	32.8
Jordan	min	ns	38.7	38.7	18.9
	max	ns	40.2	40.2	23.1
	average	ns	39.4	39.4	21.0
Lebanon	min	ns	31.8	31.8	0.0
	max	ns	33.0	33.0	0.0
	average	ns	32.4	32.4	0.0
Tunisia	min	ns	24.3	24.3	12.3
	max	43.1	28.9	59.5	15.1
	average	21.5	26.6	41.9	13.7
Morocco	min	ns	23.0	23.0	39.7
	max	ns	24.5	24.5	48.5
	average	ns	23.8	23.8	44.1
Israel	min	ns	–	–	0.0
	max	ns	–	–	0.0
	average	ns	–	–	0.0
Turkey	min	ns	–	–	0.0
	max	ns	–	–	0.0
	average	ns	–	–	0.0

Notes
ns = insignificant parameter estimate.

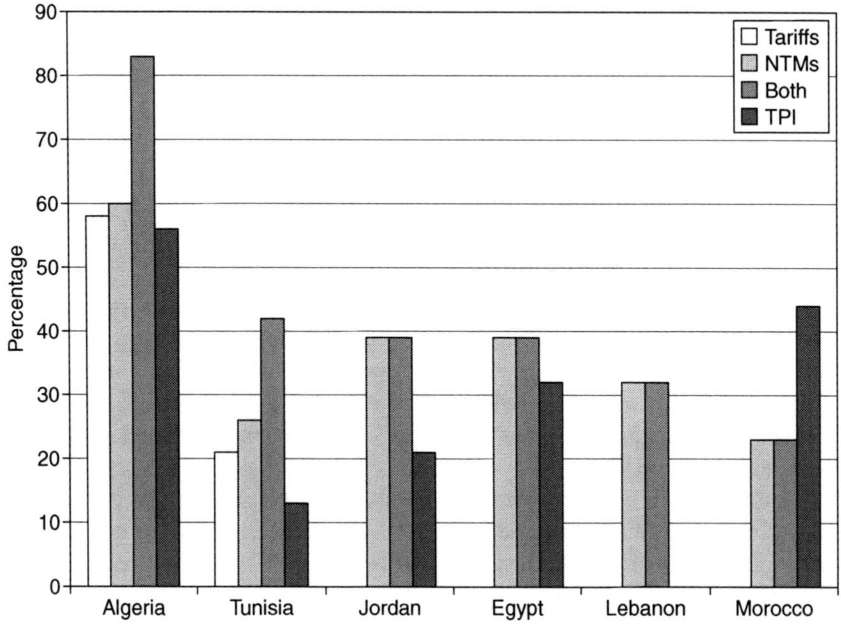

Figure 3.5a Percentage change in Mediterranean countries' imports (optimistic scenario) (average from significant parameter estimates only).

LPI data from 2007 and does not take into account the efforts of the Moroccan authorities to increase their logistics performance in the very recent years. As a result, the gain expected in Table 3.5a may be overestimated compared to the other countries for which LPI data are updated. Egypt and Jordan also show significant effects expected from logistics improvement (increase in imports by 32% and 21% respectively), whereas gains for Tunisia are smaller (14%) since this country is already close to the LPI level of 3.05. No gain is expected for Turkey, Israel and Lebanon, which have already surpassed this LPI level.

To sum up, deep integration is expected to lead to significant import increases in MENA countries, because of both NTM reduction and logistics improvement.

A second interesting result is related to **shallow integration**, through tariff removal. In this regard, the trade creation is very significant for Algeria, i.e. 59%. Again, there is a strong correlation between this result and the fact that Algeria still applies very high tariffs, as shown in Section 2. Results for Tunisia are very sensitive to the estimator used in Table 3.3. As a matter of fact, Tunisia is a country which still showed significant tariffs, but to a lesser extent than Algeria. As a result, the parameter estimates are not always significant. This is why the calculation of trade creation exhibits a minimum of 0% (this corresponds to insignificant parameter estimates) and the maximum is 43% (for the highest significant parameters). For the other countries, parameter estimates related to tariffs show the expected sign, but are insignificant. This suggests that the complete tariff removal is not expected to add a significant trade creation. This is an expected result, since we have shown that these countries have already strongly reduced their tariff protection (Section 2). As a result, no significant additional trade creation is expected. However, these results do not say that marginal effects of further reduction in tariffs are insignificant, as will be shown in Section 4.2).

In other words, tariffs do not have such a significant effect as NTMs because parameter estimates are often insignificant. This reflects the fact that tariffs have been reduced in most MED countries, except mainly in Algeria.

Finally, the combination of both tariffs and NTMs' removal provides an overall trade creation which is huge for Algeria (83%), intermediate for Egypt, Jordan, Lebanon and Tunisia (from 32% to 42%), and smaller for Morocco (24%). Again, these results reflect pretty well the overall liberalization level reached by Mediterranean countries. This will have important policy implications, as developed later.

At this stage, it must however be noticed that we considered that positive but statistically insignificant parameters corresponding to tariffs lead to insignificant trade effects. However, the results are affected by the threshold below which parameters become statistically insignificant.

In Table 3.3, for example, the parameter corresponding to tariffs is statistically significant down to 0.564 (Tunisia) but becomes statistically insignificant below, i.e. for Egypt (0.490). Consequently, we assumed above that trade creation due to tariff removal is insignificant for Egypt, even if the parameter estimate is not equal to zero.

Table 3.5b and Figure 3.5b provide the results by using the value of all parameter estimates, even if they are not significant. This has the advantage of solving the problem of the significance threshold. On the other hand, the drawback is that we consider that a trade creation can be positive even if the corresponding parameter estimate is insignificant.

The results are slightly different to those presented in Table 3.5a and Figure 3.5a, since shallow integration provides positive gains not only for Algeria and Tunisia but also for Egypt and Morocco (which are slightly below the statistical threshold). However, results for Jordan and Lebanon as well as Israel and Turkey are similar to the previous ones with very small gains. Again, the country distribution of trade gains due to shallow integration is closely linked to the tariff levels applied by the countries concerned. This means that the gains are higher for countries like Algeria and Tunisia which show the highest tariff levels, as shown in Section 2.

Results for deep integration are identical to those presented above, since all the corresponding parameter estimates are significant. Overall, trade creation due to shallow and deep integration is very high for Algeria. It is intermediate for Tunisia and Egypt, and smaller in Morocco, Lebanon and Jordan.

A final set of results can be provided concerning MENA countries' exports. Figure 3.6 summarizes the export increases expected from shallow and deep

Table 3.5b Percentage change in Mediterranean countries' imports (optimistic scenario) (from all parameter estimates)

		Tariffs (%)	*NTMs (%)*	*Both (%)*	*TPI (%)*
Algeria	min	57.2	59.6	82.7	51.2
	max	60.1	61.2	84.5	62.6
	average	58.6	60.4	83.6	56.9
Egypt	min	33.9	38.4	59.3	29.5
	max	38.7	40.0	63.2	36.1
	average	36.3	39.2	61.3	32.8
Tunisia	min	40.1	24.3	54.7	12.3
	max	43.1	28.9	59.5	15.1
	average	41.6	26.6	57.1	13.7
Jordan	min	6.8	38.7	42.8	18.9
	max	9.6	40.2	45.9	23.1
	average	8.2	39.4	44.4	21.0
Morocco	min	17.1	23.0	36.2	39.7
	max	33.7	24.5	49.9	48.5
	average	25.4	23.8	43.1	44.1
Lebanon	min	6.9	31.8	36.5	0.0
	max	7.9	33.0	38.3	0.0
	average	7.4	32.4	37.4	0.0
Israel	min	0.1	–	–	0.0
	max	0.1	–	–	0.0
	average	0.1	–	–	0.0
Turkey	min	2.3	–	–	0.0
	max	4.4	–	–	0.0
	average	0.1	–	–	0.0

integration. As expected, tariffs have no impact on MENA countries' exports since the EU has already removed its tariffs applying to these countries' exports. This means that the shallow integration is already completed on the EU side. The export increases due to the removal of NTMs in the EU are significant (18.5%) but limited by the fact that the AVE in the EU (13.4%) is much lower than the AVEs in MENA countries, as shown previously. This suggests that the removal of NTMs in MENA countries and in the EU is expected to lead to a more important increase in MENA countries' imports than exports.[9] However, considerable export increase is expected from the improvement of MENA countries' LPI toward middle-income countries' level. In this regard, the export effects shown in Figure 3.6 are greater that the import effects calculated previously, because the parameter estimate corresponding to LPI is equal to 2.96 for exports and only 1.95 for imports. In other words, the logistics improvement in MENA countries should help them increase their exports more than their imports.

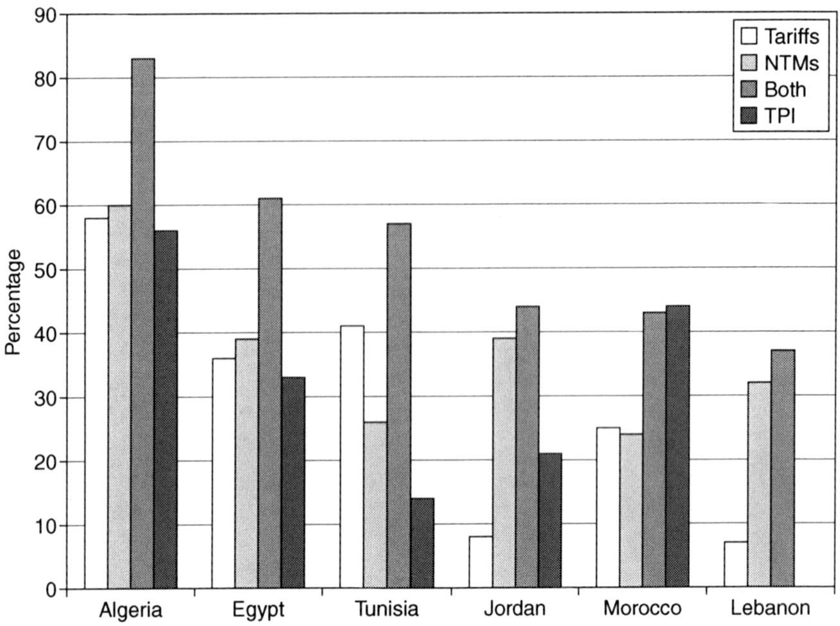

Figure 3.5b Percentage change in Mediterranean countries' imports (optimistic scenario) (average from all parameter estimates).

4.2 Marginal effects of shallow and deep integration (partial integration): the pessimistic scenario

Table 3.6 shows the marginal effects of shallow and deep integration, directly based on the parameter estimates derived in Table 3.4. It provides the percentage effects on exports to Mediterranean countries due to (i) a 1% tariff cut; (ii) a 1% reduction in the number of NTMs and (iii) a 1% increase in LPI. In this regard, the magnitude of the parameters corresponding to tariffs, NTMs and LPI are not strictly comparable across themselves, since the measurement of these variables is not similar (percentage for tariffs, numbers for NTMs and value index for LPI). In addition, the results cannot be strictly compared to those presented in Section 4.1, not only because the methodology is different but also because the proxy variables for tariffs and NTMs are different too, due to methodological requirements. However, Tables 3.5 and 3.6 provide complementary results.

First, 1% **reduction in the number of NTMs** does not increase trade very much (the maximum increase is 0.12%, for Algeria, and the minimum is insignificant, for Jordan). This result does not contradict the one developed in Section 4.1. It only suggests that a marginal (1%) reduction in the number of NTMs (for example from 20 to 19.8 barriers) does not strongly improve trade. This means that trade is less sensitive to the intensity of NTMs than to their existence. In other words, a

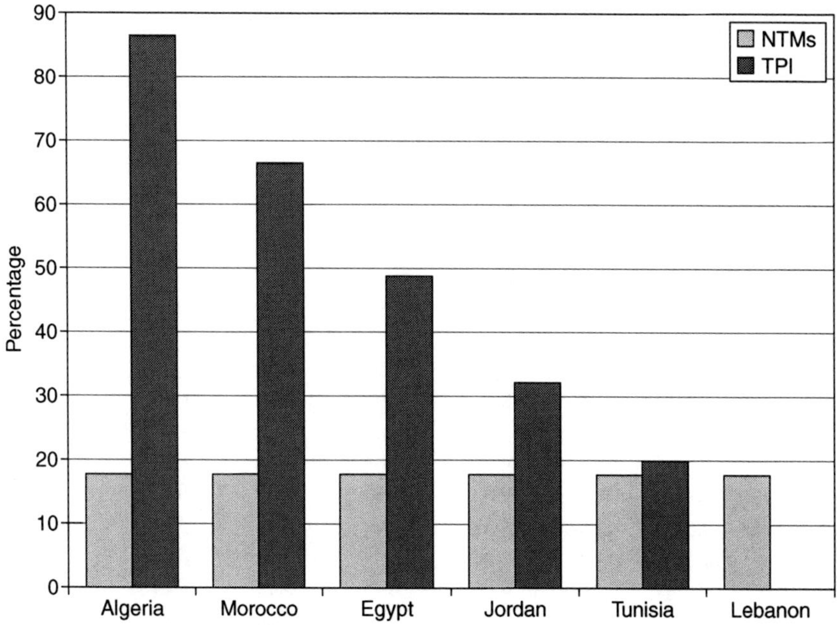

Figure 3.6 Percentage change in Mediterranean countries' exports (optimistic scenario) (average from all parameter estimates).

significant trade creation is expected to occur provided that a significant amount of NTMs are removed whatever their initial number. Having said that, the country scaling shown in Table 3.6 is consistent with that found previously. Indeed, the greatest effects are found for Algeria whereas the smallest ones involve Morocco, Tunisia (and Jordan). Again, this result will have strong policy implications.

As a second result, **a 1% tariff reduction** on MED countries' imports has significant effects for Algeria and Tunisia to a lesser extent, since it increases imports by 1.06% and 0.9%, respectively. This is not surprising since these countries have the highest tariff levels. A moderate impact is expected for Egypt (0.68%), as well as Morocco and Jordan to a lesser extent (about 0.3%). Conversely, these effects are less important in the other countries, especially Israel, Turkey and Lebanon (0.06%). These results can be compared to those found in Section 4.1. In fact, the country scaling is very similar. Besides, as already mentioned, no gain is expected for MED countries' exports, since the EU has already removed its tariffs for imports from MED countries.

Finally, trade gains due to deep integration can also be reinforced further through the improvement of logistics in MENA countries. As already mentioned, since the parameter estimates are greater for exports than for imports, MENA countries are expected to increase their exports more than their imports due to logistics improvements.

Table 3.6 The pessimistic scenario: percentage change in trade due to: 1% reduction in tariffs rates, 1% reduction in the number of NTMs and 1% increase in LPI)

		MED countries' imports			*MED countries' exports*		
		Tariffs	*NTMs*	*LPI*	*Tariffs*	*NTMs*	*LPI*
Algeria	min	1.06	0.12	1.75	0.00	0.06	2.66
	max	1.08	0.12	2.05	0.00	0.06	2.26
	average	1.07	0.12	1.95	0.00	0.06	2.96
Egypt	min	0.67	0.01	1.75	0.00	0.01	2.66
	max	0.68	0.02	2.05	0.00	0.01	3.26
	average	0.68	0.02	1.95	0.00	0.01	2.96
Jordan	min	0.24	0.01	1.75	0.00	0.01	2.66
	max	0.26	0.01	2.05	0.00	0.01	3.26
	average	0.25	0.01	1.95	0.00	0.01	2.96
Lebanon	min	0.06	0.05	1.75	0.00	0.03	2.66
	max	0.06	0.05	2.05	0.00	0.02	3.26
	average	0.06	0.05	1.95	0.00	0.02	2.96
Tunisia	min	0.87	0.01	1.75	0.00	0.01	2.66
	max	0.92	0.01	2.05	0.00	0.01	3.26
	average	0.90	0.01	1.95	0.00	0.01	2.96
Morocco	min	0.29	0.01	1.75	0.00	0.01	2.66
	max	0.30	0.01	2.05	0.00	0.01	3.26
	average	0.30	0.01	1.95	0.00	0.01	2.96
Israel	min	0.04	–	1.75	0.00	–	2.66
	max	0.05	–	2.05	0.00	–	3.26
	average	0.05	–	1.95	0.00	–	2.96
Turkey	min	0.03	–	1.75	0.00	–	2.66
	max	0.04	–	2.05	0.00	–	3.26
	average	0.04	–	1.95	0.00	–	2.96

5 The case of South–South integration

This section provides specific insights into integration between MED countries. For that purpose, the model is estimated from a restricted country sample, which only includes MED countries as reporters and partner countries. This makes it possible to appraise the impact of tariffs, NTMs and transport costs within the MED countries' area. As shown in Section 2, tariffs across MENA countries have been phased out during the GAFTA integration process (except Algeria). Consequently, all tariffs have been eliminated since 2005. However, some recent surveys indicate that previous tariff protection has sometimes been replaced by additional NTMs for specific products (Ghoneim and Péridy, 2009). As a result, trade liberalization across MED countries is not complete.

Figure 3.7 provides the simulation results due to full and marginal liberalization with regard to MENA countries' imports. Since bilateral tariffs across MED

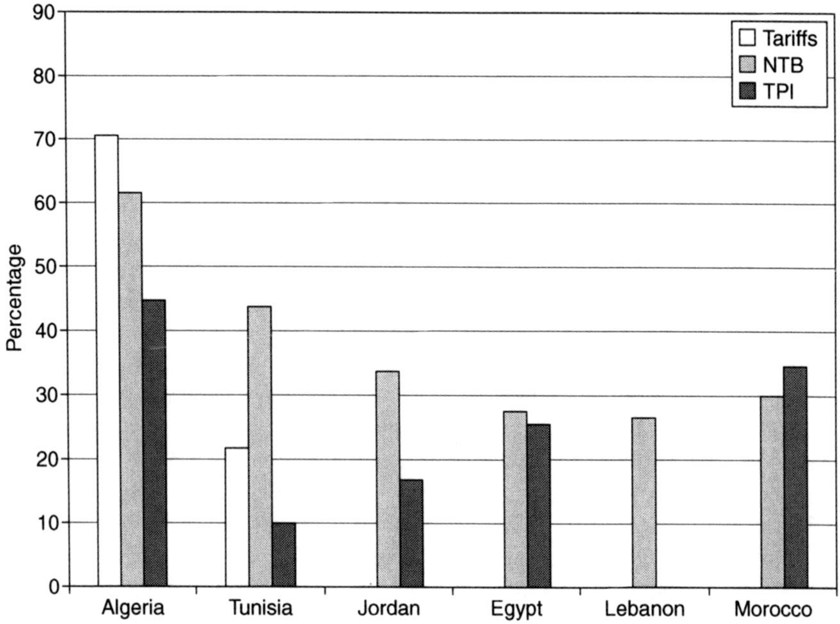

Figure 3.7 Percentage change in Mediterranean countries' imports (optimistic scenario).

countries have been removed since 2005, there is no effect of tariffs on trade. There are, however, three exceptions: the first is Algeria, which has joined the GATFA area but has not started removing its tariffs in 2005. The other exceptions concern Israel and Turkey, which are outside the GAFTA area.

The results concerning trade effects of NTMs are similar to those found in Section 4. For example, in case of full liberalization, all MED countries show a significant impact of NTM reduction. In the same way, as in Section 4 and for the same reasons, NTM reductions provide smaller marginal gains because, as already discussed, marginal cuts in NTMs are not enough to increase trade.

In addition, any improvement in LPI leads to significant import increases, especially in Algeria due to its poor logistics performance. As in Section 4, the import effects for Morocco may be over-estimated because estimations are based on data from 2007. This means that the recent improvement in LPI is not taken into account in the simulations.

Results concerning exports clearly indicate that in case of full liberalization, the removal of NTMs provides significant export increases – generally about 35% (Figure 3.8). This means that MENA countries can take advantage of the NTB removal across themselves in order to increase their exports. Interestingly, Algeria shows smaller gains, because the other MENA countries apply lower NTBs than Algeria. This means that the remaining export potential is a bit smaller for Algeria, i.e. less than 30%.

These gains must be added to those corresponding to LPI improvement. Given the high export elasticity corresponding to LPI (2.39), the export increases are particularly significant, especially for the countries which show the lowest logistics performance. As a matter of fact, the expected export increase is equal to about 70% for Algeria, 50% for Morocco and 40% for Egypt.

To sum up, the optimistic scenario for deep integration shows very significant trade increases across the MED partners, because of both NTM removal and increase in LPI. Conversely, the shallow integration process is almost fully achieved through the GAFTA Agreements. This is why the trade increase is more limited. With regard to imports, Algeria only is expected to enjoy significant import increases, since this country has not applied the GAFTA Agreement. Tunisia shows more limited gains, whereas in the other countries, no import increases are expected since they have already removed all tariffs for imports originating from the GAFTA area. Turning to exports, gains are also limited. Most countries are expected to increase their exports by about 10%. This is due to the effects of the expected tariff liberalization in Algeria.

Turning to the pessimistic scenario (Table 3.7), marginal effects of both tariffs and NTMs reduction are limited, as in the previous section. However, LPI improvement is expected to provide significant gains for most countries.

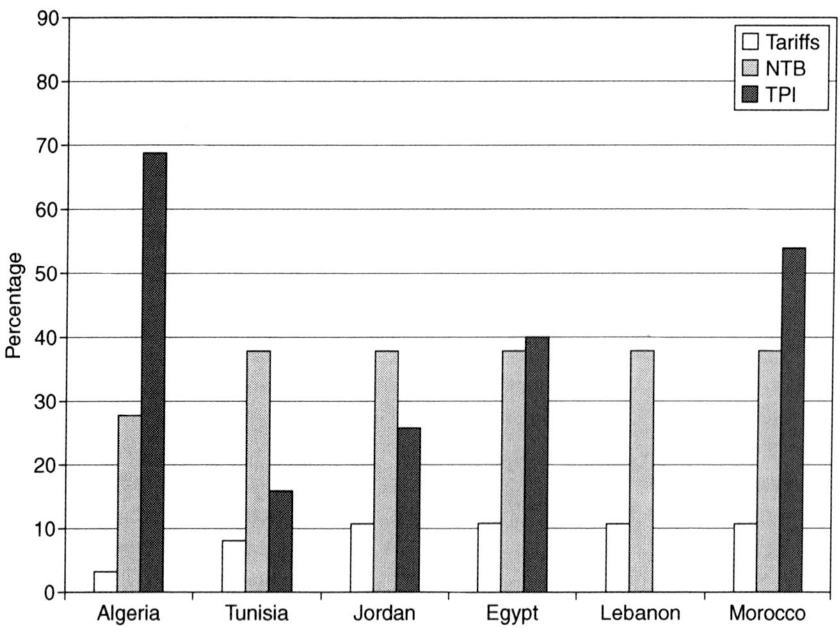

Figure 3.8 Percentage change in Mediterranean countries' exports (optimistic scenario).

Table 3.7 The pessimistic scenario: percentage change in trade due to: 1% reduction in tariffs rates, 1% reduction in the number of NTMs and 1% increase in LPI)

		MED countries' imports			*MED countries' exports*		
		Tariffs	*NTMs*	*LPI*	*Tariffs*	*NTMs*	*LPI*
Algeria	min	1.05	1.06	1.40	0.01	0.01	2.15
	max	1.10	0.06	1.70	0.01	0.01	2.63
	average	1.08	0.06	1.55	0.01	0.03	2.39
Egypt	min	0.00	0.02	1.40	0.00	0.01	2.15
	max	0.00	0.03	1.70	0.00	0.01	2.63
	average	0.00	0.03	1.55	0.02	0.03	2.39
Jordan	min	0.00	0.01	1.40	0.00	0.01	2.15
	max	0.00	0.01	1.70	0.00	0.01	2.63
	average	0.00	0.01	1.55	0.02	0.03	2.39
Lebanon	min	0.00	0.03	1.40	0.00	0.01	2.15
	max	0.00	0.04	1.70	0.00	0.01	2.63
	average	0.00	0.04	1.55	0.02	0.03	2.39
Tunisia	min	0.00	0.01	1.40	0.00	0.01	2.15
	max	0.00	0.01	1.70	0.00	0.01	2.63
	average	0.00	0.01	1.55	0.02	0.03	2.39
Morocco	min	0.00	0.01	1.40	0.00	0.01	2.15
	max	0.00	0.04	1.70	0.00	0.01	2.63
	average	0.00	0.03	1.55	0.02	0.03	2.39
Israel	min	0.17	–	1.40	0.17	0.01	2.15
	max	0.18	–	1.70	0.18	0.01	2.63
	average	0.18	–	1.55	0.25	0.03	2.39
Turkey	min	0.15	–	1.40	0.15	0.01	2.15
	max	0.19	–	1.70	0.19	0.01	2.63
	average	0.17	–	1.55	0.19	0.03	2.39

6 Conclusions and policy implications

The main findings of this research project are as follows. First, the analysis of tariffs in Mediterranean countries shows that they are still significant in Algeria and Tunisia to a lesser extent. In the other countries tariffs are much lower, especially in Israel and Turkey, which have almost completed their tariff liberalization. In addition, the protection due to NTMs is generally much greater than that due to tariffs (except for Algeria and Tunisia). In particular, the calculation of AVEs shows high tariff-equivalents for Algeria but also Jordan. Conversely, Morocco, Tunisia but also Egypt exhibit the lowest AVEs (less than 25%).

The implementation of a specific gravity model shows that trade costs significantly reduce MED countries' *imports* from their partners in the Euromed area. In particular, tariffs are trade-reducing, but mainly in the countries which showed the highest tariff levels (Algeria and Tunisia). This suggests that shallow integration was not fully achieved in these countries. Moreover, NTMs are significantly trade-reducing in all countries, especially in Algeria. On the other hand, they are less trade-reducing in Morocco and Tunisia, though significant. This means that eliminating NTMs in Mediterranean countries as a move toward deeper integration in the Euromed area is expected to provide significant gains. Besides, logistics inefficiencies significantly reduce trade in Maghreb countries.

In the same way, trade costs significantly reduce *exports* from MENA countries to their partners in the Euromed area. In particular, transport costs and logistics inefficiencies are especially trade-reducing. This is due to the gap between LPI in most MENA countries on the one hand and the EU on the other. In addition, NTMs are also export-reducing, but to a lesser extent as for imports. This can mainly be explained by the fact that NTMs applied to MENA countries' exports (especially by the EU) are lower than those applied to MENA countries' imports (by themselves). Moreover, tariffs have small effects on exports, mainly because they have been removed in most countries in the Euromed area.

The calculation of trade creation due to shallow and deep integration reveals that **tariff removal is expected to produce moderate or limited gains**, except in Algeria and Tunisia to a lesser extent, since both countries show higher tariffs than the other Mediterranean countries. For these countries, import increases are estimated to amount to 59% in Algeria and 42% in Tunisia. Egypt and Morocco show moderate import increases due to tariff removal (about 30%). For the other countries (Lebanon, Jordan, Israel and Turkey) only a limited import increase can be expected from further shallow integration, since the potential gains have been almost fully achieved due to past tariff liberalization, both multilaterally (GATT) and regionally (Barcelona Agreement). The effects of tariff removal concerning MENA countries' exports are also small, because most of their partners in the Euromed area have already removed their tariffs.

Conversely, the elimination of NTMs is expected to lead to strong trade gains (while a marginal reduction in NTMs leads to much smaller gains because NTMs must be importantly reduced in order to provide significant gains). With regard to imports, the expected increase ranges from about 25% in Morocco and Tunisia to 60% in Algeria. The other countries are in intermediate positions, showing import increases which scale from 32% (Lebanon) to 39% (Egypt and Jordan). Exports increases, although significant (35%), are smaller than import increases because the NTMs applied to the EU to MED countries' exports are lower than those applied by MED countries to their own imports. Overall, a strong trade creation is expected from deep integration. This result is consistent with that found in De Wulf and Maliszewska (2009). The main reason is that almost no progress has been made so far concerning the reduction in NTMs.

Trade gains due to deep integration can also been reinforced further through the potential reduction in trade and logistics costs: as a matter of fact, import increases are expected to amount up to up to 30% for Morocco and 45% for Algeria. Export increases are even more important due to higher export elasticities to LPI than import elasticity. In any case, the trade gains are particularly significant for the countries which show the greatest inefficiencies in their logistics, i.e. Algeria, Egypt and Morocco.

The particular case of South–South integration provides similar results, i.e. gains from deep integration (NTMs and logistics) are important, whereas gains due to shallow integration are moderate (except in Algeria, which has not started its tariff liberalization process vis-à-vis the other GAFTA members).

These results lead to the following policy implications: [10] First, Mediterranean countries should complete their shallow integration with their EU partners and across themselves as a means of capturing the remaining trade gains available. In particular, Algeria should make particular efforts to reduce its tariffs, which currently remain at high levels.

Dealing with deep integration is a more difficult task. First, NTMs must be addressed altogether, since we have shown that the removal of a particular NTM while keeping the other ones provides very small trade. As a result, each Mediterranean country should identify precisely all NTMs for each product, and decide whether to remove all NTMs for this product or not. Of course, the removal of all NTMs for all products is not necessarily the right solution, since some NTMs may be useful at product level for specific reasons (sanitary, etc....).

However, it seems that there are numerous NTMs in Mediterranean countries which strongly reduce trade. In particular, Technical Barriers to Trade (TBTs) seem particularly significant, as pointed out by a recent study implemented by the World Bank (Augier and Péridy, 2010). This study shows that TBTs account for more than 50% of the total number of NTMs in Lebanon and Egypt, especially in agriculture and food products, as well as in textiles/clothing.

Consequently, some questions must be addressed with regard to their removal for specific products, by moving toward mutual technical standard recognition or eliminating para-tariff measures. In any case, a cost–benefit analysis should be undertaken at product level before NTM elimination (especially in terms of short-term costs due to an increased competition with EU products).

A second aspect of deep integration relates to logistics efficiency. In this regard, significant additional gains can be achieved through the extension of the Euro-Mediterranean integration as a means of improving LPI (port infrastructures, logistics services, etc.). In this regard, an increased cooperation in industrial policies and FDI is required. In addition, extending the financial cooperation between the EU and Mediterranean countries (through specific EIB loans) can also help in improving logistics performance.

Appendix A: The calculation of AVEs

The KNO methodology is applied in two stages. The first includes an estimation of the quantity impact of NTMs on imports. Then, this impact is transformed into price effects, using import demand elasticities calculated in Kee *et al.* (2008).

In the first stage, the basic equation to be estimated is as follows:

$$\log(m_{n,c}) = \alpha_n + \sum_k \alpha_{n,k} C_c^k + \beta_{n,c}^{ntb} ntm_{n,c} + \varepsilon_{n,c} \log\left(1 + t_{n,c}\right) + \mu_{n,c} \qquad (1.1)$$

where $m_{n,c}$ is the import value of good (or industry) n in country c (MED countries) from EU countries (i), and C^k_c denotes a vector of country characteristics variables in MED countries. They include relative factor endowment[11] and the sum of GDP (of the reporter and the partner country), which captures economic size. The geographic distance between MED countries and their Mediterranean partners is also included. $ntm_{n,c}$ is a dummy variable which reflects the existence of bilateral NTMs. $t_{n,c}$ is the bilateral tariff on good n in country c (for imports from the EU), and $\varepsilon_{n,c}$ corresponds to the import demand elasticity.

Using the dataset completed by Lopez Gonzalez and Mendez Parra (2010), several proxies are available for tariffs, namely MFN, PREF (preferential) and AHS (effectively applied tariffs), which is the minimum between MFN and PREF. As a sensitivity analysis, all proxies have been tested. However, since preferential tariff data are often unavailable,[12] this introduces two problems. The first is that it significantly increases the number of unavailable observations. Second, it introduces a bias in AHS measure. As a matter of fact, the measure of AHS will be correct when the preferential tariff is available, but when it is not, the AHS tariff takes the value of the MFN one (since, in the formula, the minimum between MFN and unavailable PREF becomes MFN). Consequently, the measure of the AHS is very volatile in time since it sometimes captures MFN only. Given these problems, the MFN tariff seems to be the most reliable measure for the calculation of AVEs. Therefore, the results presented later only include MFN tariffs.

In the same way, several proxies are available for NTMs. As noticed in the text, eight groups of measures are available. For simplicity, we aggregate all these NTM types (except the first category which includes tariffs). In addition, a distinction is also made according to the products and/or countries the NTM applies to. Indeed, some NTMs apply regardless of the origin (e.g. sanitary requirement), some others regardless of the product, whereas some others are product-specific or country-specific. In order to capture the full range of NTMs, the latter have also been aggregated, including country- and product-specific NTMs as well as country- and product-non-specific NTMs. As a final step, this NTM variable is transformed into a binary variable which takes the value of zero in case of no NTM and unity if there is at least one NTM. This transformation is necessary to fit the model described in equation (1.1). However, when testing the trade impact of NTMs in Section 4, we will not use any longer a dummy variable.

The initial model is subsequently modified as follows. First, import-demand elasticities estimated in Kee *et al.* (2008) are substituted into (1.1). Second, the tariff term is moved to the left-hand side to address the endogeneity of tariffs. This introduces a new error term, $k_{n,c}$. Third, a White correction is introduced in order to tackle heteroskedasticity of the error term. Fourth, product-specific effects are also introduced so as to capture the variation of βs across tariff lines. Fifth, appropriate instrumental variables are included to address the endogeneity problem related to NTMs. Indeed, as shown in Lee and Swagel (1997), such endogeneity may lead to a downward bias on the estimated impact of NTMs on imports, which would result in underestimating AVEs. Sixth, a two-step estimation procedure is implemented to estimate the β coefficients, following a Heckman two-stage procedure.[13]

After these transformations, the final estimated equation becomes:

$$\log(m_{n,c}) - \varepsilon_{n,c}\log\left(1+t_{n,c}\right) = \alpha_n + \sum_k \alpha_{n,k} C_c^k + \left(-e^{\beta_{n,c}^{ntb} + \sum_k \beta_{n,c}^{ntb} C_c^k}\right) ntm_{n,c} + \kappa_{n,c} \quad (1.2)$$

The left-hand side of this equation reflects the value of imports once tariffs have been taken into account. This value of imports depends on country characteristics as well as on the remaining barriers to trade, i.e. NTMs.

Estimating equation (1.2) with the two-step Heckman procedure (TSHP) relies on the assumption that zero trade flows in the dataset do not occur randomly but are the outcome of a selection procedure. As a result, the TSHP estimator makes it possible to correct for this selection bias. The first stage estimates a Probit model (test for the probability of country *i* to exports to country *j*). In a second stage, when exports occur, the effects of trade barriers and other variables can be estimated through the choice of an appropriate estimator (Heckman, 1979; Greene, 2006).

The last step consists of calculating the AVEs after transformation of the quantity impact derived from equation (1.2) into price-equivalents. This leads to:

$$AVE = \frac{\partial \log P^d}{\partial NTM} \quad (1.3)$$

where P_d denotes the domestic price. This equation defines AVEs as the effects of NTMs on prices. The introduction of the price variable is necessary since, like *ad-valorem* tariffs, NTM effects must be calculated on prices and not on quantities. After differentiation of equation (1.1), it is easy to obtain:

$$AVE_{n,c}^{ntb} = \frac{e^{\beta_{n,c}^{ntb}} - 1}{\varepsilon_{n,c}} \quad (1.4)$$

Appendix B: Theoretical background of the gravity model

The gravity model developed in Section 3 has been implemented as a basis for getting the impact of shallow versus deep integration. From a theoretical point of view, the gravity equation has been considerably renewed in recent years. Indeed, it has been increasingly recognized that this equation can be derived from various international trade theories, notably Ricardian, Heckscher-Ohlin and monopolistic competition models (Helpman and Krugman, 1985; Bergstrand, 1989; Markusen and Wigle, 1990; Evenett and Keller, 2002), but also the reciprocal-dumping model (Feenstra *et al.*, 2001).

The gravity equation proposed here is based on this renewal. It starts from a modified version of the theoretical equation developed by Anderson and van Wincoop (2003, 2004), with special emphasis on trade costs which are the crucial point in our research study:

$$X_{ijt} = \left(\frac{Y_{it}^{\alpha} Y_{jt}^{\gamma}}{Y_{wt}^{\mu}}\right)\left(\frac{T_{ijt}}{P_{it} P_{jt}}\right)^{1-\sigma} \tag{1.5}$$

X_{ijt} corresponds to country i's exports to country j at year t. The first term in brackets includes the mass variables, namely country i's GDP (Y_{it}), country j's GDP (Y_{jt}) as well as world GDP (Y_{wt}). The second term in brackets reflects trade costs. They include the bilateral trade cost (T_{ijt}) as well as implicit prices (P_{it} and P_{jt}) which measure multilateral trade costs (Anderson and van Wincoop, 2003).

In the same way, implicit prices can be written as: [14]

$$P_{jt}^{(1-\sigma)} = \sum_i P_{it}^{\sigma-1} \theta_{it} t_{ijt}^{1-\sigma}, \forall j \tag{1.6}$$

$$P_{it}^{(1-\sigma)} = \sum_j P_{jt}^{\sigma-1} \theta_{jt} t_{ijt}^{1-\sigma}, \forall i \tag{1.7}$$

With θ_i and θ_j denoting country i and j's income shares.

Since prices depend on the trade barriers applied to all countries, they reflect multilateral trade resistance, i.e. the trade barriers that an exporter faces with all importing countries, not only its bilateral partner j. As a result, a rise in the trade costs vis-à-vis all its partners leads country i to trade more with its bilateral partner j.

Appendix C: Calculating trade creation from the gravity model

Basically, the gross trade creation due to the full removal of tariffs (shallow integration) or NTMs (deep integration) is defined by replacing the gravity equation

$$\begin{aligned} \ln X_{jk} &= \alpha_0 + \alpha_1 \ln SUMGDP_j + \alpha_2 \ln TAR_{jk} + \alpha_3 NTMs_{ijk} + \\ &\alpha_4 \ln TRANSCOST_j + \alpha_5 \ln LANG_j + \alpha_6 \ln COL_j + \varphi_j + \phi_k + \varepsilon_{ijt} \end{aligned} \tag{1.8}$$

by

$$\ln X_{jk} = \ln HX_{jk} + \alpha_2 \ln TAR_{jk} \tag{1.9a}$$

or

$$\ln X_{jk} = \ln HX_{jk} + \alpha_3 NTMs_{ijk} \tag{1.9b}$$

where $lnHX_{jk}$ reflects the hypothetical exports to Mediterranean countries, assuming no tariff (equation 1.9a) or no NTM (equation 1.9b). Indeed, $lnHX_{jk}$ is equal to

$$\begin{aligned} \ln HX_{jk} &= \alpha_0 + \alpha_1 \ln SUMGDP_j + \alpha_3 \ln NTM_{jk} + \\ &\alpha_4 \ln TRANSCOST_j + \alpha_5 \ln LANG_j + \alpha_6 \ln COL_j + \varphi_j + \phi_k + \varepsilon_{ijt} \end{aligned} \tag{1.10a}$$

or

$$\begin{aligned} \ln HX_{jk} &= \alpha_0 + \alpha_1 \ln SUMGDP_j + \alpha_2 \ln TAR_{jk} + \\ &\alpha_4 \ln TRANSCOST_j + \alpha_5 \ln LANG_j + \alpha_6 \ln COL_j + \varphi_j + \phi_k + \varepsilon_{ijt} \end{aligned} \tag{1.10b}$$

On the other hand, the specific effects of tariffs and NTMs are captured by the *TAR* and *NTM* variables in the right-hand side of equations (1.9a) and (1.9b). These variables must be defined as dummies which take the value of unity in case of no tariff (or NTMs) and zero otherwise (in log terms). Defined like this, these variables show the impact of the presence or the absence of tariff (NTMs), and will be used for simulating the impact of full integration versus the current situation.

Indeed, the gross trade creation due to the removal of tariffs and NTMs can now be defined as the difference between observed and hypothetical trade to Mediterranean countries:

$$G = X_{jk} - HX_{jk} \tag{1.11}$$

Replacing HX_{jk} from equation (1.11) into equations (1.9a) and (1.9b) and giving TAR_{jk} and NTM_{jk} the value corresponding to full integration ($lnTAR_{jk}$=1 and $lnNTM_{jk}$=1), it becomes:

$$\ln X_{jk} = \ln(X_{jk} - G) + \alpha_2 \ln e \tag{1.12a}$$

or

$$\ln X_{jk} = \ln(X_{jk} - G) + \alpha_3 \ln e \tag{1.12b}$$

This makes it possible to derive *G* as follows:

$$G = X_{jk}\left(1 - \frac{1}{e^{\alpha_2}}\right) \tag{1.13a}$$

in case of full shallow integration (tariff removal), or

$$G = X_{jk}\left(1 - \frac{1}{e^{\alpha_3}}\right) \quad (1.13b)$$

in case of full deep integration (NTM removal). In equations 1.13a and 1.13b, the term in brackets corresponds to the trade creation as a percentage of observed exports. It ranges from 0 to 1, i.e. from 0% to 100%. It equals zero when there is no trade effects of tariffs (or NTMs). In this case, $\alpha_2(\alpha_3)$ is insignificant. Conversely, as α increases towards infinity, the gross trade creation increases exponentially toward 100%.

The model can also be solved in order to calculate simultaneously the impact of shallow and deep integration. In this case, it is easy to show that the gross trade creation is equal to:

$$G = X_{jk}\left(1 - \frac{1}{e^{\alpha_2 + \alpha_3}}\right) \quad (1.14)$$

Please note that the trade creation is not an additive function. This means that the gross trade creation calculated separately for tariffs and NTMs in equations (1.13a) and (1.13b) does not add together to that calculated simultaneously in equation (1.14). This is due the mathematical properties of the trade creation function.

With regard to LPI, as already mentioned, it is expected that MENA countries reached the level of middle-income countries. The parameter estimate is that used from equation (1.8).

Notes

1 This work was produced in the context of the MEDPRO (Mediterranean Prospects) project (www.medpro-foresight.eu), a three-year project funded under the Socio-economic Sciences & Humanities Programme of DG Research of the European Commission's Seventh Framework Research Programme and coordinated by the Center for European Policy Studies (CEPS). We are grateful to Luc De Wulf (CASE, Centrum for Social and Economic Research, Warsaw, Poland) and Ahmed Ghoneim (Cairo University) for very helpful suggestions and comments.

2 The countries considered include Morocco, Algeria, Tunisia, Egypt, Jordan, Syria, Lebanon, Israel and Turkey. Libya and Palestinian territories have not been included in this analysis because of data unavailability.

3 The term 'Non Tariff Measures' (NTMs) has recently gained acceptance. It now tends to replace the term 'Non Tariff Barriers' (NTBs) since some measures do not always intend to be explicitly protectionist (e.g. some regulations or standards designed at increasing consumer safety (Cadot *et al.*, 2011).

4 The import demand elasticity is equal to −1.16 in Jordan whereas it is −1.78 for Egypt. This explains that although these two countries exhibit similar parameter estimates, the AVE is greater for Jordan (see Appendix A).

5 As in Anderson and van Wincoop (2003), world GDP is passed on to the intercept α_0.

6 As there are no reliable cross-country price indicators, the country-specific effects have been most commonly used in the empirical literature since Anderson and van Wincoop (2003) (refer to Appendix B)
7 The only change that must be made is the replacement of the binary variable corresponding to NTMs by a variable which shows the number of NTMs. The corresponding parameter shows the percentage change in trade due to the 1% reduction in the number of NTMs.
8 Please note that the parameters corresponding to tariffs and NTMs are positive in Table 3.2. This is expected since these parameters are calculated as dummies which take the value of zero in case of positive tariffs (or NTMs) and 1 otherwise. These dummies will be used for the calculation of trade creation following equations (1.13a) and (1.13b) in Appendix C.
9 Due to a lack of data concerning NTBs in all EU countries, we rely on the AVE calculated by Kee *et al.* (2009). Moreover, the export increase has been estimated assuming that trade effects for a given AVE are the same for all countries. For example, since the AVE in the EU is roughly half the AVE calculated for MENA countries, it is expected that the trade effect for EU imports will be half that calculated for EU exports.
10 A broader analysis about policy implications of border management may also be found in McLinden *et al.* (2011).
11 Factor endowment is measured by a proxy which is the difference in GDP per capita between the reporter and the partner country.
12 This may be because of zero flows or because data are unavailable for a given product in a given country.
13 For additional details, refer to Kee *et al.* (2009: 177).
14 See Anderson and van Wincoop (2003) for the complete derivation of the model.

References

Anderson, J. and van Wincoop, E. (2003) 'Gravity with Gravitas: A Solution to the Border Puzzle', *American Economic Review*, 93(1), 170–192.

Anderson, J. and van Wincoop, E. (2004) 'Trade Costs', *Journal of Economic Literature*, 42(3), 691–751.

Augier, P. and Péridy, N. (2010) 'Inventory and Assessment of Non-Tariff Measures in MENA Region', Report for the World Bank, Washington, DC: The World Bank.

Bergstrand, J.H. (1989), 'The Gravity Equation in International Trade: Some Microeconomic Foundations and Empirical Evidence', *Review of Economics and Statistics*, 23: 143–153.

Cadot, O., Maliszewska, M. and Sáez, S. (2011) 'Non Tariff Measures: impact, regulation and trade facilitation', in G. McLinden, E. Fanta, D. Widdowson and T. Doyle (eds), *Border Management Modernization*, Washington, DC: World Bank Publications, pp. 215–231.

CEPII (2007a) Database on international distances, www.cepii.fr, Paris: CEPII.

CEPII (2007b) CHELEM database for international trade, population and GDP, Paris: CEPII.

De Wulf, L. and Maliszewska, M. (2009) 'Economic Integration in the Euro-Mediterranean Region', CASE and CEPS Report, September.

Egger, P. (2004) 'On the Problem of Endogenous Unobserved Effects in the Estimation of Gravity Models', *Journal of Economic integration*, 19(1): 182–191.

Evenett, S. and Keller, W. (2002) 'On Theories Explaining the Success of the Gravity Equation', *Journal of Political Economy*, 110(2): 281–316.

Feenstra, R., Markusen, J. and Rose, A. (2001) 'Using the Gravity Equation to Differentiate among Alternative Theories of Trade', *Canadian Journal of Economics*, 34(2): 430–447.

Ghoneim, A. and Péridy, N. (2009) 'Regional Integration, Imperfect Competition and Welfare: The Experience of the Greater Arab Free Trade Area', *Economie Appliquée*, 52(4): 131–156.

Greene, W. (2006) *Econometric Analysis* (6th edn), New York, NY: Prentice-Hall International.

Heckman, J. (1979) 'Sample Selection Bias as a Specification Error' *Econometrica*, 47(1): 153–161.

Helpman, E. and Krugman, P.R. (1985) 'Market Structure and Foreign Trade: Increasing Returns, Imperfect Competition and the International Economy', Cambridge, MA: MIT Press.

Kee, H., Nicita, A. and Olarreaga, M. (2008) 'Import Demand Elasticities and Trade Distortions', *Review of Economics and Statistics*, 90(4): 666–682.

Kee, H., Nicita, A. and Olarreaga, M. (2009) 'Estimating Trade Restrictiveness Indices', *Economic Journal*, 119(534): 172–199.

Lee, J. and Swagel, P. (1997) 'Trade Barriers and Trade Flows across Countries and Industries', *Review of Economics and Statistics*, 79(3): 337–368.

Lopez Gonzalez, J. and Mendez Parra, M. (2010) *Description of the Mediterranean Trade and Protection Database*, MEDPRO-WP5.

Lucke, B. and Nathanson, R. (2007) 'Assessing the Macro Economic Effects of the Barcelona Initiative's Liberalization Process', FEMISE Report, Vol. 31–10.

Maersk Line, online rates. Available at: https://www.maerskline.com/globalfile/?path=/pdf/our_services/rates_onlin

Markusen, J. and Wigle, R.M. (1990) 'Explaining the Volume of North–South Trade', *Economic Journal*, 100(403): 1206–1215.

McLinden, G., Fanta, E., Widdowson, D. and Doyle, T. (eds), *Border Management Modernization*, Washington, DC: World Bank Publications

Péridy, N. (2005) 'Assessing the Euro-Mediterranean Partnership: What are the Lessons for ASEAN Countries?', *Journal of Asian Economics*, 16(1): 125–139.

Péridy, N. (2010) 'Evaluation de l'impact du partenariat euro-méditerranéen 15 ans après Barcelone: Quels enseignements? Quelles actions?', in: A. Gallal and J.L. Reiffers (eds), *Rapport du FEMISE sur le Partenariat Euro-méditerranéen: Le Partenariat Méditerranéen à la croisée des chemins*, pp. 3–20.

World Bank (2007) *Connecting to Compete: Trade Logistics in the Global Economy*, International Bank for Reconstruction and Development, Washington, DC: The World Bank.

World Bank (2011) *Connecting to Compete: Trade Logistics in the Global Economy*, International Bank for Reconstruction and Development, Washington, DC: The World Bank.

Part II

Liberalization and macroeconomic performance in the Mediterranean

4 The transmission of growth shocks in the EU to MENA[1]

Reinout De Bock, Daniel Florea and Joël Toujas-Bernaté

1 Introduction

This chapter examines the effect of growth shocks in European countries on economic activity in Morocco and Tunisia.[2] Both Morocco and Tunisia have taken significant steps to open up their economies and signed association agreements with the European Union (EU) in the mid-1990s.[3] In the past decade, these countries have attracted significant inflows of foreign direct investment (FDI), liberalized trade, and lowered the entry barriers for foreign banks into domestic financial markets. Today, they rely on Europe for a large share of their external receipts (exports, tourism receipts, workers' remittances and FDI), and growth is likely to be significantly influenced by events in their main European partners. Although the global crisis in 2008–2009 did not cause a recession in Morocco or Tunisia, the recession in the EU had a clear impact on their external receipts.

In the context of increasing globalization, there has been a renewed interest in examining business synchronization and spillovers of economic activity across countries. Recent studies have developed an approach to identify common shocks and spillovers. In line with these studies, we use structural vector autoregression (SVAR) models to measure the response of Tunisian and Moroccan growth to an innovation in the growth rate of key partner countries. While simple contemporaneous correlations suggest strong business cycle co-movement, SVARs have the additional advantage that they capture dynamic patterns present in the data and allow for a structural interpretation of impulse responses. Following Bayoumi and Swiston (2009), we also use our baseline SVARs to gauge the contribution of different factors such as trade, revenues from tourism and remittances. A wide literature has suggested that these variables can be the source of important transmission channels of shocks across regions.[4]

We find that positive shocks to a growth composite of trade partners have significant expansionary hump-shaped effects on growth in Morocco and Tunisia. Our analysis suggests noticeable differences in the transmission channels of these shocks in the two countries. For Tunisia, exports, and to a much lesser extent tourism, appear to be the major channels. Exports are also important in Morocco, but an equally important role is played by remittances and tourism. Our results are consistent with the evolution of the different macroeconomic aggregates in the wake of the 2008 recession in Europe. Moreover, an analysis by sector supports these results. In particular, re-estimating the VARs with sectoral data shows that the export-oriented sectors are the ones with significant responses to external growth shocks in Tunisia. In contrast, service-related sectors appear to be the most sensitive to external growth shocks in Morocco.

The chapter is organized as follows. The first subsection of Section 2 provides background information on the economic policy of both countries in the past decades and the role of the European Union as an export destination, and a source of tourism revenues, remittances and FDI. The second subsection describes the GDP data and looks at contemporaneous correlations between the different growth rates. In Section 3, we estimate the spillovers using a SVAR analysis and we check the robustness of the results examining an alternative identification scheme for the structural shock. Section 4 analyzes the role of different transmission channels, while in Section 5 we redo the SVAR analysis with sectoral data. Finally, Section 6 identifies a number of policy issues in light of these results, while taking into account growth forecasts for Europe. Section 7 concludes.

2 Background and data description

2.1 Economic policy and links with partner countries

In the past decades, Morocco and Tunisia have taken significant steps in opening up their economies. Aside from a similar geographical position, both countries are small open economies with important historical and cultural ties with Europe. Tunisia signed an association agreement with the European Union in 1995, and implemented it in 1998. Morocco signed an association agreement in 1996, which entered into force in 2000 (Box 4.1). Both agreements are part of a broader approach of the European Union (EU) towards widening its relations with neighboring countries from the south of the Mediterranean and aiming at the long-term objective of building a Euro-Mediterranean economic area. The implementation of the association agreements produced important changes for the two economies. Since then, trade flows have increased exponentially (Figure 4.1).[5] Although other factors, such as globalization and structural reforms adopted in both Morocco and Tunisia after 2000, are also at play, the impact of the association agreements on both countries appears to be significant.

Exports, tourism and remittances are sizable in both Morocco and Tunisia, although their importance varies between the two countries (Figure 4.2). Relative to GDP, exports are substantially higher in Tunisia than in Morocco. In contrast, tourism and remittances appear to be more important in Morocco. For example, the ratio of remittances to GDP in Morocco is double the ratio in Tunisia.

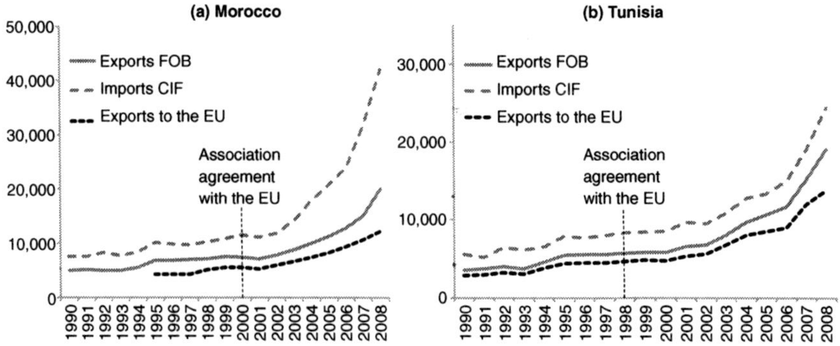

Figure 4.1 Total imports and exports (millions of USD, 1990–2008) (source: countries' authorities, and IMF staff estimates).

Box 4.1 Association Agreements

(a) The Association Agreement between Morocco and the European Union

The EU–Morocco Association Agreement was signed in February 1996, and entered into force in March 2000, following its ratification by the Parliaments of the EU Member States, the European Parliament and the Moroccan Parliament.

The Agreement aims at gradually creating a free trade area for industrial products. The EU committed to give instantaneously free access to products originating from Morocco, while Morocco implemented a gradual dismantling of its trade tariffs, according to a specific schedule. Furthermore, progressive and reciprocal liberalization of trade for a number of agricultural products started in January 2004. The Agreement also includes provisions on freedom of establishment and the liberalization of services, and free movement of capital and competition rules. From a political perspective, respect for human rights and democratic principles constitutes an essential element of the Agreement. The text equally refers to regular political dialogue at senior official level on peace, security, and regional cooperation. Another important chapter of the Association Agreement refers to the question of migration and social affairs. Following the entry into force of the agreement, a constant dialogue at Ministerial and expert level on migration and related areas has been held.

In 2008, Morocco obtained 'advanced status' relations, a move which provides greater access to the EU's internal market and which places Morocco a notch above the members of the 'neighborhood policy'. Under the terms of the advanced status, Morocco will also participate in European civil and military crisis management operations, as well as in a number of European agencies, such as Europol, the European Air Security Agency, and the European Monitoring Center for Drugs and Drug Addiction.

(b) The Association Agreement between Tunisia and the European Union

Tunisia signed a bilateral Association Agreement with the EU in July 1995, and implemented it in March 1998. An amendment covering agricultural products was implemented on January 1, 2001.

The Agreement has three main features. First, it liberalized trade relations through the immediate abolition of quantitative restrictions and a gradual reduction of trade barriers which culminated in free trade for industrial goods in 2008. Trade liberalization pertaining to agriculture products and negotiations to liberalize the trade of services are still ongoing. Second, it contributed to harmonizing Tunisia's regulatory framework with the one in place in the EU, particularly for trade-related policies, norms and standards including in transport and telecommunications, accounting and financial services, and statistics. Third, it provided support for sectors facing more difficulties to adjust to the trade liberalization (the 'mise à niveau' program) and enhanced cooperation, notably in the development of infrastructure.

The European Neighborhood Policy builds on the Association Agreement by focusing the bilateral cooperation between Tunisia and the EU on more targeted programs. It was developed in 2004 and concluded with Tunisia in 2005. It provides increased financial support, and favors enhanced regional cooperation for trade integration and the development of infrastructure (particularly for energy, transport, and information technology); improvements in the business climate (particularly through streamlined taxation and customs procedures, and strengthened intellectual and property rights); and a consolidated macroeconomic framework.

The EU is the main destination of exports for both Morocco and Tunisia (Figure 4.3). The EU's average share in Moroccan exports for the period 2005–2008 was 70%. For Tunisia this share is slightly higher, at 77%. The EU plays an even more prominent role when it comes to tourism and remittances. The average shares for tourism revenues and remittances originating from the EU during the same period (2005–2008) are between 80% and 90%. Moreover, these shares appear to be relatively stable over time.

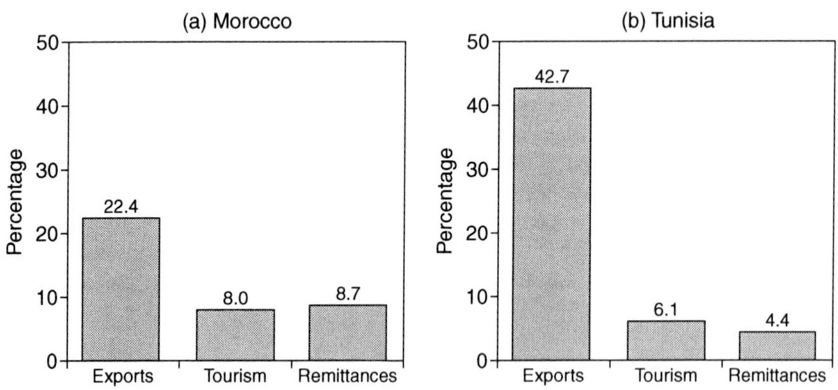

Figure 4.2 Shares of exports, tourism and remittances, 2008 (in percent of GDP) (source: countries' authorities, and IMF staff estimates).

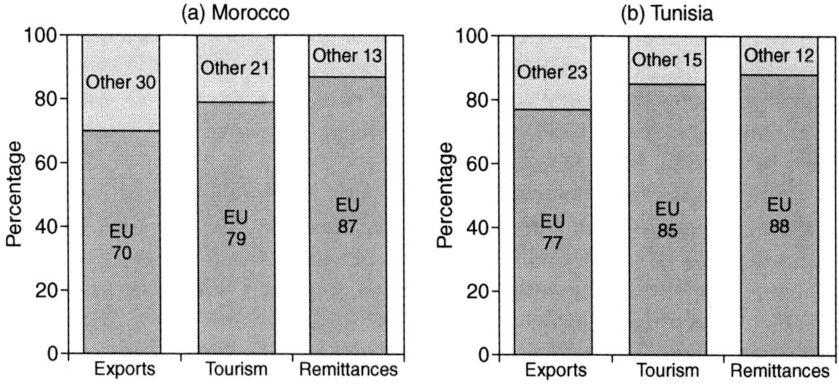

Figure 4.3 EU shares in exports, tourism and remittances (%), average 2005–2008) (source: countries' authorities, and IMF staff estimates).

Other channels might also be explored to examine the interrelation between the European Union and Morocco and Tunisia's economies, such as imports, foreign direct investment (FDI) flows, as well as financial linkages. Regarding FDI, although these flows are generally volatile, Figure 4.4 suggests that they represent a potentially important transmission channel between the EU and the Moroccan and Tunisian economies. We consider, however, that the effect of FDI is mainly structural and manifests itself in the medium to long term. As such, it is less suited for an analysis centered on business cycles correlations.

Turning to the transmission of shocks through financial channels, the Moroccan and Tunisian banking systems have limited links with international markets. Banking activities are funded in large part with domestic deposits (75% of

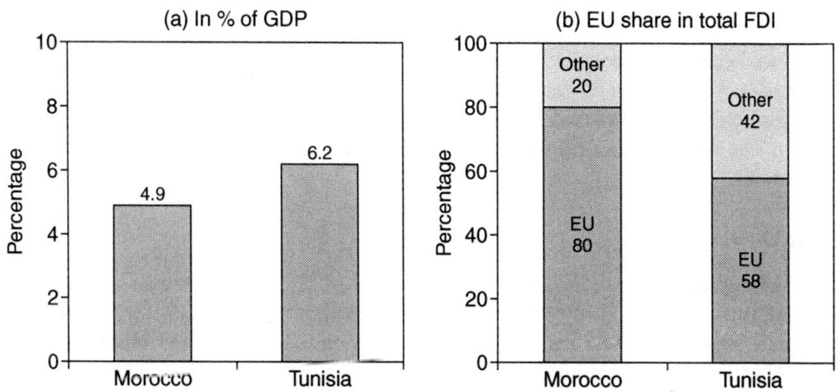

Figure 4.4 FDI in Morocco and Tunisia (average 2005–2008) (source: countries' authorities, and IMF staff estimates).

banks' resources in Morocco and 80% in Tunisia) and cross-border financing is small. In 2009, short-term foreign liabilities of Moroccan and Tunisian banks to external counterparts reported to the Bank for International Settlements (BIS) represented only 3.3% and 1.2% of their respective GDP (Table 4.1). Moreover, in both countries the capital account is only partially open. Several restrictions apply to transactions in foreign currency, foreign borrowing and foreign investment by domestic firms (Box 4.2).

Foreign banks have non-negligible presences in the two countries' banking systems. Majority-owned foreign banks accounted for 21.4% of total banking assets in Morocco (2008) and for 29.4% in Tunisia (2009). This presence might play a role in terms of increased competition, improved banking practices and diversification of funding sources, but, as in the case of imports and FDIs, these effects are more likely to appear in the long run. Nevertheless, the impact of the opening of the domestic market to foreign banks in Morocco and Tunisia is a subject that deserves a multifaceted analysis which goes beyond the purpose of this our chapter.

Box 4.2 Some of the Remaining Restrictions on Foreign Currency Transactions and Capital flows

(a) Morocco

Moroccan exporters of goods and services may open foreign exchange accounts domestically and deposit up to 50% of the repatriated foreign exchange receipts from exports. Foreign residents and corporations may open foreign exchange accounts without limitations.

Commercial banks may borrow abroad only to finance foreign trade or investment operations on behalf of customers or as part of the introduction of the forward cover for customers' foreign exchange swaps, with maturities equal to the duration of the hedging operations offered.

There are no controls on inward direct investment. Outward direct investments are subject to approval, but resident corporations in operation for more than three years benefit from certain facilities. Resident foreign nationals are free to invest abroad, provided the operations are financed from their own funds abroad or from their holdings denominated in convertible dirham or foreign exchange.

A number of measures were taken during 2009 to further liberalize the capital account.

(b) Tunisia

Professional accounts in foreign currency may be opened by resident individuals, Tunisian legal entity and foreign legal entity in Tunisia with foreign currency assets in connection with its activities. Authorization by the Central Bank of Tunisia (BCT) is required for residents to open accounts abroad. Export proceeds must be repatriated within a time limit from the payment due date. However, resident exporters may retain up to 100% of their foreign exchange export proceeds.

The acquisition of assets (capital and money market instruments) abroad by residents is subject to authorization. Residents are also required to repatriate all income from investment abroad, as well as all proceeds from the divestiture or liquidation of such investments.

Stocks in existing companies in Tunisia may be acquired freely with foreign exchange transferred from abroad by foreign non-residents. However, the acquisition by foreigners of shares with voting rights is subject to the approval of the High Investment Commission. Non-residents may also sell freely shares of companies established in Tunisia. They may also transfer freely net real proceeds from the sale of shares that were purchased with foreign exchange transferred from abroad.

Source: International Monetary Fund, 2009, *Annual Report on Exchange Arrangements and Exchange Restrictions (AREAER)*

2.2 Correlation of growth rates with European partners

Growth rates of Morocco and Tunisia on one hand and their key European partners on the other appear strongly positively correlated in the last decade. In our econometric analysis, we use real non-agricultural year-on-year growth rates of GDP series for Morocco $g_t^{MOR,NA}$ and Tunisia $g_t^{TUN,NA}$.[6] These series are seasonally adjusted and available on a quarterly basis. For the EU, a country-specific composite GDP growth rate $g_t^{EU}(\cdot)$ is calculated as a weighted average of growth rates of the main EU partners based on the weights these countries take in Morocco's and Tunisia's exports of goods respectively. The country weights are constructed by the IMF for the Global Economic Environment (GEE). The Appendix contains the formula for $g_t^{EU}(\cdot)$ and tables with the GEE weights used for Morocco and Tunisia.

Table 4.2 shows a strong positive correlation between the growth rates $g_t^{EU}(MOR)$ and $g_t^{MOR,NA}$ and $g_t^{EU}(TUN)$ with $g_t^{TUN,NA}$.[7] This correlation is 46% for Morocco and 63% for Tunisia. Statistical tests reject the hypothesis that these correlations are equal to zero. The table also shows that there is no strong correlation between growth in real petroleum spot prices, $g_t(Oil)$, and Moroccan or Tunisian growth rates. This suggests that the correlations of $g_t^{MOR,NA}$ and $g_t^{TUN,NA}$ with growth in their European partners are not hiding the effect of a global cycle.[8]

Table 4.1 Banks' external debt statistics, 2000–2009 (in percent of GDP)

	2000	*2001*	*2002*	*2003*	*2004*	*2005*	*2006*	*2007*	*2008*	*2009*
Morocco										
Liabilities to BIS banks	17.7	16.1	15.3	11.9	10.8	8.9	7.5	7.9	8.4	9.8
S-T Liabilities to BIS banks	4.8	5.3	4.7	2.7	2.6	2.6	3.2	2.9	2.1	3.3
Tunisia										
Liabilities to BIS banks	7.7	7.0	7.2	7.3	7.5	5.6	6.1	5.7	5.2	4.8
S-T Liabilities to BIS banks	2.6	2.0	1.7	1.7	1.7	1.5	2.0	1.4	1.2	1.2

Source: Bank for International Settlements, country authorities, and IMF staff calculations.

Table 4.2 Volatility and correlation coefficients of growth rates, 2000Q1–2009Q4

	$g_t^{MOR,NA}$	$g_t^{EU}(MOR)$	$g_t^{TUN,NA}$	$g_t^{EU}(TUN)$	$gt(Oil)$
$g_t^{MOR,NA}$	1.69				
$g_t^{EU}(MOR)$	0.46 (3.21)	2.08			
$g_t^{TUN,NA}$			1.59		
$g_t^{EU}(TUN)$			0.63 (5.06)	2.05	
$g_t(Oil)$	0.16 (0.98)		−0.07 (−0.43)		14.60

Source: IMF staff estimates.

Notes
Standard deviations are on the diagonal and correlations off-diagonal. Between brackets are the T-stats for the null hypothesis that a single correlation coefficient is equal to zero. *Oil* is the spot petroleum price (average of Fateh, Brent and WTI) in US$ scaled by US CPI.

3 Estimating the spillovers

3.1 Identification scheme

We proceed with a VAR-based identification scheme in order to estimate the impact of an innovation in EU growth on Morocco and Tunisia nonagricultural GDP growth. More specifically, for country j, the variables included in the baseline VAR are:

$$Z_t = \left[g_t^{EU}(j), g_t^{j,NA} \right]'$$

The reduced-form VAR is:

$$Z_t = c + \sum_{j=1}^{p} B_j Z_{t-j} + u_t, E(u_t u_t') = V,$$

where c is a constant and Z_t is the matrix with variables. The reduced-form residuals u_t are mapped into the structural shocks ε_t by the structural matrix A_0:

$$\varepsilon_t = A_0 u_t.$$

We use the inverse of the Choleski factor of the variance-covariance matrix V to identify structural shocks that are orthogonal to each other, $E[\varepsilon_t \varepsilon'_t] = I$, where I is the identity matrix. This corresponds to the assumption that on impact, structural shocks in Tunisia have a zero effect on shocks in European partner countries. It is important to note that changing the ordering of the variables in Z did not change our results.

3.2 Responses to external growth shock

For each country, we use the longest available quarterly data for the VAR estimation. For Morocco, the sample covers the period 1990Q1 to 2009Q4, whereas for Tunisia the dataset is from 2000Q1 to 2009Q4.[9] Despite covering a relatively short time span, these datasets allow us to capture the recent period of high growth with important structural changes followed by the adverse shock of 2008–2009. We include two lags in the estimated VARs. According to the Schwarz information criteria, this is the optimal lag length for both Morocco and Tunisia.

Figure 4.5 shows impulse response functions (IRFs) of growth in Morocco and Tunisia to a one standard deviation shock in the growth of GDP in the economic partners. The graph also includes standard error bands encompassing the 95% confidence interval. The impulse response of both Morocco and Tunisia GDP growth to EU GDP growth is significantly different from zero in the first four quarters. A variation of one percentage point in EU GDP growth produces a similar peak response in Morocco (0.59 in the second quarter) compared to Tunisia (0.62 in the third quarter), but generates a more abrupt and short-lived response for Morocco, while the response is more persistent in the case of Tunisia.

As a robustness check, we also reversed the order of the growth rates in the VAR, and found similar results. As expected, in all the SVARs, growth shocks in Morocco and Tunisia generate non-significant responses in growth in the EU partner countries.[10]

The variance decompositions reported in Table 4.3 show how much of the forecast error variance of a country's GDP growth can be explained by the structural shocks to GDP growth in EU partner countries. The share explained by $g_t^{EU}(MOR)$ and $g_t^{EU}(TUN)$ increases at longer horizons. At a ten-quarter forecast horizon, shocks to $g_t^{EU}(MOR)$ explain 11% of Morocco's GDP growth whereas shocks to $g_t^{EU}(TUN)$ explain 38% of Tunisia's GDP growth.

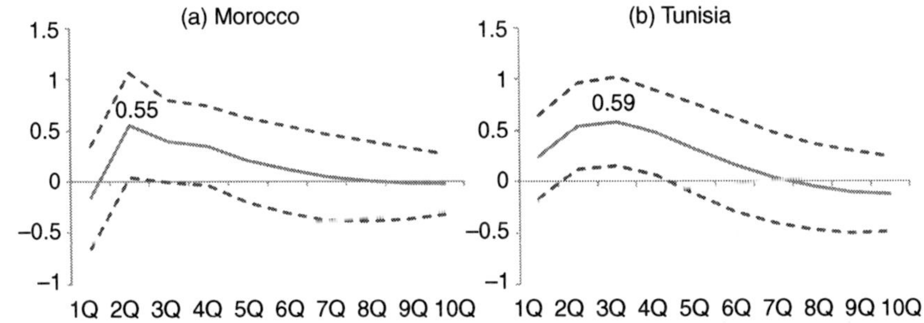

Figure 4.5 Response of domestic growth to an external growth shock (source: IMF staff estimates).

Table 4.3 Forecast error variance decompositions explained by $g_t^{EU}(\cdot)$ (in %)

Quarter	*Morocco*	*Tunisia*
1	0.49	3.78
2	6.01	17.20
3	8.12	28.94
4	9.91	34.55
5	10.51	36.71
6	10.71	37.28
7	10.74	37.31
8	10.74	37.36
9	10.74	37.58
10	10.75	37.90

Source: IMF staff estimates.

3.3 Alternative identification of shocks

We analyze the robustness of the earlier results by considering a long-run identification scheme for the structural shocks in EU partner countries. Specifically, rather than identifying the structural shock in EU partner countries by imposing a zero response on impact, we identify this shock by assuming that growth in Morocco or Tunisia has no long-run impact on GDP in partner countries. This assumption can be motivated by the size of Morocco or Tunisia's economy compared to that of partner countries. Following Blanchard and Quah (1989), the variables included in the baseline VAR are ordered as before:

$$Z_t = \left[g_t^{EU}(j), g_t^{j,NA} \right]'$$

The long-run effects of the structural shocks are given by:

$$Z_\infty = \Theta\varepsilon_t \, .$$

The identification assumption for the long-run restriction is then:

$$\Theta(1,:) = [\Theta(1,1) \quad 0]$$

Figure 4.6 shows that the IRFs to structural shocks in EU partner countries identified using this long-run restriction scheme resemble the shocks identified in the short-run identification scheme. We also added IRFs to a one standard deviation shock of the reduced-form residual, so without making any identifying restriction on the correlation matrix of the residuals u_t. The figure suggests that both the short-run and long-run restrictions do not impose big transformations.

4 Decomposing the spillovers by transmission channels

To get a sense of the relative importance of different transmission channels, we follow the approach proposed in Bayoumi and Swiston (2009). The SVARs are

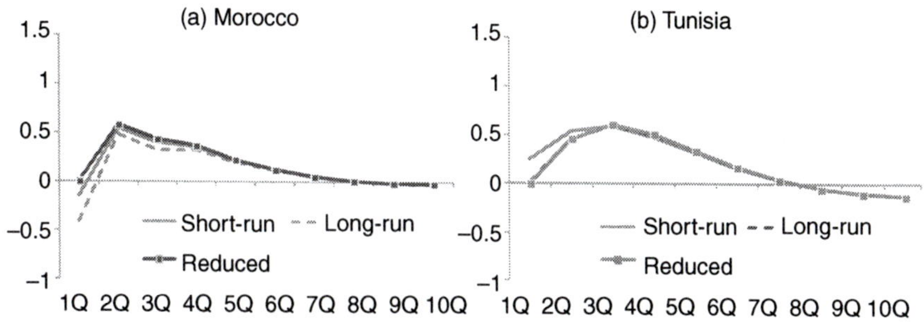

Figure 4.6 Short-run versus long-run restrictions (source: IMF staff estimates).

augmented one at a time with data on trade, tourism and remittances as exogenous variables. The potential contribution c_k of a particular channel k is then calculated as:

$$c_k = r - r_k.$$

The contribution c_k is the difference between the responses of growth in Morocco or Tunisia to growth in partner countries (r) minus the response of growth when the spillover is included as an exogenous variable (r_k). The idea is that adding the exogenous variable to the VAR leaves in r_k the part of the response that is not associated with the transmission channel k (Figure 4.7).

This approach does not exclude the existence of other relevant transmission channels and does not account for the collinearity between the different channels. This also implies that the sources of spillovers c_k are not necessarily required to sum up to the impulse response r. As such, we prefer to think of this technique as a gauge providing an indication of the relative importance of the major channels and not as a precise breakdown of the impulse response.[11]

Figure 4.8 shows the cumulative impact of the different contributions c_k determined with this method for Morocco and Tunisia, where the structural shocks

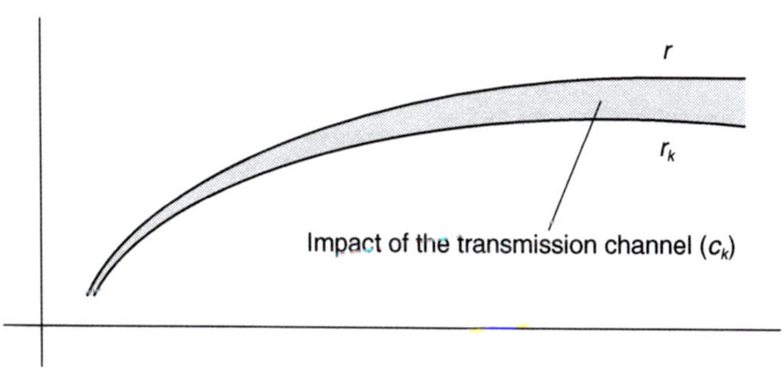

Figure 4.7 Bayoumi and Swiston approach (source: IMF staff estimates).

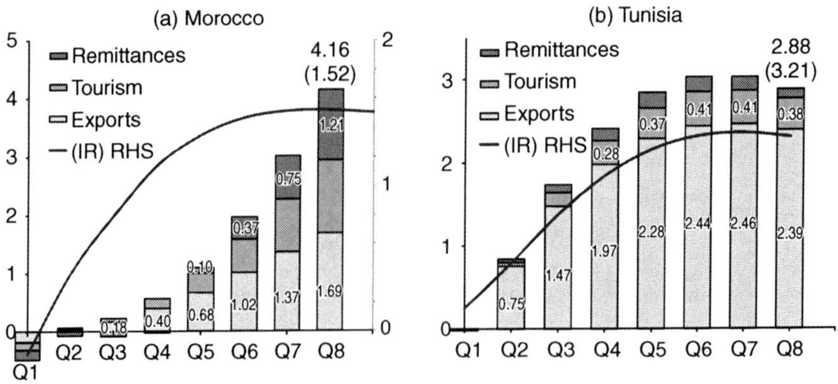

Figure 4.8 Cumulative responses to growth innovation in partner composite (source: IMF staff estimates).

are identified as in Section 3.1. We also include the cumulative impulse response function of the SVARs estimated in Section 3.2. The analysis suggests that, in the case of Tunisia, exports, and to a much lesser extent tourism, are the major transmission channels. Remittances seem to play a very limited role at these frequencies. For Morocco, the results show that besides exports, which still play an important role, remittances and tourism are also major transmissions channels for spillovers. Cross-correlations between the three flows are significant in the case of Morocco.

These results are in line with the actual evolutions in exports, tourism and remittances observed during the recent slowdown in Europe (Figure 4.9). In Morocco, all the three variables strongly responded to the sharp drop in EU GDP.[12] In Tunisia, on the other hand, exports were the most affected. Tourism receipts in Tunisia were less affected, while remittances showed a remarkably strong resilience.

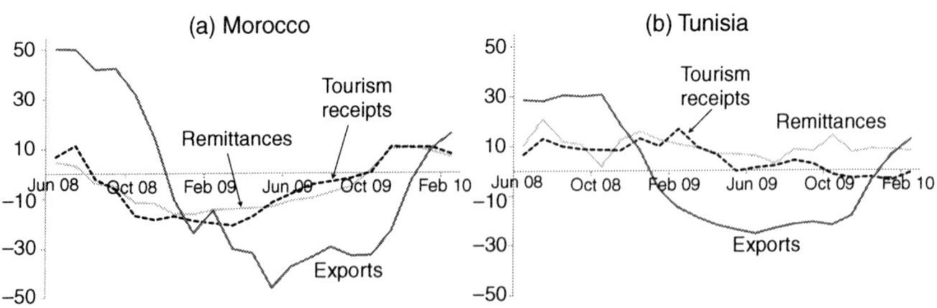

Figure 4.9 Reactions to the recent slowdown in Europe (three-month moving average year-on-year growth rates of variables in local currency (%)) (source: countries' authorities, and IMF staff estimates).

5 Sectoral analysis

In this section, we test the robustness of the previous results by examining the response of growth in different sectors to growth shocks in EU partner countries. To this aim, we re-run the SVAR and replace the non-agricultural *GDP* growth rates for Tunisia and Morocco with the GDP growth rates $g_t^{j,SECTOR}$ in particular sectors. As in Section 3.2, the impulse response measures the reaction of these sectors' value added growth rate to the country-specific EU GDP composite. For country *j*, the variables included in the VAR are then:

$$Z_t = \left[g_t^{j,SECTOR}, g_t^{EU}(j) \right]'$$

In line with the results presented in Section 4, Figure 4.10 shows that in Morocco service-related sectors, which are more significantly influenced by tourism and transfers, appear to be more sensitive to the European cycle. Sectors such as manufacturing, construction, mining and energy do not seem to be significantly influenced. By contrast, in Tunisia export-oriented sectors, such as manufacturing and energy, are the most responsive. Agriculture, mining and other services show weak reactions to the variations in EU GDP.

6 Policy implications

The econometric analysis demonstrates that, for both Tunisia's and Morocco's economies, the European Union plays a key role. Our analysis confirms the robustness of this connection, and examines the relative importance of its different transmission channels. While these close ties with the European Union have been a central factor contributing to the process of opening up the two economies and improving their competitiveness, they might also represent a challenge for the future.

Real output dropped by more than 4% in the Euro Area in 2009. Moreover, current forecasts are that the rebound in the EU area will be modest and slow. Growth in both domestic demand and real GDP will stay below their pre-crisis

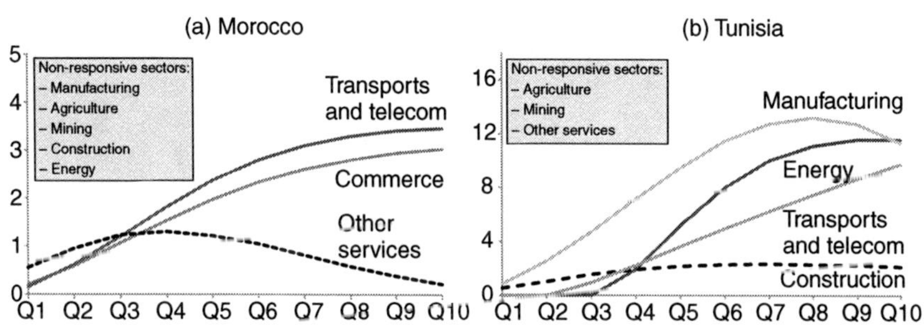

Figure 4.10 Cumulative response of sector growth to an external growth shock (source: IMF staff estimates).

levels in the years to come (Figure 4.11). Recent concerns about sovereign debt and the sustainability of public finances in Southern European countries add further downside risks to this outlook.

Not only will real GDP growth in Europe be lower, but the engines of growth in Europe are expected to change, with a lesser contribution coming from the domestic demand. As a result, growth in European imports – which represent the main source of external demand for Morocco and Tunisia – is projected to be less than half compared to the pre-crisis period in 2010 and 2011 (Figure 4.11).

It is noteworthy that, following the Association Agreements, the market shares of Morocco and Tunisia in EU merchandise imports have not increased since 1999. Table 4.4 shows that these market shares have remained fairly stable or slightly decreased over the past decade. Several factors can explain this evolution, such as the increased liberalization of world trade under the WTO Agreements and the fierce competition from fast-growing exporters such as China and Eastern Europe. Against this backdrop, maintaining market share is more than honorable.

Morocco and Tunisia have weathered the recent slowdown in Europe well, due to relatively insulated financial systems, exceptional agricultural production and strong domestic demand in 2009. In fact, growth accounting exercises suggests that domestic demand has become a more dynamic source of growth in both countries from 2008 onwards. However, increasing competitiveness and a further diversification of trade flows represent key challenges to sustaining growth in the future.

Table 4.4 Morocco and Tunisia shares in EU imports (%)

EU (27 countries)	*1999*	*2000*	*2001*	*2002*	*2003*	*2004*	*2005*	*2006*	*2007*	*2008*
Morocco	0.8	0.6	0.7	0.7	0.7	0.6	0.8	0.5	0.6	0.5
Tunisia	0.7	0.6	0.6	0.7	0.7	0.7	0.6	0.6	0.6	0.6

Source: Eurostat. Data excludes intra-EU trade flows.

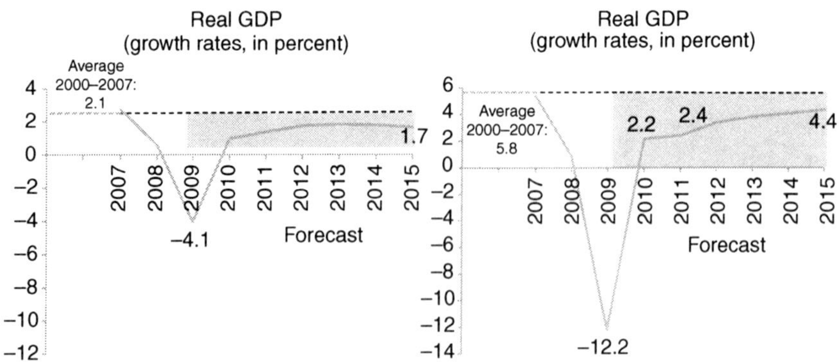

Figure 4.11 Euro area: real GDP and real imports growth (%) (source: IMF, World Economic Outlook (April 2010) and World Economic Outlook Update (July 2010)).

Figure 4.12 shows the shares of the EU and Maghreb in exports, imports and the destination-specific cover ratio (exports to over imports from a region). The figure shows that trade with other Maghreb countries is marginal for both Morocco and Tunisia, and represents an unexploited potential, especially in the context of the more subdued growth projections for the European market.

7 Conclusion

We have shown that for both Morocco and Tunisia, non-agricultural GDP growth rates are significantly influenced by the variations in GDP of their main European partners. However, the transmission channels appear to be different between the two countries. In the case of Tunisia, growth shocks are mainly transmitted through exports and, to a much lesser extent, tourism. Exports, tourism receipts and remittances play equally important roles in Morocco. These results are confirmed by the evolution of export, tourism and remittances in the wake of the recent slowdown in Europe. A similar exercise at the sectoral level indicates that the sectors related to services are the most responsive to EU's GDP in Morocco, while in Tunisia the most responsive sectors are more export-oriented.

While our findings show a remarkable coherence, there are a number of limitations to keep in mind when interpreting these results. First, it should be emphasized that a VAR analysis is not a growth accounting exercise. It shows the sensitivity of the dependent variable to external shocks rather than the influence of different components on growth. Moreover, the results of the breakdown by transmission channel are only tentative. Other potentially important channels, such as FDI, imports and financial sector linkages, which have structural impacts on the economy in the long run, certainly warrant further study.

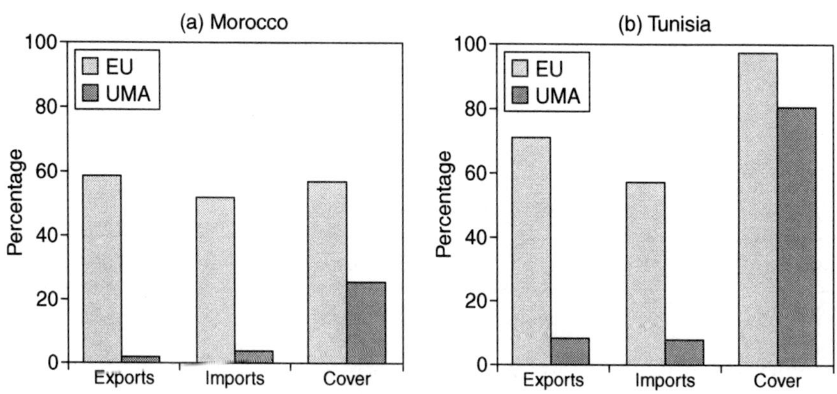

Figure 4.12 EU and UMA shares in imports, exports and cover ratio, 2008 (%) (source: countries' authorities and IMF staff estimates).

Note
UMA = Union du Maghreb Arabe (Algeria, Libya, Mauritania, Morocco, Tunisia).

Our analysis confirms the important role played by the European Union for the Moroccan and Tunisian economies. We note, however, that this close tie might also represent a challenge for the future. For the two countries, enhancing competitiveness and diversifying trade flows is essential for sustaining future growth.

Appendix: trade weights from the Global Economic Environment (GEE)

Global Economic Environment (GEE) data are group composites, based on weighted averages of selected World Economic Outlook (WEO) variables from the country databases. The trade weights are derived from the IMF's Direction of Trade (DOT) database. Every country has four sets of trade weights, i.e., the imports and exports weights for all countries as partners, and the imports and exports weights for only the advanced economies. The weights are calculated from the GEE reporting country's trade with partners which comprise 95% of the reporter's total exports or imports. The additional 5% partner countries of the reporter's trade data do not warrant any improvement in the overall trade weights. The GEE calculates a reporting country's series not from the reporting country's data but from the aggregated sum of the weighted percentage changes of its partners' data for a given WEO series.

The above tables show the GEE weights used for calculating the country-specific composite EU growth rates $g_t^{EU}(\cdot)$. As we want to attribute weights to the GDP growth of the EU countries, the EU countries' weights have been normalized such that the sum is 100. The country-specific composite GDP growth rate $g_t^{EU}(\cdot)$ can be expressed as follows, based on the weights α_t^i the EU countries take in Morocco's and Tunisia's exports of goods, respectively, and on these countries' growth rates g^i:

$$g_t^{EU}(\cdot) = \frac{\sum_{i=1}^{n}(g_t^i \alpha^i)}{\sum_{i=1}^{n}\alpha^i}.$$

Table 4.5 Table 5: GEE country weights for Morocco and Tunisia

Morocco		*Tunisia*	
France	36.36	France	42.2
Spain	33.42	Italy	29.1
United Kingdom	8.22	Germany	10.9
Italy	7.87	Spain	7.6
Belgium	5.33	Belgium	3.7
Germany	5.20	United Kingdom	3.5
Netherlands	3.60	Netherlands	2.9
Total	100	Total	100

Notes

1 We thank participants of the 2010 CREMed Workshop on 'Economies of the Mediterranean and the Euro-Mediterranean Process' at the Universitat Pompeu Fabra for helpful discussions. We also benefited from comments from Patricia Alonso-Gamo, Ralph Chami, Mohammed Daïri, Juan Carlos Jaramillo and Sadok Rouai. All errors are the sole responsibility of the authors. The views expressed in this chapter are those of the author(s) and do not necessarily represent those of the IMF or IMF policy.
2 There is a large literature examining linkages and sources of spillovers between countries. See, for example, Canova and Dellas (1993), Kose, Otrok, and Whiteman (2003), Baxter and Kouparitsas (2004), and Bayoumi and Swiston (2009). Toujas-Bernaté, Loko, and Simard (2009) investigate growth spillovers from Europe into Tunisia.
3 In 2009 MSCI Barra classified Morocco as an emerging market and Tunisia as a frontier market.
4 See, among others, Imbs (2004), Arezki, Cherif, and Piotrowski (2009), and Barajas, Chami, Fullenkamp, Montiel, and Gapen (2009).
5 Unless otherwise specified, by exports we mean exports of goods.
6 We exclude agricultural output from GDP as this component remains largely dependent on climatic factors in both countries. In what follows, unless otherwise specified, we mean nonagricultural GDP when referring to Morocco and Tunisia's GDP.
7 We found similar numbers when calculating the correlation of Moroccan and Tunisian growth rates with eurozone GDP reported by Eurostat.
8 t-tests also fail to reject the hypothesis that correlations of Moroccan or Tunisian GDP growth rates with US real GDP growth are significantly different from zero.
9 Simulations run for Morocco on the 2000Q1–2009Q4 time interval led to very similar results to the ones presented in this chapter.
10 Furthermore, forecast error variance decompositions show that the shocks in Morocco and Tunisia do not explain the shocks in EU partner countries.
11 For more details on this approach, see Bayoumi and Swiston (2009).
12 Total export performance in Morocco is also influenced by sharp fluctuations in international prices and volumes of phosphate exports. The share of phosphate in total exports was 8% in 2007, 14% in 2008, and 7% in 2009. Quantities decreased 16% in 2008 and 50% in 2009, whereas prices more than tripled in 2008 and fell 41% in 2009.

References

Arezki, R., R. Cherif, and J. Piotrowski (2009) 'Tourism Specialization and Economic Development: Evidence from the UNESCO World Heritage List,' IMF Working Paper 09/176, Washington, DC: International Monetary Fund.

Barajas, A., R. Chami, C. Fullenkamp, P. Montiel, and M. Gapen (2009), 'Do Workers' Remittances Promote Economic Growth?' IMF Working Paper 09/153, Washington, DC: International Monetary Fund.

Baxter, M. and M. Kouparitsas (2005) 'Determinants of Business Cycle Comovement: a Robust Analysis,' *Journal of Monetary Economics*, 52(1): 113–157.

Bayoumi, T. and A. Swiston (2009) 'Foreign Entanglements; Estimating the Source and Size of Spillovers Across Industrial Countries,' *IMF Staff Papers*, 56(2): 353–383.

Blanchard, O. and D. Quah (1989) 'The Dynamic Effects of Aggregate Demand and Supply Disturbances,' *American Economic Review*, 79(4): 655–673.

Canova, F. and H. Dellas (1993) 'Trade Interdependence and the International Business Cycle,' *Journal of International Economics*, 34: 23–47.

Imbs, J. (2004) 'Trade, Finance, Specialization, and Synchronization,' *Review of Economics and Statistics*, 863: 723–734.
Kose, M.A., C. Otrok, and C.H. Whiteman (2003) 'International Business Cycles: World, Region, and Country-specific Factors,' *American Economic Review*, 93(4): 1216–1239.
Toujas-Bernaté, J., B. Loko, and D. Simard, 2009, 'Investigating Growth Spillovers from Europe,' Tunisia Selected Issues Paper, IMF Country Report No. 10/109.

5 Have the promises used to sell the Euro-Mediterranean partnership come true?

Illustration from the Tunisian experience

Mohamed A. Chemingui and Hedi Bchir

1 Introduction

Under the pressure of the WTO's regulations (Article 24), the European Union (EU) has embarked with its partners from the developing world in the negotiations of Free-Trade Agreements (FTAs) since the mid-1990s. While the unilateral preferences[1] were progressively and clearly prohibited by WTO rules, the concerned developing countries had to choose between giving up their preferential access to the European markets and creating quasi-reciprocal trade concessions with their European counterparts.

At the time when most of the Southern Mediterranean Countries (SMCs)[2] started implementing their FTAs with the EU, analysts were looking to Tunisia's experience in the context of the agreement implemented since 1996, as a trial of how a North–South trade agreement could function among economies with wide variations in size, development level and wealth.

The model on which the Euro-Mediterranean Partnership (EMP) was based is not similar to the one that prevailed in the EU, which favored the free movement of workers and transferred funds from the wealthier countries to the least-advanced nations to reduce the initial disparities between members. There is an important development gap between Tunisia and most of the European countries, and any assessment of the impact of this trade agreement on Tunisia will depend on the length for which it is observed. Accordingly, since its effective inception in 1995, the EMP has been one of the most debated trade agreements. In the SMCs, the EMP is considered as a vehicle for boosting the inflows of foreign investments despite the fact that they already enjoyed free access to the European markets for most of their manufacturing exports. In Europe, the delocalization of investments to SMCs will negatively affect unemployment, given the low labor costs in these countries where the average wage ranges from less than one-tenth to one-fifth that of most of European countries (mainly France, Germany and Italy). Others see the EMP as a boon to European employment and living standards through greater trade and investment opportunities. For the SMCs, these agreements have provided for the first time a reciprocal treatment for European exports to their markets, which are considered as serious competitors to their domestic manufacturing industries, and thus may induce additional unemployment.

These opposite expectations from the implementation of the EMP have been largely subject to speculation in terms of experiences drawn from other trade agreements or from the results of simulation models. However, since the free trade component of the EMP has been in operation in the Tunisian case for more than three years, the question is not what the FTA is likely to do but what it has done.

Despite the debate over FTAs around the world having focused mainly on jobs, it is important to first answer the most fundamental question on what effect it has had on trade. Changes in trade patterns caused by a lowering or complete removal of trade barriers are ultimately the mechanism by which jobs and living standards are influenced through changes in production, specialization and diversification, productivity, investment ... etc. This chapter examines how the FTA with the EU affected the Tunisian economy based on an assessment of what did and did not work for Tunisia. Accordingly, it contributes to the active debate regarding how to approach the review of the EMP in a situation where most of the SMCs are experiencing radical political changes, which may affect their economic development model.

This chapter is organized as follows; the second section provides some basic background on the EMP, with a special focus on the Tunisian case; the third section discusses briefly the most often used techniques to determine FTA's impact and what was expected, in the Tunisian case, from the implementation of the EMP; the fourth section analyzes the effective implications of the EMP on the Tunisian economy; the fifth section draws the main shortcomings of the partnership agreement; and, finally, the last section includes an evaluation of the EMP's success and discusses the way forward.

2 Overview of the Euromed partnership

2.1 A regional view

Except for Libya and Syria, all the other SMCs have signed FTAs with the EU and are in the process of their implementation. Turkey is the most integrated country with the EU through the Custom Union Agreement implemented in 1996, while Tunisia was the first country to have fully implemented its FTA, in January 2008.

In general, all the EMP agreements display the same structure, as they include three main parts. The first concerns political and security cooperation, while the second deals with trade cooperation among the partners and the third covers economic and cultural cooperation. The security cooperation part of the EMP is limited to some general declarations of principles, and does not include a clear commitment. The trade component defines the modalities of trade liberalization among the partners through a mechanism of gradual tariff dismantlement schemes associated with a number of lists of products. Generally, under the FTAs, the EU maintained the existing preferences accorded to SMCs' exports of manufactured products without any significant improvement in agricultural market access. At the same time, the SMCs committed themselves to eliminating all the existing barriers on market access for the majority of non-agricultural products imported from the EU. Practically, all the SMCs have chosen to implement tariff dismantlement in a gradual manner over a maximum transition period of 12 years. Depending on the specific level of sensitivity to the European competition, the SMCs have classified their imports into different lists. Generally, the first list is dominated by equipment goods and inputs that are not produced locally, for which tariffs dismantlement is the fastest – instantaneous, sometimes. For the remaining commodities, usually classified into two to three lists, more gradual dismantlement schemes are applied. However, the SMCs excluded from trade liberalization some highly sensitive products, which have been classified into a 'negative' list. However, these negative lists are expected to be regularly revised.

Table 5.1 shows the macroeconomic performances of the SMCs involved in the EMP. Except for Egypt, Jordan and Morocco, GDP growth rates were heterogeneous among the countries. In addition, it seems that the majority of the SMCs that have embarked on the EMP have not moved into a new growth path. Moreover, their growth performance has been much lowers than countries with less orthodox trade and development policies, such as India, Brazil and China. Over the same period, these countries have achieved growth rates much higher than in SMCs. The difference in growth performance can be partially attributed to the economic policies followed by each group of countries. Accordingly, and contrary to SMCs' emphasis on deficit-reduction policies, the dynamic countries adopted a package of pro-growth policies, including higher levels of public investment to GDP and more pro-cyclical monetary policies. Moreover, and despite relative high growth rates, most of the SMCs have not been able to generate more jobs and to reduce unemployment pressures. Indeed, and when unemployment rates are compared between the periods before and after the entry into force of the EMP, it appears that, with the exception of the Algerian case,[3] the impact of the EMP on employment is too small and even negative in countries like Egypt (increase of unemployment). However, the only positive effect of the EMP on the SMCs seems to be the increase of FDI inflows in terms of percentage of GDP (Table 5.1). The growth in FDI inflows is largely due to the confidence that these types of agreements provide to foreign investors (European and non-European) on the sustainability of economic policies in the SMCs and to the durability of trade preferences, which they are enjoying on the European markets. However, the significant surge in FDI inflows in some countries is largely explained by the receipts from privatization of public enterprises to foreign investors, rather than new foreign investments.

2.2 The FTA between Tunisia and the EU

The EU is Tunisia's first trading partner. In 2008, it accounted for 64.5% and 72.1% respectively of Tunisia's imports and exports. Tunisia was the first SMC to sign the FTA with the EU, in July 1995.[4] The trade provisions of the

Table 5.1 Growth performance of the partners' SMCs

	Entry into force of the FTA	*GDP growth*			*FDI/GDP*			*Unemployment*		
		Total	*Before FTA*	*After FTA*	*Total*	*Before FTA*	*After FTA*	*Total*	*Before FTA*	*After FTA*
Countries that have signed Euro Med agreement										
Algeria	Sep. 2005	4.3	4.4	2.7	0.61	0.57	1.39	22.2	22.9	12.3
Egypt	Jun. 2004	5.4	5.3	5.9	2.09	1.56	6.45	8.7	8.6	11.0
Israel	Jun. 2000	5.5	6.0	3.2	1.47	0.90	4.02	7.9	7.5	9.3
Jordan	May 2002	6.2	6.1	6.8	2.74	1.30	11.67	14.3	14.3	13.9
Lebanon	Mar. 2010	4.8	4.9	4.7	5.39	3.10	11.53	8.3	8.5	8.1
Morocco	Mar. 2000	4.3	4.2	5.2	0.79	0.44	2.38	14.7	17.0	11.1
Tunisia	Mar. 1998	5.2	5.3	5.0	2.26	1.79	3.79	15.2	16.0	15.0

Source: World Development Indicators (World Bank, 2009).

Note
The 'After FTA' period covers the years 1998–2008 while the 'Before FTA' period includes the years 1990–1997.

agreement confirm the existence of free trade in manufactured goods and seek to reinforce it by initiating a dialogue in a number of related areas, mainly provisions for the freedom of establishment, free movement of capital, trade facilitation and the approximation of legislation.

The Agreement phases free trade in industrial goods over 12 years. However, under the previous trade and cooperation agreements, nearly all of Tunisia's industrial exports had free access to the EU markets. The main exemption was textiles, for which a voluntary export restriction was implemented, although it was rarely binding. In addition to maintaining the privileged access of Tunisian manufactured exports to the EU market, the free trade has been extended to textiles. However, Tunisia committed to remove all tariff and non-tariff barriers against industrial imports from the EU, subject to a number of safeguard provisions. Accordingly, quantitative restrictions and tariffs were abolished immediately after the enforcement of the agreement on a large number of items, mainly equipment goods and inputs (List 1), while tariff reduction has been gradual on the remaining products and based on three different lists (Lists 2–4). List 2 covers essentially raw materials and intermediate goods, none produced locally, for which duties have been removed gradually over a period of five years starting from the first year of implementation of the agreement. Tariffs on imported goods from the EU under this list were completely removed in December 2000. For List 3, which covers goods that compete with domestic production, tariff reduction has been implemented over the whole transition period (12 years). Finally, for List 4, which is composed of industrial products that are deemed highly vulnerable to foreign competition, tariffs have been removed over the past eight years of the transition period. Finally, a negative list has been annexed to the agreement. It contains all other products not covered by the previous four lists of products at HS6 level.

For trade in agricultural products, a transitory agreement was implemented in January 2001. It provides Tunisia with better access to the EU markets for many products, in the forms of higher annual free quota rates (mostly for olive oil, cut flowers and citrus). Simultaneously, the EU benefited from better access for its exports of vegetable oils and wheat under the preferential quota rates committed by Tunisia under the GATT Agreement. However, further liberalization of agricultural trade between Tunisia and the EU is conditional on the progress made under the Doha Round of WTO negotiations on modalities of agricultural trade liberalization, which is still not yet concluded.

The FTA also covers the right of establishment, the liberalization of services, and an effective protection of intellectual and commercial property rights. It also goes well beyond the previous framework of cooperation by calling for a comprehensive harmonization of the regulatory framework, with a plan to phase out any practices that distort trade between both parties, such as monopolies, government subsidies, or privileges granted to public enterprises. Economic and financial cooperation is strengthened, particularly to support industries that face difficulties in adjusting to trade liberalization, to promote intra-Maghreb regional integration, and to enhance environmental protection. The FTA calls for the harmonization of norms and standards (in transport, telecommunications, etc.), and for regulations and rules concerning accounting and financial services, statistics, and customs.

For trade in services, Tunisia's commitments under the FTA with the EU go hand in hand with its commitments under the GATS Agreement. For the World Bank (2004), liberalization of trade in services is the most difficult task in the Agreement for two main reasons. The first is that State monopolies are much more prevalent in the services sectors, which complicates their liberalization. The second reason is directly linked to Tunisia's commitments themselves under the GATS that are limited to only three sectors (tourism, financial services, and communications). In fact, there are no commitments in the other key services sectors, such as transport and distribution.

3 Lessons from the ex-ante assessments of the impact of the FTA with the EU on Tunisia's economy

The previous studies on how the FTA with the EU affects jobs, trade and growth in Tunisia were carried out either before or during the Agreement's implementation, all of them are forward-looking, which contrasts with the backward-looking approach of more recent studies, including the present one. The used techniques to determine FTA's impact fall into two broad categories. The first is based on quantitative simulation models, including computable general equilibrium (CGE) modeling techniques, where analysts model a simplified economy and simulate what would happen to it if tariffs and no-tariff barriers fall. Most of the ex-ante studies based on static or dynamic CGE models have found an increase in income and trade under the FTA. Because Tunisia's initial tariffs are high, the efficiency gains are also expected to be high as result of a better allocation of resources. However, when the models integrate a more realistic market of production factors, mainly labor market, the gains were expected to be smaller compared with the assumption of full mobility of production factors.[5]

Partial equilibrium models have been also used to examine the effects of the FTA. Contrary to the CGE model, they focus on particular sectors and assume that the rest of the economy is unaffected. Most of applications in Tunisia focused on the case of extending trade liberalization to agricultural products. Most of the applications show that Tunisia will generate more gains if the EU's markets are completely open to Tunisian agricultural exports under the condition that domestic support and export subsidies provided by the EU's Common Agricultural Policy (CAP) will be removed. The third and final category of models used for trade assessment is based on gravity models usually built to estimate export potential.

Unlike the studies based on simulation models, this chapter's intention is to measure how the FTA has already affected the Tunisian economy. To do so, the changes in major economic variables are empirically estimated with pre- and post-FTA data. The analysis is based on the estimation of the changes that have occurred in the Tunisian economy since the implementation of the FTA.

However, two main shortcomings of this approach should be highlighted. First, this ex-post analysis attributes all the observed changes to the FTA, despite many economic reforms and trade agreements having been implemented over the same transition period as the FTA. Second, the most significant changes in Tunisian trade policy have been introduced since the sixth year of the transition period, except for the first and the second lists, where initial protection was the lowest. Despite these shortcomings, two advantages could be attributed to the methodology used in this chapter. First, it allows the estimation of changes in trade flows and other major macroeconomic economic variables using relatively long time series data. Second, it captures most of the important aspects of the FTA, such as changes in tariff and no tariffs, in administrative regulations, and expectations about the sustainability of free trade that cannot be easily quantified. For Gould (1998), changing expectations for the sustainability of free trade are potentially among the most important aspects of an FTA agreement. In fact, if the FTA did not create a credible commitment to free trade, new investment would not flow into export industries to take advantage of reduced trade barriers. Accordingly, expectations for a sustainable open trading environment affect trade by providing the incentive for firms to make long-term capital commitments.

Since the FTA between Tunisia and the EU officially came into effect in 1998, employment, foreign investment, economic activity, technological transfers, FDI inflows and exports – especially to the EU – are all expected to have improved. However, when Tunisia started the implementation of the FTA in 1998, its economy was already relatively diversified and economic reforms were well underway.

While there is continuous debate about whether the FTA with the EU has been good for Tunisia, it is often believed that Tunisia will be the undisputed winner. In fact, through sustaining its preferential access to the European market, foreign investments have risen and productivity gains have improved. In turn, exports will be boosted and unemployment reduced.

Despite the expected positive gains from the FTA with the EU, the impact on Tunisia's unemployment has been disappointing, and on its economic growth has been at best neutral. Thus, and even after its full implementation, it is believed that the FTA's promise of broad-based dynamic growth did not come true in Tunisia. The next section describes the observed changes in the Tunisian economy that have occurred since the implementation of the FTA. Moreover, and given that the EU is the major trade partner for Tunisia, it can be assumed that the observed changes attributed to trade policy reform can be exclusively attributed to the FTA between Tunisia and the EU.

4 The outcomes of the FTA with the EU from an ex-post assessment

In Tunisia, tariffs on industrial goods originating from the EU were abolished on 1 January 2008, except for a few commodities that are excluded from the Agreement. In order to evaluate the observed impacts of the FTA on the Tunisian economy, economic performance has been compared between two periods. The first one precedes the implementation of the Agreement, while the second starts from the beginning of the tariff dismantling process and extends until the latest year for which data are available.

Important lessons and insights could be drawn from this type of analysis, in terms of guidelines for countries that are in the process of negotiating similar agreements, or in the ongoing debate concerning the reinforcement of the EMP for Tunisia under the Privileged Partner position, the European Neighbourhood Policy, or the initiative of the Mediterranean Union. However, and as highlighted previously, implementation of the FTA with the EU cannot be entirely responsible for Tunisia's economic changes since the mid-1990s. As an illustration, the rising competition from Chinese products in European markets put a brake on Tunisia's export growth. Moreover, successive reforms of macroeconomic policies in Tunisia since the mid-1990s may have had a far more decisive impact on Tunisia's economy than the FTA itself. In this respect, the gradual devaluation of the Tunisian currency vis-à-vis the Euro during the 2000s may explain much more of the export growth than the trade liberalization measures themselves (Bchir *et al.*, 2009). For these reasons and others, the present analysis of economic changes that have occurred in Tunisia since the gradual implementation of the FTA does not attempt to discern the narrow effects of the FTA from the broader impacts of the economic strategy of which they were a part. Nor do we ascribe to FTA either the credit or the blame for those impacts. Drawing from a number of studies and from various statistical sources, this chapter assesses what did and did not work for Tunisia.

4.1 Impacts on trade-creation and -diversion across partners

Trade is the first channel by which the FTA with the EU is expected to affect the Tunisian economy. At the time of initiating the implementation of the FTA with the EU, there was a real concern on trade diversion to the benefit of the EU. In other words, did the FTA create new trade opportunities for the EU in Tunisia? If the increased trade (if any) caused by the FTA was simply a shuffling of trade from other partners that were previously more competitive than the EU, than the benefit from the FTA would shrink. Despite this issue not being within the scope of this chapter, a glance at how the distribution of trade flows has changed since the FTA can tell us whether the FTA has been associated with trade diversion or not. Moreover, there was concern that there may be intensification of Tunisia's trade deficit as a result of increasing imports from the EU. However, and after the full implementation of the FTA, all these fears have been negated. First, the trade balance deficit has not registered any particular degradation. Between the two periods 1990–1998 and 1999–2008, the trade deficit of goods in Tunisia improved from 11.3% to only 9.5% (World Bank, 2009). Moreover, even the trade surplus in services improved between the same two periods, from 6.2% to 6.5% (World Bank, 2009). The overall impact on the trade deficit has been positive since the implementation of the FTA.

Figure 5.1 shows the structure of Tunisian imports by major trade partners over the period from 1994 to 2007. It shows that the significance of the EU in Tunisia's imports has decreased compared with imports from the rest of the world. Imports from the EU dropped from 69.5% to 64.9% between 1994 and 2007. The increase in Tunisian imports from China and Arab countries contributed to the decline of the EU position in the Tunisian market. Over the period 1994–2007, the EU's exports to Tunisia reduced by around 4.4 percentage points. During the same period, imports from China and Arab countries increased by 12.8% and 5.2% respectively.

The decline in the share of Tunisian imports originating from the EU suggests the absence of a trade-diversion effect. However, Table 5.2 shows that Tunisian imports increased from all origins, which means a significant trade-creation effect. China is the greatest winner from the expansion of Tunisian trade, followed by Arab countries, the USA, and the rest of the world (RoW), while imports from the EU registered a smaller increase. These findings contradict most expectations of the FTA, and this needs specific investigation. For the Tunisian case, the reason is directly linked to the historical trade relations between Tunisia and the EU. In fact, Tunisia's imports were dominated by products from the EU. With the conclusion of the Uruguay Round and the implementation of many other FTAs (such as with Arab countries, Turkey…), imports from non-EU countries have grown. The case of importation of cars is very illustrative. Before the FTA with the EU, Tunisia imported cars exclusively from European countries – mostly from France, Italy and Germany. With the conclusion of the Uruguay Round and for many other reasons (mainly corruption), imports of cars from other origins increased faster than from the EU. This is mostly the case regarding imports from the USA, Japan and Korea, despite Tunisia not being associated with them under any preferential trade agreement.

Regarding exports, the European market still represents the main destination of Tunisian exports. Its share has remained stable at around 80% (Figure 5.2). However, Table 5.3 shows that Tunisian exports to the European market grew at only 12.6% on a yearly average basis over the period 1998–2007, which is too small compared with the registered growth of exports to the USA and China (30.6% and 445.1% respectively). Despite the high growth of Tunisian exports to non-EU countries, the corresponding volume is still too small, given that the initial volume itself, before concluding the Uruguay Round, was also too small.

Table 5.2 Average growth in imports since 1998

Region	*(%)*
EU	9.7
USA	10.6
China	28.0
Arab countries	14.9
ROW	14.3

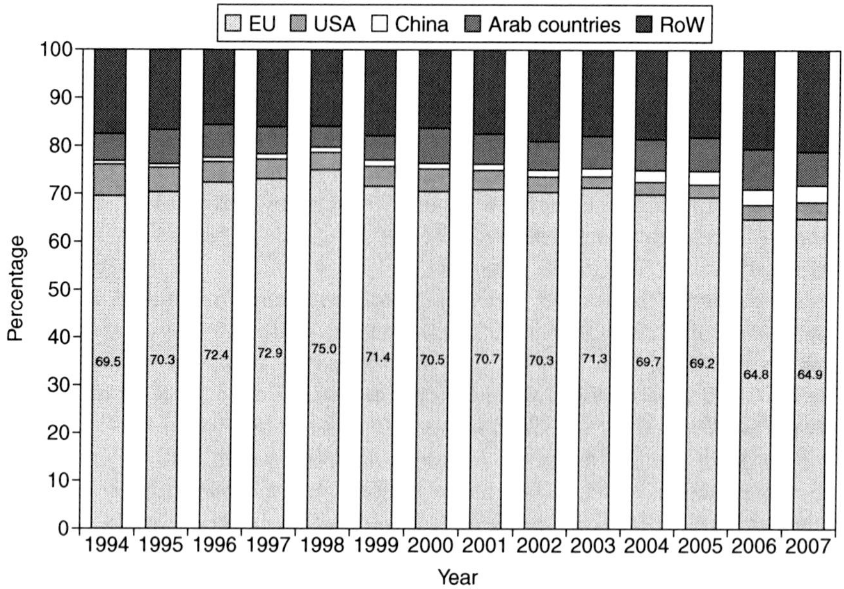

Figure 5.1 Trend in Tunisian imports by main origins (source: Tunisian National Statistics Institute (INS)).

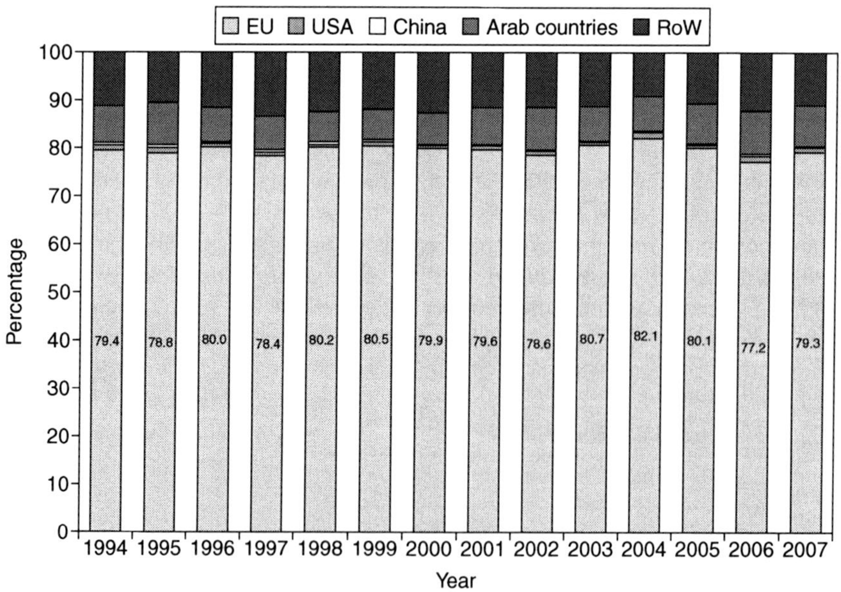

Figure 5.2 Trend in Tunisian exports by main destinations (source: Tunisian National Statistics Institute (INS)).

Table 5.3 Average growth in exports since 1998

Region	*(%)*
EU	12.6
USA	30.6
China	445.1
Arab countries	15.0
Row	10.6

4.2 Reinforcement of the contribution of private consumption to GDP against a decline of exports' role

Private consumption is still the main driver for growth and plays a key role in Tunisia's development strategy. Furthermore, its contribution to growth improved with the implementation of the FTA with the EU. The volume of private consumption increased at a yearly average rate of 4.6% during the period pre-FTA (1999–2007), against 4.3% for the period 1992–1998. Consequently, the share of private consumption to GDP passed from 62% to 61.4% over the two periods. For public consumption, and despite the intensification of the privatization of public enterprises and the stabilization program initiated since the adoption of the structural adjustment program in 1986, public consumption declined slightly but remained relatively high, passing from 16% to 15.5% of GDP on average respectively for the periods 1992–1998 and 1999–2007. Thus, final domestic consumption has intensively contributed to growth and in some extent compensated for the decline in foreign demand observed during periods of international crisis such as the recent global recession (Table 5.4).

Export is the second driver of economic growth in Tunisia. Its importance is a direct implication of the export-led growth policy followed by Tunisia since its independence. This competitive export-oriented manufacturing sector was

Table 5.4 Share in GDP of demand elements

	Share in GDP		*Average growth rate*	
	1992–1998	*1999–2007*	*1992–1998*	*1999–2007*
GDP	100.0	100.0	4.7	5.0
Imports	46.7	44.5	4.7	4.4
Internal demand	102.8	100.8	4.3	4.6
Final consumption	77.4	77.5	−0.4	0.1
Public consumption	16.0	15.5	−0.7	−0.3
Private consumption	61.4	62.0	−0.3	0.2
Investment	24.7	22.6	0.0	−1.0
Exports	43.6	43.1	0.6	0.9

Source: Tunisian National Statistics Institute (INS).

developed thanks to foreign direct investments attracted by a package of fiscal incentives implemented since 1972. However, and despite the implementation of the FTA with the EU, the contribution of exports to GDP experienced a slight decline, passing from an average of 43.6% of GDP during the period 1992–1998 to 43.1% in 1999–2007. Many factors contributed to the stagnation of the contribution of manufacturing exports to GDP in Tunisia. They include higher international competition on European markets, insufficient upgrading efforts of the Tunisian economy, a lack of diversification of export markets, and the high costs of doing business and making foreign trade.

Finally, investment appears at the third rank in term of its contribution to economic growth in Tunisia. However, its share of GDP dropped by 2.2 percentage points between the pre- and post-FTA periods, from an average of 24.7% to 22.6%. The highest drops in fixed capital formation have been observed for private investment (domestic and foreign) despite the several incentives provided to private investors. However, the contribution of the public sector to total investment continues to play an important role in the Tunisian economy. In 2008, public investment represented 38% of total the investment.

4.3 Economic growth has been pro-poor in urban areas

Since 1995, three surveys on household expenditures have been carried out in Tunisia (1995, 2000, and 2005). Analysis of trends in poverty incidence and economic growth is among the approaches usually used to capture the linkage between the two. In the pre-FTA period, the incidence of rural poverty grew in comparison, while urban poverty declined slightly. GDP grew faster but agricultural output declined due to three consecutive years of drought that resulted in more rural poverty. In the post-FTA period, poverty has continued to decline but inequality has risen. Rural households are the most negatively affected, as result of declining producer prices. However, urban households have profited more from the sustained economic growth through the successive rise in wages and improvement in capital incomes (see Table 5.5).

When successive surveys are available, as is the case for Tunisia, this is very useful in calculating the share of the total change in poverty which is due to the change over time in mean income (growth effect), and the share that is due to change in income inequality (distribution effect). This type of analysis allows checking of whether these two factors work in the same or in opposite directions, and to what extent growth has been pro-poor. The most popular approach used to achieve this goal is that of Datt and Ravallion (1991). The change in any poverty measure between two periods t and $t-1$ can be decomposed, being the sum of a growth component, a redistribution component and a residual term. According to Ayadi *et al.* (2005) and Lahouel (2007), the growth component was the major factor in the continuous poverty headcount reduction from 1980 to 2000. The distribution effect was generally either weak or opposite to that of growth.

Table 5.5 Poverty incidence and inequality trends in Tunisia, 1980–2005

	1990	*1995*	*2000*	*2005*
Poverty incidence (% of the population)				
Urban	7.3	7.1	4.9	1.9
Rural	5.7	4.9	2.9	7.1
Total	6.7	6.2	4.2	3.8
Gini coefficient	0.401	0.417	0.409	0.400

Source: INS.

4.4 Trade reforms contributed to sustain public finances

Public finance has remained fragile because of mandatory expenditures. Volatility of world prices for oil and food has also generated an additional cost to the government budget and the financial balances of public companies operating in these sectors. The phasing out of tariff protection on imports from the EU and other partners has also considerably reduced the government's income from duties payable. The reform of the VAT system and better collection of taxes on income and profits have allowed the government to compensate for the reduction in its tax revenue, and even to afford a fiscal gain. However, the government has had to rely relatively more on domestic borrowing to finance its deficit, even though the level of national savings is relatively low.

Maintenance of the budget deficit within tolerable limits has been seen as a pre-condition to achieve sustained growth and improve the effectiveness of state intervention to support economic and social development. This has been achieved through tax reforms to rationalize tax incentives and continue with the progressive reduction of the inclusive tax regime; improving the allocation of public resources; enhancing private–public partnership in the fields of infrastructure and the delivery of some services previously provided solely by the state; and limiting fuel subsidies through the continued control of energy use and the progressive adjustment of domestic prices as the economic situation requires. The fiscal discipline was expected to result in a reduction of the national debt to approximately 54.4% of GDP in 2011.[6]

4.5 The economy is less vulnerable to external shocks

The commitment of Tunisia to trade liberalization introduced two main challenges for its economy. There was concern on the one hand about the likely impact of tariff reductions on tax revenue, and on the other about the possible impact of increased imports on trade and payment balances. However, export promotion policies combined with relative higher inflows of remittances and FDI enabled reduction of the current account deficit to 2.6% of GDP in 2007, down from 5.8% of GDP during the period 1992–1996. Moreover, they made it possible to increase foreign-exchange reserves to cover more than five months of imports of goods by late 2007, compared to only two months in 1996. Finally, the government succeeded in substituting the loss in imports' tariff revenues with a sound policy of domestic taxation, mainly through extension of VAT and reinforcement of its collection. Moreover, these macroeconomic performances allowed Tunisia to face the various external trade shocks that have affected its economy over the past two decades. These shocks cover the increase in world prices of imported products (mainly food and energy) and the erosion of preferences in its traditional market, the EU. The relative high diversification of the Tunisian economy makes it less vulnerable to external shocks. Contrary to most of the MENA countries, Tunisian exports are greatly diversified and cover agriculture, energy, other mining products, services, various manufactured products, etc. The second factor that contributed to mitigating the impacts of trade shocks on the Tunisian economy is monetary policy through a flexible management of the exchange rate and maintaining its overall real stability.

These performances are also attributed to the consolidation of the State budget resources insofar as the tax burden reached 21% of GDP during the period 1997–2006 against 19.8% in 1996, thanks to the stabilization program followed by the government.

5 Shortcomings of the model

5.1 Macroeconomic vulnerabilities and economic imbalances persist

While macroeconomic management improved significantly following the implementation of the FTA with the EU, particularly in terms of taming inflation and decreasing public deficits, Tunisia has not been successful enough in removing all macroeconomic vulnerabilities and some concerns still provide a challenge. First, Tunisia's tight fiscal policies have reduced inflation, but they have also slowed economic growth. Second, tight monetary policy has also led to a persistently overvalued currency, making it more difficult for producers to compete with other developing-country exporters, such as China. Third, the objective to control the public deficit and external debt has not allowed the country to implement countercyclical pro-growth policies based on boosting public spending, mainly in infrastructures. Fourth, the government control of many productive activities represents a real barrier towards improving their development through a competitive environment.

By various indicators, Tunisia is a moderately indebted country. Total external debt was estimated at 54.9% of GDP as of the end of 2007, up from about 52% of GDP in the early 1990s. The debt service ratio payment of principal and interests as a share of exports of goods and services was about 13% at the end of 2007 versus an average of 25% in the 1990s.

To ensure that external balances remain sustainable in the future, Tunisia is pursuing a three-pronged strategy. It is encouraging export development (through the *mise à niveau* or upgrading program) and foreign direct investment (covering privatization and BOT projects). It is also trying to deepen the domestic financial markets to ensure adequate budgetary financing from domestic sources. Third, Tunisia is strategically managing its resort to international capital markets to consolidate its past record as a good credit risk able to borrow at the lower end of emerging market spreads.

In the medium term, the main risk to Tunisia's external outlook would come from a failure of this three-pronged strategy. A serious deterioration of external balances – as could be brought about by a concurrent surge in imports from the EU, a drop in exports because of weak international demand and domestic competitiveness, or a drop in foreign direct investment – would lead to significantly larger borrowing requirements accompanied by worsening borrowing conditions. With the exception of a surge in imports from the EU, Tunisia is currently facing an impressive decline in FDI and remittance inflows conjoined with a drop in its exports. If the situation is not reversed soon, the risk of deterioration of its external accounts is very possible.

5.2 Governance has not improved

How trade liberalization affects public governance is one of the key issues in terms of economic development. Experts from a number of disciplines have attempted to define what these two terms mean and, perhaps even more importantly, what they do. The fact that national governments are progressively losing their control of their national economies will make private operators much more powerful in economic regulation. We might expect an improvement in the governance level as a result of economic partnership, mainly with developed countries, which requires a better business environment, more transparent economic policies, and lower public intervention.

The perceived Corruption Index (CPI) computed by Transparency International (TI) gives an overall idea of the corruption level in absolute and relative terms in more than 180 countries. This index has become a standard tool in the analysis of changes in corruption for a particular country. It is the main instrument currently used to assess the performance of public governance. For Tunisia, the changes in this index between 1998[7] and 2009 (Table 5.6 and Figure 5.3) confirm that, even with the implementation of the FTA with the EU, corruption has worsened and Tunisia has seen its score decrease from 5.3 in 2001 to 4.2 in 2009, with its ranking dropping from 31 to 65 over the same period.

5.3 Private investment has dropped

Boosting private investment has been among the top priorities of the Tunisian government over the past two decades. Many programs have been implemented, mainly through investment schemes, which started with the offshore-oriented program of incentives to investment implemented in 1972 and amended respectively in 1993 and 2008. This program provides a package of incentives and tax exonerations mostly for fully exporting firms. It succeeded in developing the manufacturing sector in the country, initially dominated by textiles and clothing firms, and was then extended to the electronics and electric industries.

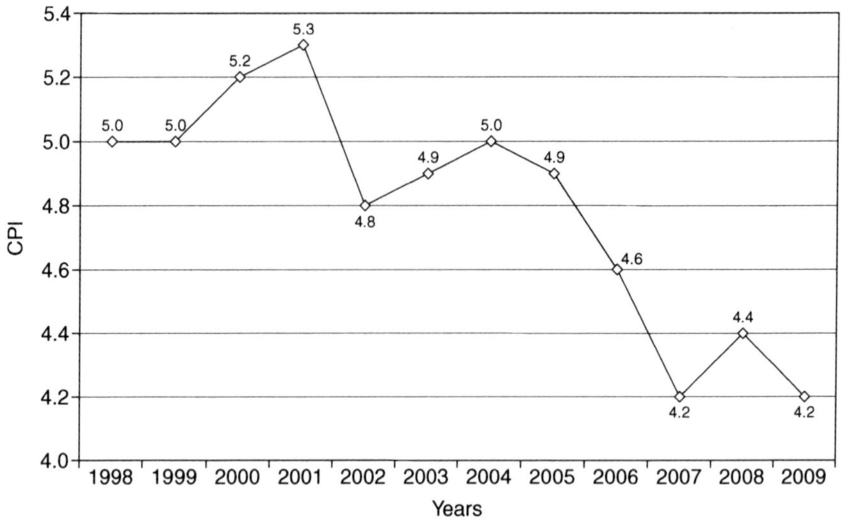

Figure 5.3 Evolution of the CPI of Tunisia (source: Corruption Perception Index (CPI) by transparency International).

With the implementation of the FTA with the EU, Tunisia amended its incentives for private investments to become a regional targeted program. However, and for the first time, exporting firms were taxed on their exports (10% against 35% for onshore firms). This last reform, coupled with the enlargement of the EU and the erosion of preferences, has affected negatively the volume of FDI inflows in Tunisia, which show a significant decline in the 2000s. However, and despite official statistics showing a total increase in FDI inflows that occurred with the phase of implementation of the FTA compared to the period 1990–1998

Table 5.6 Trend in the Tunisia ranking according the CPI

Year	*Rank*	*Number of countries covered by the survey*
1998	33	85
1999	34	99
2000	32	90
2001	31	91
2002	36	102
2003	39	133
2004	39	146
2005	43	159
2006	51	163
2007	61	179
2008	62	180
2009	65	180

(see Table 5.7 below), it is important to clarify that these statistics already cover new investments, privatization receipts and revenues from selling licenses for foreign operators.

In fact, Tunisian authorities proceeded to privatization in such a way as to keep statistics related to total FDI increasing over years. Even domestic investment is highly dominated by public investments. As shown by Table 5.7, the ratio of domestic private investment to GDP dropped from 14% on average during the period 1990–1998 to 13% in the post-FTA period (1999–2008)

5.4 Weak job creation

With relatively high and sustained economic growth achieved since the implementation of the FTA with the EU, it was expected that employment growth would be also high. However, recent figures suggest that the Tunisian economy absorbed around 1 million job-seekers between 1995 and 2009, which represents average annual job creation of 2.7% per year. Haddar (2010) analyzed the labor-intensity of economic growth in Tunisia through the estimation of the labor elasticity of economic growth. He shows that the highest level of elasticity was achieved in 1988 (0.98), and then declined continually until 2005, to only 0.53. The decline in the labor intensity of economic growth in Tunisia resulted from two mains changes that have been observed in the economy. The first is relative to the structural change that affected the productive capacities of the Tunisian economy both among sectors and between subsectors. Second, the opening of the Tunisian market to foreign competition with the erosion of preferences on its traditional foreign markets pushed local firms to reduce their costs through improving labor productivity.

However, it is striking that the FTA with the EU could bring Tunisia such large increases in trade and FDI but generate relatively low employment growth. Figure 5.4 shows the trends in GDP and employment growth rates over the period 1990–2008. These confirm that GDP growth is not well correlated with employment growth – more particularly, in 1993, GDP grew by 9% while employment increased by only 4%. Furthermore, the 6% economic growth achieved in 2005 was even accompanied by a reduction of jobs. Compared with the relatively small level of job creation, the higher increase in labor supply

Table 5.7 Evolution of the net FDI/GDP, gross domestic private investment/GDP and total investment/GDP

Average:	*1990–1998*	*1999–2008*
Foreign direct investment, net outflows (% of GDP)	2.0	3.8
Gross private investment (% of GDP)	14.0	13.0
Gross domestic investment (% of GDP)	26.5	25.2

Source: WDI.

accentuates the overall impact on the unemployment rate during the 2000s, which reached 14.2% in 2008 according to official estimates, and around 20% according alternative sources. However, limited employment creation in the manufacturing sector along with the volatility of employment in agriculture has been partially offset by the large employment creation in the service sectors. With an unemployment rate of roughly 14.2%, it appears that FTA with the EU has failed to deliver what Tunisia needs most. To understand the reasons behind this weak job creation, a closer look at the employment changes in the manufacturing sector is undertaken given, that this sector was the one most directly affected by the FTA with the EU.

The period 1985–1995 was characterized by an accelerated pace of job creation in manufacturing activities at an average yearly rate of 4.1% – well above the 2.6% achieved during the period 1995–2008. The declining contribution of the manufacturing sector to job creation in Tunisia is mainly due to two major changes. First, the increased opening of the Tunisian economy to products from the EU and other countries negatively affected the development of this sector in the form of lower investments and consequently lower job creations. Second, the accession of new countries to the WTO, mainly China, increased competition on the European market for products traditionally exported by Tunisia, which reduced the growth rate of its manufacturing exports to the EU. More particularly, job creation in the textile sector, clothing and leather, declined from an average annual growth of 3.3% over the period 1991–2000 to only 1.7% during the period 2001–2008. However, it was initially expected that these sectors would be much more negatively impacted by the erosion of preferences on the EU market thanks to the high appreciation of the Euro vis-à-vis the TND that relatively offset the losses of competition of Tunisian products on these markets (see Bchir *et al.*, 2009).

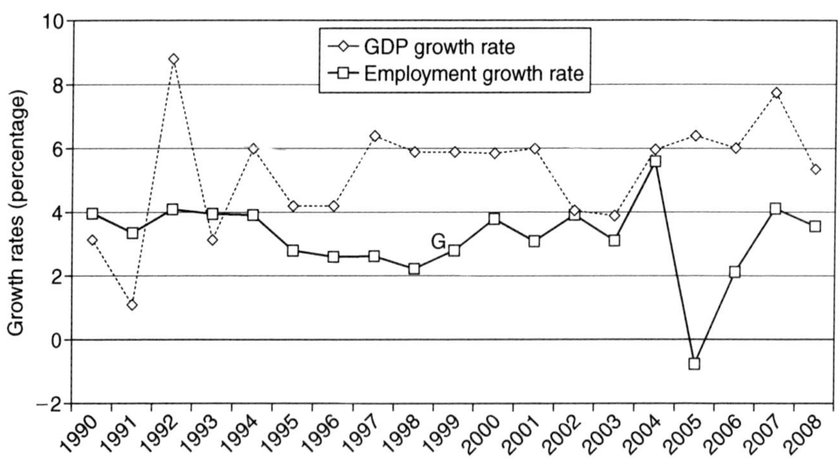

Figure 5.4 Trends in growth rates in GDP and employment (1990–2008).

An alternative approach to appreciate the changes in labor intensity of economic growth is to compare the gains in labor productivity to economic growth. When the later exceeds that of productivity, economic growth is accompanied by job creation. However, if growth is lower than productivity gains, growth is then accompanied by job destruction. The changes in labor productivity over the period 1990–2008 show that the economic growth of all market-oriented activities, excluding agriculture and fisheries, grew at a faster rate than that of productivity except for 2005. The relationship between economic growth and employment has followed two periods of development. The first period, 1990–1995, was characterized by relatively moderate economic growth at annual average rate of 4.6% and an acceleration of job creation at an average rate of 3.6%, which is lower than GDP. This development reflects a slowdown in industrial growth and a decline in capital efficiency which entails a very small productivity growth (0.1%).

However, over the second period, 1996–2008, the Tunisian economy was characterized by a combination of high GDP growth (5.8%), lower job creation (3%) except in 2005, and an increase in productivity (2.7%).

5.5 Slight economic transformation and diversification

A sectoral analysis of GDP reveals four major changes for the period 1990–2008. First, the ratio of services to total GDP passed from on average 59.8% during the period 1999–2008 to 57.1% over the period 1990–1998. These changes are mainly ascribable to the emergence of new sectors with a high potential in the services activities such as ICT and banking.

Second, the growth of manufacture's GDP has been smaller in the post-FTA compared to the pre-FTA period, while the highest growth has been achieved by the subsector of electrical and mechanical industries. Despite the continued growth of manufacturing GDP, its share in total employment has been stable at 32.3% over the two periods However, there have been significant structural changes within the manufacturing sector itself. This the case in the textiles and clothing sectors, which are losing jobs, while at the same time the electronics and electric subsectors are improving their role in labor absorption.

Third, agriculture's contribution to GDP has declined between the periods 1990–1998 and 1999–2008. The drop in the share of agriculture in GDP is mostly the result of increased contribution of services to GDP rather than an absence of dynamics in the agriculture sector (Table 5.8).

5.6 Higher GHG emissions but lower emissions intensity

Tunisia's GHG emissions are still weak compared to the industrialized countries. Indeed, GHG emissions per capita have evolved from 1.75 metric tonnes-equivalent of CO_2 (TECO_2) in 1980 to 2.69 TECO_2 in 2004. Hence, over the period 1980–2008 the average rate of increase of Tunisia's CO_2 emissions has been about 1.5% per annum. Expressed per unit of GDP, GHG emissions

Table 5.8 Trends in structural contribution to GDP

	Average share in GDP	
	1990–1998	*1999–2008*
Agriculture, value added (% of GDP)	14.1	11.4
Industry, value added (% of GDP)	28.8	28.8
Of which Manufacturing, value added (% of GDP)	17.8	17.7
Services, etc., value added (% of GDP)	57.1	59.8

Source: World Bank (2009).

evolved from 1.48 in 1980 to 1.11 $TECO_2$/1000 TD in 2008 – that is, an average reduction of carbon intensity by 1% per annum over the whole period (1980–2008).

The bulk of CO_2 emissions are produced by energy industries, followed by the transport then the manufacturing sectors. Given that the manufacturing sector in Tunisia is intensively oriented to the European market, it was expected that the implementation of European certification for Tunisian exports of manufacturing products would gradually reduce the emission intensity of CO_2. Chemingui and Thabet (2010) show that decline in GHG emissions has accelerated since 2000, with a 2.1% average annual decrease, thanks to the conjunction of several factors. Among them are the progressive and continued orientation of the Tunisian economy towards less pollutant energy intensive sectors, the improvement of energy efficiency mainly in manufactured industries, the development of the use of natural gas instead of fuel oil, and the shift in electricity production technology towards a combined cycle. Moreover, the role of the FTA with the EU cannot be omitted as a major factor explaining the reform in energy policy in Tunisia towards greater adaptation to European standards in terms of reducing air pollution through the adoption of a certification process for products sold on the European market.

6 Conclusions and policy implications

Developing countries are progressively motivated to implement FTAs with their main trade partners in the developing world. For the EU, and further to the EMP with its partners in the SMC, it is currently negotiating many FTAs with other regional blocs such as the ACP countries, MERCOSUR and the GCC. Preliminary assessment of the effects of the FTA between Tunisia and the EU provides an important lesson to other developing countries on the extent to which this type of agreement may contribute to their strategies of sustained economic growth for employment and poverty reduction through a more diversified and competitive economy. For the EU itself, the findings of this chapter may contribute to the understanding of how this type of agreement works towards achieving the original objectives for which it was initiated. Among these objectives are the increase of

European exports to the associated countries, the improvement of the international competitiveness of European firms through horizontal integration with the partner countries, and a higher and sustained economic growth in the SMCs as a means of controlling migration inflows to the EU.

For Tunisia, as well as similar developing countries seeking to develop FTA with the EU, the evidence here suggests the need for serious reviews of national development strategies. Tunisia has all the advantages that came with its early preferential agreement and its proximity to the European markets. No other SMCs can expect even the meager gains Tunisia saw under the FTA with the EU unless the trade agreement is reframed in the context of pro-growth and pro-development strategies. The role of domestic reforms and a transparent implementation of the various components of the FTA is also a key determinant of the success of the partnership, mainly in giving the required and positive signals on the real commitments of Tunisian authorities to radically transform its economy from a state-controlled to a competitive and open economy.

The reform in domestic policies should draw on the more successful strategies of other developing countries that have opted for free-market policies. Countries in the process of negotiation or implementation of FTAs with developed countries should avoid some of Tunisia's key mistakes, such as over-emphasizing tight fiscal policy and exchange rate control over international competitiveness and economic growth; weak tax collection on capital and wages; falling public investment in key sectors which could have helped pull in private and foreign direct investments; failure to implement a transparent competition policy; and the complicated regulations of trade operations even from the EU. None of these domestic policies was appropriate in the context of a free trade agreement with the major trade partner of the country. They are largely inconsistent with the model of economy in which trade liberalization and deregulation are advanced as top policy objectives.

The chapter's findings show that the FTA did not deliver to expectations in terms of employment and labor productivity, despite the various programs implemented by the government with financial support from the EU and other international donors. Unemployment is growing, mostly among skilled job-seekers, and productivity is not improving, contrary to what was recently argued by the IMF (2009):

> The Association Agreement with the EU was instrumental in raising trade openness and inducing productivity gains by exposing the industrial sector to global competition. Tunisia's prudent macroeconomic policies and structural reforms have improved its resilience to economic slowdowns with lower public and external indebtedness and much higher reserves coverage of short-term external debt.

A rigorous assessment of employment and skill development programs should be carried out, and alternatives need to be identified and implemented. Growth has also not improved, and the structure of the Tunisian economy has not changed much. Inflows of FDI and private investment have stagnated and environmental pollution has increased despite the improvement in pollution intensity.

In conclusion, the FTA did not deliver its promises, largely because of inappropriate domestic policies. The objectives of stabilizing public finances and controlling the foreign current account were advanced, instead of pro-growth and employment-generation policies. The role of the government in the economy should be intensified in two main domains: efficient spending on human capital and infrastructure on one side, and provision of more sound signals to private operators (both nationals and foreigners) on the sustainability of government policies, their transparency, and their effective implementation on the other. The removal of the wide existing barriers in investments, mainly in the service sectors, and the disengagement from many competitive activities, should constitute the basis of government actions in the coming years.

Notes

1 Except if granted on a non-discriminatory basis (enabling the clause of 1979).
2 SMCs include Morocco, Algeria, Tunisia, Libya, Egypt, Jordan, Syria, Lebanon, Palestinian Authority, Turkey and Israel.
3 Algeria largely benefited from the stabilization of the political situation and the surge of gas world prices to boost job creations in the public sector.
4 While the agreement came into force officially on 1 March 1998, Tunisia started dismantling tariffs on EU manufacturing products in January 1996.
5 See, for instance, Dessus *et al.* (2001), Boughanmi (1997), Brown *et al.* (1997), Chemingui and Dessus (1999), Rutherford *et al.* (1995), Dessus and Suwa (2000) among others for applications of CGE models to assess the FTA between Tunisian and the European Union.
6 For a further analysis on the fiscal policy changes in Tunisia, see Bchir *et al.* (2009) and Chemingui and Sanchez (2010). However, with the political change occurring in January 2011, the government deficit is expected to reach a historical level of between 5% and 7% as result of increasing social transfers and lower economic growth that negatively affect tax incomes.
7 The first year Tunisia was covered by the survey.

References

Ayadi, M, G. Boulila, M. Lahouel and P. Montigny (2005) *Pro-Poor Growth in Tunisia*, Paris: International Development and Strategies.

Bchir, M.H., M.A. Chemingui and H. Ben Hammouda (2009). 'Ten Years after Implementing Barcelona Process: What can be Learned from the Tunisian Experience?', *Journal of North African Studies*, 14(2): 123–144.

Boughnami, M. (1997) 'Impact de l'accord de libre-echange entre la Tunisie et l'Union Europeenne: Evaluation en Equilibre General Calculable', in M. Boudhiaf (ed.), *Integration Economique Regionale*, Tunis: Faculty of Economics and Management.

Brown, D., A. Deardoff and R. Stern (1997) 'Some Economic Effects of the Free Trade Agreement between Tunisia and the European Union', in A. Galal and B. Hoekman (eds), *Regional Partners in Global Markets: Limits and Possibilities of the Euro-Med Agreements*, London and ECES, Cairo: CEPR.

Chemingui, M. and S. Dessus (1999). 'La Liberalisation de l'agriculture tunisienne et l'Union Europeenne: une vue prospective', Paris: OECD Development Centre Working Paper No 144.

Chemingui, M.A and M.V. Sanchez (2010). 'Assessing Development Strategies to Achieve the MDGs in Tunisia', background paper produced for the report 'Assessing Development Strategies to Achieve MDGs in Arab Countries' produced jointly by the World Bank and UN-DESA.

Chemingui, M.A and C. Thabet (2010). 'Trade Liberalization, Environmental Degradation, and Public Health in Tunisia: Assessing the Ancillary Health Benefits of Pollution Abatement Policy'. Paper produced for the ERF Research Program on Environmental Economics

Dessus, S. and A. Suwa (1999). 'Regional Integration and Internal Reforms in the Mediterranean Area', Paris: OECD Development Center Studies.

Dessus, S., J. Devlin and R. Safadi (eds) (2001). 'Towards Arab and Euro-Med Regional Integration', OECD Development Centre Seminars, Paris

European Training Foundation – ETF – (2007) 'The Contribution of Human Resources Development to Migration Development in Tunisia', Research Report. Available at: www.etf.europa.eu/pubmgmt.nsf/(getAttachment)/5CD26BB43A026CD8C12573DB004D8AD2/$File/NOTE7B7KG6.pdf.

Gould, D.M. (1998). 'Has NAFTA changed North American Trade?', Dallas, TX: Federal Reserve Bank of Dallas, Economic Review, First Quarter 1998.

Haddar, M. (2010). 'Economic Growth and Job Creations in Tunisia', background paper for the Economic Report on Africa 2010, 'Promoting high-level sustainable growth to reduce unemployment in Africa', United Nations Economic Commission for Africa and The African Union, Addis Ababa.

IMF (2009) 'Tunisia: 2009 Article IV Consultation – Staff Report, and Public Information Notice', Washington, DC: IMF.

Lahouel, M.H. (2007) 'The Success of Pro-Poor Growth in Rural and Urban Tunisia', in T. Besley and L.J. Cord (eds), *Delivering on the Promise of Pro-Poor Growth. Insights and Lessons from Countries Experiences*, Basingstoke: Palgrave Macmillan and the World Bank, pp. 199–218.

Ravallion, M. and G. Datt (1991). 'Growth and Redistribution Components of Changes in Poverty Measures', Papers 83, World Bank – Living Standards Measurement

Rutherford, T., E. Rustrom and D. Tarr (1995) 'L'accord de libre-echange entre la Tunisie et l'Union Europeenne', Confidential Final Report, Tunis.

World Bank (2004). 'Republic of Tunisia: Making Deeper Trade Integration Work for Growth and Jobs', Washington, DC: Development Policy Review, Report No. 29847-TN.

World Bank (2009) *World Development Indicators*, Washington, DC: The World Bank.

6 The global financial crisis and the Euro-Mediterranean partnership[1]

Simon Neaime

1 Introduction

The 2007 United States (US) financial crisis, which started in the subprime market, has developed into the most severe worldwide economic crisis since the 1927 Great Depression.[2] What has prevented an even more important fallout was the introduction of a spectacular fiscal and monetary stimulus package in the more advanced economies. However, the price tag for the crisis still remains a record-breaking high. In addition to its severe effects in North America and the European Union (EU) countries, the crisis has put pressure on emerging markets worldwide, contributing to fast declines in their stock markets, Gross Domestic Product (GDP) growth rates, oil prices and revenues, commodities exports, Foreign Direct Investment (FDI), tourism revenues and workers' remittances. While some developed countries and a number of large emerging market countries are now showing some signs of recovery, the effect of the crisis on Mediterranean Partner Countries[3] (MPCs) has not yet fully unfolded. It is possible that the negative economic and social consequences of the crisis, for example on employment, will be felt for some time to come – especially given that a double-dip recession in the more advanced economies cannot be ruled out.

Weaknesses in the financial sectors of some MPCs made the transmission of the financial crisis in the region a source of concern, and have undermined the recent integration efforts of those countries with the EU. Moreover, lower growth prospects in the more advanced economies, higher financing costs and a decrease in remittances are leading to soaring current account and budget deficits, and are a source of concern for the sustainability of the current exchange rate regimes in several MPCs. On the other hand, some MPCs still suffer from the absence of bond markets, a combination of inadequate financial sector supervision, poor assessment and management of financial risk, and the maintenance of fixed exchange rates. These factors, among others, have accentuated the effects of the crisis in the region. Although trade and globalization issues and the financial integration of the MPCs' financial systems with the more mature financial markets of the EU and US are among the main reasons why the crisis affected the region, this has been accentuated by domestic macroeconomic, fiscal, monetary and financial issues, notably the existence of fixed exchange rates, weak domestic stock and bond markets, high real interest rates and limited fiscal space in some of those countries.

The rest of the study is divided as follows. The next section highlights the impact of the crisis on MPCs, emphasizing the declines in goods and capital flows to the region. Fiscal space and related fiscal stimulus packages introduced are also discussed. Finally, the implications of the crisis on stock and bond markets are also carefully analyzed. Section 3 looks at the monetary and exchange rate responses of MPCs to the crisis. The implications of the current crisis on the type of exchange rate regime in place are thoroughly assessed. The implications on the real and nominal effective exchange rates are carefully analyzed. Finally, the last section concludes with some policy implications.

2 Impact of the crisis on MPCs

The crisis brought down the majority of stock market indexes worldwide. Subsequently, lower GDP growth prospects in the most developed economies brought down the world's average real growth rate of GDP from about 4% in 2007 to −2.5% in 2009. These negative rates are, however, expected to pick up again in 2010 to about 3% (Figure 6.1). Subsequently, the crisis directly affected MPCs mainly through the trade and exchange rate channels, and through declines in GDP growth rates of the region's main trading partners, as well as declines in commodity prices and cross-border capital flows. However, and relative to other emerging regions, the impact of the crisis on MPCs has been limited, with growth slowing modestly to 3.6% on average in 2009 from a peak of 6% in 2008.

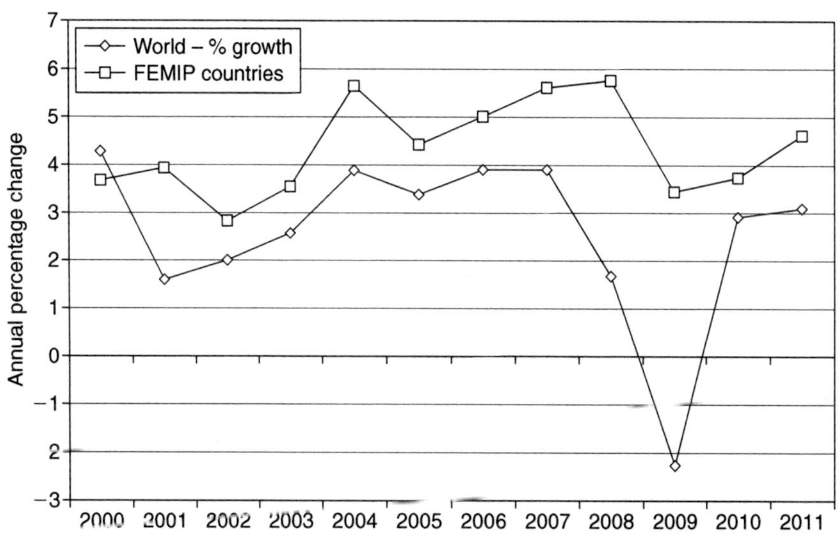

Figure 6.1 MPCs' real GDP growth rates (annual percentage change) (sources: International Monetary Fund, and International Financial Statistics).

Figure 6.2 indicates that real GDP growth prospects in 2009 in MPCs have been negatively affected because of weak growth prospects (−3.2% in the EU and −2.5% in the US) in major trading partners, mainly the EU, which accounts for about 40% of MPCs' total trade, followed by the US and the Gulf Cooperation Council Countries (GCC) accounting for about 10% of the region's total trade, respectively. Figure 6.3 shows the 2009 specific MPCs' total exports' destination as a ratio to GDP. It is clear that the North African countries' major trading partners are the EU-27 countries. It is through this trade channel that Morocco, Tunisia, Algeria and Egypt have been affected by the crisis.

Weak growth prospects affected world demand for the MPCs' exports, especially the EU's demand for the region's exports. The most affected MPCs are the North African countries of Algeria, Tunisia, Morocco and, to a lesser extent, Egypt. The ensuing global recession has not only dried up liquidity but also reduced financial inflows and export revenues, threatening the fiscal and current account balances and subsequently macroeconomic stability of several MPCs. Some of them have been facing liquidity challenges since the beginning of the financial crisis, which may evolve into solvency problems for a number of them. For MPCs with weak financial linkages with the developed market, the multiple external shocks have started to reveal gaps between revenues and spending, and outflow of capital has put downward pressure on their exchange rates coupled with a decline in foreign exchange reserves. Lower export earnings and inability to impose counter-cyclical taxation measures will worsen their budget deficits and will widen their gap of foreign exchange needs.

With tight budgets and current account deficits, and exports under pressure, future growth will hinge on private consumption, which is the highest contributor to the growth rate of real GDP (Figure 6.4).

Similar to export of commodities, tourism and remittances revenues constitute an important source of foreign exchange and contribution to economic

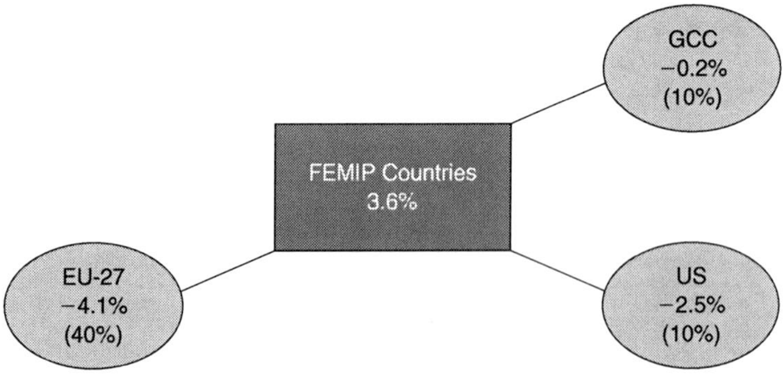

Figure 6.2 Growth in MPCs' trading partners, 2009 (source: International Monetary Fund, Regional Economic Outlook Report, and World Economic Outlook. The numbers in brackets are the trade shares of MPCs in total trade, while the numbers without brackets are the IMF's real GDP growth rates for 2009).

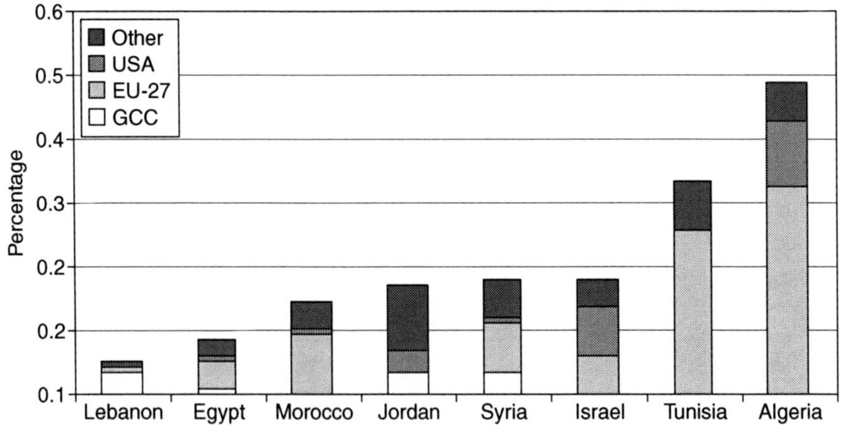

Figure 6.3 MPCs' export destinations, 2009 (in percent of GDP) (sources: IMF, Regional Economic Outlook Report, World Economic Outlook, and Euromonitor International).

growth for the MPCs of Egypt, Morocco, Tunisia, Jordan and Lebanon. However, the knock-on effect of the crisis on remittances in all MPCs, with the exception of, perhaps, Lebanon, has been profound. Remittances provide valuable foreign exchange for the MPCs that is used to finance current account deficits and foreign debt service payments, not to mention meeting consumption demands of the domestic market. In Lebanon, for instance, remittances account for about 22% of GDP, followed by Jordan, where they account for 16% of GDP. Therefore, any decrease in remittances, resulting from the crisis, will have a detrimental effect on the above two countries' rate of growth of real GDP (Figure 6.5), and on their ability to service their foreign public debt.

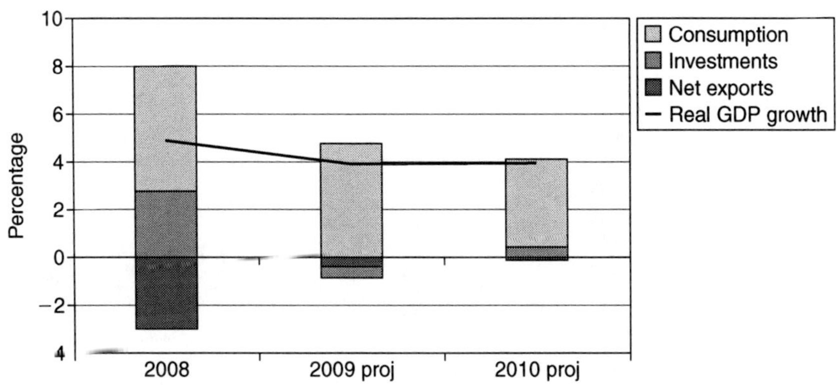

Figure 6.4 MPCs: contribution to real GDP growth (%) (sources: IMF and IFS).

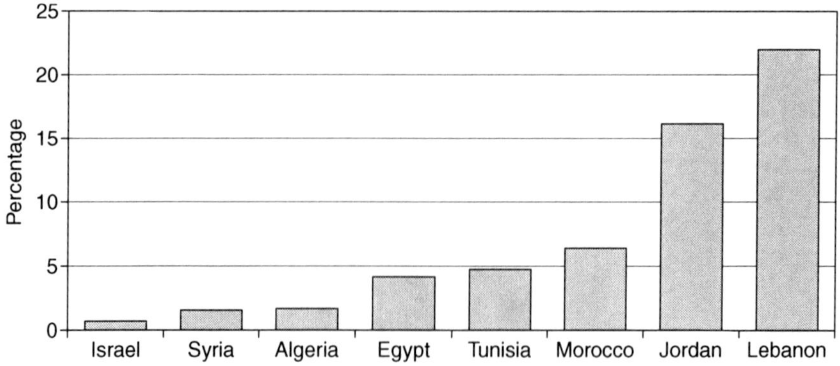

Figure 6.5 Remittances 2009 (inflows in percent of GDP) (sources: IMF and Euromonitor International).

Even though most MPCs have recently undertaken some financial reforms and pursued sound macroeconomic policies, the current financial crisis, which is not of their making, is disproportionately penalizing them and putting more pressure on the recent macroeconomic efforts devoted towards achieving macroeconomic and financial stability. Some MPCs are still facing a sharp decline in both domestic and international liquidity coupled with other aftershocks of the financial crisis, thus weakening their debt servicing capabilities. Export revenues declined by about $20 billion between 2008 and 2009, with related declines – although not quite as significant – in tourism revenues, remittances and FDI inflows (Figure 6.6).

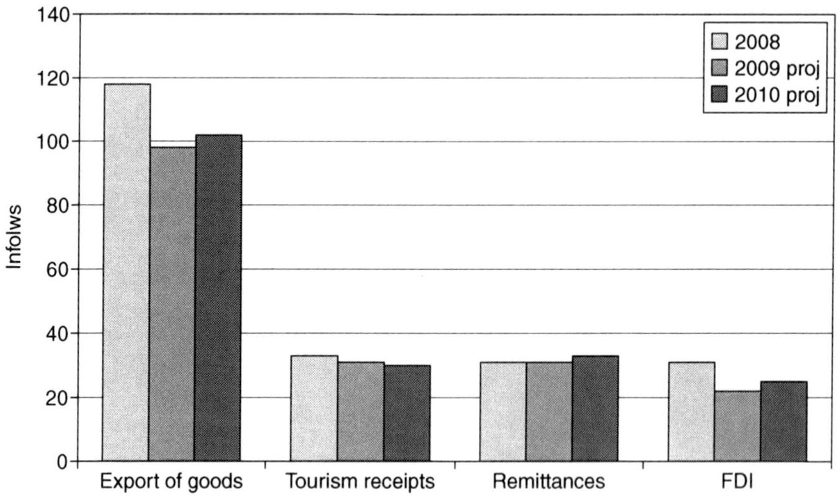

Figure 6.6 MPCs' capital inflows (sources: IMF and IFS).

Some MPCs, namely Morocco, Tunisia, Algeria and Egypt, entered the crisis either with robust fiscal space (see Figure 6.7) or with a significant amount of accumulated foreign exchange reserves. Those countries were able to implement counter-cyclical macroeconomic policies to dampen the effects of the crisis on their respective economies. On the fiscal side, this was achieved through mainly fiscal impulse[4] and automatic stabilizers.[5] However, other MPCs such as Lebanon and Jordan, both with fixed exchange rate regimes and with relatively high debt to GDP ratios (160% for Lebanon and about 70% for Jordan) and high real interest rates, were in a much weaker position and were not able to respond to the crisis with adequate policy actions. As a consequence, the severity of the external shocks passed directly through to their economies, in particular to the Jordanian economy. Lebanon managed to benefit from political stability, which helped boost its domestic economy by making it more attractive to international capital inflows.

Figure 6.8 indicates that the change in the non-oil primary fiscal deficit is expected to be negative in 2010 in each of Jordan, Lebanon, Syria and Tunisia, pointing to limited fiscal space. In addition, automatic stabilizers are expected to contribute only less than 1% to the non-oil GDP in each one of those countries respectively.

The spillover effects of the global financial and economic crisis on MPCs and its effects on the PMCs' financial markets varied according to their degree of financial integration with the EU/US capital markets. Egypt and Morocco, with large exposure to EU/US banks, bonds and equity markets, were the first to suffer (Figure 6.9). These countries are facing a four-edged sword, i.e. plunging asset prices, higher cost of borrowing, capital outflows and a decrease in exports. Other MPCs, namely Tunisia and Israel, have become more resilient with respect to past crises, owing to the building up of adequate foreign exchange reserves and a robust fiscal stance. The current financial crisis has also reversed the gains made in the past decade in reducing the debt burdens of some MPCs, and might also carry the risk of new debt/exchange rate crises because of a dangerous

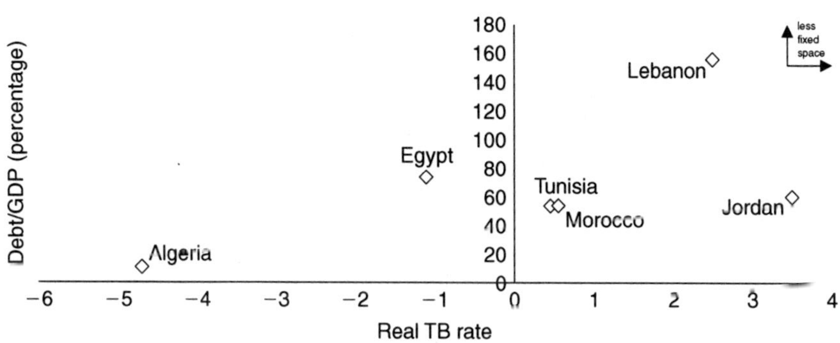

Figure 6.7 Real Treasury-Bill (TB) rates and total public debt/GDP, 2009 (%) (sources: IMF and IFS, and Audi Bank, Lebanon).

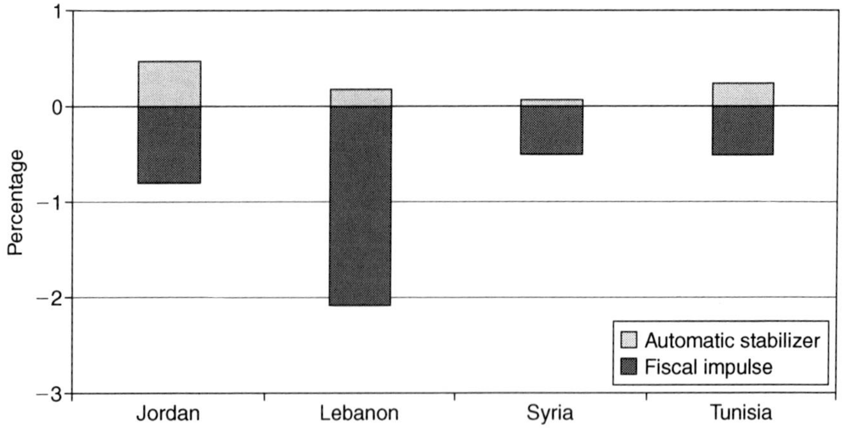

Figure 6.8 Change in non-oil primary fiscal deficit, 2010 (percent of non-oil GDP) (sources: IMF and IFS).

combination of fixed exchange rates, external shocks, the higher cost of debt servicing, and the pressing need for increasing new external and domestic borrowing.

While some MPCs have been hit by the worst exogenous financial shock in decades, other countries were ill equipped to fight the economic and social consequences of the crisis given their poor financial markets, especially their bond markets. Alleviating the liquidity problems of those countries and providing them with the fiscal space needed to combat the economic and financial crisis would also help stabilize European demand, and should thus be regarded as an

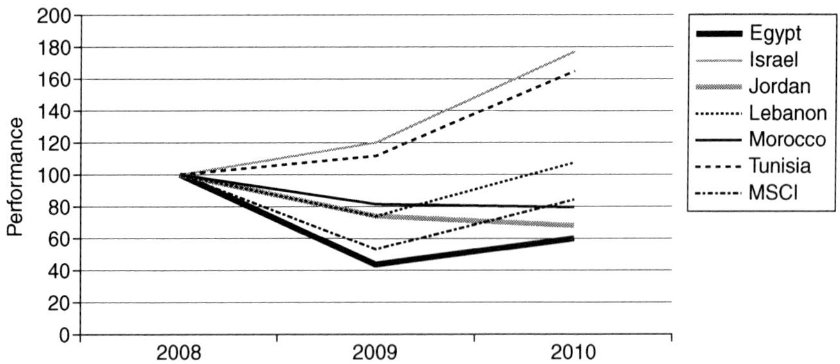

Figure 6.9 MPCs' stock market performance, 2008–2010 (sources: Egyptian Stock Exchange, Tel Aviv Stock Exchange, Amman Stock Exchange, Beirut Stock Exchange, Casablanca Stock Exchange, Bloomberg, and Wikinvest. MSCI is the Morgan Stanley Capital International Index for Emerging Markets).

integral component of EU countries' stimulus package. However, the limited reliance on international financial flows in the majority of MPCs – with the exception of perhaps Egypt – has contained the disruption of local financial markets. MPCs' bond markets are still primitive and their bond issuance constitutes a relatively very small portion of other emeging markets' bond issuance (Figure 6.10).

Figure 6.11 indicates that with the exception of Egypt and Tunisia, cross-border loans have remained low and in some instances totally insignificant in all MPCs. This contained, to some extent, the financial fallout in all these countries.

Most MPCs also suffered from the negative spillover effects emanating from the GCC countries through the workers' remittance channel, as well as through the liquidity, trade, and real GDP growth channels. The sharp decline in oil prices has had a ripple effect on foreign reserves, the exchange rate, coupled with declining capital inflows and shrinking export markets in all GCC countries. This is mainly due to having a low export base, concentrated in few commodities, and great reliance on oil export revenues for debt servicing and government expenditures. Moreover, the recent record oil price decreases and revenues have negatively affected the growth outlook of all MPCs. Lower oil revenues since 2008 will continue to generate low liquidity in GCC countries[6] – with negative spillover effects into the MPCs – and are expected to contribute to increasing further the region's interest rates. Higher interest rates have led to nominal exchange rate appreciations, losses in international competitiveness, large trade and budget deficits, and the accumulation of sizable external debts,

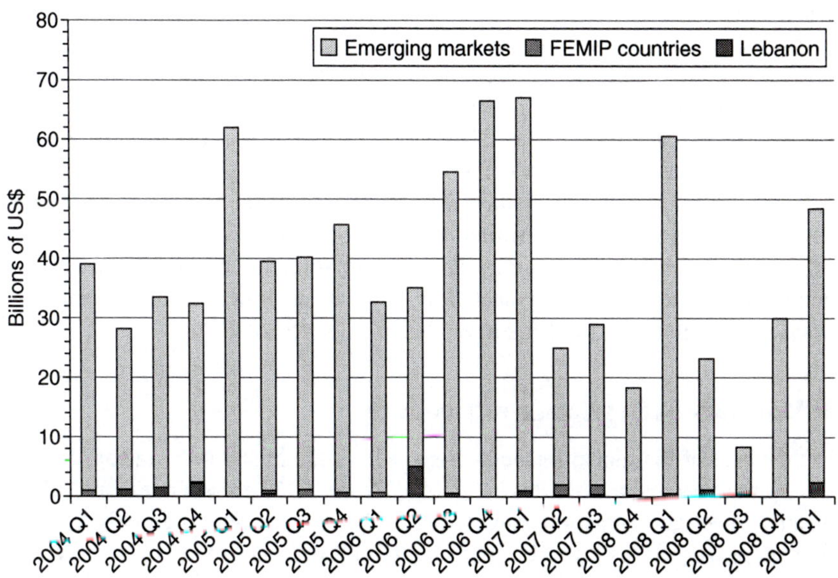

Figure 6.10 MPCs' bond issuance, 2004–2009 (in billion US$) (sources: IMF and IFS).

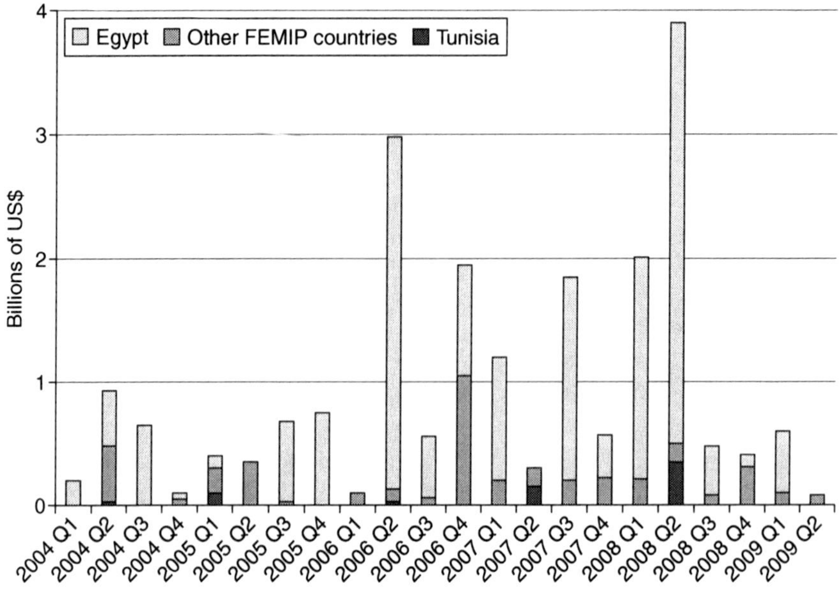

Figure 6.11 Cross-border loans, 2004–2009 (in billion US$) (sources: IMF and IFS).

and in some instances have increased the potential for a currency crisis. The implications have also been felt on the balance sheets of private sector's corporations.

Moreover, the accelerating growth of money supply through central banks, extensively increasing the net credit to the banking sector, has had little impact on the credit crunch in those countries, and there is no pick-up in bank lending because of the ongoing balance sheet adjustment process (de-leveraging), and the persistent risk aversion and insistent tendency of flight to quality in most MPCs. Currently, financial markets that fueled growth in MPCs are drying up. This constitutes an extremely serious constraint for those countries, as this is the time when external inflows are needed most to stimulate economic growth and employment and to roll over debt. Private financial flows (including financial flows and remittances) to MPCs have also fallen since 2008.

3 Monetary and exchange rate policies

In the wake of the global financial crisis, MPCs are bound to be facing the following macroeconomic hurdles in 2010: (1) lower GDP growth rates, and subsequently lower government revenues, and further budget deficits and higher rates of unemployment; (2) lower levels of capital inflows/FDI; and (3) lower level of exports, and subsequently further current account deficits, and more difficulties in servicing the portion of the debt that is denominated in foreign currency.

Lebanon,[7] Syria and Jordan, with fixed exchange rates regimes, limited fiscal space and underdeveloped financial markets, have been the most affected by the crisis due to: (1) losses of foreign reserves in trying to maintain their pegged exchange rate regime; and (2) the inability to use effectively monetary policy to absorb the effects of shocks emanating from the crisis, since monetary policy is totally geared towards preserving the exchange rate peg. It is well known that under a fixed exchange rate regime, monetary policy is geared solely towards maintaining the pegged regime. If, for whatever reason, the central bank fails in maintaining its peg, then a sudden devaluation may lead to a debt crisis similar to the Russian crisis of 1998.[8] In this case, domestic macroeconomic policies alone will not be sufficient and the EU's intervention is warranted. Those MPCs may face an exchange rate crisis and a subsequent default on foreign debt, and may also experience a balance of payment crisis due to the terms of trade shocks, the decline in export demand, the reduction in tourism and remittances flows, and real exchange rate appreciations, as was the case in Jordan, Lebanon and Syria (see Figure 6.12). There is also the potential for bank failures, depending on the exposure of commercial banks to public debt – which is most significant in Lebanon – and to the real estate sector, as was the case in some GCC countries, or due to the bad performance of outstanding loans (non-performing loans), all this being coupled with considerable difficulties posed in tapping international financial markets.

Egypt, Morocco, Tunisia and Algeria, with flexible exchange rate regimes and with more mature banking and financial markets, have been less affected by the crisis. Those countries had more room to manoeuvre domestically with counter-cyclical monetary policies, due to the effective use of monetary policy to absorb the effects of the external financial shocks emanating from the crisis. Instead of being used solely towards defending the pegged exchange rate regime, foreign reserves were available as a first line of defence to weather the negative effects of the global financial crisis.

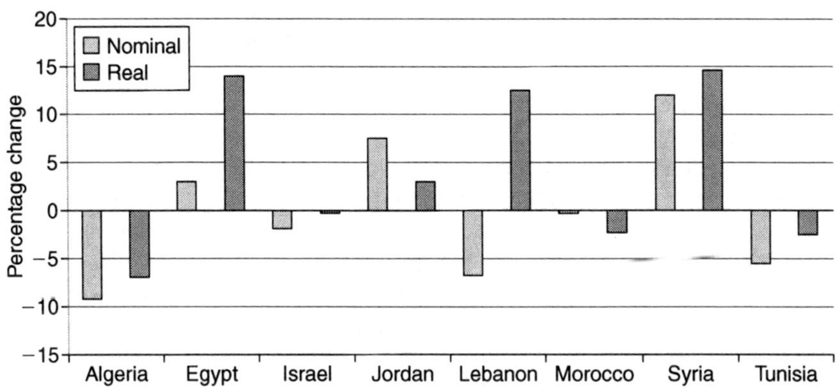

Figure 6.12 Effective real and nominal exchange rates (percentage change 2009) (sources: IMF and IFS).

A case in point is Egypt, which was able to adequately absorb the effects of shocks emanating from the current crisis, although its stock market could not escape incurring considerable losses due to its integration with the more mature financial markets. The recent float of Egypt's currency has rendered monetary policy more effective, easing up the pressure on domestic interest rates, and contributing subsequently to lowering debt service, and in the containment of the recurrent budget and current account deficits. Through a series of controlled devaluations prior to the crisis, Egypt was able to stimulate exports and generate enough foreign currency to reduce the levels of its foreign debt. The recent success of Egypt in adopting flexible exchange rates has paved the way for a smooth transition to targeting inflation.

The current financial crisis has accentuated the current account and budget deficits of several MPCs. This, coupled with a fixed exchange rate system in place, implies explicitly that those countries will have to generate foreign currency from sources other than exports to: (1) cover a widening huge gap between exports and imports; (2) service a fast-growing external debt; and (3) maintain their pegged exchange rate regime. If such hard currency is not generated, given the current financial crisis, then the by-product will be the continuous accumulation of unsustainable external debt, and a subsequent exchange rate crisis. In all cases if, for whatever reasons, these countries still opt for maintaining fixed exchange rate arrangements, they will have to implement crisis-prevention measures, namely by exercising fiscal discipline, managing properly their debts and foreign reserves, and avoiding future real exchange rate appreciations.

The structure of emerging countries' public debt highlights the extent of vulnerability of their debt burden to abrupt movements in the exchange rate, and hence is crucial when assessing future debt sustainability. The sustainability of debt that is denominated in foreign currency goes beyond the domestic conduct of fiscal and monetary policy mix per se to become dependent also on the outcomes of exchange rate policies. MPCs need to closely coordinate the optimality of the fiscal and monetary policy mix, which will have important implications for the existent exchange rate arrangements, and on how those countries can in the future be more resilient to potential external financial shocks.

For MPCs with a debt structure that is mostly domestic, the smooth transition to a flexible exchange rate regime may be one way to dampen the negative effects of the crisis. In the short run, those countries will have to keep fiscal policy tight if they seek to continue reducing their large government debt and ensure its sustainability. Before introducing more flexibility into the exchange rate, those countries will need to introduce proper fiscal adjustment measures and debt management policies to reduce the level of their external debt. They will also have to continue strengthening the financial and banking sectors to further address the fiscal imbalances, and to further mitigate any potential for a future debt or currency crisis.

The enhancement of local capital markets, especially stock markets, is another way to dampen the effects of the crisis, and will help reduce the exposure of private corporations to currency mismatches due to foreign borrowing. Those corporations will be able to raise funds locally and reduce their exposure to external financial shocks. They will also reduce any currency mismatch (exchange rate risk) in their balance sheets, and dampen the implications of any sudden outflows of capital emanating from the current crisis.

In light of the ensuing financial crisis, some MPCs will have to start implementing a monetary policy regime shift known as inflation targeting as an explicit monetary policy objective. This shift would be justified by the difficulties posed by the implications of the current financial crisis. At the same time, this move will pave the way for those countries to control the current inflationary pressures emanating from the crisis, and to make their monetary policies more transparent and effective. Given the various fiscal and monetary stimulus packages introduced as a result of the crisis, inflation in all MPCs has started to pick up since early 2010, despite its containment during the financial crisis (see Figure 6.13).

One MPC that is very close to explicitly adopting inflation targeting as its main monetary policy goal is Egypt. Other MPCs, such as Morocco and Tunisia, are implicitly targeting inflation, and are slowly moving towards an inflation targeting regime. They are already targeting the real exchange rate rather than the nominal rate in order to maintain competitiveness and avoid currency overvaluation, while opening their capital markets to international capital flows. Jordan, Lebanon and Syria will have to introduce more flexibility into their exchange rates before they can shift to an inflation targeting monetary policy regime. Inflation in Lebanon has already exceeded the 10% threshold, and is expected to worsen even further in 2010.

In light of the current crisis, it is now well established that targeting inflation may have improved the effectiveness of monetary policy in sterilizing the effects of the crisis, as opposed to discretionary monetary policies aiming at targeting

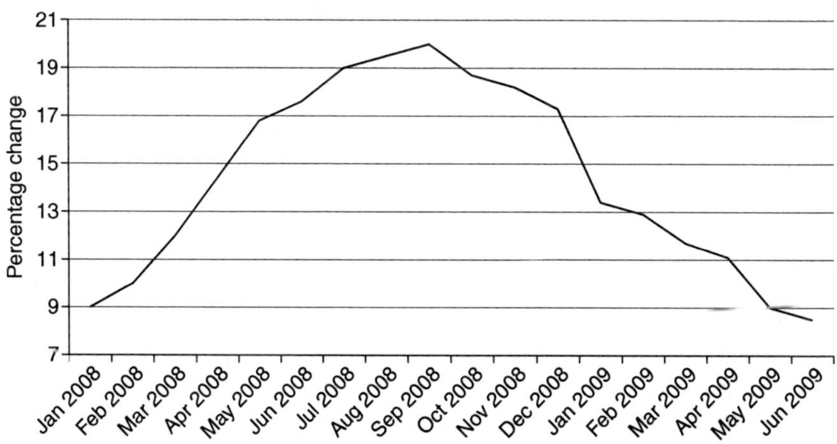

Figure 6.13 MPCs' consumer price index (annual percentage change) (source: International Monetary Fund and International Financial Statistics (IFS)).

the nominal exchange rate, which has increased uncertainty and which turned out to be ineffective on the real side of all MPCs due to the existence of time lags and other monetary and macroeconomic imbalances.

With the further integration of the Mediterranean region with the EU's economy, the increased regional and inter-regional monetary and financial economic integration, and the fast liberalization of the respective capital account, Jordan's and Lebanon's central banks should consider shifting to more flexible exchange rates regimes, if they wish to render their monetary policy more independent, and deal at the same time more effectively and swiftly with any future potential financial or monetary shock. An independent monetary policy constitutes an important prerequisite that needs to be implemented before inflation targeting can be adopted. Moreover, given the high debt levels accumulated in both MPCs, monetary policy set by the respective central bank should optimally interact in the future with public debt policy determined by the fiscal authorities, in order not to undermine any potential decision to shift to a monetary policy regime which targets inflation.

On the other hand, following the signing of the Barcelona Declaration between the EU and the MED region, most MPCs have been aiming for increased regional and inter-regional monetary and financial economic integration. A significant part of economic integration is the liberalization of the capital account and the enhancement of cross-border capital flows. However, when capital becomes increasingly mobile across national borders, and nominal exchange rates are fixed, monetary policy becomes increasingly subordinated to defending the nominal exchange rate peg.[9] In the extreme case, free capital movements and pegged exchange rates render the independence of monetary policy obsolete, as interest rates will have to shadow the interest rate of the anchor currency to which national currencies are pegged, irrespective of whether this foreign interest rate level suits the economic situation of the country. Under these circumstances, shifting to inflation targeting in some MPCs may become even more difficult to implement.

By and large, the EU has long been involved in cooperation initiatives in favor of MPCs within the framework of the Euro-Mediterranean Partnership Agreements launched in 1995, and different instruments have been put in place to support modernization and financial market reforms (recent examples are include Political Mediterranean Partnership relations with regard to Barcelona (MEDA), the Neighbourhood Policy Instrument, FEMIP, and the 2008 transition conference held in Brussels). However, the limited results obtained so far in bridging the gap between the shores of the Mediterranean have stimulated a reflection on the interventions necessary to make the EU's action more effective, especially in light of the current financial crisis, and the consequent drying up of capital inflows into MPCs.

Between 1995 and 2006, the European Commission allocated 9 billion euros to support modernization and economic reforms in MPCs. New capital of about 3.2 billion euros had been allocated to the region for 2007–2010, before the crisis. The sizeable credit interventions of the European Investment Bank (EIB), channeled, since 2002, through the Facility for Euro-Mediterranean Investment and Partnership (FEMIP), have recently registered a further increase, with 10.7 billion euros allocated for the period 2007–2013, against 6 billion euros invested between 2002 and 2006 in the nine MPCs. Moreover, it is believed that weaknesses in the MPCs' financial sector are also behind the poor results achieved so far, and the current financial crisis has worsened the current problems even more. Among future priorities, the need is particularly felt to better coordinate the use of funds allocated by different EU sources, and strengthen the relationship among various international institutions operating in the region (e.g., the European Commission, European Investment Bank, European Bank for Reconstruction and Development). In addition, the various stimulus packages introduced during the crisis in EU countries will need to account for the current financial imbalances in some MPCs to prevent further fallout in those economies, and revert all the gains that have been achieved so far through the various above-named funding programs.

4 Conclusion and policy implications

This chapter has shown that MPCs have been moderately hit by the crisis. A low degree of integration with international capital markets was instrumental in preventing a severe financial crisis. Limited exposure of the banking system to derivative products, and positive spillovers from increased public spending in GCC countries, have helped MPCs so far in avoiding a debt and exchange rate crisis. The negative spillover effects from advanced economies has been through a reduction in goods and capital flows (exports, FDI, remittances and tourism revenues). MPCs in North Africa (Algeria, Egypt, Morocco and Tunisia) have been highly exposed to the slowdown in the European Union – their main partner for trade and remittances – while the remaining MPCs of Lebanon, Jordan, Syria, and Gaza and West Bank have been highly exposed to slowdowns in the GCC region, mainly through the workers' remittances channel. For 2010, a slow recovery in partner country economies, combined with limited scope for further counter-cyclical government policy action, implies that growth – projected at 3.8% – will remain relatively flat. Policy-makers need to focus more on supply-side reforms that will help boost private sector activity and employment and enhance competitiveness.

The global economy is beginning to recover, but recovery is likely to be slow. Sustained fiscal and monetary policy support is still needed, and premature withdrawal of government support could have a negative impact on progress achieved so far. It is, however, important to have exit strategies to be adopted once the crisis is over, dealing effectively with the inflationary pressures that have resulted from the crisis, as well as increasing unemployment rates. Like other emerging countries, MPCs have been affected by the global financial crisis, but to different degrees.

Expansionary monetary and fiscal policy will continue to underpin the recovery in all MPCs. However, to safeguard price and financial stability and the soundness of public finances, credible exit strategies will be needed. Two key factors for the medium-term are private demand replacing public demand; and demand in external surplus EU economies rising to make up for shrinking demand in external deficit MPCs. Mediterranean commercial banks are generally well capitalized, but non-performing loans remain high in some cases. In the long run, enhancing MPCs' bond markets should become a priority to reduce the reliance on international financial flows and contain the exchange rate risk.

In the short run, MPCs need to maintain public spending in countries with fiscal space and flexible exchange rates, and strengthen the orderly workout of financial/corporate balance sheet effects of asset price falls on one hand, and promote financial markets development on the other. It is clear that low integration with advanced stock markets has contained the fallout, coupled with effective monetary and fiscal policy responses. However, in some MPCs, limited fiscal space, real exchange rate appreciation, and sluggish external receipts imply recovery will be slow. As the recovery takes place, policy focus will need to shift towards private sector development. However, if private demand and consumption fail to pick up, this, coupled with a limited scope for continued policy stimulus, would imply a worsening of the unemployment problem.

In the long run, the focus will need to shift toward raising MPCs' productive capacity. Addressing unemployment calls for greater private sector-led growth. Low integration with the EU's economies means losing out on the upside potential. As the recovery takes place, Mediterranean government policy focus will need to shift towards enhancing the private sector's productivity.

Potential risks for MPCs are as follows: weaker exports, tourism and remittances revenues, and sudden stops or reversal in capital flows. Moreover, slowdown in EU countries will continue to impact North Africa, while slowdown in GCC countries will continue to impact the whole region. In 2010, all MPCs are likely to suffer the impact of slower growth (which will hamper 'growing out of debt'), lower receipts from oil-producing countries, and further increases in government debt due to spending in the context of fiscal stimuli packages.

Notes

1 This paper is based on a project that received the financial assistance of the Facility for the Euro-Mediterranean Investment and Partnership (FEMIP) and the European Investment Bank (EIB) within a collaboration agreement with FEMISE. The contents of this paper are the sole responsibility of the author(s) and can under no circumstances be regarded as reflecting the position of the EIB.

2 The past two decades have witnessed monetary, fiscal and exchange rate crises in many emerging market countries: (1) The Mexican crisis of 1994. This was triggered by a devaluation of the peso to correct for a real exchange rate overvaluation, which was behind the contracting economic growth; the devaluation led to a contraction in the economy, and was followed by a debt crisis. (2) The Asian crisis of 1997, which was triggered by a combination of poor financial governance, the maintenance of pegged exchange rate regimes, the fast capital account liberalization, and weaknesses in the Asian financial systems. (3) The Russian crisis of 1998, where the steep devaluation of the Rouble by about 260% in December 1998 led to a significant growth of Russia's

external debt and its service costs; the collapse of the Treasury bill market, coupled with a commercial banking crisis which paralyzed the payment system; a worsening of the budget deficit caused by reduction of the tax base; and the impossibility of further debt financing of the budget deficit. (4) The Brazilian crisis of 1999, and the Argentinian crisis of 2001, where the result of many years of deficit financing through printing money in Brazil and Argentina led to hyperinflation and to the subsequent default of Argentina on its external debt. (5) The Turkish crisis of 2001. Turkey also experienced hyperinflation as a result of deficit financing, but managed not to default on its external debt obligations.

3 In this study, the nine MPCs also known as FEMIP countries are: Algeria, Egypt, Gaza West Bank, Israel, Jordan, Lebanon, Morocco, Syria and Tunisia.

4 This is a quantitative indicator to gauge the direct expansionary impulse that fiscal policy causes. It is designed to measure the magnitude of the change in the budgetary stance – that is, whether budgets are moving towards expansion or contraction.

5 These are changes in fiscal policy that stimulates aggregate demand (government expenditures and taxes).

6 GCC countries have been directly hit by the financial crisis through a sharp decline in oil prices and revenues. But the impact has been mitigated to a great extent by counter-cyclical monetary and fiscal policies coupled with substantial reserves built up prior to the crisis during the oil boom period 2003–2008.

7 However, Lebanon was able to weather the effects of the crisis through political stability achieved and the consequent inflow of tourists, plus the fact that the majority of commercial banks' assets were in the form of government T-Bills as opposed to investments in structured financial instruments.

8 The steep devaluation of the Rouble had led to significant increases in Russia's external debt and in its related service costs.

9 The relationship between fixed exchange rates, perfect capital mobility and independence of monetary policy (usually referred to as the 'impossible trinity' as the three cannot exist at the same point in time) is considered the main reason for the European Monetary System (EMS) crisis of 1992, as well as the breakdown of the Argentinean currency board, in addition to the 1998 Russian crisis and the 2001 Turkish crisis.

References

Euro monitor International.

International Monetary Fund, *International Financial Statistics*, Various Issues.

International Monetary Fund, *Direction of Trade Statistics*, Various Issues.

International Monetary Fund, *Regional Economic Outlook Report*, Various Issues.

International Monetary Fund, *World Economic Outlook Report*, Various Issues.

World Bank, World Development Indicators Data Base.

Part III

Privatization, labour markets and productivity in the Mediterranean

7 The political economy of privatization in the Maghreb region

How domestic and external factors have shaped the privatization process and outcomes

Mhamed Biygautane and Mohammed Lahouel

1 Introduction

This chapter examines the political economy of privatization in Algeria, Morocco and Tunisia. It uses these three countries as cases to test how political history, macroeconomic considerations and the role of International Development Agencies (IDAs) were for or against the privatization process. Its theoretical framework is based on the Pollitt (1995, 2004) and Haque (2000) arguments that these three factors significantly affect the results of any attempt to introduce new management practices. Algeria, Morocco and Tunisia have experienced similar developmental, economic and, to some extent, political paths. Internal and external political and economic factors have been pivotal in determining the outcomes of liberalization of their economies and their general outcomes. This chapter focuses on privatization as one of the main pillars of these reforms, and traces its evolvement from 1980s till 2007. It will answer these questions: What were the underlying political-economic factors behind the implementation of the privatization process? How instrumental and successful was it in achieving the promised economic growth, efficiency and equity?

The structure of this chapter is as follows: the first section starts with a brief overview of privatization, especially in the context of developing countries. The second section is divided into subsections. The first subsection justifies the rationale behind the selection of these three countries in particular, and how the abovementioned contextual factors led to different outcomes of the privatization program despite the socio-economic and historical similarities that have shaped these countries for long. The second subsection analyzes in detail the contextual factors of each country separately, and the process of privatization and its outcomes. Finally, a discussion and a conclusion follows to demonstrate the positive or negative effects of the contextual factors on the privatization process and justify how they determined the fate of the program and its results in each of the three countries.

2 Privatization: an overview

2.1 Definition and historical development

Hughes (2002) argues that privatization means many things. It could be defined as returning publically owned assets to the private sector or the reduction of government involvement in general; as reduction in both production and provision, subsidies, and regulation; or these four elements all together. Jackson and Price's (1994) definition of privatization is more precise and comprehensive; they argue that the menu of activities that constitute the definition of privatization range from the sale of public assets, deregulation, opening up of state monopolies to greater competition, contracting out and the private provision of public services. The first waves of privatization emerged in the UK during the 1980s as a component of the NPM package, and quickly reached both the developed and developing countries. It has been widely adopted for its positive effects, which are believed to be to increase business efficiency; expose companies to market forces and competition which substantially enhance the quality of products and decrease their prices; and reduce both government spending and the public sector borrowing requirements (Hughes 2002). In the context of this chapter, privatization stands for the sale of all or part of a government's equity in state-owned enterprises (SOEs) to the private sector, or the replacing of SOEs under private management through leases and management contracts (Vuylsteke 1988).

Developing countries caught up with the privatization trend which had been prevalent in the developed countries during the 1990s for a variety of reasons, which to some extent were similar to those in the developed countries. First, they were persuaded that their economic inefficiency, which was caused by the low operating state enterprises, could be improved by enhancing competition (Cook and Kirkpatrick 2003) and introducing new managerial methods. Second, privatization was considered a solution to reduce the continuous losses incurred from poorly performing state enterprises which cost governments heavy fortunes from subsidies. Therefore, privatization was considered a means both to generate revenues to reduce fiscal deficits and also to increase the share of the private sector involvement in the economy (Cook and Kirkpatrick 2003).

Empirical evidence suggests that privatization has had significant positive impacts on the economies of developing countries in terms of ownership performance, macro–micro level performance and the social impact of privatization (Cook and Kirkpatrick 2003). The assessment of previously stated objectives, like expanding the share of the private sector, improving micro–macroeconomic performance and financial profitability, mostly shows positive indicators. Shirley and Walsh (2001) conducted a comprehensive review of 52 studies that looked at the performance of publicly owned enterprises before and after privatization, and they found that 61% of these studies (32) conclude that the performance of these firms improved significantly after they were privatized. At the macro level, a World Bank study (1995) found that there was no significant decline of government spending as share of GDP after privatization during the period from

1987–1991. However, a growing body of literature discusses the adverse impacts of privatization in developing countries where it was implemented disregarding the readiness of the country politically and economically to implement a successful privatization program. Haque (2000) warns that privatization, if not implemented correctly, could lead to increasing poverty and unemployment rates, and foster social inequalities. Moreover, privatization could result in depriving citizens of basic services that were once provided by the state.

2.2 Why these three countries in particular?

Algeria, Morocco and Tunisia are challenging as cases for cross-country analysis. Although the three countries have a number of important characteristics in common, the outcomes of the same reform instrument are markedly different. As background information, the three countries share borders and occupy the same geographical space located in North Africa, both facing the Mediterranean Sea and constituting a bridge between the African and European continents. Given this geographical aspect, the three countries share a rich historical heritage influenced by the Roman occupation of the whole of North Africa, and the French colonization of the three countries from the early 1900s till late 1956, when Morocco and Tunisia gained their independence followed by Algeria in 1962. Independence did not translate into real liberation for the three societies; it only allowed the apparatus of power to be transferred from the hands of the colonial forces to the local authoritative regimes that prevented the countries from flourishing democratically. The three countries have Islam as their official religion, and a mixture of both majority Arab and minority indigenous *Amazigh* populations. They looked at least as much towards Europe as towards the Middle East to define their identities and their geopolitical roles (Mednicoff 2003). All three countries consider Europe their primary trade partner and depend on it heavily for the export of raw materials and agricultural products, and as a valuable source of foreign currency.

2.3 Privatization in Algeria

Algerian political history differs significantly from that of its two North African neighbors. The country was colonized by the French for 150 years – the longest colonization period, compared to the other two countries. Independence was not gained through intense diplomatic dialogues between the leaders of the resistance movements and the French authorities, as was the case in Morocco and Tunisia, but through severe violent confrontations between the Algerian fighters and the French Army (Chourou 2002).

When the war with France ended and the country gained independence in 1962, there were very few civilian politicians in the country and the standing of the army was higher and stronger. There were only two political institutions: the Front de Liberation National (FLN) and the Provisional Government of the Algerian Republic (PGAR). Both parties were formed in 1985 and were made up of members of the National Liberation Army. The members of each party were in disagreement about who should run the country, and actual fights took place between them. The FLN, under the leadership of Ben Bella, managed to rule the country only for two years before being overthrown by Boumediene, who was the Minister of Defense (Chourou 2002). For 30 years the state held firm control over its populations, until 1988, when violent demonstrations took place and succeeded in breaking the tradition of a one-party state and several political parties were founded. However, political instability and the absence of rule of law made the country the most scattered and fragmented in North Africa. The army in Algeria, with the different aspirations and interests of its generals, constitutes the kernel of the government, its ultimate power and the main decision-making mechanism (Cavatorta 2001).

Since independence, the Algerian economy has gone through various stages of formation, each stage completely different from the other and with repercussions that would be borne by the national economy for a long time. In 1962, the country's first President, Ben Bella, defined the country's economic policy, implementing a self-management model in agriculture and industry. The proclaimed objective of this policy was to remove the economic heritage of the French occupation and reliance on its administration of the state affairs, and to prepare the country for handling its own economic interests. However, his regime and policy did not last for long. Boumediene conducted a military coup in 1965, overthrowing the regime of Ben Bella and ending his short-lived economic policy which was replaced by a socialist policy (Ayubi 1995). This policy focused on establishing large state enterprises and investing heavily in the public sector while not allowing for any significant role for the private sector. This gave the Algerian economy of that time the label of 'Algerian socialism' or 'Algerian social-statism' (Boukaraoun 1991). The private sector was the scapegoat in this process, and its role was not revisited until the country faced major economic turbulence that left the government with no choice but to liberalize. As in other natural-resource based economies, long-lasting reliance on the public sector was the result of the nationalization of foreign oil companies (in 1967 in the case of Algeria), predominance of oil revenues and the availability of foreign lending to the state. Hence, the lack of domestic private capital, the lack of a culture that promotes entrepreneurialism and coherent national economic policies that guide the process made the public sector the main player in the Algerian economic arena. As a result, the share of the private sector fell from 153.71% in 1965 to about 11% in 1974 (Boukaraoun 1991). The ensuing economic failure led Algeria to question the relevance of the socialist system and switch to a drastically different approach to stabilize the economy and ensure long-term growth.

The Algerian economy, thus, suffered under the dominance of the public sector from misdirected public investments undertaken especially in the 1970s, when the country benefited from a sharp rise in oil revenues. The reversal of oil and gas prices in 1986 made the situation even worse. The state-owned industrial sector remained a heavy burden for the government because of its low productivity and lack of competitiveness, while the private sector faced difficulties in coping with the implications of the economic reforms embarked on since the late 1980s (Joffe 2002). Even though imports were cut sharply to alleviate the balance of external accounts and services, foreign debt continued to climb to reach $12.5 billion in 1984 and $23.8 billion in 1989 (Boukaraoun 1991). This negatively affected the daily lives of Algerians, as food supplies, which were mostly imported, shrank substantially, causing inflation to rise to an average of 15%. In October 1988, the shortages in food supplies, skyrocketing prices and fewer jobs led to riots in the main Algerian towns. More than 500 people were killed and 1000 injured (Addi 2006). Between 1985 and 1993 unemployment rose to alarmingly high rates that reached 190%, while purchasing power fell by 20% between 1989 and 1995. By 1998, 40% of the population was living below the poverty line (Joffe 2002). Under these troublesome and shaky political and economic atmospheres, privatization was introduced – or rather imposed – on the country in early 1980s by the IMF, as a policy that would rescue the country from its financial crisis and enhance the efficiency and accountability of the state-owned companies, once they were privatized (Addi 2006).

Algeria had no choice but to commence implementing the seeds for economic liberalization that would be carried out by: (1) encouraging the private sector, (2) applying severe austerity programs and (3) launching privatization programs (Boukaraoun 1991). Yet plans for economic liberalization were characterized by fragmentations and strong divisions within the political elite (Dillman 2002). The main objectives behind the privatization process as they were outlined in the 1982 Domestic Private Investment Act were: (1) employment creation, (2) participation in the enlargement of national productive initiatives, (3) complementing the public sector in the transformation of industry and subcontracting activities, and (4) filling the gap in regional development (Boukaroun 1991). The privatization process; however, was marked by confusion and arbitrariness (Dillman 1998), and has been hindered by legislative and administrative confusion as well as strong resistance from the ruling class and civil society. In fact, conflicts emerged between ministries like the Conseil National de Participation de l'Etat (CNPE) and the Conseil National de Privatisation (CNP) because it was unclear to them how many companies were actually being privatized and who their buyers were (Dillman 1998). There were no clear administrative and legislative rules that would define how the process would be carried out and the main players who would evaluate its performance. Furthermore, the forces that opposed privatization outweighed those who supported it. In Parliament, the majority of political parties were opposing privatization – something which blatantly explains the reason behind the slowness in passing privatization laws. Only one of the political parties, the Modernist Islamist Party (MSP), backed by some small entrepreneurs and businessmen with Islamist 'leanings', backed the privatization process outside the hydrocarbon and public service sectors (Werenfels 2002). Resistance also came from elites and workers; public sector managers who united in National Union of Public Entrepreneurs (UNEP) to fiercely oppose privatization (Dahmani 1999, as cited in Werenfels 2002); part of the private sector; and, more importantly, from civil society, which in 2003 managed to oblige the government to suspend the 'Fuel Act' which aimed to provide partial privatization of the giant governmental SONTRAC company. As Werenfels (2002) rightly argues, the only players that seemed to be pushing the process of privatization without hesitation were the external operators like the IMF, the World Bank and the Clubs of Paris.

After the first privatization law was passed in 1995, only the tourist sector underwent the privatization of few companies. Moreover, although four joint ventures with foreign companies were created, they resulted in the breaking up of 1000 small public companies and the loss of 450,000 jobs, reducing the number of public sector employees in the non-oil sector by half. By 1998, the process of privatization had thrown an additional 180,000 people out of their jobs and intensified the economic crisis of the country while benefiting the interests of Algerian commercial shady interests (Joffe 2002).

From 2000 to 2007, Algeria managed to earn only $1.5 billion dollars from privatizing its state-owned companies – which is very insignificant (Privatization Data Base 2011). Demonstrating the lack of interest by foreign capital, CNP head Abderrahmane Mebtoul estimated the rate of successful privatization of local public enterprises at less than 25%, as the private sector was very reluctant to buy companies due to lack of information, high bureaucratic measures, high risk, lack of bank loans and lack of a fiscal amnesty. The mediocre performance and achievement of the privatization program can be attributed to a myriad of factors. Joffe (2002) argues that foreign trade and the pharmaceutical sector have become a major scandal over the way in which privatization was carried out, as it created an oligopoly in which businessmen close to the army were the main beneficiaries for their personal sake. Moreover, foreign investors were discouraged from buying shares from the privatizable deals since they involved bribing officials who controlled the decision-making process related to the privatization programs. The role of the army and members of the elite who did not want to lose state sector rents was considerable in blocking the privatization plan and making it an inevitable failure.

2.4 Privatization in Morocco

Morocco is usually described by Moroccan authorities and legislative documents as a 'constitutional monarchy'. Yet close observation of the King's influence over the decision-making processes will reveal a different reality. The King, the Head of State and the Supreme Representative of the Nation, appoints the Cabinet members and the Prime Minister, and has the authority to dismiss them and even dissolve the legislature on his own personal initiative. The government consists of a bicameral Parliament with a lower house and Chamber of Representatives along with a Chamber of Advisors. Despite this structure of government, which tries to mask itself as a constitutional monarchy, all the decisions are made by the King; the government literally does nothing but to approve them. Desrues and Moyano (2001) stress that although Morocco has a multiparty system, the political parties are marginalized and assigned subordinate positions, allowing the King, instead of the Parliament, to be the only representative of the nation and to monopolize the relations between all the interest groups. Hence, the monarchy becomes 'an institution above the constitution', which is a blatant aspect of an authoritative regime (Desrues and Moyano, 2001).

Morocco's public portfolio was established by the French Protectorate during the period 1912 to 1956, to achieve two goals: to control natural resources, and to provide needed social and institutional infrastructure to the French settlers (Saulniers 1993a). After independence in 1956, Morocco was one of the few newly independent states to embark on a market economy (Maghraoui 2002). In fact, as Owen 1992 argues, unlike other MENA countries, Morocco never adopted the fully state-dominated developmental paradigm. The private sector always existed in the country. The Moroccan economy benefits from a great deal of natural resources: it has fertile agricultural land, significant phosphate reserves and minerals (Morocco is the biggest exporter of phosphate in the world), and fisheries. Morocco is a country where numerous and significant structural reforms have been undertaken since 1980s in the financial sector, in trade, in the fiscal sphere, in infrastructure and in the stock exchange (Cherkaoui and Ben Ali 2007).

The combination of various reasons led the country to adopt privatization as a response to severe economic difficulties. During the 1970s Morocco was the world's leading exporter of phosphates, accounting for almost 30% of total exports (Saulniers 1993b). More importantly, phosphate prices increased by 41% in the period 1973–1977, which brought massive income to the country and encouraged the government to invest more in public enterprises. However, this did not last long. The prices of phosphate dropped significantly and abruptly in 1978, and the state enterprises did not generate the expected outcomes. These two main reasons caused the country to enter a sharp economic recession. The repercussions were devastating following the short-lived economic prosperity the country had experienced in the previous years. From 1983 and 1984 investment as a percentage of GDP fell from 25% to 20% (Pfeifer 1999), and the country had to raise taxes, reduce government spending and curtail imports. Moreover, unemployment increased significantly, and economic growth and living standards fell as well. Moreover, the capital-intensive nature of state investment in the public sector did not result in the expected number of manufacturing jobs (Pfeifer 1999).

By September 1983, Morocco had failed to secure the financing of its budget deficit through borrowing from the international financial markets and had to seek further IMF and World Bank support. However, the economic reform process was not an easy one. It required nine interventions by the IMF between 1980 and 1993, and six official debt-rescheduling operations through the Paris Club with an extra three commercial debt-rescheduling operations through the London Committee. Actually, it was not till early the 2000s that external debt started to fall; between 1980 and the early 1990s it rose from \$20 to \$48.9 billion, and in 2006 it dropped all the way down to \$16.63 billion (IMF 2008). As a percentage of GDP, it fell from 125% to 80% in 1993, and to 53.6% in

2007 (IMF 2008). As Joffe (2010) explains, liberalizing the economy through privatization contributed significantly to the reduction of external debt, and was also a major player in making the Moroccan economy 'one of the most open economies in the region'(p. 11).

King Hassan II's role was instrumental in introducing the privatization program and steering it. In the 1988 spring parliamentary session he dedicated his entire speech to privatization, stressing that privatization 'could modernize the economy, help regional development, increase the well being of people, unleash an entrepreneurial spirit barred by public enterprises and open the economy to the international market' (Saulniers 1993a). The King later emphasized in a speech in front of the Parliament that: 'the decision to transfer to the private sector important parts of state owned enterprises does not stem from a short term vision or imported ideas' (Younis 1996). The conclusions that could be drawn from the Kings' speech are: first, the reform had been carefully considered and its perspective results envisioned; second, it was a long-term vision with long-term aspirations, and not just a prescription to cure the economy temporarily; third, the willingness to implement it came from a strong political will and it was not imposed by external factors.

The main objectives behind the implementation of privatization in Morocco were: (1) to generate income to reduce the government's debt and fiscal deficit; (2) to create a vibrant private sector and foster employment; (3) to attract foreign investment; and (4) to reduce inequality in the distribution of wealth and empower new socio-economic groups within the Moroccan society (Khosrowshahi 1997). The King took steps to establish a strong political basis for the success of the privatization process. The Moroccan Parliament authorized privatization on 11 December 1989, and the privatization law, which provided the framework for the program, was enacted and the government established the Ministry of Privatization. Its role was both as a facilitator of the privatization process and as a watchdog to secure the transparency of the privatization operations and a safe transfer of earned money to the government budget (Khosrowshahi 1997). On July 1991, the King named the Valuation Authority whose role was to oversee the propriety of the evaluation process and set prices for privatizations on the basis of independent evaluations of company's activities (Saulniers 1993b). In September 1991 the King named the Inter-ministerial Transfer Commission, whose role was to provide greater transparency by associating with those ministries concerned with the transfer in each case in all decisions relating to the transfer (Saulniers 1993b). The appointment of this commission completed the privatization structure.

Generally speaking, proceeds from privatization have been substantial. From 1993 to 2005, Morocco accumulated more than $6.3 billion. Naceur *et al.* (2007) argue that the 'bulk of privatization' in Morocco was achieved after 2000, as it produced 78% of revenues from the privatization program. From the year 2000 to 2007, massive privatization actions took place in different sectors ranging from telecommunications to infrastructure to finance. In 2000, the Moroccan government transferred 35% of the capital of Maroc Telecom to Vivendi

Universal and gained $2.1 billion, which was considered a great success by international standards (Privatization Data Base 2011). In 2004, 14.9% of the capital of the same company was sold on the Stock Exchange for $800 million, followed by another sale of a 16% share, again to Vivendi Universal, for $1.2 billion (Privatization Data Base 2011).

Yet in terms of the social impact of the privatization process, the government, headed by the King, favored and enforced the involvement of the domestic Fassi elite which traditionally held strong connections with the Alaouit Royal family (Joffe 2009, Khosrowshahi 1997). Several state-owned companies ended up in the hands of those who had strong ties with the palace and had access to the needed funds. As Hibou (2005) argues, the privatization process in Morocco did not pose any challenge to the *Makhzan*; on the contrary, it served its interests and strengthened the ties between the monarchy and its loyal elites: 'In Morocco, the privatization of state run companies has reinforced the *Makhzanian* modes of government in the economic domain, which entail the manipulation of vagueness and uncertainty between rules and incompatible conflicting norms' (p. 87). Implementation of the privatization program was therefore biased towards specific interest groups, while the socio-economic objectives that were announced at the outset of the process turned out to be only political slogans (Najem 2001).

2.5 Tunisia

Since gaining independence in 1956, the country had been ruled by President Bourguiba. He was a key figure in gaining independence from the French, but ended up as an enlightened dictator. He implemented a highly centralized and personalized system of governance where he appointed himself President for life and amended the Tunisian constitution to give him this right (Mednicoff 2003). However, in 1987 Zine 'Abidin Bin Ali, a military figure, overthrew Bourguiba in a 'medical-military coup', and remained the absolute ruler until the popular uprising and Jasmine Revolution of January 2011. Bin Ali initially showed good will and determination to transform Tunisia into a democratic country, yet only a few years after his rule began his governance started to take a different path. His regime gradually became more repressive than the previous, which was a source of grave disappointment to the Tunisians and to the international community as well. Although the Parliament allows the plurality of political parties, its role in the political system is merely cosmetic. The year 1994 witnessed the entrance of opposition parties to the Parliament for the first time since the country's independence, which was a result of the President's decision to allocate 20% of the seats for the 'opposition'. However, this was just for form, as in reality the opposition parties had no say in the decision-making process, which was strictly monopolized by the President.

The centralized form of the Tunisian political structure would be reflected in its macroeconomic orientation, policies and direction. The Tunisian public sector dates back to independence in 1956, when Tunisia embarked on a process of decolonization and transfer of the French private companies to the state (Saghir

1993, Ayubi 1995). This allowed the government to inherit and acquire facilities of the infrastructure, like transportation, railways, ports, telecommunications and banking. The dominant role of the state in guiding the economy and fostering the role of the public sector would be the ultimate result of this process of transformation from the colonial acquisitions to the state. Tunisia adopted an interventionist policy known as '*dirigisme planifié*', whereby the central role is given to the public sector and the role of the private sector is confined to small-scale services (Al-Mahjub 1989, as cited in Ayubi 1995). The state took control of natural sources, notably phosphates and hydrocarbons, and finance and banking before it started investing in tourism, textiles and even agriculture (Saghir 1993, Pfeifer 1999).

However, the years of positive economic performance would end as Tunisia entered a phase of crisis similar to its neighbors, for both internal and external reasons (Pfeifer 1999). The inefficiency of the public sector was one of the main factors behind this declining performance. From 1977 to 1981 the public sector made significant losses that reached 20% of government outlays, and could not meet its tax payments and social security obligations (Grissa 1991). Moreover, the poor agricultural season of 1986 and the sharp decline in tourism added more pressure to the already ailing economy. The difficulties were compounded by the adverse effects of the recession that was taking place in Western Europe on Tunisia's exports, and the very stringent conditions and high interest rates of borrowing from the international financial markets and financial institutions. Added to these unfavorable international developments were the sharp declines in the prices of oil and phosphate. Petroleum was then a major source of export earnings, accounting for about 55% of all exports during the 1970s.

The ailing economy and the increasing budget deficit and external debt forced the government to change economic policies. The IMF was the destination of Tunisia for a standby agreement in 1986, and the country then went to the World Bank as well for a structural adjustment program. The remedies were reducing public expenditures in order to curtail the budget deficit, gradual removal of trade barriers, and privatization of state-owned companies. These objectives were spelled out in the VIIth Five-Year Plan (1987–1991), which stipulated the liberalization of external trade, the removal of investment restrictions and the promotion of the private sector. Yet, according to Pfeifer (1999), the structural adjustment programs led to three significant changes in the Tunisian economic model: (1) an unequal distribution of costs and benefits; (2) access for Tunisia to external finance; and (3) higher exposure of the Tunisian economy to the international trade system and markets. A significant feature of the adjustment was the sharp reduction in government subsidies and public spending. Another significant effect was the rise in unemployment, which reached 15% of the labor force in 1990.

The objectives of privatization were to enhance the efficiency, profitability and productivity of ill-performing public entities, and to alleviate the burden on government budget. The privatization program was decentralized at its beginning, and was centralized in its later years of implementation. As Belev (2001) argues, during the period 1987–1989 there were three commissions responsible for privatization process. The first was an inter-ministerial commission called the

'*Commission d'Assainissement et de Restructuration des Entreprises à Participation Publique*', chaired by the Prime Minister. The main function of this was to approve the proposed privatizable companies. The second was an interdepartmental commission which was headed by the 'Director General of Participations' and included representatives of the Prime Ministry; its main function was to coordinate the activities of the agencies involved in the privatization program. The third was a technical commission headed by high-level government officials who had the responsibility to advise privatizable companies and to assess the social and economic risks involving each transaction. However, all this organizational structure did not result in the desired outcomes. Its complex nature made it difficult to coordinate and to put processes in motion, as it was time-consuming and bureaucratically demanding. Hence, in 1993 the Ministry of Planning and Regional Development was assigned to manage the implementation of the privatization program as a whole (Belev 2001).

The government faced strong resistance from many sources, especially from labor unions. The Minister of Social Affairs and the General Inspectorate of Labor played a significant role in alleviating the consequences of privatization on labor, especially the shedding of redundant workers (Grissa 1991, Saghi 1993). The Tunisian government stressed that employees of state-owned enterprises would have priority in buying shares from the privatized companies, and their rights would be protected in case they had to be laid off. Hence, by 1989, of the 7509 of employees in the privatized state-owned companies, 3039 kept their jobs (around 40%), 2102 were transferred to other state-owned companies, and 324 received severance payments (4%) which were determined by the length of the employee within the organization, ranging from one to three months' salary for each 12 months served in the public sector. Only 103 workers were laid off (1.5%) (Belev 2001).

The process of privatization started with the divestiture of loss-making companies especially in the tourism, transport, food and construction sectors. The state made around $134 million from 1987 to 1994 by selling 48 state-owned companies, and a 20% share in its air company, Tunisair. In 1998, the privatization of large and profitable companies started. Between the years 2000 and 2008, the main transaction that took place was the sale of Tunisie Telecom (35% of its shares) to a United Arab Emirates company (Privatization Data Base 2011). These mediocre results could be explained by many factors; resistance from workers and labor unions was not a destabilizing element, as were others that will be further explained in this chapter. In fact, Tunisia had a weak entrepreneurial community and a culture where the private sector did not have the required financial capacity and was not able to play a significant role in the national economy. Its reliance on the government and its subsidies can be justified by the fact that in 1987 several privatized companies went bankrupt or had to shut down due to their incapability of surviving in a new business environment where the public sector no longer provided subsidies (Ayubi 1999, Saghir 1993). Lack of skilled staff who could take over the public companies and manage them was a major destabilizing factor for the success of the privatization program. Moreover, Tunisia had the smallest stock exchange market in the region and in developing countries – an element that prevented systematic and successful transfer of shares from the public ownership to the hands of private investors and stakeholders. Another obstacle was the issue of patronage and the 'state bourgeoisie' who tried to stay away from taking market risks and preferred to profit from the opportunities publicly owned companies provided them. According to a Price Waterhouse report (1989), Tunisian business owners are not risk-takers and strongly prefer to deal with their family members or business associates, being unlikely to invest with strangers, which was a major barrier towards strengthening the role of private sector entities.

3 Discussion and conclusion

The main objective of this chapter was to analyze the effects of various contextual factors, political history, party politics, macroeconomic consideration and role of IDAs on the success or failure of the implementation of privatization in Algeria, Morocco and Tunisia. The question the chapter addresses is not whether or not privatization was the right tool to rescue the ill-functioning economy of these three countries, but whether these countries had the political, economic and developmental requirements to efficiently benefit from privatization programs. Privatization proved to be both successful and unsuccessful; its outcome is primarily contingent on the availability of political will, processes, and careful implementation and auditing of the whole process. The first question that comes to mind after the presentation of the achievements of the privatization programs under the political, economic and foreign factors is: Was the Maghreb region ready and mature enough to implement a privatization program – did it have the necessary prerequisites to operate successfully? It is undeniable that the period of the 1960s and 1970s was that of *etatisme* and bureaucratic expansion while that of the 1980s and 1990s was one of liberalization and privatization, although the transition from one to the other did not take a smooth and slow path. It was dictated by the burden of financial difficulties and urged by external players, mainly the World Bank and the IMF.

The analysis undertaken in this chapter supports the decisive role of these factors and their effect on any reform initiative. At the time of introducing privatization in Algeria, the political spectrum was characterized by fragmentation, instability, conflicts and constant disruptions. These aspects made any attempt at change impossible, as there were many influential bodies and vested interests in the decision-making process, ranging from the military to the state and the administration. Each of these had its own agenda and list of priorities it wanted to protect for its own sake. When privatization was imposed by the IMF and the World Bank, the army, who had a strong presence and influence in the country, was the first to resist the change as it would lose the rents it obtained from public companies. The absence of strong political leadership hindered the process of privatization in the country. Public officers in Algeria and the army generals had a high stake in the rents derived from oil and gas revenues. Therefore, privatization would constitute a threat towards securing the continuity of these substantial incomes and profits. In Morocco, although its political history had been characterized by the authoritative rule of the King and his centralized use of power, the country enjoyed substantial political stability and leadership in the region and was considered one of the safest as well. The strong political leadership embodied in the person of the King and his strong hold on the political parties enabled the implementation of privatization to be smooth and effective. However, despite the substantial economic gains of the privatization process, its outcomes served mainly the loyal elites of the Palace rather than benefiting the overall population of Morocco. Thus, it is hard to prove that the program contributed to empowering the middle class and giving them equal opportunities and gains from the program. Similarly, privatization in Tunisia was supported by the President and his government. The business environment, however, was not sufficiently strong financially and the human capital was not equipped with the necessary skills to run the newly privatized firms or to operate without the support of the public sector and its subsidies. Hence, none of these countries, in fact, can be considered as a success story in harvesting the financial and economic gains that a successful privatization program provides as is the case in some developed countries. The political landscape in these three countries was headed by leaders who were strongly tied to their close elite families and were more concerned about their personal gains rather than those of the general populace. Moreover, the macroeconomic conditions that urged privatization of the public sector entities made the program an end rather than a means of improving the efficiency and performance of these companies. Hence, the main objective was to sell the companies, and not to make sure that the transition from the public to the private sector was well monitored and scrutinized to avoid adverse repercussions for both the companies and their employees. Also, the role of the IDAs was an important factor behind these results of the privatization program. Their familiarity with the social, economic and cultural landscapes of these countries was limited, and their main target was to cut public spending and transform companies to the hands of the private sector. They failed to look closely at the process and ascertain that transparency, equal opportunities and the benefits of privatization were shared by the whole populace and not just by few influential political and military figures, as was the case mainly with Morocco and Algeria.

Before implementing any reform instrument, it is imperative to examine its conformity with the existing contextual factors of any given country. Understanding the context, its strengths and weaknesses would at least make policy-makers aware of the challenges they need to address when they implement a novel policy. In the case of Algeria, Morocco and Tunisia, the different points where the three countries initiated their reforms could not be better expressed than by Pollitt's (2004) words: '...countries start from different places with different capacities and implement changes that may not suit their contextual setting' (p, 8). The significance of the contextual factors is also emphasized by Pollitt (1995) and Haque (2000) when they argue that the reforms are mainly determined by the 'characteristics of the political and administrative systems in place'.

References

Addi, L. (2006) 'The political contradictions of Algerian economic reforms', *Review of African Political Economy*, 108: 207–217.

Ayubi, N. (1995) *Etatism versus Privatization: The Changing Role of the State in 9 Arab Countries*. Economic Research Forum.

Belev, B. (2001) 'Privatization in Egypt and Tunisia: Liberal outcomes and/or liberal policies?', *Mediterranean Politics*, 6(2): 68–103.

Boukaraoun, H. (1991) 'The privatization process in Algeria', *The Developing Economies*, XXIX(2): 89–124.

Cavatorta, F. (2001) 'Geopolitical challenges to the success of democracy in North Africa: Algeria, Tunisia and Morocco', *Democratization*, 8(4): 175–194.

Cherkaoui, M. and Ben Ali, D. (2007) 'The political economy of growth in Morocco', *The Quarterly Review of Economics and Finance*, 46: 741–761.

Chourou, B. (2002). 'The challenge of democracy in North Africa', *Democratization*, 7(1): 17–39.

Cook, P. and Kirkpatrick, C. (2003) 'Assessing the impact of privatisation in developing countries', in D. Parker and D. Saal (eds), *International Handbook on Privatization*, Cheltenham: Edward Elgar.

Desrues, T. and Moyano, E. (2001) 'Social change and political transition in Morocco', *Mediterranean Politics*, 6(1): 21–47.

Dillman, B. (1998) 'The political economy of structural adjustment in Tunisia and Algeria', *The Journal of North African Studies*, 3(3): 1–24.

Economist Intelligence Unit (2009) 'Morocco economy: privatization portfolio shrinks'.

Grissa, A. (1991) 'The Tunisian state enterprises and privatization policy', in W. Zartman (ed.), *Tunisia, The Political Economy of Reform*, Boulder, CO: Lynne Rienner Publishers.

Haque, S. (2000) 'Privatization in developing countries: formal causes, critical reasons, and adverse mpacts', in A. Farazmand (ed.), *Privatization or Public Enterprise Reform?* Westport, CT: Greenwood Press, pp. 217–238.

Hibou, B. (2005) 'The privatization of the state: North Africa in comparative perspective', in K. Schlichte (ed.), *The Dynamics of the States: The Formation and Crises of State Domination*, Aldershot: Ashgate.

Hughes, O. (2002) *Public Management and Administration: An Introduction*, New York, NY: Palgrave Macmillan.

International Monetary Fund. Available at: www.imf.org.

Jackson. P.M. and Price, C. (1994) *Privatization and Regulation: A Review of the Issues*, London: International Thomson Press.

Joffe, G. (1991) 'The political economy of privatization in Morocco', *Moroccan Studies*, 1.

Joffe, G. (2002) 'The role of violence within the Algerian economy', *Journal of North African Studies*, 7(1): 1–20.

Joffe, G. (2009) 'Morocco's reform process: wider implications', *Mediterranean Politics*, 14(2): 151–164.

Khosrowshahi, C. (1997) 'Privatization in Morocco: politics of development', *Middle East Journal*, 51(2): 242–255.

Maghraoui., M.A. (2002) 'Depoliticization in Morocco', *Journal of Democracy*, 13(4): 24–32.

Mednicoff, M.D. (2003) 'Think locally – act globally? Cultural framing and human rights movements in Tunisia and Morocco', *The International Journal of Human Rights*, 7(3): 72–102.

Naceur, S., Ghazouani S and Omran, M. (2007) 'The performance of newly privatized firms in selected MENA countries: the role of ownership structure, governance and liberalization policies', *International Review of Financial Analysis*, 16: 332–353.

Najem, P.T. (2001) 'Privatization and state in Morocco: nominal objectives and problematic realities', *Mediterranean Politics*, 6(2): 51–67.

Owen, R. (1992) State, Power and Politics in the Making of the Modern Middle East, London: Routledge.

Pfeifer, K. (1999) 'Parameters of economic reform in North Africa', *Review of North African Political Economy*, 26(82): 441–454.

Pollitt, C. (1995) 'Justification by works or by faith? Evaluating the new public management', *Evaluation*, 9(2): 133–154.

Pollitt, C. (2004) 'From there to here, from now till then: buying and borrowing public management reforms'. Conference paper presented at the Clad International Conference, Madrid, 3 November 2004.

Price Waterhouse (1989) *Privatization: Learning the Lessons from the UK Experience*, London: Author.

Privatization Data Base, World Bank Group (2011) Available at: http: //rru.worldbank.org/Privatization/.

Saghir, J. (1993) 'Privatization in Tunisia', CFS Discussion Paper Series.

Saulniers, A. (1993a) 'Privatization in Morocco', in *Privatization, A Global Perspective*, London: Routledge, pp. 293–318.

Saulniers, A. (1993b) 'Privatization in Morocco', in *Constraints and Impacts of Privatization*, London: Routledge, pp. 210–225.

Shirley, M. and Walsh, P. (2001) 'Public versus private ownership: the current state of the debate', Washington, DC: The World Bank.

Sobel, R. (1999) *The Pursuit of Wealth*, New York, NY: McGraw Hill.

Vuylsteke, C. (1988) *Techniques of Privatization of State Owned Enterprises*, Vol. I, *Methods and Implementation*, Washington, DC: World Bank Technical Paper No. 88.

Werenfels, I. (2002) 'Obstacles to privatization of state-owned industries in Algeria: the political economy of distributive conflict', *The Journal of North African Studies*, 7(1): 1–28.

Younis, T. (1996) 'Privatization: a review of policy and implementation in selected Arab countries', *International Journal of Public Sector Management*, 9(3): 18.

8 The impact of trade policy on wages

Evidence from Egypt

Mona Said

1 Introduction

Although it is now well accepted that growth constitutes the most important channel through which poverty can be affected, the relationship between trade and growth remains empirically elusive, leaving little hope that a direct link between trade and poverty can be further established.[1] A more fruitful approach to studying the impact of macroeconomic and trade policy changes on poverty is therefore to examine their differential effect on labor market rewards of various income categories in the earning distribution, particularly those classified as low-waged or poor. This chapter investigates the effect of trade reform on the incomes of low-waged and poor workers in Egypt over the period of rapid trade liberalization between 1998 and 2006. The availability of trade openness and protection measures at the two-digit industry levels, together with a rich panel of labor market data, allows us to accomplish this task for the manufacturing sector in Egypt.

Limiting this study to the manufacturing sector, it can be argued that we might be missing the bulk of the non-waged poor concentrated in rural and agricultural settings. Yet our analysis is still informative about the potential for trade reforms to change the income and poverty status of the groups of workers in Egypt that are most likely to be directly affected by those measures, namely skilled and unskilled wage workers employed in the manufacturing industry. It also allows us to examine the interaction between various industry characteristics (including trade openness) and individual characteristics (such as education and labor market experience) in influencing incomes of the poor and low-waged workers over a period of rapid trade liberalization.

2 Review of related literature

The relationship between trade and wages follows theoretically from the Hecksher–Ohlin–Samuelson (HOS) framework. According to HOS, trade will affect the relative payments to factors of production by changing relative prices of commodities. A reduction in tariffs, for example, would lower a commodity's relative price, which would lower the demand for factors of production used in that sector. If the sector happens to be labor-abundant, then the decline in prices will disproportionately lower the demand for labor and hence lower their wages. Hence, trade liberalization would lead to increasing inequality between factors of production. However, this model does not predict that trade will alter industry-specific returns since it assumes perfectly competitive markets with perfect factor mobility across uses. These assumptions do not seem to be valid for many developing countries, where markets are characterized by widespread imperfections and factors of production are extremely immobile. The short-run Immobile Factors model or the medium-run Ricardo–Viner model that assume constrained factor mobility across sectors are arguably more suited to the situation in developing countries with extreme labor and product market rigidities, such as Egypt.

The Immobile Factors model assumes that all factors are completely immobile in the short run. It predicts that tariff reductions and increased trade will lead to a decline in the earnings of factors in the import-competing sectors and an increase in earnings in the export sector. Similarly, workers in sectors that experience a larger decline in tariffs, and hence a larger decline in the price of their output, will face a decline in their wages relative to the economy-wide average, while those in sectors with smaller tariff reduction will face a relative welfare gain. The Ricardo–Viner model (sometimes referred to as the Specific Factors model) is a middle-ground model which allows one factor to be mobile across sectors while the other one is sector-specific. In this case, the factor specific to the import competing industry will lose from lower tariffs, that specific to the export-competing industry will gain from freer trade, while the effect on the real wages of labor (the mobile factor) will be ambiguous depending on the consumer's preferences for the two goods. The real wage will rise in terms of the imported good, which is now cheaper, but will fall in terms of the exportable good, which is now more expensive.

Several studies have attempted to test the relationship between trade reform, employment and relative wages for both developing and advanced economies. For the United States, Revenga (1992), Katz and Freeman (1992) and Gaston and Trefler (1994) provide some of the first attempts to measure the effect of the expansion of trade in the 1980s on industry wages. These studies point to a negative relation between tariff protection and industry wages or wage premia.

For developing countries, Hanson and Harrison (1999) used firm panel data to investigate whether the rising skilled–unskilled wage gap in Mexico in the 1980s could be explained by trade reforms. They did not find a significant correlation between producer price changes and relative white-collar employment. However, they found that reductions in tariffs were much lower in skill-intensive sectors, which were originally less protected than the low-skilled sectors. This in turn meant that reductions in prices in the low-skilled sectors were larger, which would explain the increase in wage differentials. In another paper, Harrison and Hanson (1999) found no significant relation between the ratio of white-collar to blue-collar workers' average annual wages and the level and change of industry tariffs and import licenses in the manufacturing sector between 1984 and 1990.

Revenga (1997), using the same firm panel data for Mexico, found that tariff reductions were associated with a decline in both employment and wages. Currie and Harrison (1997) investigated the impact of trade reform on wages and employment in Morocco during the 1980s. They found no significant effect of tariff reduction on employment or wages in private sector firms. Government-owned enterprises, on the other hand, responded to tariff reductions by raising employment and lowering wages.

All of these studies relied on data that did not include information on worker characteristics. This does not allow for separating the effect of the reduction in trade barriers on wages from that on returns to education. Feliciano (2001) is one of the first studies that used individual-level data to study the impact of trade reform on wages. She follows a two-step procedure, first estimating the wage equation for each individual industry observation, as a function of individual characteristics such as years of schooling, experience, marital status, gender, enterprise (public/private) and industry. Next, she estimates the relationship between this calculated industry wage differential and measures of industry protection levels (tariffs and license coverage, as well as trade openness, producer prices and import penetration). Her results indicate that reductions in tariffs, changes in producer prices and import penetration did not have a significant effect on industry wage differentials. She found that the reduction in import licenses decreased relative wages of workers in reformed manufacturing industries by 2%. Her results also indicate no significant effect of trade reform on employment or hours of work. Moreover, her evidence suggests that trade reform was associated with greater wage dispersion and a decrease in the relative wages of skilled workers.

Attanasio, Goldberg and Pavcnik (2004) investigated the effects of tariff reductions in Columbia in the 1980s and 1990s on wage inequality. They also use a two-stage estimation technique similar to that of Feliciano to calculate the effect of tariff reductions on industry wage premiums. Their results indicate a positive and significant effect of both tariff levels and first differences in tariffs on industry wage premiums. These results also point to an economically significant effect, with a 50% reduction in tariffs being associated with 6% decrease in the industry wage premium in that sector. They also find that the sectors that experienced the highest reduction in tariff protection and hence in industry wage premiums were also the same sectors with the highest share of unskilled workers and the lowest wages. Another interesting finding of Attanasio *et al.* (2004) is related to the increased rate of informal employment in Columbia following trade reforms. They found that reductions in tariffs are associated with an increase in informal employment, although this effect was more pronounced before Columbia implemented labor market reforms that made it less costly to fire workers.

Dutta (2007) performed a similar analysis for wages in India's manufacturing sector following large-scale trade reforms in the 1980s and 1990s. She calculated industry wage premiums, after accounting for observable worker characteristics and potential selection bias, as the difference between the wage received by the average worker in a given industry and that received by the average worker in the economy. She then used these wage premiums to determine the effect of trade reform. She found a positive and significant effect of tariffs on wage premia, and of changes in tariffs on changes in wage premia. This provides evidence that wages declined significantly following the reduction in protection levels in the affected industries. Acosta and Gasparini (2007) investigated the effects of capital accumulation and trade liberalization on rising wage inequality in Argentina during the 1990s. They found that the capital accumulation effect on rising inequality was larger than the trade liberalization effect as measured by import penetration. However, they did not use a direct measure of trade liberalization as embodied in tariff rates. Import penetration rates and other trade flow measures are arguably endogenous since they depend on factor costs, and hence most studies cited above rely on tariffs and changes in tariffs as the main measure of trade policy changes while import and export measures are used in robustness check regressions with tariffs.

Other studies have relied on comparing the degree of wage inequality and employment effects on various groups of workers using a 'before–after' approach, not controlling specifically for the effect of trade reform (Robertson, 2000; Green *et al.*, 2001; and El-Hamidi, 2008), to name a few). The obvious drawback with these studies is that many other policy changes typically accompany trade reform, such as public sector downsizing, privatization, structural adjustment, etc., and unless direct measures of trade reform are included in the analysis clear-cut conclusions about the effects of *trade reform* per se cannot be made with any degree of confidence.

3 Trade reform in Egypt

Although Egypt has taken a gradual approach to trade liberalization, the once highly restrictive trade regime has been reversed, from the initiation of reforms in 1986 to the beginning of WTO agreements in 1994/1995 and the signing of several multi- and unilateral trade agreements in the mid-1990s – for example, COMESA, TIFA and PAFTA. The Egyptian maximum tariff fell from 100% to 70%. It then continued to fall, reaching 40% in 1998. The next two years saw a slight increase to 43% in the most highly protected industries, including textiles, clothing, leather products, cars, transportation, furniture, glass and pottery and beverages, while cotton ginning has consistently been negatively protected (Refaat, 2003).

Having pledged to be in full compliance with WTO commitments, Egypt has had a policy of removing non-tariff barriers and replacing them with tariffs. In 1998, Egypt reduced the maximum tariff rate for most imports from a high of 50% to 40%. Refaat (2003) calculated the unweighted average tariff rates and the import-weighted average. Both display a significant fall between 1994 and 1998, when the unweighted average fell from 25.9% to 19.9%. After a slight rise up to 21.5% in 2000 it declined to 20.4% in 2002, showing that trade reform slowed after 2000. Import-weighted averages follow the same trend, but at a lower level, indicating that imports are skewed toward low-tariff goods. In addition to tariffs, Egyptian customs charges a fee, for service and inspection, of 1% on all imports plus an additional fee of 2% on goods that are subject to tariffs between 5% and 29%, or 3% on goods that are subject to tariffs of 30% or more. During the 1990s, Egypt passed legislation protecting its industries. This includes only allowing cars to be imported in their year of manufacture, increasing the local component requirement for car assembly to 45% from 40%, and encouraging government bodies to buy domestic products.

Despite concerted efforts to liberalize a highly restrictive trade regime since the early 1990s, Egypt's tariffs remain relatively high, especially when compared to other developing countries with large internal markets and diversified industrial economies. Most manufacturing sectors continue to be highly protected, mainly via a high and escalating tariff structure. Between 1998 and 2005 the simple average tariff rate for manufacturing fell from 27.6% to 21.1%, while that for agricultural products increased from 64.9% to 66.4%. Since WTO accession in 1995, Egypt's commitments have been more or less to bind tariff rates at levels that in many cases have exceeded existing levels. While 98% of Egypt's tariff lines are bound, the average bound rate fell from 45% in 1998 to 38.6% in 2005. The average bound rate on agricultural products stands at 92.2% in contrast to 29% for non-agricultural products (WTO, 2005).

Table 8.1 shows data regarding tariff reductions over the period 1997–2005. The average tariff decline was from 18.6% to 12.3% over this period. The biggest declines were in motorized vehicle manufacturing, rubber products and paper manufacturing. On average, the import penetration index did not change substantially or declined for other industries over this period; however, it has increased for coke and petroleum products, leather goods, motorized vehicles and furniture manufacturing.

The most notable is the increase in the export promotion index from an average of 10.2 to 14.4 for coke and petroleum, non-metallic minerals, and metallic products. Moreover, export promotion also increased in food and beverage and furniture manufacturing, followed by office equipment and chemical products.

4 Data and descriptive statistics

The empirical analysis is based on the recent Egypt Labor Market Panel Survey (ELMPS 06), a follow-up survey to the Egypt Labor Market Survey of 1998 (ELMS 98) that was carried out by the Economic Research Forum (ERF) in cooperation with CAPMAS.[2] ELMS 1998 was carried out on a nationally representative sample of 4816 households. The ELMPS 2006 sample consists of a total of 8349 households. The data provide information on monthly earnings, worker characteristics (such as age, education, gender, marital status, occupation, industry, and sector of employment), as well as region of residence. The working sample is restricted to manufacturing sector workers between the ages of 15 and 65 who report positive monthly earnings. Hourly real wages are calculated as the sum of wages earned in the reference month from primary jobs,

Table 8.1 Measures of trade reform in Egypt 1997–2005

ISICR 3		*1997*			*2005*			*Change 1997–2005*		
		wghtd avg tariff	*import_ penet*	*export_ orient*	*wghtd avg tariff*	*import_ penet*	*export_ orient*	*tariff*	*import_ penetr*	*export oriental*
15	Food and Beverage	21.89	26.88	3.60	12.62	25.02	11.48	9.26	−1.86	788
16	Tobacco Manufacturing	19.92	6.37	0.01	21.72	3.96	0.04	−1.80	−2.41	0.04
17	Textiles Manufacturing	24.03	14.76	32.31	13.87	10.54	19.74	10.16	−4.22	−12.57
18	Garment Manufacturing	39.71	1.73	30.29	37.00	2.76	19.96	2.71	1.03	−10.32
19	Leather Goods Manufacturing	37.15	19.89	32.30	30.76	33.19	26.18	6.39	13.30	−6.12
20	Wood Product (except Furniture) Manufacturing	11.10	91.76	6.00	5.85	92.40	9.27	5.24	0.64	3.27
21	Paper Manufacturing Publishing and Printing	16.94	52.98	2.43	5.11	34.63	6.53	11.83	−18.36	4.10
22	Manufacturing Coke and Petroleum	8.94	11.83	3.35	7.62	17.15	2.59	1.32	5.33	−0.76
23	Products Manufacturing	16.30	1.86	1.42	2.52	33.03	49.25	13.78	31.17	47.83
24	Chemical Product	11.02	46.47	11.20	9.44	47.41	16.14	1.58	0.95	4.94
25	Rubber Product	26.49	41.29	11.99	11.46	31.44	8.58	15.03	−9.86	−3.41
26	Non-metallic Mineral Manufacturing	19.11	14.89	8.82	15.93	9.45	22.05	3.18	−5.44	13.23
27	Basic Metal Manufacturing	10.64	44.77	15.41	3.03	27.34	15.5	7.61	−17.44	0.14
28	Metallic Product (Except Machinery and Equipment)	23.36	40.60	10.71	13.48	41.16	24.58	9.88	0.55	13.87
29	Machinery and Equipment (Others) Manufacturing	10.48	67.88	1.50	7.81	58.34	4.69	2.67	−9.54	3.19
30	Office Equipment and Computer Manufacturing	4.73	100.11	–	0.22	95.27	7.53	4.51	−4.83	7.53
31	Electrical Equipment (Others) Manufacturing	18.36	48.06	1.68	8.20	39.28	5.02	10.16	−8.78	3.33
32	Radio, Television and Communication Equipment Manufacturing	8.32	63.70	0.44	1.30	60.87	3.00	7.02	−2.83	2.56
33	Medical Equipment	7.67	85.41	2.78	4.98	81.02	3.48	2.69	−4.39	0.70
34	Motorized Vehicle	39.80	50.54	4.14	23.38	59.43	6.16	16.42	8.88	2.02
35	Other Transport Equipment Manufacturing	12.28	45.80	0.41	13.55	40.12	5.96	−1.27	−5.68	5.4
36	Furniture Manufacturing	20.91	53.25	33.47	20.47	74.99	48.41	0.44	21.74	14.94
	Average	18.60	42.31	10.20	12.29	41.76	14.37	6.31	−0.55	4.17

adjusted for average number of work days per month and average hours per day. For comparability purposes, wages of 1998 are inflated to 2006 Egyptian pounds using the consumer price index (the inflation factor is 1.43 from 1998 to 2006).

Moreover, to measure household income poverty for the ELMS 98 and ELMPS 06 household samples, two additional datasets are used in this study: the 1999/2000 Household Income and Expenditure Consumption Survey (HIECS 99) and the 2004/2005 Household Income and Expenditure Consumption Survey (HIECS 04). Both datasets were collected by CAPMAS. The HIECSs are household budget surveys that contain information regarding consumption expenditures on more than 550 items of goods and services. These budget surveys are generally considered the major source of information on household income and expenditure in Egypt. We use the methodology laid out in Assaad and Roushdy (2006), which consists of combining information from the HIECSs and LMSs to estimate the poverty status of households in the labor market surveys.

To identify poor earners, a low earning line is computed using the official national poverty lines listed in Table 8.2.[3] First, the individual regional specific poverty lines are converted to real terms using the consumer price index (taking 2006 as the base year). Second, the per-capita region-specific poverty lines are scaled up by the regional median ratio of household members to working-age employed household members to account for the fact that each worker's earnings are used to support not only him/herself but also other non-working members of their household. For the sake of comparability and to abstract from changes in dependency ratios that may have occurred during the 1998–2006 period, the 2006 low earning line is used to identify low earners in both the ELMS 1998 and ELMPS 06 samples. The monthly per-capita regional specific poverty lines and the corresponding low earning lines are shown in Table 8.3.

Table 8.4 presents summary descriptive statistics of variables used in regressions. As noted in the introduction, the sample of estimation is limited to wage workers currently employed in the manufacturing sector. All figures are properly weighted to reflect the population distribution. A comparison of 1998 and 2006 figures reveals that on average, real hourly wages increased, whereas all three measures of job quality recorded a marked decline over this period.

As for the explanatory variables, the share of public enterprises in the manufacturing sector in Egypt has declined from 30% to 20%, and this shift coincides with a slight decline in average years of experience (from 18 to 16.8), a more notable reduction in the share of workers with a university degree (from 8% to 12%), and a substantial increase in the proportion of workers with a vocational secondary degree (from 26.5% to 35%). Figures in both years reflect a high concentration of manufacturing activity in greater Cairo and rural Lower Egypt, together accounting for over 50% of employment in the sector.

As for trade-related and other industry variables, the average figures indicate a 6% decline in average tariffs, a 15% increase in export orientation and hardly any change in import penetration. Manufacturing industries also on average become more feminized, unionized and staffed by an increasing portion of white-collar and more skilled (secondary degrees and above) workers.

Table 8.2 Estimated per-capita region-specific poverty lines (L.E. per year) for 1999/2000 and 2004/2005.

Region	*Lower poverty line (LE. per capita per year)*		*Governorates*
	1999/2000	*2004/2005*	
Metropolitan	1109	1453	Cairo, Alexandria, Port Said, Suez
Lower Egypt Urban	1015	1430	Damiette, Dakhalia, Sharkia, Kalyoubia, Kafr El-Shaikh, Gharbia,
Lower Egypt Rural	978	1429	Menoufia, Behera, Ismaila
Upper Egypt Urban	1031	1416	Giza, Beni-Suef, Fayoum, Menia, Assyout, Suhag, Quena, Aswan
Upper Egypt Rural	964	1408	

Source: Asaad and Roushdy (2006).

Table 8.3 Real monthly per-capita region-specific poverty lines and real monthly region-specific low earning line by region (in 2006 L.E.)

Region	*Real monthly per-capita region-specific poverty lines 2004/2005*	*Real monthly region-specific low earning lines 2006*
Metropolitan	125	376
Lower Egypt Urban	123	370
Lower Egypt Rural	123	411
Upper Egypt Urban	122	366
Upper Egypt Rural	121	364
Total Egypt	123	368

Source: Asaad and Roushdy (2006).

Table 8.4 Means and standard deviation of variables used in regressions

Variable	*1998*			*2006*		
	No. Obs.	*Mean*	*Std. Dev.*	*No. Obs.*	*Mean*	*Std. Dev.*
LnRHrWag	836	0.25	0.66	1189	0.73	0.78
Percent female	1027	0.11	0.14	1533	0.14	0.14
pub_gov	1027	0.29	0.45	1533	0.19	0.39
Priv	1027	0.71	0.45	1533	0.81	0.39
Expr	1027	18.14	13.02	1533	16.81	12.16
Exprsq	1027	498.40	585.24	1533	430.22	542.66
Illiterate	1027	0.20	0.40	1533	0.18	0.38
Read/Write	1027	0.15	0.35	1533	0.08	0.28
Primary	1027	0.17	0.37	1533	0.14	0.35
Preparatory	1027	0.08	0.27	1533	0.07	0.26
GeneralSec~y	1027	0.01	0.12	1533	0.01	0.10
Vocational~c	1027	0.27	0.44	1533	0.35	0.48
PostSecond~y	1027	0.05	0.21	1533	0.05	0.21
univabove	1027	0.08	0.27	1533	0.12	0.32
Greater Cairo	1027	0.28	0.45	1533	0.26	0.44
Alex	1027	0.12	0.32	1533	0.13	0.33
Rur. Up. Egypt	1027	0.15	0.36	1533	0.16	0.36
Urb. Up. Egypt	1027	0.05	0.22	1533	0.05	0.22
Rur. L. Egypt	1027	0.27	0.44	1533	0.28	0.45
Urb. L. Egypt	1027	0.14	0.34	1533	0.13	0.33
Tariff	1027	0.19	0.10	1533	0.13	0.09
imp_penet2	1027	0.40	0.26	1533	0.39	0.25
export_ori~t	1027	0.10	0.12	1533	0.15	0.14
chng_tariff	–	–	–	1533	−0.06	0.05
chng_imp_p~2	–	–	–	1533	0.00	0.12
chng_expor~t	–	–	–	1533	0.04	0.12

5 Empirical methodology and results

We use the inter-industry wage differentials approach to determine whether workers in less heavily protected industries have lower wages than workers of similar observable characteristics in the more heavily protected industries. Let $i=1, 2, 3. \ldots I_j$ index workers in industry j. We regress the log of worker i's wages at time t ($\ln(w_{ijt})$) on a vector of worker characteristics H_{ijt} (age, age squared, gender, education indicators, sector indicators and region of residence) and a set of industry indicators (P_{ijt}) reflecting the degree of international trade and protection. We estimate the following equation:

$$\ln(w_{ijt}) = H_{ijt}\beta_H + P_{ijt}\beta_P + \varepsilon_{ijt} \tag{1}$$

for $i=1, \ldots, I_j$; $j=1, \ldots, J$, and $t=1998$ or 2006.

We estimate the above equation for all waged workers in the manufacturing sector as well as for workers classified as low-waged and poor.

We also employ quantile regression methods to gain more insight into the wage distribution by percentile of wages, and hence distinguish between higher-paying and lower-paying jobs in the manufacturing sector. This allows us to examine the differential impact of trade reforms on across five quantiles (10th, 25th, 50th, 75th and 90th) of the earning distribution.

Quantile regression methods are used to facilitate the estimation of several alternative quantiles of the wage distribution. This provides a more detailed account of the conditional (log) wage distribution. Quantile methods are also preferred over, or alongside, least square estimation due to the higher degree of robustness in estimation and reduced sensitivity to outlying observations (Koenker and Bassett, 1978) and for detecting and correcting (in combination with bootstrap methods) for heteroskedasticity (Deaton, 1997). The quantile regression method can be written in equation form as the qth quantile of the conditional log distribution of wages as a linear function of the regression variable, X:

$$\text{Quantile}_{qs}(\ln w|x) = X\beta_q (s=g,p,r) \tag{2}$$

The model can be estimated by finding the vector (β_q) that minimizes the following expression,

$$\sum_{r<0} q\,|\ln w - x'\beta_q| + \sum_{r>0}(1-q)\,|\ln w - x\beta_q|$$

where r is the residual, $r_i = \ln w - x'\beta_q$.[4]

Table 8.5 presents the regression results for all workers in the manufacturing sector in Egypt. In this as well as all of the following regressions, the log hourly wage equations are estimated for three models: 1998 levels, 2006 levels of trade

Table 8.5 Ordinary least square estimates of log hourly wages, 1998 and 2006: all manufacturing workers

VARIABLES	*(1)*	*(2)*	*(3)*
	1998:level	*2006:level*	*2006:change*
Tariff	−0.839***	−0.858***	−0.429
	(0.310)	(0.259)	(0.360)
Chngtariff			0.260
			(0.522)
Imp_penet2	−0.039	0.017	−0.069
	(0.090)	(0.094)	(0.109)
chngimp_penet2			0.640*
			(0.357)
Exp_orient	0.058	0.913***	0.089
	(0.172)	(0.162)	(0.268)
chngexp_orient			0.707***
			(0.254)
Female	−0.042	−0.149**	−0.152**
	(0.063)	(0.064)	(0.064)
Expr	0.051***	0.043***	0.043***
	(0.005)	(0.006)	(0.006)
Exprsq	−0.001***	−0.000***	−0.000***
	(0.000)	(0.000)	(0.000)
ReadWrite	0.191***	−0.034	−0.018
	(0.067)	(0.090)	(0.089)
Primary	0.356***	0.088	0.095
	(0.065)	(0.074)	(0.074)
Preparatory	0.345***	0.151*	0.166*
	(0.080)	(0.090)	(0.090)
GeneralSecondary	0.610***	0.106	0.100
	(0.176)	(0.201)	(0.200)
VocationalSec	0.474***	0.256***	0.255***
	(0.062)	(0.065)	(0.064)
PostSecondary	0.506***	0.391***	0.369***
	(0.094)	(0.101)	(0.100)
Univabove	1.072***	0.774***	0.757***
	(0.085)	(0.081)	(0.080)
Alex	−0.026	−0.054	−0.059
	(0.062)	(0.065)	(0.064)
Ruegypt	−0.107*	−0.130**	−0.126*
	(0.061)	(0.066)	(0.066)
Uuegypt	−0.047	−0.231**	−0.249**
	(0.093)	(0.104)	(0.103)
Rlegypt	−0.175***	−0.214***	−0.207***
	(0.052)	(0.053)	(0.053)
Ulegypt	−0.119*	−0.128*	−0.104
	(0.062)	(0.067)	(0.067)
pub_gov	−0.043	0.137***	
	(0.045)	(0.052)	
Constant	−0.425***	0.039	0.290*
	(0.112)	(0.109)	(0.171)
Observations	835	1189	1189
R-squared	0.402	0.280	0.291

Notes
Standard errors in parentheses.
*** $p<0.01$, ** $p<0.05$, * $p<0.1$.

variables, and 2006 changes in trade variables. Based on goodness-of-fit statistics, the human capital model appears to explain well both wage-setting and job quality outcomes in the manufacturing sector in Egypt. As expected, there is a significant negative wage differential associated with being female in both years. Compared to 1998, the female disadvantage in wages worsened and became more significant in 2006. There is a positive and significant wage differential in 2006 in the public sector. The experience wage profiles follow the expected inverted U-shape implied by human capital theory. There are also increasing returns to education, and they particularly jump at the university or above levels. Finally, there are mostly negative and significant differentials due to residence outside of greater Cairo.

As for trade variables, level of tariff protection is significantly negatively related to wages in both 1998 and 2006. Export orientation as well as the change in export orientation are both significant and positively related to wages in 2006. In other words, for all manufacturing, trade liberalization in form of lower tariffs and trade openness in terms of export orientation (but not import penetration, which is insignificant) appear to exert a positive influence on wages for the average worker in the manufacturing sector in Egypt.

Table 8.6 shows that the same results are more or less maintained when we limit the regression to only the group of low waged workers. In fact the negative impact of tariff protection in 1998 and 2006, and the positive impact of the change in export orientation in 2006 is much more pronounced for the group of low waged workers. It is also interesting to note that almost none of the human capital varianles, including gender, experience and level of education are significant for this group of workers, especially in 2006. Experience and Vocational education had a positive significant effect in 1998, but lost their significance in 2006.

If we limit the regression to only the poor in the manufacturing sector, as in Table 8.7, then we still get a negative impact of tariff on wages in 1998, but the results are not maintained in 2006. Export orientation is no longer significant. Finally, it interesting to note that there is a large and significant negative wage differential for the group of poor female workers in the manufacturing sector in Egypt.

Finally, Tables 8.8–8.10 report estimates of the above models using quantile regression methods for five quantiles of the earning distribution (10th, 25th, 50th, 75th and 90th). The results confirm again that tariff protection is consistently negative for all quantiles, and the impact is largest for the lowest and highest quantiles in 1998 (10th, 25th and 90th), and for the highest quantiles in 2006 (75th and 90th). The positive impact of increased export orientation on wages is only prevalent for the 50th percentile of the earnings distribution, and is not so at higher or lower quantiles. Hence we found a significant effect in OLS results.

Table 8.6 Ordinary least square estimates of log hourly wages, 1998 and 2006: low-waged manufacturing workers

VARIABLES	*(1)*	*(2)*	*(3)*
	1998:level	*2006:level*	*2006:change*
Tariff	−91.668**	−62.777**	−2.923
	(43.013)	(31.391)	(40.623)
Chngtariff			−33.666
			(62.915)
Imp_penet2	3.524	2.783	2.851
	(11.714)	(10.885)	(12.727)
chngimp_penet2			−2.393
			(43.633)
Exp_orient	−20.620	25.050	−14.570
	(21.347)	(20.964)	(31.024)
chngexp_orient			77.253***
			(28.111)
pub_gov	−0.002	0.106	0.131*
	(0.060)	(0.067)	(0.067)
Female	−0.038	−0.077	−0.065
	(0.075)	(0.062)	(0.062)
Expr	0.033***	0.007	0.007
	(0.007)	(0.007)	(0.007)
Exprsq	−0.001***	−0.000	−0.000
	(0.000)	(0.000)	(0.000)
ReadWrite	0.065	−0.203**	−0.192**
	(0.075)	(0.096)	(0.096)
Primary	0.178**	−0.003	−0.006
	(0.076)	(0.082)	(0.081)
Preparatory	0.203**	−0.087	−0.067
	(0.098)	(0.111)	(0.110)
GeneralSecondary	0.292	0.143	0.094
	(0.227)	(0.291)	(0.292)
VocationalSec	0.259***	0.003	0.010
	(0.071)	(0.070)	(0.070)
PostSecondary	0.126	0.033	0.024
	(0.119)	(0.145)	(0.145)
Univabove	0.258	−0.068	−0.086
	(0.198)	(0.111)	(0.111)
Alex	−0.006	0.001	−0.004
	(0.091)	(0.085)	(0.085)
Ruegypt	−0.052	0.092	0.084
	(0.082)	(0.085)	(0.085)
Uuegypt	−0.082	0.043	0.024
	(0.124)	(0.115)	(0.114)
Rlegypt	−0.070	0.143**	0.134**
	(0.069)	(0.064)	(0.065)
ulegypt	0.009	0.070	0.089
	(0.086)	(0.083)	(0.084)
Constant	−0.380***	0.044	−0.031
	(0.144)	(0.119)	(0.155)
Observations	366	483	483
R-squared	0.198	0.092	0.109

Notes
Standard errors in parentheses.
*** $p<0.01$, ** $p<0.05$, * $p<0.1$.

Table 8.7 Ordinary least square estimates of log hourly wages, 1998 and 2006: poor workers

VARIABLES	*(1)*	*(2)*	*(3)*
	1998:level	*2006:level*	*2006:change*
Tariff	−299.689**	−55.386	28.830
	(137.092)	(69.175)	(90.478)
Chngtariff			13.777
			(151.983)
Imp_penet2	8.574	−10.105	13.261
	(37.813)	(24.439)	(30.149)
chngimp_penet2			−146.488
			(99.307)
Exp_orient	15.442	55.766	74.861
	(57.257)	(51.969)	(66.938)
chngexp_orient			84.411
			(58.162)
pub_gov	−0.105	0.108	0.179
	(0.169)	(0.140)	(0.156)
female	0.321	−0.461***	−0.444***
	(0.256)	(0.152)	(0.152)
expr	0.073***	0.022*	0.024*
	(0.023)	(0.013)	(0.013)
Exprsq	−0.001***	−0.000	−0.000
	(0.001)	(0.000)	(0.000)
ReadWrite	0.198	−0.176	−0.166
	(0.160)	(0.147)	(0.147)
Primary	0.240	−0.014	0.000
	(0.178)	(0.133)	(0.133)
Preparatory	0.577*	0.179	0.165
	(0.334)	(0.179)	(0.180)
GeneralSecondary	0.310	0.000	0.000
	(0.997)	(0.000)	(0.000)
VocationalSec	0.238	−0.107	−0.076
	(0.198)	(0.129)	(0.131)
PostSecondary	0.000	0.426	0.426
	(0.000)	(0.345)	(0.366)
Univabove	0.000	0.507	0.558
	(0.000)	(0.855)	(0.856)
Alex	−0.092	−0.026	−0.020
	(0.395)	(0.256)	(0.259)
Ruegypt	−0.151	0.025	−0.032
	(0.347)	(0.149)	(0.152)
Uuegypt	−0.134	−0.081	−0.135
	(0.375)	(0.172)	(0.178)
Rlegypt	−0.506	−0.122	−0.152
	(0.363)	(0.167)	(0.172)
Ulegypt	0.195	−0.151	−0.142
	(0.448)	(0.215)	(0.214)
Constant	−0.067	0.253	0.001
	(0.579)	(0.230)	(0.343)
Observations	84	137	137
R-squared	0.490	0.337	0.359

Notes
Standard errors in parentheses.
*** $p<0.01$, ** $p<0.05$, * $p<0.1$.

Table 8.8 Quantile regression estimates of log hourly wages, 1998: all manufacturing workers

VARIABLES	*(1)*	*(2)*	*(3)*	*(4)*	*(5)*
	10th	*25th*	*50th*	*75th*	*90th*
Tariff	−122.744**	−153.648***	−82.220***	−42.140	−159.774***
	(53.011)	(45.432)	(29.301)	(49.373)	(47.396)
Imp_penet2	−17.294	−7.516	9.380	12.916	−22.843*
	(11.313)	(14.965)	(11.207)	(10.860)	(13.429)
Exp_orient	−2.728	28.468	16.661	31.141*	45.421
	(33.720)	(17.907)	(19.649)	(17.721)	(30.490)
pub_gov	−0.039	−0.000	0.001	−0.013	−0.178***
	(0.050)	(0.055)	(0.088)	(0.078)	(0.068)
Female	−0.098	−0.128	−0.083	−0.020	0.006
	(0.128)	(0.109)	(0.091)	(0.098)	(0.129)
Expr	0.064***	0.051***	0.045***	0.044***	0.047***
	(0.010)	(0.010)	(0.010)	(0.006)	(0.008)
Exprsq	−0.001***	−0.001***	−0.001***	−0.000***	−0.000***
	(0.000)	(0.000)	(0.000)	(0.000)	(0.000)
ReadWrite	0.012	0.108	0.219	0.228**	0.155**
	(0.107)	(0.126)	(0.142)	(0.105)	(0.077)
Primary	0.235*	0.247**	0.267***	0.234***	0.206*
	(0.141)	(0.123)	(0.089)	(0.079)	(0.107)
Preparatory	0.297*	0.260**	0.304***	0.210	0.246
	(0.164)	(0.126)	(0.089)	(0.139)	(0.154)
General-Secondary	0.759***	0.482***	0.463**	0.368	0.642
	(0.127)	(0.125)	(0.188)	(0.241)	(0.598)
VocationalSec	0.432***	0.357***	0.445***	0.420***	0.503***
	(0.101)	(0.124)	(0.103)	(0.092)	(0.073)
PostSecondary	0.135	0.342	0.445***	0.514***	0.534***
	(0.122)	(0.212)	(0.162)	(0.146)	(0.186)
Univabove	0.911***	0.886***	0.931***	1.027***	1.123***
	(0.147)	(0.118)	(0.108)	(0.121)	(0.176)
Alex	−0.187**	−0.066	0.018	0.094	0.160
	(0.093)	(0.086)	(0.074)	(0.095)	(0.147)
Ruegypt	−0.135*	−0.151*	−0.048	−0.021	−0.083
	(0.079)	(0.089)	(0.120)	(0.060)	(0.124)
Uuegypt	−0.191*	−0.078	0.061	−0.060	0.023
	(0.115)	(0.082)	(0.114)	(0.095)	(0.139)
Rlegypt	−0.337***	−0.185*	−0.095	0.043	0.121
	(0.083)	(0.100)	(0.069)	(0.082)	(0.132)
Ulegypt	−0.116	−0.052	−0.074	−0.119*	−0.065
	(0.101)	(0.057)	(0.062)	(0.065)	(0.121)
Constant	−0.867***	−0.497***	−0.418***	−0.235	0.355
	(0.162)	(0.111)	(0.120)	(0.145)	(0.218)
Observations	835	835	835	835	835

Notes
Standard errors in parentheses.
*** $p<0.01$, ** $p<0.05$, * $p<0.1$.

Table 8.9 Quantile regression estimates of log hourly wages, 2006 (levels of trade variables): all manufacturing workers

VARIABLES	*(1)*	*(2)*	*(3)*	*(4)*	*(5)*
	10th	*25th*	*50th*	*75th*	*90th*
Tariff	−14.204	−2.249	−46.111*	−103.583***	−147.710***
	(47.323)	(18.427)	(26.195)	(24.884)	(49.027)
Imp_penet2	6.034	13.277	19.595*	7.728	−0.384
	(15.108)	(13.043)	(10.290)	(12.663)	(13.031)
Exp_orient	57.999**	70.728***	82.442***	116.075***	127.736***
	(23.899)	(15.997)	(14.034)	(18.714)	(25.675)
pub_gov	0.153**	0.166***	0.094	0.137***	0.062
	(0.070)	(0.062)	(0.059)	(0.053)	(0.145)
Female	−0.350***	−0.357***	−0.324***	−0.180*	0.043
	(0.097)	(0.062)	(0.065)	(0.104)	(0.444)
Expr	0.043***	0.047***	0.045***	0.045***	0.047***
	(0.009)	(0.007)	(0.005)	(0.006)	(0.010)
Exprsq	−0.000**	−0.001***	−0.001***	−0.001***	−0.000**
	(0.000)	(0.000)	(0.000)	(0.000)	(0.000)
ReadWrite	−0.071	0.008	0.003	0.004	−0.079
	(0.198)	(0.129)	(0.075)	(0.082)	(0.249)
Primary	−0.022	0.009	0.051	0.088	0.032
	(0.113)	(0.072)	(0.060)	(0.071)	(0.127)
Preparatory	0.057	0.051	0.072	0.111	0.132
	(0.115)	(0.107)	(0.108)	(0.106)	(0.195)
GeneralSecondary	−0.119	0.159	0.276**	0.075	0.445
	(0.313)	(0.236)	(0.127)	(0.459)	(0.288)
VocationalSec	0.257***	0.200***	0.222***	0.227***	0.348***
	(0.088)	(0.062)	(0.063)	(0.072)	(0.126)
PostSecondary	0.497***	0.324***	0.391***	0.446***	0.451***
	(0.191)	(0.077)	(0.087)	(0.125)	(0.145)
Univabove	0.593***	0.707***	0.717***	0.847***	1.159***
	(0.119)	(0.082)	(0.078)	(0.128)	(0.253)
Alex	−0.090	0.046	0.054	0.034	−0.094
	(0.081)	(0.067)	(0.062)	(0.067)	(0.147)
Ruegypt	−0.262*	−0.133*	−0.015	0.042	−0.164
	(0.155)	(0.078)	(0.080)	(0.066)	(0.123)
Uuegypt	−0.352***	−0.132**	−0.144**	−0.162***	−0.408***
	(0.131)	(0.059)	(0.073)	(0.047)	(0.117)
Rlegypt	−0.179***	−0.166***	−0.145***	−0.174***	−0.307**
	(0.069)	(0.040)	(0.054)	(0.048)	(0.139)
Ulegypt	−0.211***	−0.140**	−0.123*	−0.116*	−0.218
	(0.069)	(0.062)	(0.067)	(0.063)	(0.156)
Constant	−0.584***	−0.442***	−0.113	0.263**	0.641***
	(0.159)	(0.108)	(0.092)	(0.115)	(0.244)
Observations	1189	1189	1189	1189	1189

Notes
Standard errors in parentheses.
*** $p<0.01$, ** $p<0.05$, * $p<0.1$.

Table 8.10 Quantile regression estimates of log hourly wages, 2006 (change in trade variables): all manufacturing workers

VARIABLES	*(1)*	*(2)*	*(3)*	*(4)*	*(5)*
	10th	*25th*	*50th*	*75th*	*90th*
Tariff	46.957	36.874	24.722	−62.957	−153.894*
	(49.968)	(36.199)	(54.949)	(50.832)	(84.335)
chngtariff	43.148	−8.873	−18.098	20.329	58.261
	(77.281)	(56.164)	(49.635)	(77.819)	(172.671)
Imp_penet2	7.641	13.961	24.140*	4.323	−20.183
	(16.126)	(17.956)	(13.640)	(14.610)	(26.393)
chngimp_penet2	−18.793	−4.565	−49.571	57.667	143.135
	(42.514)	(54.241)	(46.114)	(55.246)	(111.244)
Exp_orient	25.846	47.607	75.372***	44.733	22.491
	(38.157)	(31.344)	(18.179)	(30.236)	(60.689)
chngexp_orient	64.094	44.009*	75.836**	65.067*	35.128
	(45.269)	(25.777)	(33.285)	(35.323)	(54.884)
pub_gov	0.161***	0.169**	0.141***	0.169***	0.035
	(0.059)	(0.081)	(0.041)	(0.057)	(0.129)
female	−0.342***	−0.323***	−0.356***	−0.160	−0.023
	(0.120)	(0.069)	(0.044)	(0.125)	(0.394)
expr	0.046***	0.049***	0.047***	0.047***	0.042***
	(0.010)	(0.006)	(0.005)	(0.006)	(0.012)
exprsq	−0.001**	−0.001***	−0.001***	−0.001***	−0.000
	(0.000)	(0.000)	(0.000)	(0.000)	(0.000)
ReadWrite	−0.182	0.036	−0.041	0.012	−0.025
	(0.135)	(0.099)	(0.058)	(0.074)	(0.174)
Primary	−0.073	0.000	0.021	0.084	0.179*
	(0.095)	(0.077)	(0.070)	(0.064)	(0.094)
Preparatory	0.002	0.043	0.033	0.097	0.154
	(0.106)	(0.096)	(0.083)	(0.099)	(0.184)
GeneralSecondary	−0.248	0.162	0.243	0.078	0.339
	(0.299)	(0.211)	(0.221)	(0.259)	(0.248)
VocationalSec	0.154**	0.225***	0.199***	0.221***	0.346***
	(0.074)	(0.064)	(0.047)	(0.057)	(0.131)
PostSecondary	0.397***	0.315***	0.394***	0.392***	0.469**
	(0.108)	(0.094)	(0.086)	(0.104)	(0.186)
univabove	0.513***	0.699***	0.699***	0.796***	1.059***
	(0.096)	(0.097)	(0.067)	(0.089)	(0.226)
alex	−0.035	0.046	0.029	0.023	−0.181
	(0.090)	(0.075)	(0.058)	(0.067)	(0.136)
Ruegypt	−0.228	−0.142**	−0.026	0.046	−0.157*
	(0.140)	(0.071)	(0.131)	(0.068)	(0.086)
Uuegypt	−0.416***	−0.138*	−0.146**	−0.186***	−0.449**
	(0.138)	(0.082)	(0.064)	(0.068)	(0.190)
Rlegypt	−0.184***	−0.157***	−0.167***	−0.186***	−0.305***
	(0.059)	(0.061)	(0.063)	(0.061)	(0.087)
Ulegypt	−0.155	−0.145***	−0.130**	−0.116*	−0.187*
	(0.096)	(0.056)	(0.052)	(0.065)	(0.103)
Constant	−0.578**	−0.515***	−0.245	0.321*	0.981**
	(0.226)	(0.141)	(0.167)	(0.171)	(0.459)
Observations	1189	1189	1189	1189	1189

Notes
Standard errors in parentheses.
*** $p<0.01$, ** $p<0.05$, * $p<0.1$.

6 Conclusion

This chapter investigates the impact of trade openness on wage outcomes in the Egyptian manufacturing sector over a period of rapid trade liberalization. The chapter utilizes newly available panel labor market survey data for 1998–2006, merges it (at the two-digit industry level) with trade variables that capture export orientation, import penetration as well as direct policy change relating to reduction of average tariffs, and uses the merged dataset to estimate the impact of trade policy on wages of poor and low-waged workers in Egyptian manufacturing.

The results in this chapter show that for the average manufacturing worker, level of tariff protection is significantly negatively related to wages in both 1998 and 2006. Moreover, export orientation as well as the change in export orientation are both significant and positively related to wages in 2006. In other words, for all manufacturing, trade liberalization in form of lower tariffs and trade openness in terms of export orientation (but not import penetration, which is insignificant) appear to exert a positive influence on wages for the average worker in the manufacturing sector in Egypt.

The same results are more or less maintained when we limit the regression to only the group of low-waged workers. In fact the negative impact of tariff protection in 1998 and 2006, and the positive impact of the change in export orientation in 2006, is much more pronounced for the group of low-waged workers. If we limit the regression to only the poor in the manufacturing sector below, then we still get a negative impact of tariff on wages in 1998, but the results are not maintained in 2006. Export orientation is no longer significant using quantile regression methods for five quantiles of the earning distribution (10th, 25th, 50th, 75th and 90th).

Finally results using quantile regression methods again confirm that tariff protection is consistently negative for all quantiles, and the impact is largest for the lowest and highest quantiles in 1998 (10th, 25th and 90th), and for the highest quantiles in 2006 (75th and 90th). The positive impact of increased export orientation on wages is only prevalent for the 50th percentile of the earnings distribution and is not so at higher or lower quantiles.

The above results combined confirm that trade liberalization measures that resulted in lower tariff rates have thus been beneficial for manufacturing workers' incomes in Egypt, and that effect is in fact stronger for workers classified as poor or with lower earnings. Import penetration appears to have an insignificant effect on low-waged workers' earnings, whereas export orientation positively influences mean or median workers' wages, but has insignificant effects on incomes of the poor. In sum, a trade policy based on lower tariff protection appears to exert a positive influence on incomes of poor workers in the manufacturing sector in Egypt. There is evidence elsewhere, however, that this might come at the expense of greater casualization of workers and higher incidence of low-quality jobs in Egypt (see Said and al-Azzawi, 2009).

Notes

1 See Goldberg and Pavcnik (2004) for a review of this literature.
2 For more details, see Barsoum (2006).
3 The per capita region-specific poverty lines for Egypt were estimated by El-Laithy and Lokshin (2002) using the data from the 1999/2000 HIECS.
4 The above minimization problem can be easily accomplished by linear programming techniques. Standard errors are calculated from the analytic variance–covariance matrix proposed by Koenker and Bassett (1978), or in cases of suspected heteroskedasticity bootstrap methods are used (see Deaton, 1997: 84–85; Stata Corporation, 1997: 94–104).

References

Acosta, P. and Gasparini, L. (2007) *Economic Development and Cultural Change*, Vol. 55, *Capital Accumulation, Trade Liberalization, and Rising Wage Inequality: The Case of Argentina*, Chicago, IL: University of Chicago Press, 793–812.

Arbache, J.S., Dickerson, A.W. and Green, F. (2001) 'Assessing the Stability of the Inter-industry Wage Structure in the Face of Radical Economic Reforms', Studies in Economics 0103, Department of Economics, University of Kent.

Assaad, R. and R. Roushdy (2006) 'Poverty and the Labor Market in Egypt: A Review of Developments in the 1998–2006 Period', Paper prepared as a Background Paper for the *Egypt Poverty Assessment Update*, Cairo: Population Council, Egypt.

Attanasio, O., P.K. Goldberg and N. Pavcnik (2004) 'Trade Reforms and Wage Inequality in Colombia', *Journal of Development Economics*, 74(2): 331–366.

Barsoum, G. (2006) *Egypt Labor Market Panel Survey 2006, Final Report*, Cairo: Population Council, Egypt.

Buchinsky, M. (1994) 'Changes in the US Wage Structure 1963–1987: Application of Quantile', *Econometrica*, 62: 405–458.

Currie, J. and A. Harrison (1997) 'Trade Reform and Labor Market Adjustment in Morocco', *Journal of Labor Economics*, 15: S44–S71.

Deaton, A. (1997) *The Analysis of Household Surveys*, Baltimore, MD: The Johns Hopkins University Press.

Dutta, P.V. (2007) 'Trade Protection and Industry Wages in India', *Industrial and Labor Relations Review*, 60(2): 268–286.

El-Hamidi, F. (2008) 'Trade Liberalization, Gender Segmentation, and Wage Discrimination: Evidence from Egypt', ERF Working Paper No. 414.

El-Laithy, H. and M. Lokshin (2002) 'Economic Growth and Poverty: Egypt 1995–2000,' Mimeo, Background Paper.

Feliciano, Z.M. (2001) 'Workers and Trade Liberalization: The Impact of Trade Reforms in Mexico on Wages and Employment', *Industrial and Labor Relations Review*, 55(1): 95–115.

Gaston, N. and D. Tefler (1994) 'Protection, Trade, and Wages: Evidence from US Manufacturing', *Industrial and Labor Relations Review*, 47(4): 574–593.

Goldberg, P. and N. Pavcnik (2003) 'The Response of the Informal Sector to Trade Liberalization', *Journal of Development Economics*, 72: 463–496.

Goldberg, P. and N. Pavcnik (2004) 'Trade, Inequality and Poverty: What Do We Know? Evidence from Recent Trade Liberalisation Episodes in Developing Countries', Paper prepared for the 2004 Brookings Trade Forum on 'Globalization, Poverty and Inequality: What Do We Know? Where Are We Going?', Washington DC, 13–14 May 2004.

Goldberg, P. and N. Pavcnik (2005) 'Trade, Wages, and the Political Economy of Trade Protection: Evidence from the Colombian Trade Reforms', *Journal of International Economics*, 66: 75–105.

Green, F., Dickerson, A. and Saba Arbache, J. (2001) 'A Picture of Wage Inequality and the Allocation of Labor Through a Period of Trade Liberalization: The Case of Brazil, *World Development*, 29(11): 1923–1939.

Hanson, G. and A. Harrison (1999) 'Trade Liberalization and Wage Inequality in Mexico', *Industrial and Labor Relations Review*, 52(2): 271–287.

Harrison, A. and G. Hanson (1999) 'Who Gains from Trade Reform? Some Remaining Puzzles', *Journal of Development Economics*, 59(1): 125–154.

Heckman, J. (1979) 'Sample Selection Bias as a Specification Error', *Econometrica*, 47: 153–161.

Hoekman, B. and A. Winters (2005) 'Trade and Employment: Stylized Facts and Research Findings', ECES Working Paper No. 102.

Katz, L. and Freeman, R. (eds) (1992) *Differences and Changes in Wage Structures*, Chicago, IL: University of Chicago Press

Koenker, R. and Bassett, G. Jr (1978) 'Regression Quantiles', *Econometrica*, 46(1): 33–50.

Krueger, A.B. and L.H. Summers (1988) 'Efficiency Wages and the Inter-Industry Wage Structure', *Econometrica*, 56(2): 259–293.

Refaat, A. (2003) 'Trade-Induced Protectionism in Egypt's Manufacturing Sector', ECES Working Paper No. 85, Cairo: The Egyptian Center for Economic Studies.

Revenga, A. (1992) 'Exporting Jobs? The Impact of Import Competition on Employment and Wages in US Manufacturing', *Quarterly Journal of Economics*, 107(1): 255–284.

Revenga, A. (1997) 'Employment and Wage Effects of Trade Liberalization: The Case of Mexican Manufacturing', *Journal of Labor Economics*, 15(3), S20–S43.

Robertson R. (2000) 'Trade Liberalisation and Wage Inequality: Lessons from the Mexican Experience', *The World Economy*, 23(6): 827–849.

Said, M. and S. Al-Azzawi (2009) 'Trade Liberalization, Inter-industry Wage Differentials and Job Quality in Egyptian Manufacturing', Paper prepared for Population Council's Dissemination Conference on Poverty, Job Quality and Labor Market Dynamics, Cairo, July 2009.

STATA Corporation (1997) *Reference Manual to Stata 5.0*, College Station, TX: Stata Press.

WTO World Trade Organization (2005) *Trade Policy Review: Egypt*, Report by the WTO Secretariat, Document WT/TPR/G/150.

9 Trade, productivity and technical change in the MENA countries

Joaquín A. Millán

1 Introduction

Over the past decades, an issue of great concern has been the integration of Middle East and North Africa countries (MENA in the acronym introduced by the World Bank and the International Monetary Fund). In the widest definition, MENA encompasses the 21 members of the Arab League and Iran, Israel, and Turkey, which is hardly a homogeneous region, as El-Erian and Fischer questioned (2000). Recently, Devlin (2010) asks whether MENA countries are different from other developing countries, noting the diversity within the region, with striking and growing differences between the Gulf countries and the rest of the MENA countries. The Mediterranean MENA countries are a better-defined group, according to signers of the so-called Barcelona Process.

The European Union-15 (EU15) and 12 countries of the Middle East and North Africa (Algeria, Cyprus, Egypt, Israel, Jordan, Lebanon, Malta, Morocco, Syria, Tunisia, Turkey and West Bank/Gaza Strip) launched the first common European policy in the Mediterranean by signing the Euro-Mediterranean Partnership (EMP), or Barcelona Process. Later, in 2004, Malta and Cyprus became members of the European Union (EU). Oil-rich Libya, whose economy is analysed in Otman and Karlberg (2007), is generally excluded from analyses of the Mediterranean MENA countries.

The Barcelona Process set out three basic tasks, analysed in Calleya (2005): a political and security partnership, an economic and financial partnership, and a partnership in social, cultural and human affairs. In 2008, the European Council prompted the European Commission to redefine the relationship between the EU and its MENA neighbours based on the Barcelona Process.

For our purposes, the main interest is the economic partnership. Brach (2008) emphasizes that after more than a decade of the Barcelona Process, MENA countries have advanced insufficiently in development and cooperation. Pastore *et al.* (2009) suggest the existence of unexploited trade potential between the EU and MENA countries. Moreover, Romagnoli and Mengoni (2009) go further and note that the economies of the MENA region have recently fallen back on subregional trading blocs and bilateral agreements.

Fawzy (2003) surveys economic and political incentives to promote integration, emphasizing the low degree of complementarity among the trade structures. Galal and Hoekman (2003) add several political reasons, such as the asymmetrical distribution of the benefits from integration across and within countries, and issues of national sovereignty or fear of competition, as the causes for poor integration for Arab countries. Dawson (2009) analyses the main problems in trade negotiations with the EU, with an emphasis on Morocco.

Political issues are critical with Turkey and, mainly, Israel. In this sense, for Chourou (2004), Israel is the major reason for the slow progress of the Barcelona Process. The Social and Economic Council of the Arab League created the Greater Arab Free Trade Area (GAFTA) in 1997, to a great degree as a response to the Barcelona Process. Hence, Zorob (2008) judges the potential of the GAFTA as a complementary strategy for integration to be quite limited. However, although most Arab states formally boycott the State of Israel, Hofmann (2008) holds a moderately optimistic view showing how the Israeli economic agenda in the Middle East follows both 'formal and informal business channels'.

Even at the wider definition, there are fewer studies for the MENA region than for other developing regions, as Nugent and Pesaran (2006) claim, although this is changing quickly. Yousef (2004), Esfahani (2006) and the papers in Nabli (2007) and Sayan (2009), among others, analyse existing and potential institutional reforms in the MENA countries. Finally, Devlin (2010) presents a wide survey of issues concerning the MENA countries.

Recently, several analyses have focused on trade and growth. Bhattacharya and Wolde (2010a) analyse constraints on growth, in particular the lack of adequate infrastructure and labour mismatch due to disincentives, large public sectors and excessively regulated private sectors. In a parallel paper, Bhattacharya and Wolde (2010b) empirically study constraints on trade for the MENA countries; mainly transport infrastructures and customs regulations.

Several studies report weak economic growth for the MENA countries, and different interpretations appear in the literature. Sala i Martin and Artadi (2003) tackle investment quality in the Arab World, emphasizing low productivity of investment in the public sector and a hostile environment for private investment. Benhassine (2009) studies the relationship between the private and public sectors in the MENA countries. The World Bank (2006) identifies government failures and microeconomic market failures for Morocco. Makdisi *et al.* (2006), among others, have studied the sources of growth for the MENA countries.

This research focuses on the eight MENA Mediterranean countries for which data are available: Algeria, Egypt, Israel, Jordan, Morocco, Syria, Tunisia and Turkey. The period analysed follows 1985 because of the beginning of stabilization programs and claims of changes in policy. Beginning in the mid 1980s, Jordan, Algeria, Morocco, Tunisia and Egypt implemented extensive, largely unilateral, economic policy reforms, as Konan (2003) notes. Other economic policy changes in the period were due to serious economic or political problems. Israel initiated a reform program after severe inflation in 1985, which is reviewed in Agenor and Montiel (2008: 355–59) or, from a radical point of view, less favorably in Nitzan and Bichler (2002). Even more stringent were Turkey's political and economic changes in the early 1980s with the 'Third Republic' following the coup in 1980 and chronically high inflation, which is described by Zürcher (2004) and Nas (2008), among others.

The approach in this chapter, based on production theory, deals with imports as an input, with capital and labour, and exports as an output, with domestic consumption goods and domestic investment goods. This allows the estimation of export supply and import demand jointly measuring interactions (elasticities) and the effects of technical change. There are applications of this approach to developed countries, but it can also apply to less developed countries. The idea is that economic agents in the MENA countries behave similarly to those in industrial economies but operate under different technological environments. In this way, we can expect that similar ways of modelling could represent differences in production technologies in the MENA countries. The approach is richer than the more common approaches of analysing productivity as a single output and trade equations ad hoc.

The production approach to trade is of particular interest for less developed countries, as the stylized facts of development macroeconomics show. Agenor and Montiel (2008: 15) describe stylized fact (1) of the typical development economy as 'openness to trade in goods and assets', and fact (2) as 'little control over the prices of the goods they export and import'. The modelling approach in this chapter specifies these issues explicitly. Moreover, as stylized fact (9) appears as 'imported intermediate goods play an important role in the aggregate production function' and in an explicit way: 'Through the cost of imported intermediates, the exchange rate has an important influence on the position of the economy's short-run supply curve' (p. 21). Then, three of the macroeconomic features that characterize development macroeconomics are central to the modelling approach based on production theory.

In particular, our approach allows the investigation of the empirical macro consequences of changes in trade policy. There are several operating assumptions. We do not separate imported intermediate and consumption or investment goods; data are not available, and even final goods generate economic activity in trade and retail when imported. Complementarity or substitution between public and private investment or public and private consumption are not analysed; Benhassine (2009) studies this issue in depth. Finally, there is no comment on monetary issues.

Financial constraints do not appear as true problems for the MENA economies. Boulila and Trabelsi (2004) find that causality runs from the real to the financial sector, and that finance plays a minor role in the determination of long-run growth in the MENA countries. Guncavdi and Kucukcifci (2005) conclude that the production sector of the Turkish economy has increasingly become independent from the use of financial services.

In short, the empirical analysis in this chapter consists of the estimate of productivity growth and technical progress biases for specific variables for eight Mediterranean MENA countries, 1985–2007. First, there is a presentation of estimates of capital and labour shares in GDP, elasticities for trade and domestic production. Second, productivity effects and technical change biases are reported. The comparison of economic differences and similarities across countries and time is interesting for analysing the success of development in these countries. Moreover, the comparison of the interrelationship between trade and macroeconomic structure is of interest for identifying the economic effects derived from international agreements on economic cooperation. The structure of the chapter is as follows. Section 2 describes the basic National Accounts data used to analyse trade issues in the Mediterranean MENA countries. The main traits of the production structure of the MENA countries are presented in Section 3. Section 4 focuses on productivity and technical change issues. Finally, the conclusion appears in Section 5.

2 Data

This study uses yearly data from 1985 to 2007. The net outputs in the database are consumption (C) as domestic final private consumption expenditure and government final consumption, investment (I) as gross capital formation, exports of goods and services (X), and imports of goods and services (M). Exports are the total exports of goods and services, and imports are total imports of goods and services. The net outputs C, I, X and M are the demand components of the Gross Domestic Product (GDP) in the national accounts. As outputs, C denotes the production of consumer goods, I the production of investment goods, and X the production of export goods.

Since the national accounts for the different countries have been revised several times, there are different data series even for the same variable. We chose the reference data series from the World Developments Indicators (WDI) of the World Bank when data are available and there is no obvious preferable alternative. Hence, we use WDI data for Algeria, Egypt, Jordan, Syria, Tunisia and Turkey (1987–2007). For Turkey, the series for the years 1985 and 1986 are from TÜIK (2009).

For Israel and Morocco, we have used data directly from the national statistical offices. The WDI do not provide data for Israel for the period prior to 1995. The Israeli series consists of the linking the Israeli Statistical Institute series from 1985–1995 and 1995–2007. For Morocco, series from: 'Comptes Nationaux 1990–2007 base 1998' are completed for the period 1985–1990 by linking data from 'PIB de Maroc 1980–2004 base 1980'.

For all countries, the prices of exports and imports are the implicit price deflators for exports and imports respectively, without tariff rate adjustments. The base year is 2000 for the price series, and thus the corresponding quantities are in terms of 2000 domestic currencies.

Labour is the total number of workers, from the WDI. The capital stocks series come from updating the capital series data in World Penn Tables 5.6 (Heston *et al.*, 1996) by applying the perpetual inventory method, as in Easterly and Levine (2001). Finally, labour and capital are measured in index form with base 2000.

The dataset consists of prices and quantities for three outputs (exports, investment, and combined private and government consumption), one variable input (imports) and two exogenously given fixed inputs (labour and capital) for the eight Mediterranean MENA countries. Table 9.1 shows the mean rates of growth of price for variable outputs and imports, and quantity for all outputs and inputs. Moderate to high inflation is common, being very high in Turkey and lower in Jordan, Morocco and Tunisia.

It is worth noting that Israel is the only country with a significant improvement in the terms of trade (export price increases more than import price). In

Table 9.1 Volume and price rates of growth (%)

	Volumes					
	Consumption	*Investment*	*Exports*	*Imports*	*Labour*	*Capital*
Algeria	1.5	0.8	2.9	−0.8	4.2	2.0
	(4.0)	(9.9)	(3.6)	(12.6)	(0.8)	(1.6)
Egypt	3.7	2.0	8.2	4.1	2.6	5.8
	(1.2)	(11.8)	(7.4)	(10)	(1.2)	(1.9)
Israel	4.1	5.1	6.5	5.7	3.1	2.7
	(2.7)	(11.3)	(6.9)	(7.2)	(1.3)	(1.2)
Jordan	3.0	4.4	4.8	3.3	4.9	2.8
	(7.6)	(15.3)	(8)	(12.5)	(3.4)	(1.8)
Morocco	3.3	4.5	7.0	6.5	2.4	3.4
	(4.3)	(6.7)	(5.1)	(4.8)	(1.1)	(1.8)
Syria	3.9	0.3	9.6	4.5	4.3	1.9
	(6.3)	(20.6)	(12.8)	(15)	(2.8)	(2.4)
Tunisia	4.0	3.1	5.7	4.3	2.6	4.6
	(1.7)	(11.4)	(5.1)	(6)	(0.6)	(3.6)
Turkey	4.3	6.5	8.4	9.7	1.4	1.4
	(4.4)	(18.3)	(7.3)	(15.5)	(2.4)	(2.3)
Algeria	12.2	14.8	16.0	16.0		
	(9.3)	(14.1)	(27)	(13.7)		
Egypt	10.4	11.1	7.9	10.5		
	(5.7)	(14.2)	(13.9)	(14.4)		
Israel	9.5	9.1	7.8	7.4		
	(8.7)	(8.8)	(7.1)	(6.2)		
Jordan	4.7	4.7	4.9	5.8		
	(6.9)	(6.9)	(7.6)	(10.7)		
Morocco	3.4	3.8	1.7	2.0		
	(2.3)	(6.8)	(2.3)	(5)		
Syria	9.8	12.7	10.0	11.8		
	(8.6)	(20.5)	(15.1)	(14.7)		
Tunisia	4.6	4.4	5.1	6.0		
	(2.1)	(3.3)	(4.1)	(2.8)		
Turkey	42.7	40.5	39.0	37.8		
	(21.3)	(21.9)	(23.9)	(24.9)		

Notes
First row, average 1985–2007. Second row, standard deviation.

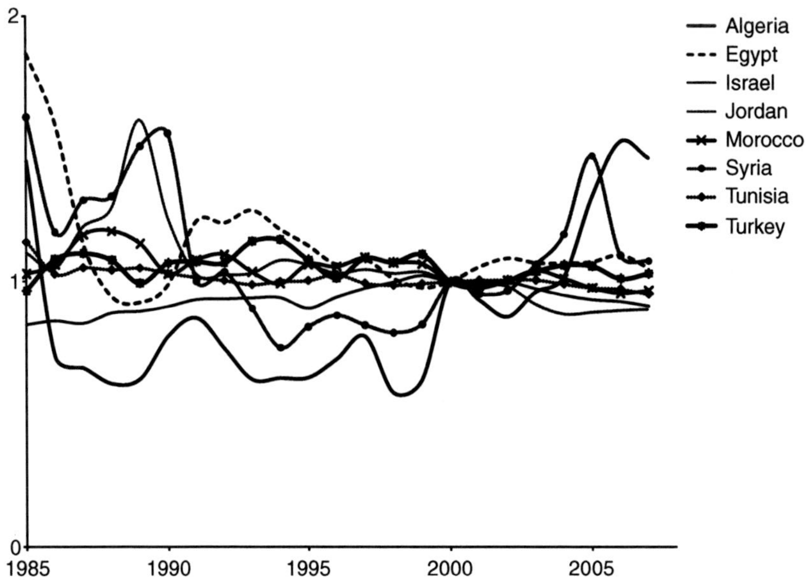

Figure 9.1 Terms of trade.

Turkey, the improvement in the terms of trade is of minor relevance due to high inflation. In general, terms of trade deteriorate slightly, the Egyptian case being remarkable. Earlier developments in the 1980s account for these results; there has been a general improvement in terms of trade since the 1990s. Figure 9.1 shows the evolution of the terms of trade with base 2000. Although there is no clear smooth trend for any country, the fluctuations are not very large.

Returning to the quantities in Table 9.1, investment growth is lower than consumption growth in Syria (very pronounced), Algeria, Tunisia and Egypt. The Egyptian case is studied in Loayza and Odawara (2010), showing the importance of investment composition (public or private). As expected, investment volatility measured by the standard deviation of the rate of growth is much higher than consumption volatility. Labour increased in all countries, but mainly in Algeria, Jordan and Syria. The moderate increase of capital, mainly in Algeria and Syria, is notable. It is worth noting the Turkish case, with low increases in capital and labour.

Concerning trade, it is worth noting that exports always increase more than both domestic consumption and investment. On the other hand, in general, imports increase more than investment and always more than consumption, except in Algeria. The decline in Algerian imports is noteworthy because the period analysed follows a period of an even more explicit import substitution strategy. Export growth is always higher than import growth, except for Turkey, where both are greater than for any other country in the sample.

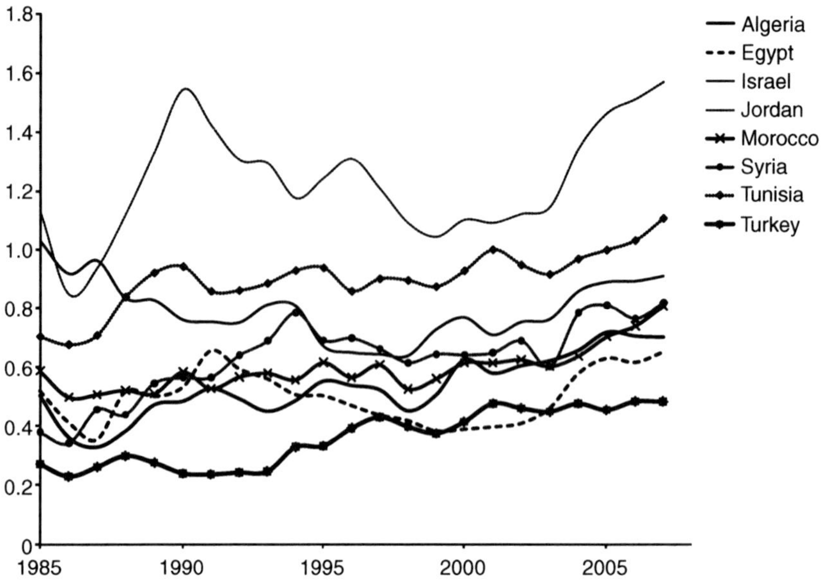

Figure 9.2 Openness.

The finding of heterogeneous patterns of input and output growth suggests the difficulty of grouping clusters of countries, by either their development level or geographical area, through patterns of trade and growth. However, Figure 9.2 shows some common patterns of evolution of openness. The measure of openness is the sum of absolute values of export and import divided by GDP. In general, openness increased for all countries in the latter ten years analysed, following a period of stability or slight decrease in the 1990s. Previous evolution shows large inter-country variability. Figure 9.2 reflects the fact studied in Esfahani and Squire (2007) of the MENA countries as remarkably open economies. There is an inverse relationship between openness and the population size of an economy. Openness is very high in Jordan, followed by Tunisia and Israel; on the other hand, openness is lower in Egypt and Turkey.

3 Trade and domestic macrovariables

The explanation of the determinants of trade evolution is the objective of an econometric analysis, whose results are summarized in this section and the following. The econometric analysis, based on Kohli (1993) and Fox and Diewert (1999), consists of the estimation of a system of equations for consumption, investment, imports and exports derived from a normalized quadratic GDP function with constant returns to scale and regularity conditions imposed.

First, concerning fixed inputs, the econometric analysis provides shadow prices and shares in GDP for labour and capital. A summary of shadow marginal shares for labour and capital appears in Table 9.2. The estimated shares of labour are low and decreasing for Morocco, and increasingly lower for Tunisia and Turkey, with opposite results for capital. They are decreasing but still very high for Egypt. The labour share is increasing in Algeria, and shows no monotonic trend in Israel or Syria. An important result is that the share of capital in some countries is close to or even above 0.5, as found for the average of the MENA countries in Makdisi *et al.* (2006), and that these shares seem very variable. These results are particularly

Table 9.2 Marginal shares for capital and labour, averages.

	Labour	*Capital*
Algeria	0.559	0.441
1985–1992	0.504	0.496
1993–2000	0.581	0.419
2001–2007	0.597	0.403
Egypt	0.728	0.272
1985–1992	0.768	0.231
1993–2000	0.756	0.244
2001–2007	0.650	0.350
Israel	0.513	0.487
1985–1992	0.455	0.545
1993–2000	0.570	0.430
2001–2007	0.514	0.486
Jordan	0.703	0.297
1985–1992	0.590	0.410
1993–2000	0.801	0.199
2001–2007	0.719	0.281
Morocco	0.291	0.709
1985–1992	0.309	0.691
1993–2000	0.300	0.700
2001–2007	0.259	0.741
Syria	0.790	0.210
1985–1992	0.726	0.274
1993–2000	0.882	0.118
2001–2007	0.757	0.243
Tunisia	0.620	0.380
1985–1992	0.661	0.339
1993–2000	0.605	0.395
2001–2007	0.592	0.408
Turkey	0.732	0.268
1985–1992	0.897	0.103
1993–2000	0.724	0.276
2001–2007	0.553	0.447

interesting from a modelling perspective. First, they show that the values used in conventional growth accounting, with labour shares around 0.6 and for capital around 0.4, as in Pissarides and Véganzonès-Varoudakis, (2006), may be inappropriate for the MENA countries. Second, these findings cast some doubts on the common practice of fitting Cobb Douglas functions for GDP with common elasticities for all countries and perhaps different technology levels.

Figure 9.3 shows the evolution of the predicted export share of GDP. The pattern is remarkable; not too smooth, in agreement with true values, which is the result of the good fit of the estimated model. There are general increases, although of very variable magnitude, since the mid-1990s. The evolution was more variable in the 1980s and early 1990s, with both strong decreases (Israel) and increases (Algeria, Egypt, Jordan). The trends of predicted import shares are shown in Figure 9.4, with increasing import shares only in the 2000s, and very variable evolution for the different countries in earlier years. Only for Jordan, Egypt and (but at very low level) Turkey is there a sustained increase in imports. The decrease in imports for Israel until the end of the 1990s is significant. Comparing Figures 9.3 and 9.4, the evolution of import shares is smoother than the evolution of export shares, suggesting lower export goods elasticities, in absolute values, than those for import goods.

The latter fact is illustrated in Figures 9.5 and 9.6, which show the evolution of own price elasticities for exports and imports, respectively. Export own elasticities are usually below 0.5, and with no clear trend except for Israel, with high but declining export elasticity. Values around 1 for Turkey and Egypt only

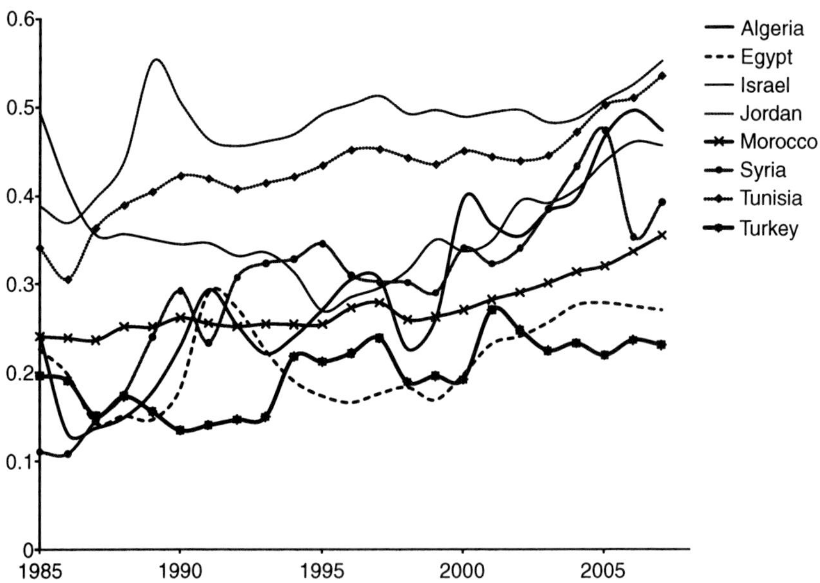

Figure 9.3 Predicted exports share in GDP.

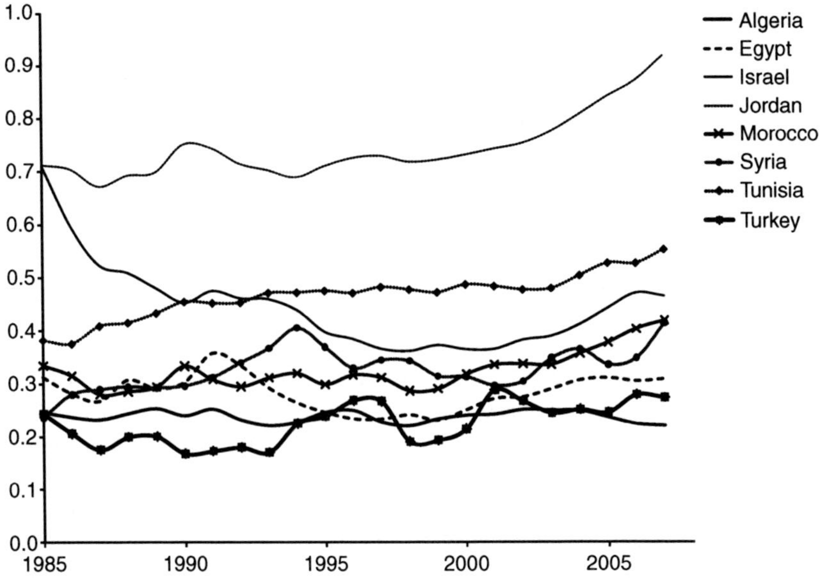

Figure 9.4 Predicted imports share in GDP.

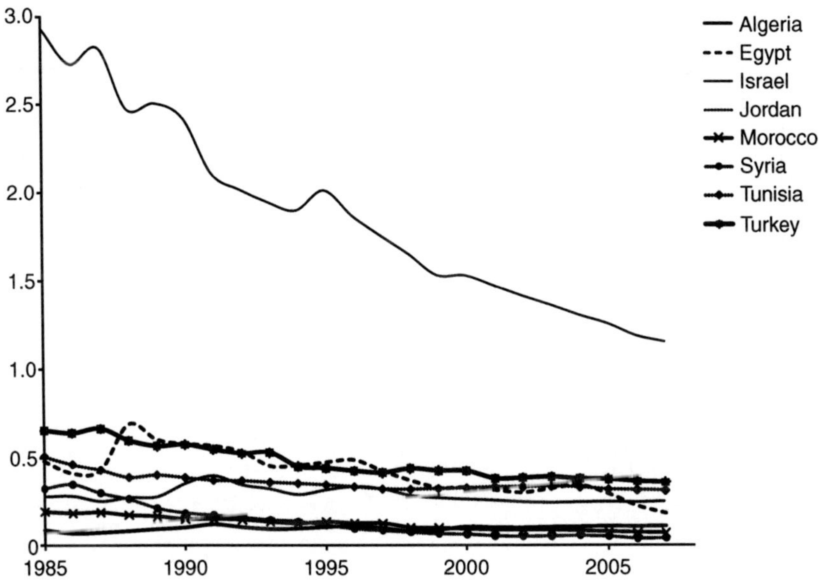

Figure 9.5 Elasticity own price exports.

appear in the 1980s and early 1990s. This is probably evidence of increased specialization due to liberal trade policies in recent years. Profiting from comparative advantages has therefore lower exports elasticity. Imports own elasticity is very high but declining too for Israel. Contrary to the findings for exports, imports own elasticities are of interesting magnitude for some countries: Egypt, Jordan and even Algeria. Exports and imports own elasticities have not been increasing since the mid-1990s.

Average values of the estimates of the own- and cross-price elasticities for all variable outputs and each country are presented in Table 9.3. Following the analysis of export and import responses, we first comment on cross-export price elasticity, taking into account the very low values. For Israel (mainly), Morocco, Tunisia and Turkey, exports and domestic consumption are substitutes; i.e. an increase in the export price has a negative effect on the supply of consumption goods and vice versa – an increase in the price of domestic goods has an adverse effect on export supply. The productions of exports and domestic consumption goods are complementary in Jordan. Exports and investment goods are also complementary in Israel, Jordan, Egypt and Morocco. However, Tunisia and Turkey show substitution between the production of exports and investment goods.

Investment goods are import-intensive, in the sense that an increase in the price of imports leads to a decrease in the supply of investment goods, for Israel, Jordan and Egypt, and to a lesser degree for the remaining countries, except Morocco. The consumption goods are import-intensive for all countries, but the effect is negligible except, perhaps, for Jordan.

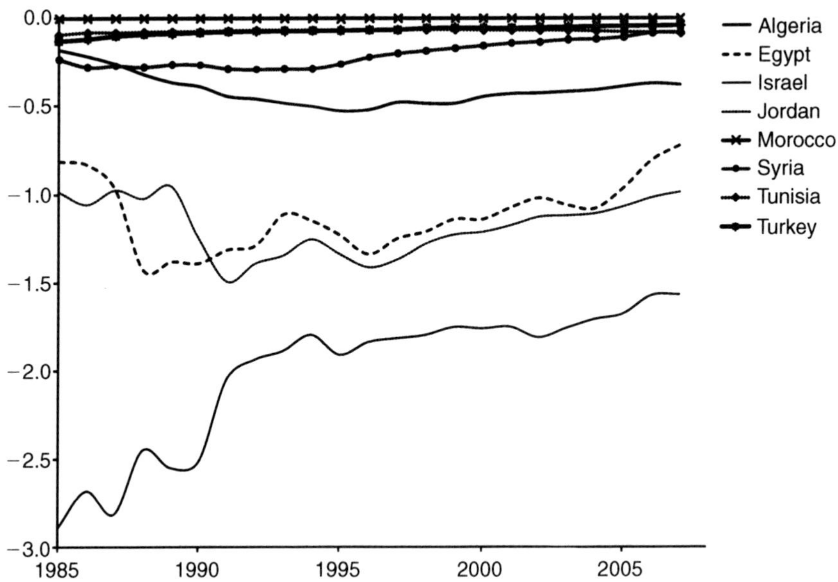

Figure 9.6 Elasticity own price imports.

Table 9.3 Price elasticities, 1985–2007 averages

	PC	*PI*	*PX*	*PM*		*PC*	*PI*	*PX*	*PM*
	Algeria					*Egypt*			
Consumption	0.02	0.01	0.03	−0.05	Consumption	0.04	0.01	0.06	−0.10
Investment	0.01	0.01	0.02	−0.04	Investment	0.04	0.18	0.10	−0.31
Exports	0.06	0.02	0.10	−0.18	Exports	0.18	0.07	0.28	−0.53
Imports	0.13	0.05	0.22	−0.41	Imports	0.29	0.20	0.47	−0.96
	Israel					*Jordan*			
Consumption	0.24	0.03	−0.17	−0.11	Consumption	0.12	0.08	0.13	−0.33
Investment	0.15	0.18	0.55	−0.88	Investment	0.29	0.18	0.31	−0.79
Exports	−0.42	0.31	1.89	−1.79	Exports	0.27	0.17	0.29	−0.72
Imports	0.21	0.39	1.41	−2.01	Imports	0.44	0.27	0.47	−1.18
	Morocco					*Syria*			
Consumption	0.17	−0.07	−0.08	−0.02	Consumption	0.00	0.00	0.01	−0.02
Investment	−0.23	0.09	0.11	0.02	Investment	0.01	0.00	0.02	−0.02
Exports	−0.25	0.10	0.12	0.02	Exports	0.04	0.01	0.13	−0.19
Imports	0.04	−0.02	−0.02	0.00	Imports	0.05	0.02	0.14	−0.21
	Tunisia					*Turkey*			
Consumption	0.10	−0.03	−0.14	0.07	Consumption	0.04	0.02	−0.05	−0.01
Investment	−0.08	0.02	0.12	−0.06	Investment	0.08	0.07	−0.17	0.02
Exports	−0.26	0.07	0.36	−0.17	Exports	−0.21	−0.20	0.47	−0.07
Imports	−0.11	0.03	0.16	−0.08	Imports	0.03	−0.02	0.06	−0.07

Consumption and investment goods are complementary in Jordan, Israel, Tunisia and Turkey, and substitutes in Egypt and Morocco. However, the cross-price effects of consumption and investment goods are very low. This is partly because the supply elasticities for consumption, mainly, and for investment goods are in general very low, almost completely inelastic, due to aggregation, the composition of public expenditure, and market imperfections.

4 Productivity and technical change biases

Next, we examine the evolution of GDP components from the estimates of productivity and technical change biases. Jorgenson and Fraumeni (1981) show that biased (non-neutral) effects of technical change are equivalent to particular price effects on total factor productivity, and that the share weighted difference between netput i technical change and TFP is the effect of changes in the price of netput i on TFP. Although biased technical change is commonly analysed in terms of share changes over time, the latter meaning is more appealing: TFP is dependent on changes in relative prices.

Figure 9.7 presents the evolution of TFP growth. It is worth noting that Diewert and Wales (1992) pointed out that flexible functions, such as the normalized quadratic in this analysis, give technical progress estimates which are smoothed versions of the estimates from growth accounting. In general, TFP growth has been increasing since the mid-1990s. In particular, TFP growth was been very high in the 2000s.

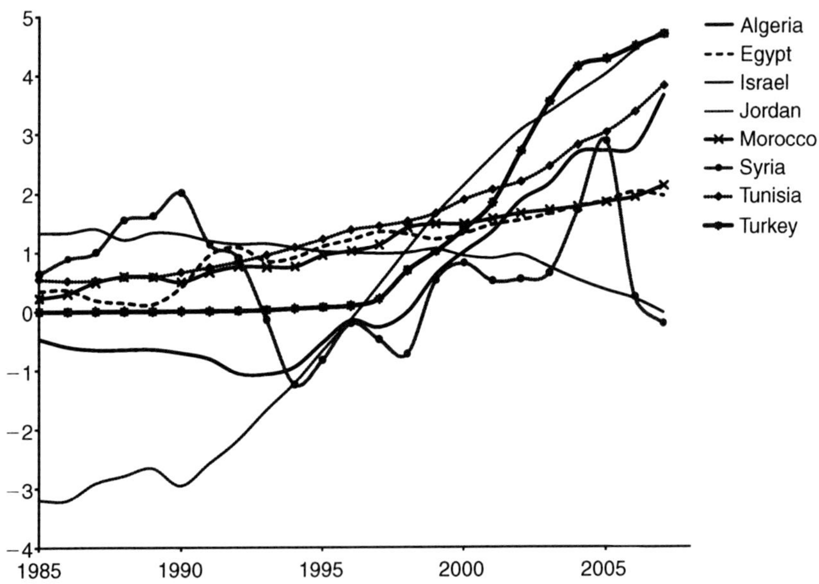

Figure 9.7 Total factor productivity.

Average values of total factor productivity (TFP) growth and technical change biases are reported in Table 9.4. For ease of interpretation, imports biases are shown as the negative of the values obtained in the estimation system, because imports are negative outputs. The comparison of the biases clearly reflects the dissimilarities in growth for the countries in the sample, because any possible combination of biases according to sign is presented.

Sekkat (2010) finds important productivity adjustments due to the phenomena of firm entry and exit for Morocco, Tunisia and Turkey. However, other causes

Table 9.4 Total factor productivity (TFP) and technical change biases; averages (%)

	TFP growth	*Biases*			
		Consumption	*Investment*	*Exports*	*Imports*
Algeria	0.4	−0.5	0.0	−0.4	−0.9
1985–1992	−0.7	−0.2	−0.2	0.1	−0.3
1993–2000	−0.2	−0.9	−0.6	−0.1	−1.6
2001–2007	2.5	−0.5	0.9	−1.3	−0.9
Egypt	1.1	−0.4	0.0	0.7	0.4
1985–1992	0.4	0.2	−0.7	0.2	−0.3
1993–2000	1.2	−0.3	−0.2	0.7	0.2
2001–2007	1.7	−1.3	1.1	1.5	1.3
Israel	1.0	−0.6	−0.3	0.7	−0.2
1985–1992	1.3	−1.2	−0.1	−0.7	−2.0
1993–2000	1.0	−0.6	−0.3	0.5	−0.4
2001–2007	0.5	0.2	−0.7	2.5	2.0
Jordan	0.2	1.1	−0.6	0.7	1.2
1985–1992	−2.8	0.0	−0.3	0.6	0.3
1993–2000	0.2	0.6	−0.8	0.8	0.6
2001–2007	3.7	3.0	−0.8	0.8	3.0
Morocco	1.1	−0.5	0.3	1.0	0.7
1985–1992	0.5	−0.3	−0.2	1.1	0.7
1993–2000	1.1	−0.5	0.3	1.0	0.7
2001–2007	1.8	−0.8	0.8	0.8	0.8
Syria	0.6	2.1	−1.4	1.2	2.0
1985–1992	1.2	0.2	−1.0	0.9	0.0
1993–2000	−0.3	3.2	−1.6	1.5	3.1
2001–2007	0.9	3.2	−1.4	1.1	2.9
Tunisia	1.6	−0.4	−0.7	0.6	−0.5
1985–1992	0.6	−0.5	0.3	0.6	0.4
1993–2000	1.4	−0.3	−0.6	0.6	−0.2
2001–2007	2.8	−0.4	−2.0	0.7	−1.7
Turkey	1.3	−0.3	0.6	0.5	0.9
1985–1992	0.0	−0.0	0.0	0.0	0.0
1993–2000	0.4	−0.2	0.2	0.2	0.3
2001–2007	3.7	−0.7	1.8	1.4	2.5

for TFP growth operate, as TFP growth has been very high in recent years, except for Israel and Syria, and always positive.

It is remarkable that technical change biases are in general stronger than the general technical change effect, in particular regarding exports and imports. Technical change is consumption-reducing or small, except in Syria and Jordan, where it is clearly consumption-augmenting and investment-reducing. Technical progress is also investment-reducing in Israel.

Figure 9.8 shows the evolution of export biases of technical change. In general, technical change is export-augmenting except in Algeria, where it is progressively reducing, and Tunisia, where it is more or less stable. Israel shows an increasingly augmenting export bias of technical change.

The evolution of import biases of technical change is shown in Figure 9.9. Technical change is import-saving in Algeria and Tunisia, and import-using in the remaining countries. Israel changed remarkably from import-saving to import-using in the mid-1990s.

The main traits for the different countries are as follows. Algeria exhibits a productivity decline until the mid-1990s and progressive improvements since then. This pattern is related to the evolution of the progressive decrease or less reducing biases for exports and imports, and to investment goods-augmenting biases.

Egypt shows a positive evolution of technical change since the early 1990s. In addition, technical change is clearly trade- and investment goods-augmenting and progressively consumption goods-reducing.

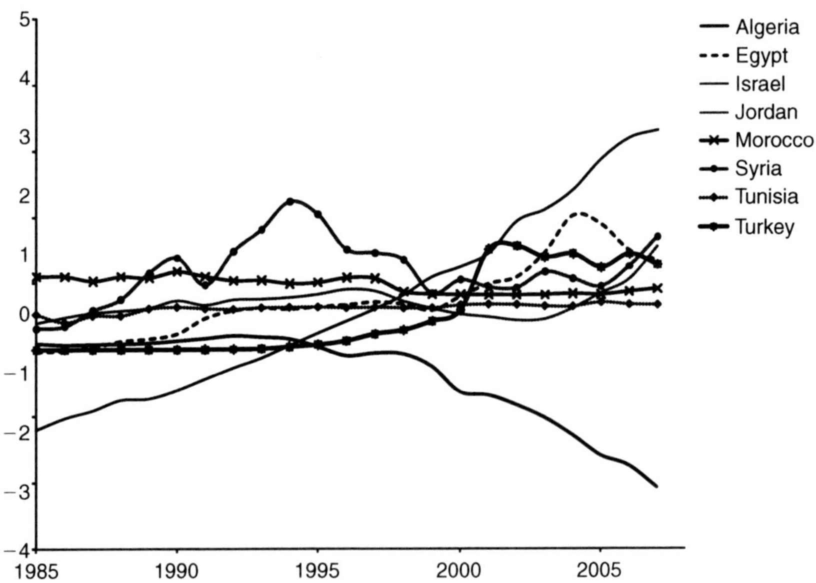

Figure 9.8 Technical change biases exports.

Productivity grew at a slower pace in Israel during the period. It is remarkable how biases evolve for trade. Technical change was import- and export-reducing until the mid-1990s, and import- and export-augmenting since the mid-1990s. A similar but lower pattern is observed in consumption goods.

Jordan exhibits technical regress and small technical change biases until the mid-1990s. and technical progress with important biases since then. In the 2000s, import- and consumption goods-augmenting biases are particularly important.

Morocco shows progressive productivity improvements. This is just the opposite of the findings in Sekkat (2004) for earlier periods, since the 1960s. Trade-augmenting biases are more or less stable. The pattern of technical change is followed in the evolution of investment goods-augmenting and consumption goods-reducing technical change biases.

Syria exhibits the most volatile pattern of productivity growth and technical change biases. The productivity decline in the 1990s is remarkable, in association with a large consumption goods-augmenting bias. The import-augmenting bias is very important, following the same pattern of general productivity change.

Progressive and important productivity improvements are found for Tunisia, but at the cost of problematic biases. High productivity growth at the sectoral level has been reported for Tunisia in Nabli *et al.* (2001), who also noted that Tunisia's trade specialization has shifted dramatically since the 1980s. The World Bank (2009) concludes that 'trade integration, mainly with the EU, has played a key role' in Tunisia's income growth. Remarkable consumption- and investment goods- and import-decreasing trends suggest that little progress is to be expected in this area.

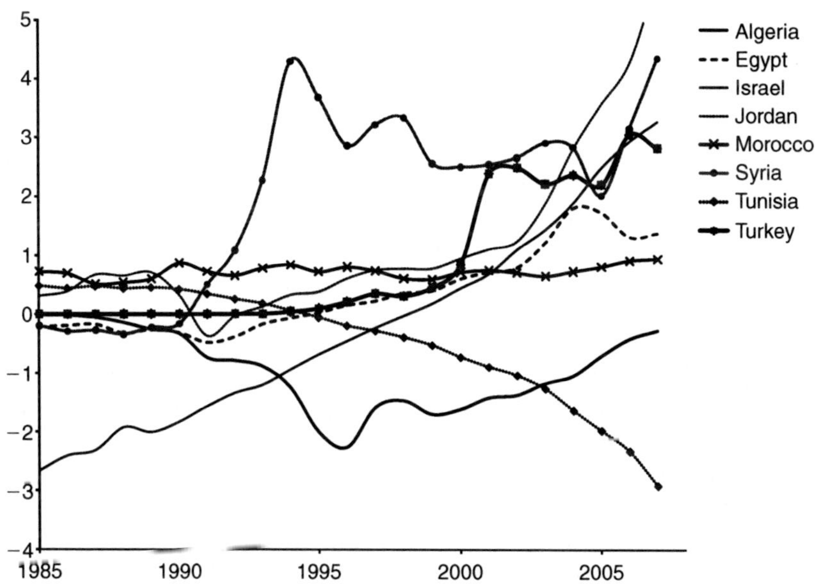

Figure 9.9 Technical change biases imports.

The evolution of TFP growth and technical change biases in Turkey is very peculiar. Technical change and biases were negligible until 1995 and have increased very quickly since then. First, we must note that this is a smooth trend and not the representation of true inter-year variations. Second, we recognize technical change effects as a composite of true technology improvements and efficiency improvements due to the closing of inefficient firms, as noted by Sekkat (2010) in a micro-econometric analysis of firm creation and destruction.

To summarize, there is in general progressive increase in productivity for most of the countries. However, the pattern of evolution and the characteristics of technical change biases are dissimilar, although clearly trade-augmenting for some countries. These results reinforce the idea behind the difficulties of the Mediterranean MENA countries in operating in an integrated way.

5 Conclusion

The characteristics of exports and imports are modelled jointly with domestic goods and investment goods in a production framework for eight Mediterranean MENA countries. Price elasticities and technical change effects summarize the evolution of trade variables. The empirical results are as comparable as possible between countries because the variables have been constructed in the same way given data availability.

The results from this chapter provide a detailed picture of the effects of technical progress on the economies of the countries analysed. Productivity is increasing in most of the countries and the trends are of increasing productivity, in particular since the mid-1990s. This fact exemplifies how productivity improvements develop quite slowly, because the main adjustment programs in the countries studied data from the mid-1980s.

The estimates of the effects of technical progress also illustrate how technical change may favour some aggregates. In particular, except for Algeria, there has been support for trade expansion for at least the past 15 years, with varying importance of export- and import-biased technical change. Biased technical change is given two simultaneous explanations: the evolution of technical change favouring some aggregates, such as exports, over time, and the higher sensitivity of this particular aggregate to evolve according to favourable price changes.

Price elasticities are also notable. Imports tend to be more elastic, suggesting better adaptation to changing economic environments. On the other hand, the low values of export elasticity, and the decline in the export elasticities in the countries with higher values, are the natural consequence of trade specialization. The results for Israel, with a strong export sector specializing in high technology, illustrate this main issue. On the same ground, Tunisia's development is particularly problematic because the number of items exported has increased greatly in the latter years, which suggests less specialization even assuming larger fragmentation in international trade. However, Tunisia concentrates its exports to a much-reduced number of EU countries, in a certain sense disregarding particular (macro-)economic conditions. This suggests a cautionary message regarding developments following the Barcelona Process: the increase in trade between Mediterranean MENA countries and EU countries could result in excessive dependence on the economic conditions of EU importers for the MENA exporter.

Although there are no clusters of countries exhibiting the same set of elasticity and technical change signs, implying that no two countries are very close in economic behaviour, a pattern of joint evolution is found. In particular, the results tend to be more similar in the final years. This means that these countries can be closer in economic evolution and, in spite of the difficulties of increasing trade due to specialization, other forms of economic cooperation could be appealing. In this line, this conclusion supports the suggestions by Hoekman and Sekkat (2010) that returns on efforts to deepen integration of services, labour and capital markets are likely to be higher than those derived from trade, and that trade openness is a secondary factor in the development of the MENA economies (Brach, 2008).

The fact that the consequences of economic reforms tend to appear in the latter years of the sample in spite of having been implemented since the early and mid-1980s suggests that transformations and adjustments in the real economy are slow. The conclusion is that diverse economic policies must be implemented without seeking an immediate payback. Moreover, it is important to develop consistent and continuous improvements over existing policies without turning back to older protectionist models. Recent improvements in productivity and trade show that even moderate success takes a long time. Moreover, because of the trend toward less flexibility when the MENA exporters benefit from natural advantages, care must be taken in production and country diversification, to enhance inner labour and capital markets without a large risk of foreign dependence.

References

Agénor, P.R. and Montiel, P.K. (2008) *Development Macroeconomics* (3rd edn), Princeton, NJ: Princeton University Press.

Benhassine, N. (2009) *From Privilege to Competition: Unlocking Private-led Growth in the Middle East and North Africa*, Washington, DC: The World Bank.

Bhattacharya R. and Wolde, H. (2010a) 'Constraints on Growth in the MENA Region', IMF Working Paper, Middle East and Central Asia Department WP/10/30.

Bhattacharya R. and Wolde, H. (2010b) 'Constraints on Trade in the MENA Region', IMF Working Paper, Middle East and Central Asia Department WP/10/31.

Boulila, G. and Trabelsi, M. (2004) 'The Causality Issues in the Finance and Growth Nexus: Empirical Evidence from Middle East and North African Countries', *Review of Middle East Economics and Finance*, 2(2): Art. 3.

Brach, J. (2008) 'Economic Development of the Arab Countries in the Middle East and North Africa Determinants, Constraints, and Implications for EU–Arab Relations', Dissertation, Fakultät für Wirtschafts- und Sozialwissenschaften der Universität Hamburg.

Brach, J. (2009) 'Technology, Political Economy, and Economic Development in the Middle East and North Africa', *Review of Middle East Economics and Finance*, 5(3): Art. 1.
Calleya, S.C. (2005) *Evaluating Euro-Mediterranean Relations*, London: Routledge.
Chourou, B. (2004) 'Arab Regional Integration as a Prerequisite for a Successful Euro-Mediterranean Partnership', in A. Jünemann (ed.), *Euro-Mediterranean Relations after September 11: International, Regional and Domestic Dynamics*, London: Frank Cass and Company.
Dawson, C. (2009) *EU Integration with North Africa. Trade Negotiations and Democracy Deficits in Morocco*, London: I.B. Tauris.
Devlin, J.C. (2010) *Challenges of Economic Development in the Middle East and North Africa Region*, Singapore: World Scientific.
Diewert, W.E. and Wales, T.J. (1992) 'Quadratic Spline Models for Producer's Supply and Demand Functions', *International Economic Review*, 33: 705–722.
Easterly, W. and Levine R. (2001) 'It's Not Factor Accumulation: Stylized Facts and Growth', *World Bank Economic Review*, 15: 177–219.
El-Erian, M.A. and Fischer, S. (2000) 'Is MENA a Region? The Scope for Regional Integration', in J.W. Wright Jr (ed.), *Economic and Political Impediments to Middle East Peace. Critical Questions and Alternative Scenarios*, New York, NY: St Martin's Press.
Esfahani, H.S. (2006) 'A Reexamination of the Political Economy of Growth in the MENA Countries', in J.B. Nugent and H. Pesaran (eds), *Explaining Growth in the Middle East*, Amsterdam: Elsevier.
Esfahani, H.S. and Squire, L. (2007) 'Explaining Trade Policy in the Middle East and North Africa', *The Quarterly Review of Economics and Finance*, 46(5): 660–684.
Fawzy, S. (2003) 'The Economics and Politics of Arab Economic Integration', in A. Galal and B. Hoekman (eds), *Arab Economic Integration: Between Hope and Reality*, Washington, DC: Brookings Institution Press.
Fox K.J. and Diewert W.E. (1999) 'Is the Asia-Pacific Different? Technical Progress Bias and Price Elasticity Estimates for 18 OECD Countries, 1960–1992', in T.-T. Fu, C.J. Huang and C.A.K. Lovell (eds), *Economic Efficiency and Productivity Growth in the Asia-Pacific Region*, Cheltenham: Edward Elgar.
Galal, A. and Hoekman B. (eds) (2003) 'Between Hope and Reality: An Overview of Arab Economic Integration', A. Galal and B. Hoekman (eds), *Arab Economic Integration: Between Hope and Reality*, Washington, DC: Brookings Institution Press.
Guncavdi, O. and Kucukcifci, S. (2005) 'Financial Reforms and the Decomposition of Economic Growth: An Investigation of the Changing Role of the Financial Sector in Turkey', *Review of Middle East Economics and Finance*, 3(1): Art. 4.
Heston, A., Summers, R. and Aten, B. (1996) *Penn World Table Version 5.6*, Center for International Comparisons of Production, Income and Prices at the University of Pennsylvania.
Hoekman, B. and Sekkat, K. (2010) 'Arab Economic Integration: Missing Links', CEPR Discussion Paper No. DP7807.
Hofmann, S. (2008) 'Regional Cooperation Under Conflict: Israeli–Arab Business Cooperation in the Middle East', in C. Harders and M. Legrenzi (eds), *Beyond Regionalism? Regional Cooperation, Regionalism and Regionalization in the Middle East*, Aldershot: Ashgate.
Jorgenson, D.W. and Fraumeni, B.M. (1981) 'Relative Prices and Technical Change', in E.R. Berndt and B.C. Field (eds), *Modeling and Measuring Natural Resource Substitution*, Cambridge, MA: MIT Press.

Kohli, U. (1993) 'A Symmetric Normalized Quadratic GNP Function and the US Demand for Imports and Supply of Exports', *International Economic Review*, 34: 243–255.

Konan, D. (2003) 'Alternative Paths to Prosperity: Economic Integration among Arab Countries', in A. Galal and B. Hoekman (eds), *Arab Economic Integration: Between Hope and Reality*, Washington, DC: Brookings Institution Press.

Loayza, N.V. and Odawara, R. (2010) 'Infrastructure and Economic Growth in Egypt', World Bank, Policy Research Working Paper No. 5177.

Makdisi, S., Fattah, Z. and Liman, I. (2006) Determinants of Growth in the MENA Countries', in J.B. Nugent and H. Pesaran (eds), *Explaining Growth in the Middle East*, Amsterdam: Elsevier.

Nabli, M.K., Bahlous, M., Bechri, M., El Abbassi, M., El Ferktaji, R. and Talbi, B. (2001) 'Trade, Finance and Competitiveness in Tunisia', in J.M. Fanelli and R. Medhora (eds), *Finance and Competitiveness in Developing Countries*, London: Routledge.

Nas, T.F. (2008) *Tracing the Economic Transformation of Turkey from the 1920s to EU Accession*, Leiden: Brill NV.

Nitzan, J. and Bichler, S. (2002) *The Global Political Economy of Israel*, London: Pluto Press.

Nugent, J.B. and Pesaran, H. (2006) 'Introduction: Explaining Growth in the Middle East', in J.B. Nugent and H. Pesaran (eds), *Explaining Growth in the Middle East*, Amsterdam: Elsevier.

Otman, W. and Karlberg, E. (2007) *The Libyan Economy. Economic Diversification and International Repositioning*, New York, NY: Springer.

Pastore, F., Ferragina, A.M. and Giovannetti, G. (2009) A Tale of Parallel Integration Processes: A Gravity Analysis of EU Trade with Mediterranean and Central and Eastern European Countries', *Review of Middle East Economics and Finance*, 5(2): Art. 2.

Pissarides, C. and Véganzonès-Varoudakis, M.A. (2006) 'Labor Markets and Economic Growth in the MENA Region', in J.B. Nugent and H. Pesaran (eds), *Explaining Growth in the Middle East*, Amsterdam: Elsevier.

Romagnoli, A. and Mengoni, L. (2009) 'The Challenge of Economic Integration in the MENA Region: From GAFTA and EU-MFTA to Small Scale Arab Unions', *Economic Change and Restructuring*, 42: 69–83.

Sala-i-Martin, X. and Artadi, E. (2003) 'Economic Growth and Investment in the Arab World', Departament d'Economia i Empresa UPF, Economics and Business Working Papers Series, 683.

Sayan, S. (ed.) (2009). *Economic Performance in the Middle East and North Africa. Institutions, Corruption and Reform*, London: Routledge.

Sekkat, K (2004) 'Sources of Growth in Morocco: An Empirical Analysis in a Regional Perspective', *Review of Middle East Economics and Finance*, 2(1).

Sekkat, K. (ed.) (2008) *Competition and Efficiency in the Arab World*, Basingstoke: Palgrave-McMillan.

Sekkat, K. (ed.) (2010) *Market Dynamics and Productivity in Developing Countries. Economic Reforms in the Middle East and North Africa*, New York, NY: Springer.

TÜİK (2009) *Statistical Indicators 1923–2008*, Turkish Statistical Institute.

World Bank (2006) *Kingdom of Morocco: Country Economic Memorandum: Fostering Higher Growth and Employment with Productive Diversification and Competitiveness* (two volumes), Washington, DC: World Bank.

World Bank (2009) *Tunisia's Global Integration. A Second Generation of Reforms Growth and Employment*, Washington, DC: World Bank.

Yousef, T.M. (2004) 'Development, Growth and Policy Reform in the Middle East and North Africa since 1950', *Journal of Economic Perspectives*, 18(3): 91–116.

Zorob, A. (2008) 'Intraregional Economic Integration: The Cases of GAFTA and MAFTA', in C. Harders and M. Legrenzi (eds), *Beyond Regionalism? Regional Cooperation, Regionalism and Regionalization in the Middle East*, Aldershot: Ashgate.

Zürcher, E. J. (2004). *Turkey. A Modern History* (3rd edn). London: I.B. Tauris.

Part IV

Social welfare and public policy in the Mediterranean

10 The financial sector and poverty in the MENA countries

Muhsin Kar, Bülent Güloğlu, Şaban Nazlioğlu and Hüseyin Ağir

1 Introduction

The link between financial development and economic growth has been one of the long-debated theoretical issues – whether the financial sector actually contributes to the real sector in the process of economic development. The empirical works reveal that there is no universal consensus on the causal relationship between financial development and economic growth. In fact, the empirical evidence suggests that the relationship between financial development and economic growth is sensitive to choice of the proxy used for the measurement of financial development in most cases.

Despite several previous studies on the MENA region having provided similar conflicting results on the causality issue, the causal relationship between financial development and poverty reduction has been neglected. Previous studies on this subject concerning the MENA countries largely utilize a bivariate causality analysis and may, therefore, suffer from the omission of variable bias. Recently it has been argued that financial development might directly cause poverty alleviation emanating from the availability of accessible financial instruments, services and institutions for poor households. Therefore, the introduction of a third variable affecting both financial and economic growth in the bivariate framework may alter not only the direction of causality between the two variables, but also the magnitude of the estimate.

To our best of knowledge, there is not any study which has gone the full distance to empirically examine the impact of financial development and economic growth on the ultimate policy goal, i.e. poverty reduction for the MENA countries. This study tries to contribute to the literature by examining the causal relationship among financial development, economic growth and poverty reduction in the MENA region. In this regard, this chapter attempts to answer two critical questions: (1) Does financial development (economic growth), which results from economic growth (financial development), lead to poverty reduction in the MENA region? (2) Which sector leads in the process of poverty reduction in the MENA – the financial sector or the real sector? In order empirically to investigate the interactions among these variables, this chapter employs a trivariate modelling framework by employing the recent developments in the panel data analysis for the period 1980–2007.

2 Financial development, economic growth and poverty reduction

The relationship between financial development and economic growth has long remained an important issue of debate in the literature (Schumpeter, 1912; Robinson, 1952; Patrick, 1966; McKinnon, 1973; Shaw, 1973; Greenwood and Jovanovic, 1990; Bencivenga and Smith, 1991; Roubini and Sala-i Martin, 1992; King and Levine, 1993a, 1993b; Pagano, 1993, Khan and Senhadji, 2003; Deidda, 2006; Trew, 2006, Yang and Yi, 2008). These theoretical discussions over several decades reveal that there is not a consensus on either the role of finance in economic growth or the direction of causal inference between finance and growth. Recently, a few theoretical and empirical studies (De Janvry and Sadoulet, 2000; Dollar and Kraay, 2001; Eastwood and Lipton, 2001; Holden and Prokopenko, 2001; Clarke *et al.*, 2002; Jalilian and Kirkpatrick, 2002, 2005; Honohan, 2004; Jeanneney and Kpodar, 2005; Quartey, 2005; Odhiambo, 2009) have added a third variable, namely poverty reduction, to the debate on the link between financial development and economic growth. Introducing a new element to the existing discussion might open new channels among the concerned variables, and deserves further investigation.

It is argued that financial development directly or indirectly leads to poverty reduction. In Figure 10.1, A and B show the indirect contribution of financial development to poverty reduction through economic growth, while C reflects direct interaction between financial development and poverty reduction.

As far as the *indirect contribution of the financial sector to poverty reduction which works through economic growth* is concerned, this is directly related with the discussion on the causal inference between finance and economic growth. The debate on this topic can be traced back to early last century. Schumpeter (1912) emphasizes the importance of financial services in promoting economic growth. This view was also supported later by Gurley and Shaw (1955) and Goldsmith (1969), who argue that more developed financial markets promote economic growth by mobilizing savings and facilitating investment. In addition, Patrick (1966) contributes to the literature by developing two new concepts: demand following and supply leading. The first one emphasizes the importance of the creation of modern financial institutions, their financial assets and liabilities, and relates financial services to the response to the demand for these services by investors and savers in the real economy (Patrick, 1966: 174). This approach implies that financial system can thus support and sustain the leading sectors in the process of growth. Here, an expansion of the financial system is induced as a consequence of real economic growth. The second one means the creation of financial institutions and the supply of their financial assets and liabilities, and relates financial services to advance demand for them, especially the demand of entrepreneurs in the modern, growth-inducing sectors. 'Supply leading' has two functions: to transfer resources from traditional (non-growth) sectors to modern sectors, and to promote and stimulate an entrepreneurial response in these modern sectors (Patrick, 1966: 75).

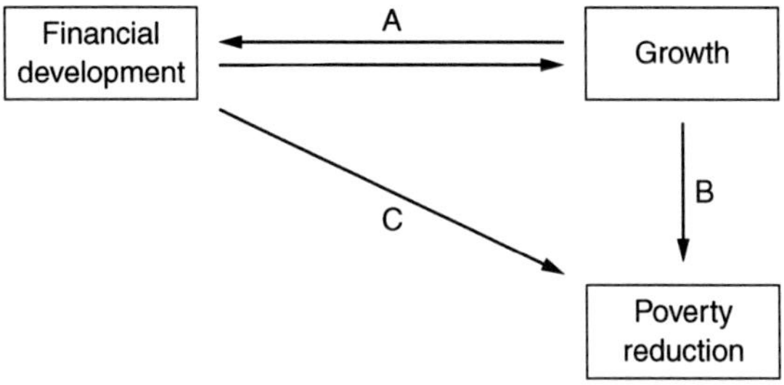

Figure 10.1 Direct and indirect relations among finance, economic growth and poverty (source: DFID, 2004).

Similarly, in the early 1970s a new paradigm in the design of financial policies emerged, and its underpinnings were provided by both McKinnon (1973) and Shaw (1973), who prescribe liberalization of financial markets by deregulating interest rates and permitting financial institutions to allocate credit on the basis of viability and productivity of borrowers, their enterprises or projects. They basically argue that financial liberalization through higher interest rates leads not only to a more efficient allocation of funds but also to an increase in loanable funds by attracting more households' savings to banking deposits. This in turn leads to greater investment and hence faster economic growth.

Moreover, the emergence of the endogenous growth theory in the 1980s (Romer, 1986, 1990; Lucas, 1988; Barro, 1991) renewed the debate regarding the link between the financial sector and economic growth. Following this new literature, attempts have been made to analyse whether the initial level of financial development and financial policies are determinants of economic growth. It is hypothesized that, following the work of Goldsmith (1969), McKinnon (1973) and Shaw (1973), countries starting with a more developed financial structure will achieve higher growth rates since a better financial structure may attract more savings, and can finance more investment and may allocate resources to the highest yielding investment projects. Several studies have attempted to show how the operation of the financial sector may affect the rate of economic growth in the endogenous framework (Greenwood and Jovanovic, 1990; Bencivenga and Smith, 1991; Roubini and Sala-i Martin, 1992; King and Levine, 1993a, 1993b; Pagano, 1993, Bencivenga *et al.*, 1996). Finance can influence growth in an endogenous growth model by increasing the savings rate (Bencivenga and Smith, 1991), by increasing the returns on investment (Greenwood and Jovanovic, 1990), and by increasing human capital accumulation (Levine and Renelt, 1992). In these studies, financial intermediaries (such as information collection and analysis, risk sharing and liquidity provision) are explicitly modelled and these models suggest that financial development is generally growth-promoting (Levine, 1997). In these analyses, it is implicitly assumed that achievement of economic growth would unambiguously contribute to poverty reduction.

Once the *causal inference between financial development and economic growth*[1] is established,[2] it is easy to argue that economic growth induces poverty reduction (De Janvry and Sadoulet, 2000; Dollar and Kraay, 2001; Eastwood and Lipton, 2001). In particular, De Janvry and Sadoulet (2000) find that although economic growth reduces rural and urban poverty on average, the negative impact of recessions was stronger than the positive impact of expansions in 12 countries in Latin America for the period 1970–1994. Dollar and Kraay (2001) show that the income of the bottom 20% of the population has a unitary elasticity with respect to growth, implying that economic growth does not disadvantage the poor by excluding them from growth-induced prosperity in a sample of 80 countries over four decades. However, the work of Holden and Prokopenko (2001) shows that economic growth may not be a sufficient condition for poverty reduction. In particular, Holden and Prokopenko (2001) argue that it is possible for a country to enjoy positive economic growth without any benefit to its poorest households, if income inequality increases. If this is the case, then the rich will get richer while the poor will get poorer.

With regard to the *direct contribution of financial development to poverty reduction*, financial development can lead to poverty reduction in developing countries in a number of ways (Odhiambo, 2009). First, financial development, by addressing the causes of financial market failure such as information asymmetry and a high fixed-cost of lending to small borrowers, can improve the opportunities for the poor to access formal finance (Stiglitz, 1998; Jalilian and Kirkpatrick, 2001). Second, a sound financial system allows the poor to access financial services, particularly the credit and insurance-risk services. This, in turn, strengthens the productive assets of the poor, enhancing their productivity and increasing the potential for achieving sustainable livelihoods (World Bank, 2001; Jalilian and Kirkpatrick, 2002, 2005; Odhiambo, 2009). DFID (2004) provides empirical support that the financial sector enables the poor to draw down accumulated savings or borrow money to start micro-enterprises. These developments eventually contribute to wider access to financial services, create more employment, result in higher incomes and thus alleviate poverty. Overall, the direct link between financial development and poverty alleviation arises from the availability of accessible financial instruments, services and institutions for poor households (Holden and Prokopenko, 2001; Odhiambo, 2009).

As regards empirical studies, there is a growing literature which investigates the causal relationship between financial development and poverty reduction (Clarke *et al*., 2002; Jalilian and Kirkpatrick, 2002, 2005; Beck *et al*., 2004; Honohan, 2004; Jeanneney and Kpodar, 2005; Quartey, 2005; Odhiambo, 2009, Bittencourt, 2009). In particular, Jalilian and Kirkpatrick (2002, 2005) show that financial development contributed to poverty reduction through a growth-enhancing effect up to a certain threshold level of economic development in 42 economies, 26 developing and 16 developed. In the same vein, Beck *et al.* (2004) reveal that the income of the poorest 20% of the population grew faster than the average GDP per capita in countries with higher financial development in 52 developing and developed countries. Jeanneney and Kpodar (2005) find that financial development is pro-poor, and financial instability specifically hurt the poor and dampened the positive effect of financial development on poverty reduction in 75 developing countries for the period 1966–2000. Quartey (2005) concludes that even though financial sector development does not Granger-cause savings mobilization in Ghana, it leads to poverty reduction. Honohan (2004) detects that there is a negative association between financial sector development and headcount poverty. In particular, a 10% point increase in the ratio of private credit to GDP should reduce poverty ratios by 2.5–3% points. Odhiambo (2009) shows that both financial and economic development Granger-cause poverty reduction in South Africa. Bittencourt (2009) concludes that financial development had a significant and robust effect in reducing inequality in Brazil for the period 1985–1994.

3 Empirical analysis

3.1 Model specification and data

The relationship between financial development and economic growth in the empirical literature is generally investigated in a bivariate framework for the MENA countries (Al-Tamimi *et al.*, 2002; Achy, 2004; Boulila and Trabelsi, 2004; Creane *et al.* 2004; Al-Awad and Harb, 2005; Abu-Bader and Abu-Qarn, 2008; Nazlioglu *et al.*, 2009). A quick review of these researches reveals that the direction of causality between finance and growth is not certain, and the links between variables are country- and indicator-specific in these countries.

Unlike the above cited studies, Caporale and Pittis (1997), Caporale *et al.* (2004) and Odhiambo (2008, 2009) argue that the causality studies based on a bivariate framework can turn out to be inappropriate because of the well-known omitted variable problem. Omitting an important variable can change both the inference and the magnitude of the estimates. In order to overcome this problem, the authors suggest using more than two variables in testing the causality. Accordingly, in this study we employ a multivariate model to investigate the linkage amongst financial development, real income and poverty reduction in the MENA region. The model in panel data form can be written as follows:

$$\ln Pov_{it} = \beta_0 + \beta_1 \ln Y_{it} + \beta_2 \ln FDI_{it} + \varepsilon_{it} \quad (i = 1, 2, 3, ..., N); (t = 1, 2, 3, ..., T) \quad (1)$$

where *Pov* stands for poverty, *Y* represents the economic growth and FDI denotes the financial development index.

The panel set covers annual data spanning the period from 1980 to 2007 for 14 MENA countries (Algeria, Bahrain, Egypt, Iran, Israel, Jordan, Kuwait, Morocco, Qatar, Saudi Arabia, Sudan, Syria, Tunisia and Turkey). Availability of the data for the MENA region countries has limited both the number of countries and the time span of the analysis.

The description of the variables used in the study is as follows. The measurement of poverty is a controversial issue to be dealt with, and a large number of proxies for poverty measure have been proposed in the empirical studies. While Deininger and Squire (1996) and Lundberge and Squire (1998) employed the Gini coefficient and headcount data for poor people, Ravallion (1992), Woolard and Leibbrandt (1999), Quartney (2005) and Odhiambo (2009) employed per capita consumption as a measure for poverty reduction. Since the use of per capita consumption as a proxy for poverty reduction appears to be more reliable, in this study per capita final real consumption expenditure is chosen as an indicator for poverty reduction. Odhiambo (2009) argues that this measure is consistent with the World Bank's definition of poverty as 'the inability to attain a minimal standard of living' measured in terms of basic consumption needs. In addition, the economic growth is measured by per capita real GDP. Both real consumption and real income in national currencies and population are collected from the Statistical Division Database of the United Nations (UN, 2010).

Another issue in the variable description stage is to construct proxy/proxies for financial development. Different measures of financial development have been suggested in the literature (King and Levine, 1993a, 1993b; Lynch, 1996; Nazlioglu *et al.*, 2009). In order to overcome a potential omitted variable bias it is convenient to use a bulk of financial development indicators. Following the literature on financial development we use three financial development indicators which were originally suggested by King and Levine (1993a, 1993b): ratio of broad money (M2) to GDP (hereafter M2Y); ratio of domestic credit to GDP (hereafter DCY), and ratio of private sector credits to GDP (hereafter CPSY). The data on financial development indicators were obtained from IMF'S International Financial Statistics.

Table 10.1 illustrates the correlation matrix among poverty reduction, income and three financial development indicators for 14 MENA countries. As can be seen, while the correlation between POV and Y is quite high, the correlations between POV and each financial development indicator are low. This correlation matrix at first glance implies a closer relationship between poverty reduction and economic growth. On the other hand, it seems that the correlations between poverty reduction and financial development indicators are modest. It can be observed that all of the correlations among the financial development indicators are high, which indicates a close relationship among the financial development indicators. According to Saci and Heldon (2008), there is some redundancy of information provided by these financial indicators because of the high correlations among them. Furthermore, the close relationship among financial development indicators can cause multicollinearity problem which can lead to the misleading inferences. To overcome these problems with the financial development indicators, recent studies have concentrated on developing a comprehensive index for financial development. In this regard, the principal component analysis – which is a statistical tool to transform a number of correlated variables into a smaller number of uncorrelated variables – has been widely used (see, for instance, Creane *et al.*, 2003; Saci and Holden, 2008; Jalli *et al.*, 2009).

Following this trend in selecting the appropriate indicator of financial development, this study constructs a financial development index (FDI) from M2Y,

Table 10.1 The correlation matrix

	POV	*Y*	*M2Y*	*DCY*	*CPSY*
POV	1				
Y	0.997	1			
M2Y	0.173	0.165	1		
DCY	0.002	−0.006	0.637	1	
CPSY	0.162	0.156	0.954	0.617	1

DCY and CPSY by means of principal component analysis. Table 10.2 reports the results obtained from principal component analysis for 14 MENA countries. The eigenvalues for three principal components show that the first principal component (PC1) explains the highest proportion of variance, which ranges from 54.7% for Egypt to 92.4% for Tunisia. Therefore, a financial development index (FDI) is constructed by using the factor loadings based on the first principal component.

3.2 The methods and findings

This study employs panel unit root, cointegration and causality analyses in order to find out the relationships among poverty reduction, economic growth and financial development. The rationale behind the use of panel data methods is that panel data analysis increases power of unit root and cointegration tests by combining information from both time and cross-section dimensions.

Table 10.2 Results for principal component analysis

Countries	*Eigenvalues*			*Variance proportion*			*Factor loadings (PC1)*		
	PC1	*PC2*	*PC3*	*PC1*	*PC2*	*PC3*	*M2Y*	*DCY*	*CPSY*
Algeria	2.165	0.725	0.108	0.721	0.241	0.036	0.619	0.445	0.647
Bahrain	2.076	0.711	0.211	0.692	0.237	0.070	0.469	0.609	0.640
Egypt	1.643	0.843	0.513	0.547	0.281	0.171	0.655	0.498	0.568
Iran	2.009	0.977	0.013	0.669	0.325	0.004	0.702	0.691	0.172
Israel	1.495	1.033	0.470	0.498	0.344	0.156	0.541	−0.437	0.718
Jordan	2.479	0.36	0.157	0.826	0.120	0.052	0.598	0.582	0.551
Kuwait	1.970	0.922	0.107	0.656	0.307	0.035	0.673	0.685	−0.279
Morocco	2.874	0.113	0.012	0.958	0.037	0.004	0.572	0.572	0.588
Qatar	2.644	0.246	0.108	0.881	0.082	0.036	0.591	0.578	0.563
S.Arabia	1.928	0.980	0.091	0.642	0.326	0.030	0.703	−0.239	0.670
Sudan	1.877	1.027	0.094	0.625	0.342	0.031	0.711	0.087	0.698
Syrian	1.848	0.751	0.400	0.616	0.250	0.133	0.544	−0.539	0.643
Tunisia	2.773	0.184	0.041	0.924	0.061	0.013	0.562	0.582	0.588
Turkey	1.881	0.780	0.338	0.627	0.260	0.112	0.650	0.593	0.474

Notes
PC: Principal component.

The modelling framework consists of four steps in this study. First, as a preliminary analysis, a test for cross-sectional dependence among the selected MENA countries is carried out and unit root properties of the variables in question are examined. Second, the long-run relationships among the variables are investigated by utilizing a panel cointegration test. Third, the long-run cointegration parameters are estimated by means of a panel cointegration estimator. Finally, causal relationships among the variables are detected by conducting the panel Granger causality testing approach.

Preliminary analysis

Before estimating the relationship among poverty reduction, economic growth and financial development, time-series properties of the variables in the study should be examined. For this purpose, in this study we use panel unit root tests, which are more powerful than the univariate time-series unit root tests. One of the important issues in panel unit root testing procedure is the cross-section dependence problem – that is, the correlations of residuals across different equations. In order to test for cross-section dependence (CD), a CD test recently developed by Pesaran (2004) is utilized. The results are illustrated in Table 10.3.

Since the results for poverty, economic growth and financial development indicate cross-sectional dependence, we use the so-called second-generation panel unit root approach to analyse the stationarity properties of the variables. More precisely, we employ the cross-sectionally augmented IPS (CIPS) test developed by Pesaran (2007). The CIPS test results are presented in Table 10.4. As can be seen, the series (except lnY with constant model) are not stationary in their level form. However, all the series become stationary when they are expressed in their first difference. In terms of econometrics, the variables are integrated of order one. Thus we can proceed with the cointegration analysis.

Panel cointegration tests

In order to empirically investigate the existence of the long-run equilibrium relationship between poverty reduction, growth and financial development, we conducted the panel cointegration tests developed by Pedroni (1999).

Table 10.3 Results for cross-sectional dependence test

Variable	*CD Statistic*	p-*value*
lnPOV	−1.97	0.025
lnY	−1.29	0.098
lnFDI	−3.07	0.001
Residuals (ε_{it})	0.69	0.487

Notes
CD test for residuals was based on the countr-by-country OLS estimation of equation (1). The CD statistic has asymptotically a standard normal distribution.

Table 10.4 Results for panel unit root test

Variable	*Constant*	*Constant and trend*
lnPov	−1.59 [0.710]	−2.56 [0.650]
lnY	−2.35 [0.025]	−2.59 [0.150]
lnFDI	−1.43 [0.860]	−2.56 [0.175]
Δ*lnPov*	−3.78 [0.000]	−3.74 [0.000]
Δ*lnY*	−3.48 [0.000]	−3.78 [0.000]
Δ*lnFDI*	−3.15 [0.000]	−3.28 [0.000]

Notes
Δ is the first difference operator. Numbers in brackets are p values. The maximum lag lengths were set to 2 and the Schwarz Bayesian Criterion was used to determine the optimal lag length.

To test for the null of no-cointegration in the panel, Pedroni developed seven cointegration statistics.[3] It is worth noting that the Pedroni panel cointegration tests are only valid under the assumption of cross-sectional independence. This assumption is supported by our dataset according to CD test for the residuals of equation (1) given by the last row of Table 10.1. Pedroni's testing approach first requires estimating equation (1) with the OLS for each cross-sectional unit. Results for the panel cointegration tests are reported in Table 10.5. All the statistics with the exception of group ρ reject the null hypothesis of no cointegration.

To confirm the results obtained with Pedroni cointegration tests, we also employ the Westerlund (2005) CUSUM panel cointegration test in which the null

Table 10.5 Results for panel cointegration tests

Test	*Panel cointegration statistic*	
Pedroni (1995)		
Panel v-statistic	1.58	*
Panel ρ-statistic	−1.50	*
Panel t-statistic (non-parametric)	−2.39	***
Panel t-statistic (parametric)	−2.82	***
Group ρ-statistic	−0.43	
Group t-statistic (non-parametric)	−2.40	***
Group t-statistic (non-parametric)	−3.26	***
Westerlund (2005)		
Panel CUSUM	0.72	

Notes
Pedroni tests: The tests were carried out with two lags. *** and * indicate the rejection of the null no-cointegration at 1% and 10% level significance, respectively. The statistics are asymptotically distributed as standard normal. The panel ν-statistic is a right-tailed test and has a critical value of 1.28 at 10% level of significance. The remaining statistics are left-sided tests and have a critical value of −1.28 at 10%
Westerlund test: The panel CUSUM test was based on Dynamic OLS estimation of equation (1). Leads and lags were set to two in panel DOLS estimation The statistic is asymptotically distributed as standard normal. The statistic is a right-tailed test and has critical value of 1.28 at 10%.

hypothesis is cointegration instead of no cointegration. The Westerlund test result illustrated at the bottom of Table 10.5 fails to reject the null hypothesis and gives support to the Pedroni tests results. To sum up, both of the two cointegration tests support evidence of long-run cointegration relationship among poverty, economic growth, and financial development in the MENA region.

Panel cointegration estimation

Once the cointegration relationship is established, the next step is to estimate the long-run parameters. In order to estimate panel cointegration parameters various methods have been proposed, such as panel OLS, panel Dynamic OLS (DOLS) and panel Fully Modified OLS (FMOLS). Pedroni (2000) compared the asymptotic properties of various panel cointegration estimation methods by pooling along 'within' and 'between' dimensions of the panel and showed that the between-dimension (group-mean) panel estimators behave well even in relatively small samples. We therefore estimate the panel cointegration parameters using group-mean panel FMOLS and DOLS estimators developed by Pedroni (2000, 2001) under the assumption of cross-sectional independency.

The group-mean panel FMOLS estimator can be constructed simply as

$$\hat{\beta}^{*}_{GFM} = N^{-1}\sum_{i=1}^{N}\beta^{*}_{FM,i}$$

where $\beta^{*}_{FM,i}$ is parameter vector obtained from the time series FMOLS estimation of equation (1) for each member of the panel. Similarly, the associated *t*-ratio can be constructed as

$$t_{\hat{\beta}^{*}_{GFM}} = N^{-1/2}\sum_{i=1}^{N}t_{\hat{\beta}^{*}_{FM,i}} \; .$$

In order to obtain the panel cointegration vector based on the group-mean panel DOLS estimator, the following model is estimated with the OLS for each member of the panel:

$$\ln Pov_t = \beta_0 + \beta_1 \ln Y_t + \beta_2 \ln FD_t + \sum_{k=-K}^{K}\alpha_k \Delta \ln Y_t + \sum_{k=-K}^{K}\lambda_k \Delta \ln FD_t + \varepsilon_t \qquad (3)$$

where $-K$ and K are leads and lags to be determined. Then, the group-mean panel DOLS estimator can be constructed as

$$\hat{\beta}^{*}_{GD} = N^{-1}\sum_{i=1}^{N}\beta^{*}_{D,i}$$

where $\beta^*_{D,i}$ is the parameter vector obtained from the individual OLS estimation of equation (3). The associated *t*-ratio can be constructed as

$$t_{\hat{\beta}^*_{GD}} = N^{-1/2}\sum_{i=1}^{N} t_{\hat{\beta}^*_{D,i}}.$$

Table 10.6 presents the panel cointegration parameters on income and financial development index. At first glance, it seems that both panel DOLS and FMOLS estimators produce similar results. More specifically, the panel DOLS (FMOLS) estimator shows that a 1% increase in the per capita income and financial development index respectively increases the per capita consumption by 0.671 (0.016) and 0.856 (0.012)%. As expected, these results show that income growth contributes more than financial development to poverty reduction in the MENA countries.

Panel Granger causality

The cointegration relationship implies the existence of causal linkages among the variables, but does not indicate the direction of causality. Once the cointegration relation is established, it is common to investigate causal interactions among the variables under study. As Engle and Granger (1987) demonstrated, inferences from a causality test based on a vector auto regression (VAR) model in first differences may lead to misleading results when the variables are cointegrated. Therefore, they suggest the use of the vector error correction model (VECM) by augmenting the VAR model with one-lagged error correction term. Following Constantini and Martini (2009), we specified the following panel VECM to investigate causal linkages among poverty reduction, economic growth and financial development.

$$\Delta \ln Pov_{it} = \delta_{1i} + \sum_{p=1}^{k}\delta_{11ip}\Delta \ln Pov_{it-p} + \sum_{p=1}^{k}\delta_{12ip}\Delta \ln Y_{it-p} + \sum_{p=1}^{k}\delta_{13ip}\Delta \ln FDI_{it-p} + \phi_{1i}\varepsilon_{it-1} + \upsilon_{1it} \qquad (4.1)$$

Table 10.6 Results for panel cointegration estimation

	lnY		*lnFDI*	
Panel DOLS	0.671	(60.53)***	0.016	(1.69)*
Panel FMOLS	0.856	(20.02)***	0.012	(3.29)***

Notes

Leads and lags were set to 2 in panel DOLS estimation. Values inside the parentheses are the absolute values of *t*-statistics. *** and * denote statistical significance at 1 and 10 percent level of significance, respectively.

$$\Delta \ln Y_{it} = \delta_{2i} + \sum_{p=1}^{k} \delta_{21ip} \Delta \ln Pov_{it-p} + \sum_{p=1}^{k} \delta_{22ip} \Delta \ln Y_{it-p} + \sum_{p=1}^{k} \delta_{23ip} \Delta \ln FDI_{it-p} + \phi_{2i}\varepsilon_{it-1} + \upsilon_{2it} \tag{4.2}$$

$$\Delta \ln FDI_{it} = \delta_{3i} + \sum_{p=1}^{k} \delta_{31ip} \Delta \ln Pov_{it-p} + \sum_{p=1}^{k} \delta_{32ip} \Delta \ln Y_{it-p} + \sum_{p=1}^{k} \delta_{33ip} \Delta \ln FDI_{it-p} + \phi_{3i}\varepsilon_{it-1} + \upsilon_{3it} \tag{4.3}$$

where p is the optimal lag length(s) and ε_{it} is the residuals from the panel FMOLS estimation of equation (1). This specification for Granger causality allows investigation of three kinds of causality. First, the short-run causality from economic growth to poverty reduction can be tested with a Wald χ^2 statistic[4] by imposing $\delta_{12ip}=0$. The same method is followed to determine the short-run causal linkages among the variables for the remaining cases. Second, the long-run causality can be analysed by examining the statistical significance of the t-statistics associated with the error correction terms. For instance, the statistically significant φ_{1i} implies that economic growth and financial development are Granger-causes of poverty reduction. Finally, the strong causality[5] can be examined by jointly testing the statistical significance of the error correction terms and the short-run coefficients. For example, the strong causality from economic growth to poverty can be tested by imposing $\delta_{12ip}=0$ and $\varphi_{1i}=0$.

Results for panel Granger causality analysis are illustrated in Table 10.7. Since we are particularly interested in determining the direction of causalities (if any) from economic growth and financial development to poverty reduction, we initially consider the first row of Table 10.7. As can be seen, there is a short-run causality from economic growth to poverty reduction and from financial development to poverty reduction. This finding is consistent with the long-run causality test result, which implies that there is significant long-run causality from economic growth and financial development to poverty reduction. The finding of short- and long-run causalities from economic growth and financial development in fact implies the strong causality from economic growth to poverty reduction, and from financial development to poverty alleviation.

The results in the first row of Table 10.7 show the presence of significant causality from economic growth to poverty and from financial development to poverty, in the short run. Significance of the error term supports the causal inference from income and finance to poverty in the long run. A joint test of significance for both the lagged variables and the error term provides further evidence for this causality in the strong form.

As far as the causality from poverty and finance to economic growth is concerned (second row in Table 10.7), the results show that while there is a

Table 10.7 Results for panel Granger causality

	Short-run			*Long-run*	*Strong causality*		
	Wald Test			*t-test*	*Wald Test*		
	$\Delta lnPov$	ΔlnY	$\Delta lnFDI$	ε_{t-1}	$\Delta lnPov; \varepsilon t_{-1}$	$\Delta lnY; \varepsilon_{t-1}$	$\Delta lnFDI; \varepsilon t_{-1}$
$\Delta lnPov$	–	32.80 [0.000]	5.17 [0.075]	0.21 [0.000]	–	56.47 [0.000]	26.86 [0.000]
ΔlnY	6.70 [0.035]	–	2.93 [0.230]	0.004 [0.362]	7.81 [0.049]	–	3.76 [0.287]
$\Delta lnFDI$	1.52 [0.467]	0.19 [0.908]	–	−1.87 [0.000]	22.29 [0.000]	21.55 [0.000]	–

Notes
The panel VECM was estimated with the OLS. The optimal lag length was selected automatically using the Akaike information criteria. Figures in brackets are p values.

causality from poverty reduction (per capita real consumption) to economic growth in the short run, this is not the case for financial development. In addition, insignificance of the error correction term indicates that the long-run causality from poverty and finance to economic growth does not exist in the MENA. Moreover, there is a strong causality from poverty to economic growth.

The results from poverty reduction and economic growth (third row) to financial development are illustrated in the last row of Table 10.7. As can be seen, although there is no short-run causality either from poverty to financial development or from economic growth to financial development, there is long-run causality from both poverty and economic growth to financial development. The long-run causality tends to dominate the short-run non-causality, which in turn leads to a strong causality from poverty and economic growth to financial development.

With respect to the causal linkages between financial development and economic growth (looking at the second and third rows together), the results show that although financial development is not cause of economic development in either the short or the long run, economic growth causes financial development in both the short and the long run. Therefore, the findings provide evidence of demand following hypothesis.

4 Conclusion

The link between the financial sector and economic growth has been a hotly debated issue for a very long time. The discussion is mainly on the direction of causality between these two variables. The contribution of financial development to poverty reduction is generally examined in a bivarite framework by investigating the direction of causality between financial development and economic growth. Empirical results provide enough evidence to force two opposite approaches on the role of finance in economic development processes to reach a firm conclusion.

Recently, there has been increasing attention as to whether financial development reduces poverty. The financial sector indirectly reduces poverty through economic growth, and directly alleviates poverty by increasing the availability and accessibility of financial funds for the poor. In other words, the direct link between financial development and poverty alleviation arises from the availability of accessible financial instruments, services and institutions for poor households (Holden and Prokopenko, 2001; Odhiambo, 2009).

The topic is investigated by adding a third variable representing poverty reduction to a bivariate framework which consists of financial development and economic growth. The introduction of a third variable affecting both financial and economic growth in the bivariate structure may alter not only the direction of causality between the two variables, but also the magnitude of the estimate.

This chapter analyses the interactions among poverty reduction, economic growth and financial development in MENA countries for the period 1980–2007 within the context of a trivariate modelling framework by employing the recent developments in the panel cointegration and causality analyses. Empirical findings imply that combination of the results for poverty reduction, economic growth and financial development clearly indicates bi-directional causal linkages between economic growth and poverty reduction and between financial development and poverty reduction in the long run, and a unidirectional causal link from economic growth to financial development. This study therefore concludes that poverty reduction in the MENA region is a consequence of and a cause for economic growth and financial development.

As far as the two questions addressed in the introduction are concerned, both the financial and the real sector not only reduce poverty but are also affected by it in the MENA and financial development results from economic growth. The empirical findings reveal that the real sector is the main source for the interactions. In order to reduce poverty, the real sector is important and alleviates poverty directly and indirectly through financial development. In addition, financial development directly contributes to the reduction of poverty and an indirect link through economic growth does not work in the MENA.

Notes

1 On the contrary, Robinson (1952) suggests that financial development follows economic growth. In addition, Lucas (1988), Stern (1989), Chandavarkar (1992), Stiglitz (1994) and Singh and Weisse (1998) question the importance of the financial system in promoting economic growth. In particular, while Lucas (1988: 6) states that 'the importance of financial matters is very badly overstressed', Chandavarkar (1992: 134) notes 'none of the pioneers of development economics ... even list finance as a factor of development'. Singh and Weisse (1998) points to risks of financial collapse and consequent economic recession that may result from rapid deregulation of once repressed financial systems. These theoretical discussions reveal that there is not a consensus on both the role of finance in economic growth and direction of causal inference between finance and growth.

2 Conflicting results from numerous empirical studies for many country groups and specific countries have not reached a firm conclusion whether finance leads (causes) economic growth yet. See the empirical surveys in this topic: Hermes (1994), Arestis and Demetriades (1997), Thiel (2001), Eschenbach (2004), Lawrence (2006), Shan and Jianhong (2006), Ang (2007).

3 See Pedroni (1999) for the details of panel cointegration tests.

4 Since all the variables are entered into the panel VECM in their stationary form, a standard χ^2 statistic can be used to test the null hypothesis of no causality (Constantini and Martini, 2009).

5 This kind of causality shows which variables bear the burden of a short-run adjustment so that a long-run equilibrium following a shock to the system is established (Asafu-Adjaye, 2000).

References

Abu-Bader, S. and Abu-Qarn, A.S. (2008) Financial development and economic growth: Empirical evidence from six MENA countries. *Review of Development Economics*, 12(4): 803–817.

Achy, L. (2004) 'Financial Liberalization, Saving, Investment and Growth in MENA Countries'. Available at: http: //129.3.20.41/eps/fin/papers/0411/0411004.pdf (10.11.2008).

Al-Awad, M. and Harb, N. (2005) Financial deepening and economic growth in the Middle East. *Applied Financial Economics*, 15: 1041–1051.

Al-Tamimi, H.A.H., Al-Awad, M. and Charif, H.A. (2002) Finance and growth: Evidence from some Arab Countries. *Journal of Transnational Management Development*, 7(2): 3–18.

Ang, J.B. (2007). 'Are Financial Sector Policies Effective in Deepening the Malaysian Financial system?' Monash University, Discussion Paper, 02/07.

Arestis, P. and Demetriades, P. (1997) Financial development and economic growth: Assessing the evidence. *Economic Journal*, 107(442): 783–799.

Asafu-Adjaye J. (2000). The relationship between energy consumption, energy prices and economic growth: time series evidence from Asian developing countries. *Energy Economics*, 22: 615–625.

Barro, R.J. (1991) Economic growth in a cross section of countries. *Quarterly Journal of Economics*, May, 407–443.

Beck, T., Demirgüç-Kunt, A. and Levine R. (2004) 'Finance, Inequality and Poverty: Cross Country Evidence', World Bank Policy Research Working Paper 3338.

Bencivenga, V.R. and Smith, B.D. (1991) Financial intermediation and endogenous growth. *Review of Economic Studies*, 58: 195–209.

Bencivenga, V.R., Smith, B.D. and Starr, R.M. (1996) Equity markets, transaction costs, and capital accumulation: An illustration. *World Bank Economic Review*, 10(2): 241–265.

Bittencourt, M. (2009) Financial development and inequality: Brazil 1985–1994. *Economic Change and Restructuring*, 43(2): 113–130.

Boulila, G. and Trabelsi, M. (2004) The causality issues in the finance and growth nexus: Empirical evidence from Middle East and North African Countries. *Review of Middle East Economics and Finance*, 2(2): 123–138.

Caporale, G. and Pittis, N., (1997). Causality and forecasting in incomplete system. *Journal of Forecasting*, 16: 425–437.

Caporale, G.M., Howells, P.G. and Soliman, A.M. (2004) Stock market development and economic growth: the causal linkages. *Journal of Economic Development*, 29(1): 33–50.

Chandavarkar, A. (1992) Of finance and development: Neglected and unsettled questions. *World Development*, 22: 133–142.

Clarke, G., Xu, L. and Fou, H.F. (2002) 'Financial and Income Inequality: Test of Alternatives Theories', World Bank Policy Research Paper, WPS 2984.

Costantini, V. and Martini, C. (2009) The causality between energy consumption and economic growth: A multi-sectoral analysis using non-stationary cointegrated panel data, *Energy Economics*, doi: 10.1016/j.eneco.2009.09.013.

Creane, S., Goya, I.R., Mobarak, M. and Sab, R. (2003) Financial development and economic growth in the Middle East and North Africa. *Finance and Development, A Quarterly Magazine of the IMF*: 4(1).

Creane, S., Goyal, R., Mobarak, A.M. and Sab, R. (2004) Evaluating financial sector development in the Middle East and North Africa: New methodology and some new results. *Topics in Middle Eastern and North African Economies*. Available at: www.luc.edu/orgs/meea/volume6/Creane.pdf (12.11.2008).

De Janvry, A. and Sadoulet, E. (2000) Growth, poverty, and inequality in Latin America a causal analysis, 1970–1994. *Review of Income and Wealth*, 46(3): 267–287.

Deidda, L.G. (2006) Interaction between economic and financial development. *Journal of Monetary Economics*, 53: 233–248.

Deininger, K. and Squire, L., 1996. A new dataset for measuring income inequality. *World Bank Economic Review*, 10: 565–591.

DFID (2004). *Financial Sector Development: A Pre-requisite for Growth and Poverty Reduction?* Department for International Development (DFID), Policy Division, June.

Dollar, D. and Kraay, A. (2001) 'Growth is Good for the Poor', Policy Research Working Paper Series 2587, Washington, DC: The World Bank.

Engle, R.F. and Granger, C.W.J. (1987) Cointegration and error correction representation, estimation and testing. *Econometrica*, 55: 251–276.

Eastwood, R. and Lipton, M. (2001) Pro-poor growth and pro-growth poverty reduction: meaning, evidence and policy implications. *Asian Development Review*, 19: 1–37.

Eschenbach, F. (2004) 'Finance and Growth: A Survey of the Theoretical and Empirical Literature', Tinbergen Institute Discussion Paper, TI 2004039/2.

Goldsmith, R.W. (1969) *Financial Structure and Development*, New Haven, CT: Yale University Press.

Greenwood, J. and Jovanovic, B. (1990) Financial development, growth, and the distribution of income. *Journal of Political Economy*, 98(5): 1076–1107.

Gurley, J.G. and Shaw, E.S. (1955) Financial aspects of economic development. *American Economic Review*, 45(4): 515–538.

Hermes, N. (1994). Financial development and economic growth: A survey of the literature. *International Journal of Development Banking*, 12(1), 3–22.

Holden, P. and Prokopenko, V. (2001) 'Financial Development and Poverty Alleviation: Issues and Policy Implications for Developing and Transition Countries', IMF Working Paper No. WP/01/160.

Honohan, P. (2004) Financial development, growth and poverty: how close are the links? In: C. Goodhart (ed.), *Financial Development and Economic Growth: Explaining the Links*, Basingstoke: Palgrave Macmillan.

Jalil, A., Feridun, M. and Ma, Y. (2009) Finance-growth nexus in China revisited: New evidence from principal components and ARDL bounds tests, *International Review of Economics and Finance*, doi: 10.1016/j.iref.2009.10.005.

Jalilian, H. and Kirkpatrick, C. (2001) 'Financial Development and Poverty Reduction in Developing Countries, Working Paper No. 30, Institute for Development Policy and Management, University of Manchester. www.man.ac.uk/idpm.

Jalilian, H. and Kirkpatrick, C. (2002) Financial development and poverty reduction in developing countries. *International Journal of Finance and Economics*, 7(2): 97–108.

Jalilian, H. and Kirkpatrick, C. (2005). Does financial development contribute to poverty reduction? *Journal of Development Studies*, 41(4): 636–656.

Jeanneney, S.G. and Kpodar, K. (2005) 'Financial Development, Financial Instability and Poverty', CSAE WPS/2005–09, University of Auvergne.

Khan, M.S. and Senhadji, A.S. (2003) Financial development and economic growth: A review and new evidence. *Journal of African Economies*, 12(2): ii89–ii110.

King, R.G. and Levine, R. (1993a) Finance and growth: Schumpeter might be right?. *Quarterly Journal of Economics*, 108(3): 717–737.

King, R.G. and Levine, R. (1993b). Finance, entrepreneurship, and growth: Theory and evidence. *Journal of Monetary Economics*, 32(3), 513–542.

Lawrence, P. (2006) Finance and development: Why should causation matter? *Journal of International Development*, 18, 997–1016.

Levine, R. (1997) Financial development and economic growth: Views and agenda. *Journal of Economic Literature*, 35: 688–726.

Levine, R. and Renelt, D. (1992) A sensitivity analysis of cross-country growth regressions. *American Economic Review*, 82, 942–963.

Lucas, R.E. (1988) On the mechanics of economic development. *Journal of Monetary Economics*, 22: 3–42.

Lundberge, M. and Squire, L. (1998) 'The Simultaneous Evolution of Growth and Inequality', Mimeo, The World Bank.

Lynch, D. (1996) Measuring financial sector development: A study of selected Asia-Pacific countries. *Developing Economies*, 34(1), 3–33.

McKinnon, R.I. (1973) *Money and Capital in Economic Development*, Washington, DC: Brookings Institution.

Nazlioglu, S., Kar, M. and Agir, H. (2009) 'Financial Development and Economic Growth in the MENA Countries', 10th Mediterranean Social and Political Research Meeting of the Mediterranean Programme of the Robert Schuman Centre for Advanced Studies at the European University Institute, March 25–28, 2009, Montecatini Terme, Florence, Italy.

Odhiambo, N.M. (2008) Financial depth, savings and economic growth in Kenya: a dynamic casual relationship. *Economic Modelling*, 25(4): 704–713.

Odhiambo, N.M. (2009) Finance–growth–poverty nexus in South Africa: A dynamic causality linkage. *Journal of Socio-Economics*, 38(2): 320–325.

Pagano, M. (1993). Financial markets and growth: an overview. *European Economic Review*, 37: 613–622.

Patrick, H.T. (1966) Financial development and economic growth in underdeveloped countries. *Economic Development and Cultural Change*, 14: 174–189.

Pedroni, P. (1999) Critical values for cointegration tests in heterogenous panels with multiple regressors. *Oxford Bulletin of Economics and Statistics*, 61: 653–670.

Pedroni, P. (2000) Fully modified OLS for heterogeneous cointegration panels, *Advances in Econometrics*, 15: 93–130.

Pedroni, P. (2001) Purchasing power parity tests in cointegrated panels. *Review of Economics and Statistics*, 83: 727–931.

Pedroni, P. (2004) Panel cointegration: Asymptotic and finite sample properties of pooled time series tests with an application to PPP hypothesis: New results, *Econometric Theory*, 20: 597–627.

Pesaran, M.H. (2004) 'General Diagnostic Tests for Cross-section Dependence in Panels', CESifo Working Paper 1229; IZA Discussion Paper 1240[970].

Pesaran, M.H. (2007) A simple panel unit root test in the presence of cross-section dependence. *Journal of Applied Econometrics*, 22: 265–312.

Quartey, P. (2005) 'Financial Sector Development, Savings Mobilisation and Poverty Reduction in Ghana', UNU-WIDER 2005, Research Paper No. 2005/71, United Nations University, Helsinki, Finland.

Ram, R. (1999) Financial development and economic growth: Additional evidence. *Journal of Development Studies*, 35(4): 164–174.

Ravallion, M. (1992) 'Poverty Comparisons: A Guide to Concepts and Methods, Living Standards Measurement Study', Working Paper 88, Washington, DC, The World Bank.

Robinson, J. (1952) *The Generalization of the General theory, the Rate of Interest and Other Essays*, London: Macmillan, pp. 67–142.

Romer, P.M. (1986) Increasing returns and long run growth. *Journal of Political Economy*, 94(5): 1002–1037.

Romer, P.M. (1990) Endogenous technological change. *Journal of Political Economy*, 98(5): 71–102.

Roubini, N. and Sala-i Martin, X. (1992) Financial repression and economic growth. *Journal of Development Economics*, 39: 5–30.

Saci, K. and Holden, K. (2008) Evidence on growth and financial development using principal components. *Applied Financial Economics*, 18(19): 1549–1560.

Schumpeter, J.A. (1911) *The Theory of Economic Development; An Inquiry into Profits, Capital, Credit, Interest, and the Business Cycle*, translated by R. Opie, Cambridge, MA: Harvard University Press, 1934.

Shan, J. and Jianhong, Q. (2006) Does financial development 'lead' economic growth? The case of China. *Annals of Economics and Finance*, 1: 231–250.

Shaw, E.S. (1973) *Financial Deepening in Economic Development*. New York, NY: Oxford University Press.

Singh, A. and Weisse, B.A. (1998) Emerging stock markets, portfolio capital flows and long term economic growth: Micro and macroeconomic perspectives. *World Development*, 26: 607–622.

Stern, N. (1989) The economics of development: A survey. *Economic Journal*, 100: 597–685.

Stiglitz, J. (1994) The role of the state in financial markets. In: M. Bruno and B. Pleskovic (eds), *Proceedings of The World Bank Conference on Development Economics*, Washington, DC: The World Bank.

Stiglitz, J. (1998) The role of the state in financial markets. In: *Proceedings of the World Bank Annual Conference on Development Economics*, pp. 19–52.

Thiel, M. (2001). 'Finance and Growth: A Review of Theory and the Available Evidence', Directorate General for Economic And Financial Affairs, Economic Paper No. 158. Available at: http: //ec.europa.eu/economy_finance/publications/publication884_en.pdf,29.05.2009.

Trew, A. (2006) Finance and growth: A critical survey. *The Economic Record*, 82(259): 481–490.

United Nations (UN) (2010) *National Accounts Main Aggregates Databases*. Available at: http: //unstats.un.org/unsd/snaama/downloads/Download-GDPconstant-NCU-countries.xls (10.01.2010).

Westerlund, J. (2005) A panel CUSUM test of the null of cointegration. *Oxford Bulletin of Economics and Statistics*, 67(2): 231–262.

Woolard, I. and Leibbrandt, M. (1999) 'Measuring Poverty in South Africa', DPRU Working Papers No. 99/33 (October), Development Policy Research Unit, University of Cape Town.

World Bank (2001) *World Development Report 2000/2001*. New York, NY: Oxford University Press.

Yang, Y.Y. and Yi, M.H. (2008). Does financial development cause economic growth? Implication for policy in Korea. *Journal of Policy Modeling*, 30(5): 827–840.

11 EU migration policy and the Euromed process

The role of traditional and new determinants[1]

Nicolas Péridy

1 Introduction

In the past decade, significant changes have occurred concerning migration patterns into the EU. In particular, there has been a tremendous increase in migration flows from SMCs to the EU, especially Southern Europe. For example, the EU has faced a rise in migration flows by 1.5 million in 2006; Spain itself has attracted 3.6 million migrants from 2001 to 2006, mainly from SMCs. Consequently, Spain, which was traditionally a country where net immigration was negative (with outflows greater than inflows) has recently experienced a situation with positive net immigration. It must also be said that this country is facing significant illegal migration flows from SMCs, together with Italy and France to a lesser extent. In this regard, policy-makers have implemented massive regularization policies. This concerned, for example, 600,000 migrants in Spain in 2005. Overall, the total number of migrants originating from SMCs and living in the EU is estimated to be about 15 million people (FEMISE, 2007).

This chapter aims to explain such a surge in EU migration from SMCs. It relies on new theoretical developments in migration theories. Indeed, the theory of international migration has experienced a considerable revival, especially with regard to migration determinants. Until the early 1990s, the standard migration theories were mainly based on the human capital model (Sjaastad, 1962; Harris and Todaro, 1970). According to this model, migration depends on the income differential between the origin and the destination countries, net of migration costs. The standard theory of international trade (Heckscher–Ohlin–Samuelson) complements this result by stating that if two countries only differ in their factor endowment (capital and labour), then international trade must equalize factor prices. In this case, trade is a substitute for migration.

The revival started with the use of self-selection models (Borjas, 1987). This makes it possible to identify new migration determinants, such as income inequality as well as migrant skills in the source and the destination countries. In this regard, it is worth mentioning that migration skills have also been taken into account in the brain drain model (Kwok and Leland, 1982; Stark, 1991).

One extension refers to the welfare magnet theory (Borjas, 1999). It predicts that once a migrant is self-selected, he can choose a place of location where social transfers are the highest. As a result, there is a positive relationship between migration and the level of social transfers offered in each destination country.

Another revival includes the specification of migration costs. In addition to the traditional location costs, such as transport costs (geographical distance), differences in languages between the source and the host countries as well as differences in the cost of living, several other costs have been identified. The first one corresponds to border effects, which measures the specific cost of crossing a frontier (Helliwell, 1997; Hunt and Mueller, 2004). This concept was first developed in international trade theory by McCallum (1995). As a second cost, the loss of human or business networks by moving to a foreign country is also increasingly discussed in the recent literature. In particular, Carrington *et al.* (1996) show that the endogenous migration cost decreases with past migration. The dynamics of migration flows has also been explored in Vergalli (2006).

A third migration cost includes migration policies. It has been shown that migration decreases when migration policy becomes more restrictive, since it reinforces migration costs (Benhabib, 1996; Bianchi, 2006). This relationship has also been tested empirically by several authors, notably Cobb-Clark (1993), Karemera *et al.* (2000), Hatton and Williamson (2005a), Ortega (2005), Clark *et al.* (2007) as well as Mayda (2007).

A final revival corresponds to the trade–migration relationship. In fact, it has been increasingly recognized that trade and migration can be complementary if countries have different technologies, if competition is imperfect and if there are economic distortions, such as production taxes. In all these cases, trade alone cannot equalize factor prices. As a result, migration flows are needed and become complementary to trade (Markusen, 1983; Venables, 1999). Recent empirical articles generally support this result (Piperakis *et al.*, 2002; Wagner *et al.*, 2002; Co *et al.*, 2004).

In spite of this revival, most of these theories have been developed and tested separately. As a result, there is a limited literature which simultaneously includes all these new migration determinants (Hatton and Williamson (2005a); Clark *et al.*, 2007; Mayda, 2007). In this spirit, this chapter relies on a generalized model of migration determinants which includes both traditional and new migration economic determinants. In particular, by including simultaneously social transfers, the trade–migration relationship, border effects as well as human networks, it includes a larger set of variables than the previous studies. In addition, it also includes non-economic migration determinants, such as climate and environment, as well as differences in religion between countries.

The rest of the chapter is organized as follows. Section 2 describes the empirical model, with particular emphasis on the presentation of the dataset, the choice of the variables as well as the econometric specification. Estimation results are presented and discussed in Section 3. The chapter concludes with discussions of the policy implications of our findings.

2 The empirical model: description of the variables and econometric specification

The econometric model developed in this section relies on a single and consistent framework which includes both the traditional and new migration determinants described previously. It is based on a database which involves the EU-15 as destination countries (Belgium and Luxembourg are counted as the same country). The countries of origin include nine SMCs (Algeria, Morocco, Tunisia, Egypt, Israel, Jordan, Lebanon, Syria and Turkey). The time period taken into consideration stems from 1993 to 2004.

2.1 Description of the variables

All the variables used in the model are described below, with a summary provided in Table 11.1. The empirical model is specified as:

$$
\begin{aligned}
M_{sdt} = {} & a_0 + a_1 \frac{W_{dt}}{W_{st}} + a_2 POV_s + a_3 \frac{\sigma_{ws}}{\sigma_{wd}} + a_4 \left(\frac{\sigma_{ws}}{\sigma_{wd}}\right)^2 + a_5 \frac{T_d}{T_s} \\
& + b_1 D_{sd} + b_2 L_{sd} + b_3 B_{sd} + b_4 \frac{H_d}{H_s} + b_5 \frac{U_d}{U_s} + b_6 N_{sdt} \\
& + c_1 Z_d + c_2 E_d + c_3 R_{sd} + c_4 COL_{sd} + c_5 C^S{}_{sdt} \\
& + d_1 P_{dt} \\
& + e_1 AGE_s + e_2 \frac{S_h}{S_d} \\
& + \alpha_s + \beta_d + \gamma_t + \varepsilon_{sdt} \qquad (1)
\end{aligned}
$$

The dependent migration variable M_{sdt} denotes migration from the source country *s* to the destination country *d* at year *t*. It is measured through the use of two main databases. The first is Carim (2006), which is specific to SMCs. It is complemented by the SOPEMI dataset developed by OECD (2006a). When data are not available, some national sources have also been used. The problem of consistency across these databases has been addressed through a careful comparison of common data. For the remaining missing data which, above all, concern zero migration flows, the 0 value has been used (in logarithm).

As a sensitivity test, two dependent variables have been alternatively specified. The first corresponds to the gross migration rate, i.e. gross migration flows as a proportion of the origin country's population. The second is the stock of migrants as a proportion of the origin country's population. Although there is no consensus in the economic literature about the choice between migration flows or stocks, the stock variable seems to be preferable in the present case for several reasons. First, there are more available data, especially in the Carim dataset.

Second, migration stocks seem to better reflect structural migration than flows, which can vary temporarily a great deal. In this regard, some theoretical articles show that there is a long-term relationship between the stock of migrants and some migration determinants, such as income, whereas this long-term relationship does not hold for migration flows (Brucker and Schroder, 2005). However, one drawback of the use of the stock of migrants is that it fits less the theoretical model since the aggregate probability to migrate applies better to migration flows.

Basically, the dependent variable includes all migrants registered in the statistics. This raises two problems. The first is that this variable does not distinguish the various motives for migration (labour migrants, tied movers, refugees, etc.). This problem is due to the lack of detailed statistics available for a large number of countries, especially developing countries. As a result, it must be assumed that equation (1) captures the various motives for each migrant category (income, social transfers, joining a network as well as non-economic motives). A second problem is related to illegal migrants. In our database, the number of legal migrants settled in EU countries and originating from SMCs is equal to 5.8 million (based on OECD (2006a) and Carim (2006)). This is far from the tentative estimation of overall migrants (including illegal ones), which ranges between ten and 15 million (Carim, 2006). Although it is impossible to include illegal migrants in our database simply because accurate statistics do not exist, some of them are still counted in case of regularization policies. These policies have been widely used in Spain and Italy, which legalized more than one million migrants in the 1990s (Péridy, 2006). Since these migrants become 'legal', they are registered in the statistics and hence taken into account in our database (refer to additional discussion in the empirical results).

Turning to the explanatory variables, the first line in equation (1) involves the economic migration determinants. W_{dt}/W_{st} corresponds to the wage ratio in the destination and source country. It is proxied by the GDP per capita ratio, measured in PPP (Source: CEPII 2006a). The parameter a_1 is expected to have a positive sign, according to the standard migration theory.

POV_s in a poverty trap indicator which complements the income variable described previously. Indeed, when income in the country of origin falls to a certain threshold, migration can no longer increase simply because potential migrants are too poor to migrate (Hatton and Williamson, 2005b). A negative value of a_2 is expected. As a statistical source, we use the United Nations human poverty index (United Nations, 2006).

The income inequality ration is represented by σ_{ws}/σ_{wd}. It has been proxied by the Gini coefficient ratio. According to the new migration theory developed by Borjas, an inverse U-shaped relationship is expected between this ratio and migration. For example, assuming that the destination country is richer than the source country, and assuming simultaneously that the wage inequality is greater in the destination country, we find an inverse U-shaped function between migration and income inequality. This means that a rise in income inequality in the source country first increases migration (because the return to skill is first greater

Table 11.1 Description of variables

Variable	*Symbol*	*Description*	*Sources*
Migration flows	M_{sdt}	Gross migration flows a proportion of the origin country's population (%)	OECD (2006a) Carim (2006)
Migration stocks	M_{sdt}	Migration stocks a proportion of the origin country's population (%)	OECD (2006a) Carim (2006)
GDP per capita ratio	W_{dt}/W_{st}	Destination to source country GDP per capita measured in PPP (US dollars)	CEPII (2006a)
Poverty trap	POV_s	Human Poverty Index	United Nations (2006)
Income inequality ratio	σ_{ws}/σ_{wd}	Source to destination country's Gini coefficients	United Nations (2006)
Social transfers' ratio	T_d/T_s	Various proxies: 1) Destination to source country's education expenses as a percentage of GDP; 2) Health expenses as a percentage of GDP; 3) Overall public expenses as a percentage of GDP	WHO (2005), UNESCO (2006), OECD (2006b), LIS (2005)
Distance	D_{sd}	Weighted distance index developed by CEPII	CEPII (2006b)
Differences in languages	L_{sd}	Probability index that a person in country s speaks a different language than in country d	Wagner and al. (2002)
Border effect	B_{sd}	Dummy variable which is equal to zero for internal migration and one for cross-country migration	Internal migration found in OECD (2000)
Cost of living ratio	H_d/H_s	Cost of living index	Mercer (2005)

Business networks	N_{sdt}	Proxied by bilateral trade of goods between country s and d	OECD (2006a)
Unemployment ratio	U_d/U_s	Unemployment rate in country d as percentage of that of country s	ILO (2006)
Climatic cost index	Z_d	National climatic index which takes into account temperature, rainfall and sunshine differences across countries (see complete description in the text)	Own calculations from data developed by The Weather Channel
Environmental cost	E_d	Two proxies: 1) CO_2 emissions total and 2) as a percentage of GDP	OECD (2006c)
Differences in religion	R_{sd}	Religion difference index (see description in the text)	Own calculations from CIA (2007)
Human network	C^S_{sdt}	Lagged stock of migrants already settled in country d	OECD (2006a) Carim (2006)
Cultural links	COL_{sd}	Colonization index which is equal to 1 in case of significant past colonial links and zero otherwise	CEPII(2006a)
Migration policy	P_{dt}	Various proxies: 1) FRDB index of migration policy; 2) enlarged FDRB index to asylum policy (Hatton, 2004); 3) total number of residence permits granted by a destination country as a percentage of its population	FRDB (2006); Hatton (2004); OECD (2006a)
Age	AGE_s	Share of people aged less than 15 years as a percentage of country's population	United Nations (2006)
Education and skills ratio	S_h/S_d	Secondary school endowment ratio	UNESCO (2006)

in the destination country). However, after a certain threshold, as income inequality in the source country goes on increasing and becomes higher than in the destination country, migration decreases (because the return to skill gets higher in the source country).

As a result, the expected signs of a_3 and a_4 are respectively positive and negative (source: United Nations, 2006). For this variable, we are limited by the type of data available. As a matter of fact, it would have been possible to use more precise variables, for example from the wage premium data developed by Freeman and Oostendorp (2000). However, these data, based on International Labour Organization (ILO) statistics, are not available for several key countries in our sample, such as Morocco, Egypt, Jordan, Gulf countries, etc. In the same way, Grogger and Hanson (2008) propose original measures of skill premium from various statistical databases (Luxembourg Income Studies and ILO) but again data proved to be unavailable for our country sample.

T_d/T_s accounts for the social transfer ratio between the destination and the source country. According to the welfare magnet theory, a positive value of coefficient a_5 is expected. Four proxies are tested for this variable: the first two proxies correspond to education and health expenses as a percentage of GDP (sources: WHO, 2005; UNESCO, 2006). The two additional proxies cover overall public expenses (including transfers) as a percentage of GDP (OECD, 2006b; Luxembourg Income Study, 2005).

The second line in equation (1) includes economic migration costs. The distance D_{sd} is measured by a weighted index which takes into account the spatial distribution of people within each country (CEPII, 2006b). As in Wagner *et al.* (2002), the difference in languages L_{sd} is measured by an index which reflects the probability that a randomly selected person in the country of origin speaks a different language than in the destination country:

$$L_{sd} = 1 - \sum_i (L_{si} \times L_{di})$$

L_{si} and L_{di} correspond respectively to the population in countries s and d which speak the language i, as a proportion of the overall population. This index varies from zero (if two countries speak the same language) to unity (if they speak two different languages). Data stem from CIA (2007). In our data sample, the main language similarities involve Maghreb countries with France (L_{sd}=0.8), Egypt and Jordan with the UK (0.85), Lebanon with France (0.9), as well as Maghreb countries with Spain (0.95).

Border effects, which are now a standard variable both in international trade and in international migration theory, measure the specific cost (for a good or a migrant) of crossing an international frontier. Some authors have shown that crossing an international border can reduce migration flows up to 100 times compared with internal migration (Helliwell, 1997; Hunt and Mueller, 2004). In equation (1), border effects B_{sd} are measured by a dummy variable which is equal to 0 for migrations within a country (M_{dd}) and unity for migrations across countries (M_{sd}). As a result, estimating the border effect requires data on internal migrations (OECD, 2000) as well as internal distance (CEPII, 2006b).

The cost of living ratio H_d/H_s is measured by the Mercer (2005) cost of living index. A negative sign for b_4 is expected. The unemployment ratio U_d/U_s is also expected to be negatively correlated with migration (b_5 negative). The statistical source is the International Labor Organization (2006).

Business networks N_{sdt} are proxied by trade (exports plus imports) between countries *s* and *d* (Razin and Sadka, 1997; Pederson *et al.*, 2004). Indeed, it can be assumed that the more trade there is between the source and the destination countries, the tighter the commercial and business links between these countries will be (statistical source: OECD, 2006c).

The third line in equation (1) includes non-economic and specific migration costs. Z_d corresponds to costs related to a possible unfavourable climate in the destination country. In order to measure this concept, an original national climatic index is used (c_1 is negative). The statistical source used for building up this index is The Weather Channel (2007). As an alternative, an original climate similarity variable is also implemented.[2]

E_d captures the migration costs related to the possible detrimental environment quality in country *d*. It is measured by the CO_2 emissions (OEDC, 2006d). Two alternative proxies have been tested, namely total CO_2 emissions and CO_2 emissions as a percentage of GDP. The expected sign for c_2 is negative. Indeed, the higher the CO_2 emissions in the destination country, the higher the cost for the migrant and the less willing he is to migrate.

R_{sd} is an original variable which measures the differences in the religion between the source and the destination country:

$$RELIGION_{sd} = 1 - i\sum \min(R_{is}, R_{id})$$

R_{is} and R_{id} respectively correspond to the population with the religion *i* as a percentage of the total population in countries *s* and *d*. This index varies between zero (if religions are the same in countries *s* and *d*) to unity (when they are strictly different). A negative sign is expected for c_3 (source: CIA, 2007).

C^i_{sd} denotes the individual specific cost related to the loss of human networks when migrating. In our macro approach, we use an inverse proxy which measures the stock of migrants already settled in the destination country at year $t-1$. It is assumed that the more numerous the community of migrants in country *d* originating from a given source country *s*, the more attractive this destination country is for potential migrants from *s* (c_5 is expected to be positive). Since the introduction of this variable may also capture the impact of omitted variables, this problem has been controlled through the introduction of country- and time-specific effects, which makes it possible to correct this bias (Egger, 2004).

COL_{sd} is an additional variable which proxies historical and cultural links between two countries. It is measured by a dummy which reflects colonial relationships over a long period of time with substantial participation in the colonized country's governance (source: CEPII, 2006a). This variable is equal to 1 in case of colonial links and 0 otherwise. The absence of colonial links can be considered as a migration cost if we assume that such links can make countries closer (development of networks, infrastructures, closer culture, etc....). As a result, a positive relationship is expected for tight colonial links, especially between France and Maghreb countries, between France and Lebanon (as well as Syria), but also between the UK and Egypt as well as Jordan.

P_{dt} reflects the destination country's migration policy. Due to the particularities and the complexity of national migration policies in EU countries, there is no direct EU measurement concerning the enforcement of migration policies in EU countries through one or several harmonized variables. As a consequence, several general proxies have been included. The first is based on an original aggregated index of migration policies (FRDB, 2006). This index is a weighted average of several measures corresponding to various migration criteria, such as the admission standard for migrating, the maximum duration of the first migration period, the quota level, the time necessary to get a residence permit, the number of ministries the migrant must contact to be admitted in a destination country, etc. ... A rise in this index means that the migration policy is more restrictive (a negative sign is expected for d_1). A second proxy combines the previous index with a specific index of asylum policy. It was developed by Hatton (2004). As a sensitivity analysis, we also use the total number of residence permits granted by a given destination country as a percentage of its population.

Equation (1) also includes two additional variables. The first is the age of the migrant, since we consider that he wants to maximize his gain over his entire working career. This assumption is derived from the standard human capital theory. As a result, the higher the share of people aged less than 15 years, the more migration (e_1 positive). The statistical source is United Nations (2006). The last variable (S_h/S_d) makes it possible to test directly the impact of skills of the migrants of country *h* relative to country *d* (source: UNESCO, 2006). If e_2 is positive, this means that migration increases with the relative skills of the migrant. This suggests that migrants are positively selected, according to Borjas' terminology.

The final line in equation (1) shows the specific effects related to the country of origin (α_s) and the country of destination (β_d). A time effect (γ_t) is also included. These effects account for the heterogeneity of data as well as for the potential bias due to omitted variables, as noted earlier.

Before turning to the econometric analysis, Table 11.2 provides basic descriptive statistics of the main variables selected in the model. Several features emerge from this table. First, there are significant and persistent GDP per capita differences between SMCs and the EU. With the exception of Israel, SMCs have a GDP per capita which never exceeds one-third of EU level. Countries like Egypt, Jordan or Morocco show the lowest levels, i.e. below 20% of the EU average. This difference is likely to have a significant impact on migration. This will be tested empirically in the next section. However, countries like Egypt or

Morocco exhibit a significant poverty index. This poverty trap is expected to reduce migration flows, as theoretically shown previously. Another characteristic of income is the limited income inequality in SMCs. This suggests that the return to skill is rather low. As a result, workers originating from SMCs may be motivated to migrate to countries showing a higher return to skills, such as the UK or the USA.

Social transfers are generally higher in EU countries, though countries like Egypt, Syria and Morocco spend more than 10% of their GDP for health expenses. However, Northern EU countries as well as France and Germany are very attractive in terms of social transfers, since total public spending accounts for more than 25% of GDP. Differences in unemployment rates are also significant, i.e. 15% in SMCs against 8% in EU countries. Maghreb countries face particularly high unemployment rates (up to 27% in Algeria). This is also expected to increase the migration pressure to the EU.

Looking at non-economic migration determinants, it appears clearly that the climatic migration cost is very low for Southern EU countries (including France), which are attractive due to generally sunny weather. In terms of environmental quality, Northern EU countries are in a favourable position. France, but also Italy and Spain to a lesser extent, are also attractive because of limited CO_2 emissions. This can be mainly explained by the choice of nuclear power as the main energy supply, especially in France.

Turning to migration policy, it is striking to observe a difference between Northern EU countries and Southern EU countries, which generally show a much less restrictive policy (especially Greece, Italy and Spain) than the Northern ones. Section 3 will assess whether these differences in migration policies are significant for explaining migration patterns.

2.2 Model specification and sensitivity analysis

The model is first specified in a semi-log basis, in which the dependent migration variable is in logarithm and the independent variables keep a linear form. This choice is motivated by the Davidson and McKinnon test. Such an approach is in line with several other studies of international migration (Pedersen *et al.*, 2004; Peridy, 2006; Clark *et al.*, 2007, etc.).

The choice of the appropriate proxies for the independent variables has been made through a step by step analysis. Table 11.3 exhibits the estimation results. Standard OLS, FEM and REM are not presented, given problems related to autocorrelation, heteroskedasticity and endogeneity. Three estimators are finally selected. First, a robust GLS is implemented in order to take into account heteroskedasticity and autocorrelation. Second, the Hausman and Taylor (HT) estimator is used so as to address the endogeneity problem. The final estimator is that developed by Arellano, Bond and Bover (Arellano and Bond, 1998; Arellano and Bover, 1995). This dynamic estimator makes it possible to include the lagged migration variable (flows or stocks) as a proxy for human networks.

Table 11.2 Descriptive statistics for the main variables used in the model (2004)

SMCs	*GDP per cap.*	*Social transfer 2*	*Unemploy. rate*	*Cost of living*	*Education*	*Gini*	*Age*	*Poverty trap*	*Social transfer 3*	*Migration policy 1*	*Climatic cost index*	*Environ. 1*	*Environ. 2*
Turkey	7262	6.01	10.3	93.8	78	40.0	29.7	9.7					
Israel	19716	1.20	10.3	87.6	89	35.5	28.0	1.8					
Algeria	5671	6.96	27.3	81.9	67	35.3	31.2	21.3					
Morocco	3607	10.99	18.3	81.6	36	39.5	32.2	34.5					
Tunisia	6865	5.22	14.9	65.2	65	39.8	27.5	18.3					
Egypt	3298	16.89	10.2	72.5	81	34.4	34.3	30.9					
Jordan	4086	6.26	15.0	80.1	80	36.4	38.0	8.1					
Lebanon	5349	9.66	18.0	84.6	75	40.0	29.5	9.6					
Syria	3128	15.00	11.7	50.0	43	35.0	38.0	13.8					
Minimum	*3298*	*1.20*	*10.2*	*65.2*	*36.0*	*34.4*	*27.5*	*1.8*					
Maximum	*19716*	*16.89*	*27.3*	*93.8*	*89.0*	*40.0*	*38.0*	*34.5*					
Mean	*6554*	*8.69*	*15.1*	*77.5*	*68.2*	*37.3*	*32.0*	*16.4*					
Standard deviation	*5162*	*4.97*	*5.6*	*13.2*	*17.9*	*2.4*	*4.0*	*10.9*					

European Union											
France	24192	6.01	8.9	102.2	94	32.7		28.8	120	0.29	0.23	6.17
Belgium/Lux	26901	6.66	7.5	87.2	97	26.0		23.8	190	0.40	0.40	10.85
Germany24125	6.25	8.70	88.4	88.0	28.3		27.3	120	0.47	0.39	10.10	
Italy	23271	4.89	9.0	104.9	91	36.0		24.1	90	0.12	0.29	7.48
Netherlands	24348	5.45	3.1	93.3	89	32.6		23.0	100	0.41	0.39	11.13
UK	24505	5.27	5.1	120.3	95	36.0		24.0	190	0.41	0.33	8.80
Ireland	31245	5.94	4.2	100.0	83	35.9		15.0	130	0.40	0.34	10.82
Denmark	26653	8.04	4.7	110.0	96	24.7		29.0	150	0.53	0.33	9.54
Finland	25546	5.76	9.1	95.2	95	26.9		24.0	100	0.71	0.46	12.29
Sweden	25378	7.73	4.0	96.8	100	25.0		30.0	100	0.65	0.21	5.89
Austria	26741	5.59	4.0	97.8	89	30.0		26.5	150	0.41	0.30	8.60
Spain	19893	3.66	11.4	86.9	96	32.5		19.0	100	0.24	0.34	7.36
Greece	18059	2.96	9.6	87.2	86	35.4		23.0	30	0.00	0.47	8.23
Portugal	15923	3.84	5.0	80.2	85	38.5		19.0	113	0.06	0.35	6.11
Czech Republic	14908	2.89	7.3	90.8	91	25.4		20.4		0.53	0.74	11.29
Hungary	13558	2.68	5.8	93.3	94	24.4		22.9		0.55	0.42	5.49
Poland	9681	1.74	19.9	91.5	83	31.6		23.5		0.59	0.69	7.35
Slovak Republic	11994	2.05	17.6	89.9	88	25.8		13.9		0.53	0.61	7.14
Minimum	*9681*	*1.74*	*3.1*	*80.2*	*83*	*24.4*		*15.0*	*30*	*0.00*	*0.21*	*5.49*
Maximum	*31245*	*8.04*	*19.9*	*120.3*	*100*	*38.5*		*30.0*	*190*	*0.71*	*0.74*	*12.29*
Mean	*21496*	*4.86*	*8.1*	*95.3*	*91*	*30.4*		*23.2*	*117*	*0.41*	*0.41*	*8.59*
Standard deviation	*6069*	*1.88*	*4.6*	*9.6*	*5*	*4.7*		*4.9*	*43*	*0.20*	*0.15*	*2.12*

Note
The variables are described in Table 11.1 as well as in the text.

Table 11.3 Estimation results for SMCs

	STOCKS			*FLOWS*		
	GLS (robust)	*HT*	*ABB*	*GLS (robust)*	*HT*	*ABB*
GDP per capita ratio	0.0028**	0.0077***	0.0015*	0.0066***	0.0011*	0.0049**
Poverty trap	−0.0087*	−0.0058	−0.0007	0.0005	−0.0009	0.0003
Income inequality ratio	24.6378***	18.7296***	5.4138	25.2832***	21.5106***	6.3515***
(Income inequality ratio)^2	−9.1535***	−6.6875***	−1.9738***	−9.3688***	−7.9533***	−2.5412***
Social transfers ratio	0.0005	0.0004	0.0001	0.0006	0.0004	0.0001
Distance	−0.0009***	−0.0010***	−0.00016	−0.0007***	−0.0008***	−0.0003***
Differences in languages	−0.5989	−0.0636	−0.4323	−0.3057	−0.0829	−0.2396
Cost of living ratio	−1.1666	−1.2894***	−0.1606*	−0.5632***	−0.5003**	−0.1887**
Unemployment ratio	−0.1995*	−0.4884*	−0.0982	−0.7634***	−0.5997**	−0.1856*
Business network (trade)	0.00016***	0.00083***	0.00014***	0.00009***	0.00012***	0.00047***
Climate	−0.4231***	−0.3295***	−0.0656**	−0.4010***	−0.3226***	−0.0584**
Environment	−0.8853***	−0.8936***	−0.1853***	−0.9425***	−0.8738***	−0.1453**
Differences in religion	−0.409***	−0.0261*	−0.0090*	−0.0366***	−0.0559***	−0.0312***
Colonies	1.7118***	1.3197*	0.1854*	0.9951***	1.0301**	0.1568*
Human networks			0.8305***			0.8471***

Migration policy	−0.0012***	−0.0011***	−0.0005*	−0.0011***	−0.0111***	−0.0006*
Age	0.0093	0.0032	0.0009	0.0012	0.0014	0.0008
Education ratio	1.0875***	0.6355*	0.0988	0.6306***	0.7133**	0.1296*
Intercept	−4.0689			−4.8086		
r^2	0.7113			0.709		
Number of observations	1188	1188	1089	1188	1188	
Davidson and McKinnon test	0.0004			0.0003		
Variance Inflation Factor	37.9			37.8		
Autocorrelation (rho)	0.951			0.943		
LM test	5556.11***			5360.99***		
Hausman test	218.24***			217.38***		
Hausman and Taylor test (theta)		0.976			0.946	
Non-linearities: – distance^2	−0.0001	−0.0001	0.0000–0.0001	−0.0001	0.0000	
– GDP per capita ratio^2	0.0002	0.0001	0.0000	0.0001	0.0001	0.0000
Alternative independent variable: climate similarity	0.1044***	0.0956***	0.0085***	0.0888***	0.0756**	0.0064**

Notes
*** significant at 1% level; ** significant at 5% level; * significant at 10% level.

Amongst the other econometric tests carried out in this chapter, the Variance Inflation Factor (VIF) gives an indication concerning mullticollinearity. In Table 11.3, the VIF is slightly greater than the upper limit generally admitted in the literature, i.e. 30. This is not very surprising, given the great number of independent variables included in the econometric model. Additional investigation reveals that multicollinearity is essentially due to two variables, namely income inequality and the square of this variable. In order to control the possible bias introduced by these two variables, the model has been re-estimated without them. The VIF statistics fall below the upper limit. In addition, the removal of these variables does not significantly modify the sign and the magnitude of the other variables. This suggests that the multicollinearity bias is not important.

Finally, several sensitivity analyses are presented. First, the choice of several alternative estimators makes it possible to compare the parameter estimates and to ensure the robustness of the result. As a second sensitivity analysis, estimations have been implemented by using alternatively migrant stocks and flows in the dependent variable. As a third sensitivity test, several proxies have been alternatively tested for some independent variables, such as migration policy, social transfers as well as environment.

3 Estimation results

Table 11.4 provides the estimation results by using alternatively migration stocks and flows as the dependent variable. As a first result, the traditional economic determinants of migration are all significant. In particular, the GDP per capita difference between SMCs and the EU is a major determinant. The corresponding coefficient is always significant whatever the estimator. Consequently, the spectacular increase in migration from SMCs to Spain can be partly explained by the exceptional rise in the Spanish GDP per capita since its accession to the EC in 1986.

As a traditional migration cost, distance also plays a crucial role in explaining migration at a macro level. As a matter of fact, a 1000-km rise in the distance between two countries leads to a decrease in the migration ratio by about 1 to 2 percentage points.[3] Differences in unemployment and cost of living are also greatly significant for explaining migration.

In addition to these traditional migration determinants, most of the new determinants are also significant. For example, in line with Borjas' theory, we find an inverse U-shaped relationship between migration and the income inequality ratio (a_3 and a_4 are respectively positive and negative). This means that as income inequality reaches a certain threshold in the destination country, a rise in this variable increases migration. This is due to the fact that migrants are attracted by favourable returns to skills in the destination country. This result is complemented by the positive sign of the education variable, which suggests that migration increases with the education level of the migrant. Consequently, this finding supports the brain drain theory.

Table 11.4a Parameter estimates related to migration policy

	GLS (robust)	*HT*	*ABB*
POL1 (stocks)	−0.0004*	−0.0005**	−0.00005*
POL1 (flows)	−0.0015***	−0.0017***–0.0010***	
POL2 (stocks)	−0.0012***	−0.0011***	−0.0005*
POL2 (flows)	−0.0011***	−0.0111***–0.0006*	
POL3 (stocks)	−6.7770***	−3.4943***	−0.3847**
POL3 (flows)	−9.6148***	−7.5252***–5.4747***	

Notes
*** significant at 1% level; ** significant at 5% level; * significant at 10% level.

Table 11.4b Parameter estimates related to migration policy *(POL2)*: breakdown by countries

FLOWS	*GLS (robust)*	*HT*	*ABB*
France	0.0006	0.0008	0.0007
Belgium-Lux.	n.a.	n.a.	n.a.
Germany	0.0003	0.0004	0.0002
Italy	−0.00030–0.0002	−0.0002	
Netherlands	−0.0010**	−0.0018***	−0.0017***
Great Britain	−0.0013***	−0.0021***	−0.0013***
Ireland	−0.0015***	−0.0019***	−0.0017***
Denmark	−0.0013**	−0.0016***	−0.0011***
Finland	−0.0009*	−0.0023***	−0.0009*
Sweden	n.a.	n.a.	n.a.
Austria	−0.0006	−0.0002	−0.0002
Spain	0.0010	0.0012	0.0008
Greece	−0.0017**	−0.0008	−0.0011**

Notes
*** significant at 1% level; ** significant at 5% level; * significant at 10% level.

Networks are also a very significant variable for explaining South–North Mediterranean migration. In the first place, the coefficient corresponding to human networks is always significant, since the lagged migration coefficient is equal to about 0.83 or 0.84, depending on the econometric specification. This result correlates some new findings concerning dynamic migration (Carrington *et al.*, 1996; Vergalli, 2006). Second, business networks (measured by trade) also increase migration. Indeed, Table 11.3 shows that US$1 million of additional trade between two countries leads to an increase in the migration rate of 0.1% to 0.5%, depending on the estimator. In other words, the model highlights a complementary relationship between trade and migration. This result supports recent theoretical and empirical findings concerning the specific trade–migration relationship (Razin and Sadka, 1997; Piperakis *et al.*, 2003; Pederson *et al.*, 2004).

As an additional migration cost variable, the migration policy in the destination country is always significant. This suggests that as the migration policy in EU countries becomes more restrictive, the migration rate is reduced. In Table 11.3, this variable is proxied by the index of migration policy which includes asylum policy (*POL2*). As a sensitivity analysis, the model has been re-estimated with two alternative proxies, i.e. the index of migration policy without taking into account the asylum policy (*POL1*) as well as the total number of residence permits as a percentage of the destination country's population (*POL3*). The coefficients corresponding to the various policy proxies are displayed in Table 11.4a. This table clearly shows that the EU migration policies significantly reduce migration as they become more restrictive. In addition, when using migration flows, the magnitude of the coefficient is greater than when using migration stocks. This suggests logically that migration policy is more efficient for regulating migration flows than migration stocks.

However, additional investigation shows that the impact of migration policy differs depending on the destination country. As a matter of fact, when re-estimating the model for each EU country with the *POL2* proxy, it appears that the migration policy coefficient is strongly negative and significant for Northern EU countries, whereas it is generally insignificant for Southern EU countries as well as Germany (Table 11.4b). This can be explained by massive regularization policies implemented by Southern countries vis-à-vis illegal migrants originating from SMCs. These policies have led to a strong increase in the total number of migrants recorded in the statistics. Another reason can be found in specific bilateral relationships involving, for example, France with Maghreb countries or Germany with Turkey.

Non-economic migration determinants are also all significant. In particular, past colonial links between two countries strongly increase the probability to migrate. In addition, the difference in the religion between the source and the destination country reduces migration. Finally, climate and environment in the destination country also play a significant role in the migration decision, even if the contribution of these variables to the r^2 is low.

However, the coefficient which accounts for social transfers is not significant. The robustness of this result is checked by the use of the four proxies related to social transfers. For all these proxies, the corresponding coefficients remain insignificant. This result shows that migrants from SMCs are essentially motivated by higher wages and returns to skills in the EU, but not by social transfers. This finding is consistent with the unemployment coefficient, which shows that an increase in unemployment in EU countries reduces migrations, despite the possibility of taking advantage of social transfers. In fact, the numerous and restrictive conditions which must be fulfilled to take advantage of these transfers may also explain why this variable is not significant.

The language difference is also insignificant. This unexpected result may be due to remaining multicollinearity problems with the variable corresponding to colonialism. As a matter of fact, re-estimating the model without the colony variable makes the language variable coefficient significant with the expected sign.

Hence, since the two variables are individually significant determinants of EU migration, the final model specification includes both variables.

In the same way, the poverty trap variable is not significant. One possible reason is that compared to many other developing countries, especially the least developed countries, Mediterranean countries are all emerging countries. Consequently, they are less concerned by poverty.

The age variable is the final insignificant variable. This can be explained by the choice of the proxy. Indeed, due to the lack of individual data related to the age of the migrant, this variable is proxied by the proportion of people aged less than 15 years old. This reflects very imperfectly the average age of the migrant. Moreover, SMCs exhibit a similar age structure of their population and the age variable barely varies over time. This low variabilility across countries and over time also explains this result.

The model estimated previously can be extended by enlarging the previous country sample to a greater number of countries of origins (including developed countries). Basically, 58 reference countries are included in addition to SMCs. These are the major developing countries as well as developed countries, i.e. the EU-15, the USA, Canada, Japan, Australia as well as New Zealand. Identically, the number of destination countries is extended to some other OECD countries. This makes it possible to test our theoretical model on a large scale and to test the border effect variable, thanks to the introduction of common source and destination countries.

Results in Table 11.5 confirm the impact of the migration determinants previously identified. In addition, several variables which were previously insignificant become significant. First, the poverty constraint exhibits the expected and significant sign. As mentioned previously, the extension of the country sample to a large number of countries leads to an increase in the variance of this variable across countries. This helps to make this parameter significant. For similar reasons, the language variable becomes significant, thanks to this enlarged sample. However, the age variable remains insignificant. Again, this can be explained by the poor quality of the proxies at a macro level.

A final interesting result concerns border effects, which strongly reduce migration. This result correlates findings in particular studies related to border effects, which all conclude that there is a significant specific cost of crossing an international border (Helliwell, 1997; Hunt and Mueller, 2004).

4 Conclusion and policy implications

To sum up, the previous estimations have shown that migration to the EU from SMCs is determined by numerous and complex factors which go far beyond the traditional migration model. As a matter of fact, it has been stressed that migration does not only depend on traditional factors, such as distance, GDP or cost of living differences; it also depends on a set of other determinants, such as human and business networks, income inequality, migration policy, education as well as non-economic factors (colonialism, religion, climate and environment).

Table 11.5 Results for the generalized model

	HT	*ABB*
GDP per capita ratio	0.0065***	0.000648***
Poverty trap	0.0279***	−0.0072***
Income inequality ratio	0.3520***	0.2898***
(Income inequality ratio)^2	−0.5077***	−0.1497***
Social transfers ratio	0.0025	0.0028*
Distance	−0.00012***	−0.000026***
Border effects	−6.2450****	−0.9430***
Differences in languages	−1.4710***	−0.2610***
Costs of living ratio	−0.3897	−0.0852
Unemployment ratio	−0.0886	−0.0027
Business network (trade)	0.0000023***	0.00000002***
Climate	−0.0759**	−0.0189**
Environment	−0.2623**	−0.0468**
Differences in religion	0.0058***	−0.0009***
Colonies	1.9893***	0.3160***
Human network		0.8338***
Migration policy	2.6508***	0.8703***
Age	0.0156	0.0058
Education ratio	−0.5294***	−0.0120*
r^2	0.7236	
Number of observations	16,882	15,475
Davidson and McKinnon test	0.0005	
Variance Inflation Factor	6.06	
Autocorrelation (rho)	0.976	
LM test	8.4681.00***	
Hausman test	2491.1***	
Hausman and Taylor test (theta)	0.984	
Non-linearities: – distance^2	−0.0001	0.0000
– GDP per capita ratio^2	0.0001	0.0000
Alternative independent variable: climate similarity	0.0122**	0.0055*

Notes

*** significant at 1% level; ** significant at 5% level; * significant at 10% level.

These findings have several policy implications. First of all, they question the objectives of migration policies in the EU. If the main objective is to restrict migration flows, there is no evidence that this aim is consistent with other EU policies with regard to Mediterranean countries and in particular the trade policy. Indeed, the Barcelona Agreement signed in 1995 has been devoted to liberalizing trade flows between the EU and SMCs. According to our empirical findings, this must lead to higher migration flows, since we have shown that trade and migration are complementary. Consequently, a restrictive migration policy seems to be inconsistent with a liberal commercial policy.

Second, it has been stressed that the impact of migration policies is differentiated within the EU. Indeed, migration policies seem to have a significant effect in Northern EU countries, whereas their impact is insignificant in Southern countries, essentially because of the massive regularization of illegal migrants. Again, there is a problem of consistency between Northern and Southern EU policies. Coordinating national policies or moving toward a migration policy at the EU level can be an opportunity to address this inconsistency.

Third, our results contradict a common opinion which states that migrants are primarily motivated to take advantage of social transfers in EU countries. In fact, we show at a macro level that people originating from SMCs are mainly migrating to EU countries in order to obtain a higher wage than in their home countries. In particular, they are looking for higher returns to skills.

As a final remark, the present model shows that the recent rise in European immigration from SMCs has been driven by several factors, such as the rise in the GDP gap (especially with Spain), the increasing human and business networks, the differences in returns to skills, the decrease in unemployment in most EU countries and the increasing education level in SMCs, as well as by specific migration policies in Southern EU countries (regularization). Given the other natural factors (short distance, similarities in languages, close links due to colonialism, favourable climate and environment especially in Southern EU countries), migration from SMCs into the EU is likely to go on increasing in the coming years. In particular, this process can be accelerated if EU countries face a shortage of labour in specific industries.

The present analysis still suffers from a lack of precision in measuring some variables at a macro level. In particular, it fails to take into account the impact of quotas or selective migration policies. It also fails to highlight the relationship between the age of the migrant and migration. Several improvements can be expected in the future, notably thanks to the additional improvement of the quality of the data at a macro level. In the meantime, this analysis can be complemented by studies at a micro level, based on individual data.

Notes

1 This paper is based on a project (FEM31-01) that received the financial assistance of the European Union through the FEMISE association. The contents of this paper are the sole responsibility of the authors and can under no circumstances be regarded as reflecting the position of the European Union.
2 For a complete description of these indexes, refer to Péridy (2010).
3 In a semi-log model, we remind the reader that a 1-unit variation of the independent variable leads to an a% variation of the explained variable, where a denotes the estimated parameters. In addition, if the independent variable is a dummy, then a one unit variation of this variable leads to $a(e^{a}-1)$% change in the explained variable, see Kennedy, 1998: 108).

References

Arellano, M. and S. Bond (1998) *Dynamic Panel Data Estimation Using DPD98 for Gauss: A Guide for Users*, Madrid: CEMFI.

Arellano, M. and O. Bover (1995) 'Another look at the instrumental variable estimation of error component-models', *Journal of Econometrics*, 68: 29–51.

Belot, M. and T. Hatton (2008) 'Immigrant Selection in the OECD', CEPR Working Paper 6675.

Benhabib J. (1996), 'On the political economy of immigration', *European Economic Review*, 40(9): 1737: 43.

Bianchi, M. (2006) 'Immigration Policy and Self-Selecting Migrants', SSE/EFI Working Papers Series in Economics and Finance No. 627, Stockholm School of Economics.

Borjas, G. (1987) 'Self-selection and the earnings of immigrants', *American Economic Review*, 77(4): 531–553.

Borjas, G. (1999) 'Immigration and welfare magnets', *Journal of Labor Economics*, 17(4): 607–637.

Brucker, H. and C. Defoort (2006) 'The Self-Selection of International Migrants Reconsidered: Theory and New Evidence', IZA Discussion Paper 2052, Institute for Labour Studies, Bonn.

Brucker, H. and J.H. Schroder (2005) 'International Migration with Heterogeneous Agents: Theory and Evidence', mimeo, DIW Berlin.

Carim (2006) *Mediterranean Migration, 2006 Report*, Euro-Mediterranean Consortium for Applied Research on International Migration, Robert Schumann Center, European University Institute.

Carrington, W., E. Detragiache and T. Vishwanath (1996) 'Migration with endogenous moving costs', *American Economic Review*, 86(4): 909–930.

CEPII (2006a) *CHELEM Database for International Trade, Population and GDP*, Paris: CEPII.

CEPII (2006b) *Database on International Distances*. Available at: www.cepii.fr, Paris: CEPII.

CIA (2007) *The World Factbook*, Washington, DC: Central Intelligence Agency.

Clark, X., J. Hatton and J. Williamson (2007) 'Explaining US immigration, 1971–1998', *Review of Economics and Statistics*, 89(2): 359–373.

Co, C., P. Euzent and T. Martin (2004) 'The export effect of immigration into the USA', *Applied Economics*, 36: 573–583.

Cobb-Clark, X. (1993) 'Immigrant selectivity and wages: the evidence for women', *American Economic Review*, 83(4): 986–993.

Egger, P. (2004) 'On the problem of endogenous unobserved effects in the estimation of gravity models', *Journal of Economic Integration*, 19(1): 182–191.

FEMISE (2007) 'Recent Migration Patterns from MENA Countries to the EU: A Quantitative Assessment and Policy Implications' – FEMISE Programme n. 31–01 with the Leonard Davis Institute of International Relations, The Hebrew University, University of Jerusalem, Israel (Prof. Alfred Tovias) and the University of Rabat Rabat, Morocco (Prof Mohammed Kachani).

FRDB (2006) *Social Reform Database, Migration Policies*, Fondazione Rodolfo Bededetti.

Freeman, R. and R. Oostendorp (2000) 'Wages around the World: Pay Across Occupations and Countries', NBER Working Paper 8058.

Grogger, T. and G. Hanson (2008) 'Income Maximization and the Selection and Sorting of International Migrants', NBER Working Paper 13021.

Harris, J. and Todaro, M. (1970) 'Migration, unemployment and development: a two sectors analysis', *American Economic Review*, 60(1): 126–142.

Hatton, T. (2004) 'Seeking asylum in Europe', *Economic Policy*, 5: 62–79.

Hatton, T. and J. Williamson (2005a) 'What fundamentals drive world migration?', in G. Borjas and J. Crips (eds), *Poverty, International Migration and Asylum*, Basingstoke: Palgrave-MacMillan, pp. 15–38.

Hatton, T. and J. Williamson (2005b) 'Refugees, Asylum Seekers and Policy in Europe', CEPR Discussion Paper 5058.

Helliwell, J. (1997) 'National borders, trade and migration', *Pacific Economic Review*, 2(3), 65–85.

Hunt, H. and R. Mueller (2004) 'North American migration: returns to skill, border effects and mobility costs', *The Review of Economics and Statistics*, 86(4): 988–1007.

International Labor Organization (2006), *Laborsta*, International Labor Organization, International Labour Office database on labour statistics, ILO Bureau of Statistics.

Karemera, D., V. Oguledo and B. Davis (2000) 'A gravity model analysis of international migration to North America', *Applied Economics*, 32: 1745–1755.

Kennedy, P. (1998) *A Guide to Econometrics* (4th edn), Cambridge, MA: MIT Press.

Kwok, V. and H. Leland (1982) 'An economic model of the brain drain', *American Economic Review*, 72(1): 91–100.

Luxembourg Income Study (2005) *Social Transfers, Basic Descriptive*, Luxembourg: Luxembourg Income Study.

Markusen, J. (1983) 'Factor movements and commodity trade as complements', *Journal of International Economics* 14(3–4): 341–356.

Mayda, A. (2007) 'International Migration: A Panel Data Analysis of the Determinants of Bilateral Flows', CEPR Discussion Paper 6289.

McCallum, J. (1995) 'National borders matter: Canada–US regional trade patterns', *American Economic Review*, 85(3): 615–623.

Mercer (2005) *Worldwide Cost of Living Survey*, London: Mercer Human Resource Consulting.

OECD (2000) *Perspectives de l'emploi de l'OCDE 2000, Rapport Annuel*, Paris: OECD.

OECD (2006a) *Trends in International Migrations, SOPEMI, Annual Report, 2006*, Paris: OECD.

OECD (2006b) *Social Expenditure Database*, Vol. 2001, *Public Expenditure* (SNA93), Paris: OECD.

OECD (2006c) *Monthly International Trade, Total Trade by Partner Country, Annual*, Vol. 7, *2005*, Paris: OECD.

OECD (2006d) *CO_2 Emissions from Fuel Combustion 1971–2004*, Paris: OECD/IAE.

Ortega, F. (2005) 'Immigration quotas and skill upgrading', *Journal of Public Economics*, 89: 1841–1863.

Pederson, J., M. Pytlikova and N. Smith (2004) 'Selection or Network Effects? Migration flows into 27 OECD Countries, 1990, 2000', IZA Discussion Paper 1104.

Péridy, N. (2006) 'Welfare magnets, border effects or policy regulation: what determinants drive migration flows into the EU?', *Global Economy Journal*, 6(4): 1–33.

Péridy, N. (2010) 'Un Modèle Généralisé des Déterminants des Migrations Internationales: Application aux Migrations des Pays Méditerranéens vers l'UE', *Revue Economique*, 61(6): 981–1010.

Piperakis, A., C. Milner and P. Wright (2003) 'Immigration, trade costs and trade: gravity evidence from Greece', *Journal of Economic Integration*, 18(4): 750–762.

Razin, A. and E. Sadka (1997) 'International migration and international trade', in M. Rosenzweig (ed.), *Handbook of Population and Family Economics*, Vol. 1B, Amsterdam: Elsevier, pp. 851–887.
Sjaastad, L.A. (1962) 'The Costs and Returns of Human Migration', *Journal of Political Economy*, 70(5): 80–93.
Stark, O. (1991), *The Migration of Labour*, Cambridge: Blackwell.
The Weather Channel (2007) *Monthly Climate Statistics*. Available at: http: //uk.weather.com.
UNESCO (2006) *Statistical Yearbook*.
United Nations (2006) *World Development Report*, Rapport Annuel, UN: United Nations Development Programme.
Venables, A. (1999) 'Trade liberalization and factor mobility: an overview', in R. Faini, J. de Melo and K. Zimmermann (eds), *Migration: The Controversies and the Evidence*, Cambridge: Cambridge University Press, CEPR.
Vergalli, S. (2006) 'The Role of Community in Migration Dynamics' Fondazione Eni Enrico Mattei, Working Paper 2006.4.
Wagner, D., K. Head and J. Ries (2002) 'Immigration and the trade of provinces', *Scottish Journal of Political Economy*, 49(5): 507–525.
WHO (2005) *World Health Report*, Geneva: World Health Organization.

12 The economic, social and environmental impacts of the Euro-Mediterranean Free Trade Area

Clive George

1 Background

The Barcelona Process and now the Union for the Mediterranean take it as a given that the progressive establishment of a Euro-Mediterranean Free Trade Area (EMFTA), along with targeted financial assistance from the European Union, will create an area of shared prosperity and make a major contribution to the parallel goals of peace and stability. The assumption prompts several questions. First, the Member States of the European Union already belong to a free trade area, and more, in the EU's single market. With the possible exception of Turkey, it is not proposed that the southern and eastern Mediterranean countries should join them. If the shared prosperity of Member States is dependent on their membership of the Union, how can partner countries achieve the same through the more limited aspirations of the EMFTA? Second, the EU has formed or is negotiating many other free trade areas throughout the world, with provisions that are much the same as those of the EMFTA. Many other countries are doing the same, including the USA, and the Mediterranean and elsewhere. Are European and Mediterranean countries' agreements with each other any more significant than their equivalent arrangements with the rest of the world? Third, the goal of shared prosperity is also being pursued worldwide through the multilateral framework of the WTO. Are preferential trade agreements like the EMFTA any more than a patchwork of second-best options? Finally, the global economic crisis and parallel concerns over food security, resource depletion, climate change and other issues affecting the region have called into question the economic, social and environmental sustainability of the global free market ideal. Are the actual and proposed provisions of the regional trade agreements suitably adapted to the global challenges that Mediterranean countries now face?

All of these questions are political as well as economic. Even from a purely economic perspective, there are no simple answers. On the one hand, Jagdish Bhagwati and others argue vehemently that any preferential trade agreement is a retreat into protectionism, with the name 'free trade area' calculated to confuse (Bhagwati, 2002). On the other hand, the WTO allows its own core principle of non-discrimination to be over-ruled by such arrangements, provided that they cover substantially all trade between the parties, on the grounds that they may improve overall economic performance by creating more trade than they divert. Sheila Page presents a different case for some of them (Page, 2007). In groups of countries with common historical, political and security ties, the wider benefits may outweigh the economic costs. Where there are no such ties, such agreements may be no more than an attempt by the stronger negotiating parties to boost their own economic performance by freezing out competitors. The question then arises of whether the Mediterranean is in the first of these categories or the second.

The Paris Declaration placed the Union for the Mediterranean firmly in the first category, with the statement that 'Europe and the Mediterranean countries are bound by history, geography and culture', and united by a common ambition for peace, democracy, prosperity and mutual understanding.[1] Is this really true? Does geography bind this corner of the world to Europe any more than it does to Africa and Asia? Is Mediterranean culture stronger than the overlapping cultures which bind one half of the region to the rest of the Middle East and the other half to the rest of the West? And does the region's history bind it any more than it divides it? It is a long history, of trade and of conflict over the profits of that trade. Ever since the Phoenicians' world-changing innovations in maritime technology and navigation opened the whole of the Mediterranean to merchant seafarers and settlers, the peoples of the east, south and north have contested its control. Trade around the sea's own shores, trade through its strategic corridor to the markets of the east, and now trade in its resources of oil and natural gas have all played their part in characterising the region as much by its conflicts as by its common interests. The Paris Declaration was right in proclaiming a common ambition for prosperity and peace, but it is less clear what kind of trade regime might help to deliver it.

2 Impact assessment

Since the mid-1990s public concerns over the potentially adverse effects of trade agreements have been addressed through government-sponsored impact assessment studies, beginning with the North American Free Trade Agreement and accelerating with the global issues raised at the WTO conference in Seattle at the end of 1999. In response, the European Commission undertook to sponsor Sustainability Impact Assessment (SIA) studies of all its proposed trade agreements, including those in the Mediterranean. The findings of these studies shed light on some of the questions raised above.

The SIA methodology combines extensive stakeholder consultation with technical analysis, to evaluate the potential social, economic and environmental effects of a proposed trade agreement. The goal of the studies is to identify measures which may be taken by the EU and its trading partners to maximise benefits and avoid or minimise potentially adverse effects. The technical analysis is based on economic modelling studies and a comprehensive review of the theoretical and empirical research literature, to identify cause and effect relationships between the proposed trade measures and potential economic, social and environmental impacts. Both static and dynamic effects are examined. The results of economic modelling studies are used to estimate the changes in static equilibrium and corresponding effects during the period of adjustment, while longer-term dynamic effects are assessed primarily through analysis of the research literature. Two main studies were undertaken for the Mediterranean, one covering all the countries involved in the Barcelona Process (SIA-EMFTA) and the other examining the proposed EU–Libya Association Agreement.[2]

3 Economic impacts

One of the most striking findings of these studies is that the economic efficiency gains from comparative advantage are small, and in some cases negative. From a review of some 80 modelling studies it is estimated that the overall effect on economic welfare of fully liberalising regional trade in industrial products, agriculture and services would be a gain of about 0.4% of GDP in the EU and an average of 2% of GDP in the Mediterranean Partner Countries (MPCs). Some of the countries may experience a net welfare loss, with a negative effect from industrial goods partially countered by gains from agriculture and services. A dedicated economic modelling study carried out as part of the EU–Libya SIA gave similar results.

The SIA methodology was derived from that defined in the US National Environmental Policy Act, and subsequently adopted in impact assessment systems throughout the world. One of its key requirements is that the significance of the likely impacts should be assessed, typically by comparison with the baseline situation and existing trends. Since the regional trade negotiations began in 1995, the combined GDP of the MPCs has grown by about a factor of two. That is about 50 times more than the static equilibrium welfare gain of fully liberalising regional trade in industrial goods, agriculture and services combined. On this basis the impact is only marginally significant, if that.

It is now generally accepted that much larger gains can occur through dynamic effects. Some of the modelling studies incorporated some of these effects, to give welfare gains two or three times bigger than from the static analysis alone. However, this is not particularly relevant. The estimated gains are still far smaller than would be needed to increase MPC growth rates to what has been achieved in East Asia and several other newly industrialising countries, through dynamic effects that are not amenable to modelling. Furthermore, although trade liberalisation has been a central component of the policies that have been pursued in these countries, it has generally followed rather than preceded the successful implementation of other critical aspects of an export-oriented industrialisation strategy. One of the studies included an analysis of the relevance of the South East Asian experience to Mediterranean countries, and concluded that many of the lessons are directly applicable. However, in order to make use of these lessons MPCs need to develop their overall development strategy first, and then negotiate fully supportive specific provisions in trade agreements, to be implemented in parallel with other key elements of the strategy. Tunisia in particular has been relatively successful in following this type of approach.

In the absence of a comprehensive development strategy to reap the potential dynamic gains, MPCs should be wary of negotiating trade agreements that benefit particular export industries with little or no overall economic benefit, at the expense of adverse social and environmental effects that can be highly significant. Although the net change in economic welfare calculated by economic models is small, the inter-sectoral production changes associated with it are much bigger. Production is projected to decline by several tens of per cent in some sectors, with similar rises in others.

4 Sectoral, social and environmental impacts

The economic modelling studies indicate a significant short- to medium-term decline in MPC manufacturing, which may be reversed in the longer term if greater competition helps to stimulate technological upgrading. However, competitive pressures may not be enough. Several of the countries have implemented government sponsored programmes to help industrial companies increase their competitiveness, derived from similar measures adopted to assist Portugal in its accession to the EU. Some of these programmes have been more successful than others. Success has generally been dependent on appropriation of the programme by national actors rather than relying on EU financial and technical support.

The industrial products for which adverse effects are greatest include transportation equipment, food and beverages. Some modelling studies show a rise in textiles and clothing in some of the MPCs, but few of these take full account of the increasing competitiveness of East Asian and South Asian exports. Diversification into other industrial sectors is likely to be necessary. The overall inter-sectoral production shifts may have a significant adverse effect on overall levels of unemployment throughout the period of adjustment.

In agriculture, MPC production is projected to decline significantly in cereals, livestock and dairy produce, and rise for fruits, vegetables and (in some countries) olive oil. The overall employment effects are expected to be small, but with significant positive and negative short-term local effects. Liberalisation is expected to stimulate a shift from small-scale to large-scale commercial farming. Unless accompanied by successful policies for integrated rural–urban development, the longer-term impact on employment may be significantly adverse in both rural and urban areas. Differential gender effects occur in both directions, with particular concerns arising for rural women.

Environmental effects associated with the inter-sectoral production changes are positive in some cases and negative in others. Most of these would be relatively small, but the adverse effects could be significant if not accompanied by appropriate strengthening of regulatory regimes. The net effect on climate change is expected be adverse, but of only minor significance in relation to overall magnitude of the problem. The greatest environmental concern is the potential impact on water resources in particular regions of those countries where agricultural exports expand. There may also be significant adverse effects on biodiversity in areas where water scarcity, land conversion or other factors are already causing pressure.

5 Government revenues

The most immediate impact of tariff reductions is a reduction in government revenue. There have been cases when liberalisation has increased the volume of imports so much that receipts have risen despite the lower tax rate, but such cases are rare, and have generally been accompanied by a rising trade deficit and serious exchange rate difficulties. The effect would be insignificant in Europe, but would have a larger impact in some of the MPCs. The revenue loss in Lebanon has been estimated at 5% of GDP, with possibly higher impacts in Egypt, Algeria and the Palestinian Territories.

The lost revenue would need to be compensated to avoid potentially adverse effects through reduced expenditure on health, education and social support programmes. In the past most middle-income countries have been able to raise revenue from other sources, and total revenues have remained broadly unchanged. However, this is not the case for low-income countries, whose total government revenue has declined in parallel with falling tariff revenue. Even if all the lost revenue is replaced by other taxes, there can still be adverse effects. One study found that if tariffs are replaced by capital taxes, the impact of liberalisation on economic welfare may shift from positive to negative. Others have indicated that replacement by VAT, a consumption tax or income tax can have an adverse effect on poverty. Revisions to the tax system therefore need to be designed carefully.

6 The case of Libya

Libya is an extreme example of some of the issues faced in the region, particularly in its acute water shortages and the major contribution of the oil and gas sector to the economy. The main potential benefits to both the EU and Libya from the proposed trade agreement come from closer cooperation in the energy sector, with potentially significant adverse effects that need to be taken into account.

In the short to medium term, closer cooperation on the development of Libya's oil and gas industries could be highly beneficial to both parties, provided it is accompanied by stronger environmental regulation. However, expansion of these industries would accelerate the long-term decline of the resource, while reinforcing Europe's dependence on fossil fuels. By contrast, closer cooperation in the development of solar energy could make a major contribution both to Europe's long-term energy needs and to the long-term prospects of the Libyan economy, while at the same time helping to tackle climate change. Since other Mediterranean countries have similar potential, a cooperative region-wide programme on solar energy development is highly desirable. The Mediterranean Solar Plan that is currently being explored through the Union for the Mediterranean warrants high priority.

Because of its water supply constraints, Libya's agricultural production is far short of meeting its own food needs and is unlikely to become an economically competitive source for processed exports. It is therefore likely that liberalisation would lead to a long-term decline of the industry, with increasing reliance on imports of both agricultural produce and processed foods. Significant concerns also arise for the rest of the Libyan manufacturing industry. The modelling scenarios project a rise in imports of over 30% of domestic production, with little economic incentive to modernise the industry.

Further concerns arise over the potential impact of fisheries liberalisation on the sustainability of the entire Mediterranean tuna industry. Subject to the details of the trade agreement, it could add significantly to the risk of a collapse in stocks of bluefin tuna, and heighten the need for much stronger conservation measures by all Mediterranean countries that exploit the resource.

7 Regional integration

The SIA studies concurred with many others in identifying potentially large dynamic gains to MPCs from more fully integrating their economies with each other. However, the deeper integration measures proposed by the EU, for investment, public procurement, trade facilitation, product standards, competition policy and intellectual property rights, may not have the desired effect. Investment agreements need to avoid allowing greater freedom for acquisitions or mergers that would make no contribution to the country's domestic capital stock or technological base, while transferring the profits to foreign investors. Public procurement reforms can have both benefits and costs, with no substantial evidence of any benefit from making commitments in a trade agreement. The same applies to competition policy, which needs to be tailored to a country's own evolving needs as it develops and implements a privatisation programme. Many measures for trade facilitation and harmonisation of standards can be highly beneficial, but those that are not already being taken can be difficult to implement. The granting of intellectual property rights for foreign companies that go beyond the WTO TRIPs agreement can do more harm than good, particularly when applied in areas where domestic industry is not already internationally competitive. All of these proposals would benefit EU exporters and financiers. It is less clear that they would benefit partner countries.

Effective integration of MPC economies would require much more ambitious action, taken on the countries' own initiative. Drastic cuts in tariff and non-tariff barriers between MPCs would help to ensure greater complementarity in agricultural and industrial production, enabling economies of scale and greater international competitiveness. However, this would be difficult to achieve without cooperative action to ensure a reasonably smooth transition. This might, for example, consist of measures similar to the EU's structural funds, along with cooperative investment in regional transport and other infrastructure. If such a programme were established, it might become practicable to integrate national industrial and agricultural development strategies into a regional strategy. Regional institutions might be created to support this, undertaking research into common issues of economic, social and environmental development. However, it is questionable whether the southern and eastern Mediterranean countries share a strong enough common identity to embark on more than a fairly limited programme of this nature. Parallel ties with the rest of Africa and West Asia need to be taken into account, varying from one end of the Mediterranean to the other, along with similarly varying ties with Europe.

8 Discussion

Throughout their history the peoples on the northern, eastern and southern shores of the Mediterranean have had their own distinct identities, characterised as much by their outward relationships as by those within the region itself. To the Romans the sea was the *mare nostrum*, their sea, the sea at the centre of their world. The free trade area that Rome established was imposed by imperial might and did not last. The peoples of the east, south and north have each had their turn at being the guiding influence, along with others from further afield. Now the balance is changing again. Regional markets are part of a global market, whose own structure is evolving as economic power shifts from west to east. The shape of the world that is emerging is not yet clear, and nor is the region's place in it.

If economics were not so closely intertwined with politics it would clearly favour multilateral liberalisation of global markets through the WTO, with little or no justification for a Euro-Mediterranean Free Trade Area or any other nominally free trade area. But that is not the world we live in. All the countries of the Mediterranean have something to gain from strengthening the economic ties between them. However, in the absence of some regional identity that over-rides other identities, each of the Mediterranean partner countries needs to tailor those ties to its own particular needs and aspirations. In doing so, they need to take account of the likely impacts of all the various options.

From the economic perspective, development dynamics are far more significant than the static efficiency gains available from reducing trade barriers. Each component of the trade negotiation agenda, whether for tariff or non-tariff barriers or any of the deeper integration measures that are proposed, has a strong influence on those dynamics, which is not necessarily positive. Each has to be examined with care, and judged against whether it would help or hinder a country's efforts to achieve its own development goals. Whatever agreement is reached will have side effects, with potentially adverse impacts on particular sections of society or the natural environment. These too need to be identified in the course of negotiating an agreement, and managed in the process of implementing it.

The Union for the Mediterranean rightly envisages a major role for Europe in this, based on a common ambition for prosperity, peace and stability. However, financial support from the EC is no more significant than the economic efficiency gains. Europe's influence on regional development dynamics is what matters. Here too, economics and politics are closely intertwined, and any attempt to separate them would be counter-productive. If the goal of peace and stability comes first in the negotiation of the region's trade agreements, the economic gains and losses to Europe must come second.

Notes

1 Joint Declaration of the Paris Summit for the Mediterranean, Paris, 13 July 2008.

2 The SIA-EMFTA study was led by IDPM at the University of Manchester, in partnership with Bocconi University, CITET, Deloitte & Touche, CIHEAM, ODI and UN ESCWA. The EU-Libya study was led by Development Solutions, in partnership with IDPM, CEPR and MEC International. All the study reports are available on the EC website, http: //ec.europa.eu/trade/analysis/sustainability-impact-assessments.

References

Bhagwati, J. (2002) *Free Trade Today*, Princeton, NJ: Princeton University Press.

Page, S. (2007) 'Using Trade Rules to Help Development: Balancing the Benefits and Costs of the WTO system for Developing Countries', International Seminar on The New Agenda for International Trade Relations as the Doha Round Draws to an End, Barcelona, 29–30 January 2007.

Index

Page numbers in italics refer to tables and those in bold type refer to figures. Numbers including "n" e.g. 138n2, refer to notes.